Nursing Ethics

Across the Curriculum and into Practice

Janie B. Butts, DSN, RN
The University of Southern Mississippi
School of Nursing
Hattiesburg, Mississippi

Karen L. Rich, MN, PhD(c), RN
The University of Southern Mississippi
School of Nursing
Long Beach, Mississippi

JONES AND BARTLETT PUBLISHERS
Sudbury, Massachusetts
BOSTON   TORONTO   LONDON   SINGAPORE

World Headquarters
Jones and Bartlett Publishers
40 Tall Pine Drive
Sudbury, MA 01776
978-443-5000
info@jbpub.com
www.jbpub.com

Jones and Bartlett Publishers Canada
2406 Nikanna Road
Mississauga, ON L5C 2W6
CANADA

Jones and Bartlett Publishers International
Barb House, Barb Mews
London W6 7PA
UK

Library of Congress Cataloging-in-Publication Data

Butts, Janie.
   Nursing ethics : across the curriculum and into practice / Janie Butts, Karen Rich.
     p. ; cm.
   Includes bibliographical references and index.
   ISBN 0-7637-4735-1 (pbk. : alk. paper)
   1. Nursing ethics.
   [DNLM: 1. Ethics, Nursing. WY 85 B988n 2005]   I. Rich, Karen, MN.   II. Title.
   RT85.B78 2005
   174.2—dc22

                                                                          2004021350

Production Credits
Acquisitions Editor: Kevin Sullivan
Production Director: Amy Rose
Associate Editor: Amy Sibley
Production Assistant: Kate Hennessy
Associate Marketing Manager: Emily Ekle
Manufacturing and Inventory Coordinator: Amy Bacus
Composition: Auburn Associates, Inc.
Cover Design: Timothy Dziewit
Cover Photograph: © Photos.com
Printing and Binding: Malloy Inc.

Printed in the United States of America
09 08 07 06 05   10 9 8 7 6 5 4 3 2 1

Acknowledgments

To Ronnie, my hero and eternal soul mate!
To my sons, David and Denny—
It seemed like only an hourglass of time
as I saw you both grow up before my eyes.
You are wonderful young men who continue to realize your dreams.
You have become everything that I could ever hope you to be!
To Copper, you are my little red Dachshund who is forever loyal.
Love you all,
Janie B.

To my kind and gentle mother who continues to believe that the flower
of my life is still blooming and to my late father who was always so
proud to say that his daughter is a nurse.

And, most importantly, my gratitude goes to Patsy, my dear friend and
Jedi Master. You have taught me more than you will ever know.
Karen

Special Acknowledgments

We want to express our sincere appreciation to the staff at Jones and Bartlett
Publishers, especially Kevin and Amy, for their continued encouragement, assistance,
and support during the writing process and publication of our book.

Table of Contents

CHAPTER 3   Adult Health Nursing Ethics   53
Janie B. Butts

CHAPTER 4   Reproductive Issues and Nursing Ethics   69
Janie B. Butts

CHAPTER 5 Nursing Ethics in the Care of Infants and Children   95

Karen L. Rich

CHAPTER 6 Adolescent Nursing Ethics   119

Janie B. Butts

CHAPTER 7   Ethics in Psychiatric and Mental Health Nursing   147

Karen L. Rich

CHAPTER 8   Ethics in Geriatric and Chronic Illness Nursing   175

Karen L. Rich

CHAPTER 9   **Community and Public Health Nursing and Leadership Ethics**   **203**

Karen L. Rich

CHAPTER 10   **End-of-Life Ethical Issues and Nursing**   **231**

Janie B. Butts

Preface

I don't like the idea of a unitary subject;
I prefer the play of a kaleidoscope:
you give it a tap and the little bits of colored glass
form a new pattern.

Roland Barthes, *The Grain of the Voice*

MORAL ELEMENTS OF NURSING PRACTICE

In our first edition of *Nursing Ethics: Across the Curriculum and into Practice*, we have reflected on three moral elements that we believe are pervasive in all of nursing practice—a kaleidoscope or variety of patterns in terms of relationships and compassion symbolized by nurturing hands. These moral elements are closely linked and form a dynamic mosaic of nurses' everyday practice.

The instrument of the kaleidoscope was so named from the Greek *kalos* (beautiful) and *eidos* (form). In Webster's Dictionary (2004), the kaleidoscope was described as:

> . . . an instrument containing loose bits of colored material (as glass or plastic) between two flat plates and two plane mirrors so placed that changes of position of the bits of material are reflected in an endless variety of patterns. [A kaleidoscope forms] a variegated changing pattern or scene, a succession of changing phases or actions, a . . . kaleidoscope of shifting values, [or] information (n.p.).

When one turns a kaleidoscope, the loose bits of colored glass or plastic fall effortlessly into a variety of patterns, shapes, and colors. A new and different image is formed with every turn of the cylinder.

We have used the *kaleidoscope* and the visual image that is formed by its colored glass as a metaphor for the intrinsic nature of nursing. The art of nursing can be likened to the kaleidoscope—a dynamic instrument that continuously creates a vision of changing patterns and shapes infused with the beauty of human relationships. Nursing is permeated by vibrant and dynamic ethical conceptions of human *good*, like bits of colored glass; but also like small pieces of glass, nursing is infused with the striking cracks and flaws of humanness. Nursing work *is* nursing ethics with all of the moral successes and moral failures of individual nurses and the whole nursing community forming the mosaic of nursing.

As the professional nursing community continues its journey of moral progress into the 21st century, we believe that the *compassionate relationships* between nurses and patients form a vital element of humanistic nursing. These compassionate relationships shape the ever-changing and vibrant kaleidoscope of nursing ethics.

Our emphasis on the *hands* of nurses and patients reflects the primary focus of nursing—the relief of suffering and well-being of patients. It is into the nurturing hands of nurses that patients lay open their vulnerabilities and suffering. Joan Erikson (1982) beautifully expressed this idea:

> When we are faced with a really troublesome problem, we sometimes resort to putting the matter "in the hands of" those more knowledgeable than ourselves. That is of course precisely what an ideal health care institution offers: hands—understanding, capable, talented hands, which have had careful training and much experience in communication with those who are limited in their modes of expressing needs. "In the hands of"—nothing could state more clearly what the importance of hands is and must be for patients everywhere. Conscious and attentive use of the hands would make all our lives more meaningful in the care and comfort of relationships with patients who feel isolated and somewhat abandoned. Hands are essential for vital involvement in living (pp. 120–121).

NOTES TO EDUCATORS, STUDENTS, AND PRACTICING NURSES

NLNAC and AACN Recommendations

Accrediting agencies have recommended that nursing educators include ethics and ethical decision-making strategies in their nursing curricula (American Association of Colleges of Nursing [AACN], 2003; National League of Nursing Accrediting Commission [NLNAC], 2003). The NLNAC (2003) competencies for the 21st century for nurses were adapted based on the *Pew Health Commission Competencies for 2005*. Specifically, the following excerpt is the core competency for practicing nurses' ethical behaviors:

> Exhibit ethical behaviors in all professional activities
>
> • Embrace a personal ethic of social responsibility and service
> • Provide counseling for patients in situations where ethical issues arise
> • Participate in discussion of ethical issues in health care as they affect communities, society, and health professions (NLNAC, Interpretive Guidelines, 2003, p. 86)

In the document, *Nursing Education's Agenda for the 21st Century*, AACN (2002) members emphasized that nursing students and practicing nurses are experiencing a new environment in healthcare and must be prepared to meet the challenges. The recommendation offered by AACN in this document is that nursing educators need to incorporate ethical principles and concepts of ethical decision making in nursing curricula for nursing students.

Before we began writing our book, we evaluated the significance of the NLNAC and AACN documents. Some of the moral issues that nurses experience on a daily basis may leave nurses on uncertain moral ground. Whether practicing nurses become bogged down in ethical situations about death, abortion, or saving premature infants, nurses will most likely experience moral suffering when they begin to question the meaning of life and death. Nurses must be prepared to attach their own meanings to life and death, and nursing students and practicing nurses need to acquire foundational knowledge about ethics and decision-making strategies to prepare them for the moral issues that they experience daily. Included in this textbook are decision-making approaches and models, rationale for decisions, and management of care for various topics.

Purposes and Readership

We have three purposes for this book. First, we wanted to provide a nursing ethics book that includes an exploration of a wide array of nursing moral issues. We wanted to include bioethical issues that nurses encounter everyday—the ones that Fry and Veatch (2002) so colorfully stated were the "flesh and blood" issues (p. 1)—but we wanted to cover the issues from a humanistic perspective. In the body of the text, we have included the most current scholarly literature, related news briefs, and research and legal findings regarding ethical issues. The content of our nursing ethics book is also based on theoretical foundations, clinical evidence, and case study.

Second, a prominent feature of this book is its "across the curriculum" format for undergraduate nursing students. The book can be used as a supplementary textbook when students use it in each nursing course. We strongly believe that if ethical concepts and bioethical issues are integrated in the beginning of nursing programs and throughout curricula, students will become more mindful of the myriad of ethical challenges that they will face in practice and become habituated to resolving moral conflicts. Ultimately, we believe nurses will want to find ways to participate in the large-scale bioethical deliberations and decision making regarding their patients' life and death issues. The book also is intended for RN to BSN students and their curricula, especially in ethics courses, professional development courses, or leadership courses. Many RN students returning to school have not been exposed to ethics classes or ethical content though they bring a wealth of real flesh and blood experiences with them into the classroom.

The third purpose of the book is connected to the last part of the book's title, "into practice." As we have stated previously in this preface, *nursing work is nursing ethics*. The content of the book was designed to stimulate the moral imagination of practicing nurses so that they can integrate ethical principles, theories, and decision-making skills *into their practice*.

Pedagogical Features

We have strived to create a nursing ethics book that is not only theoretically sound but also has practical significance. The pedagogical features that are highlighted in our book are designed to stimulate critical thinking and provide links to the art of nursing as they relate to everyday ethics for students and nurses. The features of the book include:

- Quotes at the front of each chapter
- Summary of key concepts at the front of each chapter
- Key terms in italics with their definitions throughout body of text
- Critical thinking activities, called "Ethical Reflections," at the end of most topical discussions
- Critical thinking and reflection boxes, called "Ethical Kaleidoscope" boxes throughout each chapter
- "Web Ethics" boxes in each chapter
- A case study at the end of each chapter
- Critical thinking questions linked with each case study

Special Features of the Chapters

Chapter 1: Introduction to Nursing Ethics

- Jonsen, Siegler, and Winslade's (2002) *Four Topics* approach to ethical case analysis
- Practical strategies for developing web ethics and an overview of health care on the Web

Chapter 2: Values, Relationships, and Virtues

- Rich and Butts' virtue-based *Moral Ground Model* and their view of Moral Suffering
- Relationships in nursing

Chapter 3: Adult Health Nursing Ethics

- A reflection on telling the truth by an exemplary nurse from the play *Wit*
- Organ transplantation—the newest recommendations

Chapter 4: Reproductive Issues and Nursing Ethics

- Central ethical dilemmas of abortion and reproductive technology
- Management of care for women of child-bearing age based on Bergum's (2004) "relational ethics" of environment, embodiment, mutual respect, and engagement

Chapter 5: Nursing Ethics in the Care of Infants and Children

- Concepts of "mothers" and "mothering persons" involving ethical care of infants and children
- Withholding and withdrawing treatment of children under 12 years old

Chapter 6: Adolescent Nursing Ethics

- Ethical dilemmas involving prevention education: abstinence-only and comprehensive sex education programs
- Management of care for adolescents based on the virtues of trustworthiness, genuineness, compassion, and honesty

Chapter 7: Ethics in Psychiatric and Mental Health Nursing

- Ethical implications and stigma associated with a mental illness diagnosis
- Management of care based on a humanistic nursing practice theory and a person-centered approach

Chapter 8: Ethics in Geriatric and Chronic Illness Nursing

- Moral agency related to elders' decisional capacity, autonomy and paternalism, vulnerability, dependence, and dementia
- Virtues that are needed by elders

Chapter 9: Community and Public Health Nursing and Leadership Ethics

- A view of community building, communitarian ethics, and moral imagination
- Service learning, servant leadership, health disparities, and infectious diseases

Chapter 10: End-of-Life Ethical Issues and Nursing

- An explanation of the ideal death, the history of death, and euthanasia
- An overview of types of advance directives, surrogates, and end-of-life issues

Instructor's Resources

Instructor's Resources are provided on the "catalog page" for our book at the Jones and Bartlett Publishers Web site (www.jbpub.com). Instructor's Resources will include chapter overviews and objectives, student activities, and chapter test questions.

Comments and Feedback

We are dedicated to making this nursing ethics book the one that will meet your needs for the future. We are interested in your comments about the book. Please email us at jbondbutts@comcast.net for feedback or questions concerning the textbook, questions about ethics, or any questions that you may have regarding the case studies in the textbook. We appreciate your support!

REFERENCES

American Associate of Colleges of Nursing [AACN]. (2002). *Nursing education's agenda for the 21st century*. Retrieved August 18, 2004, from http://www.aacn.nche.edu/.

Erikson, E. H., & Erikson, J. M. (1997). *The life cycle completed* (extended version). New York: W.W. Norton & Company.

Fry, S. T., & Veatch, R. M. (2000). *Case studies in nursing ethics* (2nd ed.). Boston: Jones & Bartlett Publishers.

Merriam-Webster Online Dictionary. (2004). Retrieved from http://www.merriam-webster.com.

National League of Nursing Accrediting Commission. (2003). Interpretive guidelines by program type: Core competencies for practicing nurses—adapted by NLNAC. Retrieved August 18, 2004, from http://www.nlnac.org/.

CHAPTER 1

Introduction to Ethics in Nursing

Janie B. Butts, Karen L. Rich

Live a balanced life—learn some and think some and draw and paint and sing and dance and play and work every day some. . . . When you go out into the world, watch out for traffic, hold hands, and stick together.

Robert Fulghum, *All I Really Need to Know I Learned in Kindergarten*

SUMMARY

1. Because of unavoidable social connections, every person makes moral and ethical choices in life that will inevitably affect others.
2. The foundation of deontological theory is that a person has a duty to perform particular actions and to do the right action for its own sake.
3. Utilitarianism is an ethical theory that is based on usefulness, or the greatest good for the greatest number of people.
4. The four major principles of bioethics are autonomy, beneficence, nonmaleficence, and justice.

5. The ideals of social justice are fairness and equality. In health care, the central ethical concern continues to be discovering a way to set up a health care infrastructure where equal access to health care and the fair distribution of resources can take place.

6. Nurses make independent ethical decisions on a day-to-day basis, but, at the same time, they are an integral part of a larger team of decision makers. Many complex bioethical decisions are made interdependently between nurses and others in the health care arena.

7. There are many ethical codes of conduct for Web users and Internet surfers, but if everyone would practice a primary ethic of "respect one another," there would be many fewer unethical or criminal behaviors on the Internet.

A KALEIDOSCOPE OF ETHICS AND MORALITY

As controversial and sensitive ethical issues continue to challenge nurses and other health care professionals, many of them have begun to develop a unique appreciation for the diverse ethical viewpoints of others. Moral uncertainty about many issues is at its highest level in history. Practical approaches are necessary if there is to be any hope of resolution in particular cases and situations. Although nurses make independent ethical decisions every day, they also play a critical role within the larger team of decision makers. Patients and family members participate in dialogue with nurses to resolve many bioethical and health care issues. Nurses must develop theoretical knowledge and the necessary skills to form a foundation for practicing right actions and developing moral character. In doing so, it is important that nurses be able to distinguish among the various terms, theories, and principles used in ethics and to identify and analyze ethical dilemmas.

Morality and the Ethical Way

Ethics may mean different things to different people, but generally ethics is a way to understand and examine the moral life (Beauchamp & Childress, 2001, p. 1; Gert, 2002). Ethics may be used as an overall view or set of principles. Formal ethical theories, professional codes of ethics, and codes of conduct in the military are some of the guides of human conduct provided by ethical systems.

Morals, on the other hand, are specific ways of behaving or the way that people set out to accomplish ethical practices. All individuals have ideas about what they believe is moral and how they interpret their own moral experiences. Because individuals differ, there are many conflicting doctrines or theories about how people should live and how everyday moral problems should be resolved. *Morality*, derived from the Latin word *moralis*, refers to a widely held view or social consensus about the normal conduct for human beings and society (Gert, 2002). Many ethicists define morality and ethics separately. The meaning of human decency, right and wrong, good and evil, proper and improper acts, and cruel and benevolent (or kind) acts are explained in terms of morality.

In recent years, a notion of common morality has had a revival in popularity and acceptance. *Common morality* is the belief that all persons who have a serious attitude toward morality have a "pre-thought"—a starting point about certain norms. Even before the person attempts to apply an ethical theory in order to justify a moral decision, there is "awareness that there is something morally wrong with lying, stealing, breaking promises, killing a human, and the like" (Veatch, 2003, p. 191).

As long as can be remembered, morality has had somewhat of a negative connotation, in part because of an array of "oughts" and "ought nots" that have accompanied religious decrees and the questions of Greek philosophers, such as "How shall I live?" and "What ought I do or not do?" (Landauer & Rowlands, 2001; Weston, 2001). The rationale for this thinking is related to not violating moral dictates. One of the problems with defining morality in this negative sense of "you should not" is that any behavior outside the realm of "not" may be implied to be acceptable.

A negative form of the term "morality" is *immorality*, which refers to a person's unacceptable behavior as compared to certain accepted societal moral standards or principles. The many acts of immorality include dishonesty, murder, and certain sexual acts. *Amoral* is a term that people use to refer to actions that are done with an indifference to, or no concern for, moral norms. For example, murder is immoral, but if a person commits murder with absolutely no sense of remorse or maybe even a sense of pleasure, that person can be labeled as being amoral. Acts are considered *nonmoral* if moral norms and standards do not apply. One example of a nonmoral situation is when a dog soils the walkway in a public park. The dog should not be labeled immoral or amoral; rather, the dog or situation should be labeled nonmoral because the dog's behavior is not relevant to moral behavior (Angeles, 1992).

With regard to ethics, the negative form is described as *unethical*, for instance, when a trust between two or more people is broken or when a person's practice goes against a code of conduct that has been endorsed by members of a professional group. Keeping an open mind, however, is important, because ethics is all about making moral choices that are considered best for individuals or society at certain times and in particular situations, and then evaluating the choices and outcomes.

Billington (2003) highlighted some important features about morals and ethics.

- Probably the most important feature about ethics and morals is that no one can avoid making moral or ethical decisions because the social connection with others necessitates that people must consider moral and ethical actions.
- Other people are always involved with one's moral and ethical decisions. Private morality does not exist.
- Moral decisions matter because every decision affects someone else's life, self-esteem, or happiness.
- Definite conclusions or resolutions will never be reached in ethical dilemmas or debates.

- In the areas of morals and ethics, people cannot exercise moral judgment without being given a choice; in other words, the ability to choose an option from among a group of choices is essential to making a sound moral judgment.
- People use moral reasoning to make moral judgments or to discover right actions.

Philosophical Approaches to Morality and Ethics

The subject of morality has been studied with two major approaches of philosophical inquiry: normative ethics and metaethics (Mappes & DeGrazia, 2001). The first major approach, *normative ethics*, involves an attempt by ethicists to decide what is morally right and wrong and what should be accepted as a common set of behaviors or actions. Normative ethicists make claims and statements about how humans should behave or what ought to be done in certain cases. Normative ethicists may also prescribe courses of action and make evaluative judgments about what is right, wrong, good, praiseworthy, or blameworthy (Falikowski, 1998).

When providing a reasonable justification for moral norms, a practical approach is taken. The aim of the practical approach, called *applied normative ethics*, is an attempt to resolve a specific moral problem or ethical dilemma followed by an attempt to determine if the resolution can be justified. One example of a moral problem is whether or not a physician and nurse have the right to override a mentally competent patient's adamant refusal of treatment. For instance, a physician and nurse must make an ethical decision if a patient with an acute bacterial infection that is highly contagious refuses treatment. The physician and ethics committee, upon evaluation, can justify the decision to override the patient's request because of the nature of the patient's illness. A communicable disease that is left untreated could be a threat to other people in the community.

Descriptive ethics, a subcategory of normative ethics, is an approach used when researchers or nursing ethicists want to know more about what people think about human morality. Sometimes it is referred to as the "scientific study of morality" (Mappes & DeGrazia, 2001, p. 1). In descriptive ethics, researchers attempt to describe and explain the accepted moral norms and views, such as when a nursing ethicist conducts research to explore the views of staff nurses about telling patients the truth about their terminal illnesses.

The investigation and evaluation of moral judgments, theoretical systems, and the meaning of ethical language, such as the word "good," is approached through *metaethics*, which is the second major philosophical mode of inquiry. Metaethicists do not focus on what ought to be done, prescribe behavior, or attempt to justify moral judgments. They are more concerned with the language of morality. Metaethicists analyze and examine terms and meanings, attempt to clarify moral concepts, identify the source of ethics, and obtain knowledge about what is ethical (Falikowski, 1998). Another segment of metaethics is the study of the rationale or justification of particular ethical systems of thought, such as an ethical theory. For example, a nursing metaethicist may attempt to understand how people identify and justify a human right in relation to a theory of justice.

Bioethics

The terms "bioethics" and "health care ethics" are sometimes used interchangeably in the literature. Bioethics is a specific domain of ethics that focuses on moral issues in the field of health care. Bioethics has evolved into a discipline all its own as a result of life and death moral dilemmas faced by physicians, nurses, and other health care professionals.

In his book *The Birth of Bioethics*, Jonsen (1998) designated a span of 40 years, from 1947 to 1987, as the era when bioethics was evolving as a discipline. This era began with the Nuremberg Tribunal in 1947 when Nazi physicians were charged and convicted for the murderous and tortuous war crimes they had labeled as scientific experiments during the early 1940s. The 10 judgments in the final court ruling of the trials provided the basis for the worldwide Nuremberg Code of 1947. This code became a document used to protect human subjects during research and experimentation.

The 1950s and 1960s were preliminary years before the actual birth of bioethics. A transformation was occurring during these years as technology advanced. In this era, a new ethic was emerging about life and the extension of life through technology. Many advances were made, including the discovery of the polio vaccine, better transplantation techniques, and improvements in life-support technology. Scientists and physicians were forced to ask questions such as "Who should live?", "Who should die?", "Who should decide?" (Jonsen, 1998, p. 11). Many conferences and workshops during the 1960s and 1970s dealt with issues surrounding life and death. By 1970, the public, physicians, and researchers were referring to these issues as bioethics (Johnstone, 1999). Today, bioethics is a vast interdisciplinary venture that has engrossed the public's interest since the time of its conception. The aim of bioethicists today is to continue to search for answers to deep philosophical questions about life and the significance of human beings and to help guide and control public policy (Kuhse & Singer, 1998).

Nursing Ethics

Nurses practice and use ethics on a daily basis. In a survey by the American Nurses Association (ANA) at its 1994 convention, 69% of nurses stated that they faced ethical issues daily or weekly (ANA, 1996). Ethical decisions have become a routine and inherent part of clinical practice for registered nurses. To practice nursing ethically requires that nurses first recognize ethical problems and probable conflicts and then display a moral sensitivity in all nurse–patient communications and interventions (Oddi, Cassidy, & Fisher, 1995). Many times nurses experience moral distress when faced with making ethical decisions in practice, however, partly because of lack of knowledge and education about ethical content and the ethical topic itself and partly because nurses are placed in volatile ethical situations where they feel forced to continue treatment beyond a possible cure (Habel, n.d.; Varcoe et al., 2004).

"It is the real-life, flesh and blood cases that raise fundamental ethical questions," stated Fry and Veatch (2000, p. 1) as they took a logical approach to defining nursing ethics. Nursing ethics sometimes is viewed as a subcategory of the broader area of bioethics, just as medical ethics is a subcategory of bioethics. However, controversy continues to exist over whether or not the nursing profession has its own unique moral problems in health care. Nursing ethics, as all health care ethics, usually begins with cases or problems that are practice-based.

Many nursing ethicists view nursing ethics as a unique field of ethics because of a wide array of ethical problems that surface in relationships between nurses and patients, families, physicians, and other professionals who are a part of the health care team. Many nursing ethicists distinguish bioethical issues from the general ethical issues that nurses encounter on a daily basis. Ethics in nursing involves ethical issues other than those that are traditionally thought of as bioethical in nature, such as the moral circumstances surrounding relationships between nurses and others. Because of the distinction between biomedical versus nurses' ethical issues, nursing ethics can be defined as having a two-pronged meaning. Johnstone (1999) defined it as: "the examination of all kinds of ethical and bioethical issues from the perspective of nursing theory and practice" (p. 46). The key point here is that ethical issues are viewed from a nursing perspective, mainly because the nursing discipline has matured to the point of viewing ethics as a separate and distinct field. With the field of nursing ethics, Varcoe et al. (2004) emphasized that the field of nursing ethics must now be focused on the experiences and needs of practicing nurses, the exploration of the meaning of nursing ethics, and ethical practice in terms of the perceptions of practicing nurses.

Ethical Reflections

- Identify two outstanding events in your life that you consider to have been occasions for acting in an ethical way.
- Describe the events, your feelings, and the learning processes that took place as a result of these two events.
- Compare the two events and the hard choices you had to make in each event.

ETHICAL THEORIES AND OTHER APPROACHES

Normative ethical theories function as moral guides in answering the question "What ought I do or not do?" A theory can provide individuals with guidance in moral thinking and reasoning and provide justification for moral actions. There is a normative framework with foundational statements for each ethical theory, and people who apply an ethical theory need to know the assumptions and foundations of that theory. Optimally, ethical theories and other approaches should help people discern commonplace morality and strengthen moral judgments ". . . in the face of moral dilemmas" (Mappes & DeGrazia, 2001, p. 5). The following Web Ethics box provides Internet sites related to ethical and moral theories, nursing ethics, and bioethics.

Web Ethics

Ethical Theory
http://www.walkupsway.com/ethics.htm

Jonsen's Four Topics Method
http://eduserv.hscer.washington.edu/bioethics/tools/cesumm.html

Online Guide to Ethics & Moral Philosophy
http://caae.phil.cmu.edu/Cavalier/80130/Syllabus.html

Nursing Ethics
http://www.nursingethics.ca/

Online Journal of Nursing/Ethics
http://www.nursingworld.org/ojin/ethicol/ethictoc.htm

Ethical Theories

Deontology

Deontology is an ethical theory based on dutiful actions, not actions based on rewards, happiness, or consequences (Hill & Zweig, 2003). Deontological theory encompasses natural law theory, Kantianism, and Ross's *prima facie* duties.

Natural Law Theory St. Thomas Aquinas (1225–1274), who had a great influence on the natural law theory of the Roman Catholic writers of the 13th century, was himself influenced by the works of Aristotle and Cicero (Munson, 2004). Most versions of natural law theory today have their basis in the philosophy of Aquinas. Rightness of actions, according to the natural law theorists, is self-evident and is determined by nature, not by customs and human preferences. The law of reason, which is implanted in the order of nature as opposed to being revealed through intuition or one's innate sense, commands human actions. Use of the highest right reason and rationality guides human beings to their goals and their ends.

Kantianism Probably the philosopher most influential to the deontological way of thinking was Immanuel Kant, a German philosopher of the 18th century (Munson, 2004). In his classic work, *Groundwork of the Metaphysics of Morals*, Kant (trans. 2003) attempted to define a person as a rational human being with freedom and moral worth. A person is morally good and admirable if actions are done from a sense of duty.

Because human beings are rational, they have the freedom to make moral judgments. Therefore, Kant (trans. 2003) stated, people ought to follow a universal framework of moral maxims or rules to guide right actions and duties because it is only through dutiful actions that people have moral worth. Even when individuals do not want to act from duty, it is Kant's belief that they are required to do so. Maxims apply to everyone universally and become the laws for guiding conduct. Reasoning is sufficient to lead a person to moral actions; moral actions should be undertaken as ends in themselves, not as means to ends (McCormick, 2001). In fact, when people use others as mere means to ends, such as deliberately using another person to reach an intended positive goal through health care research, people could very well be harmed, and the outcomes of such actions may be negative. Kant emphasized that people should regard everyone with dignity and respect, and when they do not, individuals feel used and demoralized.

For example, a physician asked a nurse in the clinic to monitor certain effects of a new blood pressure medication, which is not FDA-approved, on an elderly female patient who was already having a few adverse effects to the medication. The physician told the nurse that if the elderly patient could remain on the medication for 6 weeks without missing any doses, they would each receive a hefty bonus from the pharmaceutical company for their research efforts. The nurse informed the physician of the effects but, for the sake of the research outcome and the anticipated bonuses, they decided that it would be best if the elderly lady remained on the medication for the full 6 weeks if possible. As a result, the nurse and physician decided to have a home health nurse administer the elderly patient's medication every day. In this scenario, the nurse and physician were not concerned with the feelings of the patient as a person or the side effects she was exhibiting. They were using the elderly lady as a means to certain ends for their benefit.

Kant made a distinction between two types of duties: the hypothetical imperative and the categorical imperative. The two types of duties correspond to two methods of observing the maxims (rules). *Hypothetical imperatives* are duties or rules that people ought to observe if certain ends are to be achieved. Hypothetical imperatives are sometimes called "if–then" imperatives, which are conditional. For instance, "*if* I want to show compassion toward my patient, *then* I should perform a compassionate action for my patient."

However, Kant also stated that moral actions must be based on reason. Where moral actions are concerned, duties and laws are absolute, unconditional, and universal. Kant called these moral imperatives *categorical imperatives*. When acting according to a categorical imperative, one would ask, "If I perform this action, should it become a universal law?" No action can ever be judged as right, according to Kant, if the action cannot have the potential to become a binding law for all people. For example, Kant's ethics would impose the categorical imperative that one can never tell a lie for any reason, because if a person lies in any instance, the person cannot rationally wish that permission to lie become a law for everyone in the universe. Another categorical imperative, according to Kant, would be that suicide is never acceptable. A person, when committing suicide, cannot rationally wish that all people should feel free to commit suicide; the world would become chaotic.

W.D. Ross's Seven Prima Facie Duties Ross's book, *The Right and the Good*, is based on his connection of ethical intuitionism to *prima facie* (conditional) duties (Brannigan & Boss, 2001). Clearly, Ross's theory was deontological or ruled-based, in nature, but he, as opposed to Kant, considered consequences to have value in his theory of *prima facie* duties. Ross believed in two moral principles: rightness and goodness. He outlined seven *prima facie* duties. A *prima facie* duty is "one that dictates what I should do when other relevant factors in a situation are not considered" (Munson, 2004, p. 758).

Actual duties are those real duties that a person is obligated to perform. *Prima facie* duties are morally significant duties as they relate to individual circumstances at first sight. If two duties come into conflict, only one duty can become the actual duty. *Prima facie* duties are not absolute but are conditional, according to Ross. Mappes and DeGrazia (2001) clearly explained the conflict between a *prima facie* duty to keep a promise and a *prima facie* duty to assist someone in need:

> . . . it is clear (in terms of our "ordinary moral consciousness") that the duty to keep promises is usually more incumbent upon us than the duty to assist those who are in need. However, if the promise is relatively trivial and the need of another is compelling–a matter of serious distress–then it is equally clear that the priority is reversed. In the difficult cases . . . there is . . . no hard-and-fast rule . . . The best that anyone can do is to make a reflective, 'considered decision' as to which of the competing prima facie duties has the priority . . . (p. 25)

A duty to assist can override a duty to keep a promise in certain nursing duties and priorities. Suppose that Jane, an acute-care primary nurse, promised to assist her patient, Ms. Carr, with her postoperative ambulation in 15 minutes but, in the meantime, Mr. Bass, another one of her patients, had a seizure. Mr. Bass needed Jane's immediate assistance. Two hours passed before she was able to return to Ms. Carr's room. When Jane returned to Ms. Carr's room, she explained what had happened. She did the right thing by breaking her promise to Ms. Carr to help another patient in an emergency situation.

Ross described a set of moral rules that should guide a person's universal principles (Munson, 2004). These are considered to be *prima facie* duties:

- Duties of fidelity: telling the truth, keeping actual and implicit promises
- Duties of reparation: righting the wrongs we have done to others
- Duties of gratitude: recognizing the services others have done for us
- Duties of justice: preventing a distribution of pleasure or happiness that is not in keeping with the merit of the people involved
- Duties of beneficence: helping to better the condition of other beings
- Duties of self-improvement: bettering ourselves with respect to virtue or intelligence
- Duties of nonmaleficence: avoiding or preventing an injury to others.

Utilitarianism

Utilitarianism promotes the highest good that is possible in every situation; in other words, "the greatest good for the greatest number" (Rohmann, 1999, p. 76). Jeremy Bentham (trans. 1988) introduced the principle of British utilitarianism in his book *An*

Introduction to the Principles of Morals and Legislation. Utilitarianism is related to real-life, common-sense actions and their consequences, not aristocratic privilege, religious faith, or tradition. In utilitarianism, according to Bentham, each form of happiness is equal, and each object should be evaluated according to its production of happiness, good, or pleasure (Brannigan & Boss, 2001). Although happiness or benefit to others is the goal, it should be kept in mind that utilitarianism is not an "all or none" theory. Common sense approaches should be taken seriously when individuals are deciding a course of action to improve some part of society (Falikowski, 1998).

In his book *Utilitarianism*, Mill (trans. 2002) challenged Bentham's view when he clearly pointed out that objects of pleasure and happiness do have different qualities and are not equal. For example, Mill stated that pleasure and happiness should be prioritized according to a person's intellectual ability. In this way, the most prioritized, higher pleasures, such as applying the Golden Rule to one's conduct, are preferable over lower pleasures, such as immediate gratification and physical pleasure alone. Only human beings, not animals, possess the mental faculty to develop the level of happiness that results from higher pleasures. According to Mill, the greatest happiness principle is based on the greatest happiness for everyone concerned.

Because utilitarians place great emphasis on what is best for groups, not individual people, the focus is on acts that produce the most good in terms of the most happiness. By aiming for the most happiness, this theory focuses on consequences, utility, or ends.

Other Approaches

Virtue Ethics

When people practice virtue ethics, they do not use universal rules or principles to guide their actions. Since the time of Aristotle (384–322 BCE), virtues, *arête* in Greek, have referred to excellences of character (Pence, 2000). Aristotle was one of the most influential thinkers on virtue ethics. Virtue ethics deals with questions, such as "what sort of person must I be?" and "what makes an individual a good or virtuous person?", rather than "what is right or good to do?". Virtues are thought of as purposive dispositions and character traits that are developed throughout life (Mappes & DeGrazia, 2001). Schools, social institutions, and families help to shape a person's moral character.

Everyone upholds someone in their personal or professional lives as morally outstanding because that person seems to have an almost unblemished character. Although these people are judged superior in character and are seen as models for others, an infinite number of other people are also considered to be virtuous or as having the potential to develop a virtuous character. Most, but not all, virtues, are considered a mean between two kinds of vices, involving either an excess or a deficiency. For instance, Aristotle (trans. 2002) named courage as a virtue, the excess of courage as rashness, and the deficiency of courage as cowardice. One other example names truthfulness the mean; imposture the excess; and self-deprecation the deficiency (see more on truthfulness and "Truthtelling in Nursing" in Chapter 3). The mean for each virtue is unique for each situation and each person; in other words, the mean is not always the exact average. Some of the other virtues include benevolence, compassion, thoughtfulness, fairness, justice, generosity, wisdom, temperance, and patience. Aristotle and others identified many other virtues that people practice in their daily lives.

When virtuous people are faced with complex moral dilemmas, they will choose the right course of action because doing the right thing comes from a developed character. Aristotle believed that in order for moral character to be developed, an individual must make a personal effort through training and routine practice.

Ethic of Care

The ethic of care has a history in the moral experiences of women. Emphasis is placed on personal relationships and relationship responsibilities (Mappes & DeGrazia, 2001). Some of the specific concepts are compassion, empathy, sympathy, and concern for others.

People who uphold the ethic of care think in terms of particular situations and individual contexts, not in terms of universal rules and principles (Munson, 2004). In resolving moral conflicts and understanding complex situations, a person must use critical thinking to inquire about relationships, circumstances, and the problem at hand. The situation must be evaluated with "caring, consideration, understanding, generosity, sympathy, helpfulness, and a willingness to assume responsibility" (Munson, 2004, p. 788).

ETHICAL PRINCIPLES

A framework commonly used in bioethics, known as *principlism*, encompasses four guiding principles—autonomy, beneficence, nonmaleficence, and justice (Beauchamp & Childress, 2004). Principlism is not a theory or a decision-making model; rather, the principles

---

Ethical Reflections

Think about how each of the following ethical theories and approaches—deontology (natural law theory, Kantianism, and Ross's *prima facie* theory), utilitarianism, virtue ethics, and the ethic of care—could provide justification for the decisions you may make in the following debates:

- Nurses and other health care professionals, including physicians, should/ should not always tell the truth to patients and their family members, even when the truth may hurt someone.
- The death penalty is/is not moral.
- Nurses and other health care providers should/should not assist in helping people to end their lives.

(or principlism) function as guidelines for making justified moral decisions or evaluating an action or policy (Munson, 2004). In 1979, Beauchamp and Childress published their first edition of *Principles of Biomedical Ethics*, which featured these four principles. Currently, the book is in its fifth edition and the four principles have become an essential foundation for analyzing and resolving bioethical problems.

Autonomy

Autonomy involves self-determination and freedom. Autonomy is the right of a rational person to self-rule and to generate personal decisions independently (Beauchamp & Childress, 2001). Some people argue that autonomy has top priority among the four principles. However, there is no general consensus about this issue, and many argue that other principles, such as beneficence, should take priority. Ideally, when using a framework of principlism, no one principle should automatically rule supreme.

The principle of autonomy is sometimes described as *respect* for autonomy (Beauchamp & Childress, 2001). In the domain of health care, respect for a patient's autonomy includes actions, such as obtaining informed consent for treatment; facilitating patient choice regarding treatment options; allowing the patient to refuse treatment; disclosure by the provider of personal medical information, diagnoses, and treatment options to the involved patient; and maintaining confidentiality. Restrictions on autonomy may occur in cases where there is a potential for harm to others through communicable diseases or acts of violence. People basically lose their autonomy or right to self-determination in such instances.

Patient Self-Determination Act

The Patient Self-Determination Act of 1990, enacted in 1991, was the first federal statute designed to facilitate the knowledge and use of advance directives (Devettere, 2000; Guido, 2001). With the help of agencies, staff, and institutions, all health care providers must provide written information to adult patients regarding the right to make health care decisions, refuse or withdraw treatments, and write advance directives.

It is important that dialogue about end-of-life decisions and options not be lost in hospital admission processes and office paperwork. Nurses provide the vital communication link between the patient's wishes, the paperwork, and the provider. When the opportunity arises, nurses need to take an active role toward increasing dialogue in regard to patients' rights and end-of-life decisions. In addition to responding to the direct questions that patients ask, nurses would do well to look for the subtle cues that patients give that signal their anxieties and uncertainty about end-of-life care. A good example of compassion is the alleviation of suffering and fears in regard to end-of-life nursing care and decision making.

Beneficence

The principle of beneficence addresses deeds of "mercy, kindness, and charity" (Beauchamp & Childress, 2001, p. 166). *Beneficence* means taking action to promote the welfare of other people. Although there are limits to what nurses can do, they can promote the interests and well-being of their patients. Two examples of beneficent nursing actions are practicing sterile technique during postoperative dressing changes to prevent wound infection and helping postoperative patients cough and breathe deeply to prevent hypostatic pneumonia. A more subtle beneficent and kind action would be assisting a 40-year-old female patient experiencing acute inflammatory rheumatoid arthritis in both hands with her hair and makeup.

Occasionally, nurses may experience ethical conflicts when confronted with having to make a choice between respecting the patient's right to self-determination (autonomy) and the principle of beneficence. This conflict occurs if nurses decide to act in ways that they believe are for a patient's own good when the actions are opposed to the patient's autonomous preferences. The deliberate overriding of a patient's wishes is called paternalism. One example of a paternalistic action is for a nurse to administer physician-ordered oxygen with a nasal cannula to a confused hypoxic patient with labored breathing while the patient is saying "no" to the nasal cannula. In that case, the nurse was aware that the patient critically needed oxygen to improve breathing, otherwise the patient may have experienced organ damage from oxygen deficiency. Nurses must weigh carefully the value and "good" of paternalistic actions and determine if they are truly in the patient's best interest. Justified paternalism sometimes involves matters of safety to the patient.

Nonmaleficence

Nonmaleficence means to "do no harm" and is considered to be an overriding principle for everyone who undertakes the care of a patient (Munson, 2004, p. 772). Nonmaleficence is the other side of the coin of beneficence, but the two terms cannot be addressed separately (Aiken, 2004). If health care professionals ever violate the principle of nonmaleficence, it is usually in terms of a short-term violation to yield a long-term greater good. One example is when a patient undergoes debilitating cancer chemotherapy and the long exhausting process of radiation to have a longer life with more quality later.

Best practice and due-care standards are adopted by various regulatory agencies to ensure that providers of care maintain the competency and level of skill needed to care for patients. Nonmaleficence has many implications in the area of health care. These include avoiding negligent and harmful care and making decisions regarding withholding or withdrawing treatment and whether or not to provide extraordinary or heroic treatment.

Justice

Justice is a principle in health care ethics as well as the basis of a duty-based (deontological) ethical theory. In other words, the concept of justice is all encompassing in the field of ethics (Beauchamp & Childress, 2001). In terms of principlism, *justice* refers to the right and the demand to be treated justly, fairly, and equally. In this regard, however, being treated justly may not assure the best advantage for a person (Munson, 2004). Justice in health care often refers to *distributive justice*, which pertains to the distribution of scarce health care resources. Most of the time, difficult resource allocation decisions are based on attempts to answer questions regarding who has a right to health care and who will pay for health care costs. The theory of social justice and the concepts of distributive justice and allocation of resources are discussed in the next section.

SOCIAL JUSTICE

Definition

Social justice is usually thought of in terms of how units or items, whether good or bad, should be distributed among members of a society (Miller, 1999). A Sicilian priest first used the term "social justice" in 1840, but it was in 1848 that Antonio Rosmini-Serbati popularized the term (Novak, 2000). In 1900, Willoughby expanded on the definition of social justice in his book, *Social Justice*, and posed the critical question of whether or not social and economic institutions were, at that time, treating individuals fairly (cited in Miller, 1999). The mission to define and attain some measure of social justice has continued because the pursuit of social justice has been a consequence of the 18th century's Enlightenment ideals of reasoned justice. Since then, *social justice* has been defined as:

> . . . a virtue that guides us in creating those organized human interactions we call institutions. In turn, social institutions, when justly organized, provide us with access to what is good for the person, both individually and in our associations with others. Social justice also imposes on each of us a personal responsibility to work with others to design and continually perfect our institutions as tools for personal and social development (Center for Economic & Social Justice, n.d., ¶ 7).

The term has mostly been used to describe competing powers of social systems and regulative principles on an impersonal basis, such as high unemployment, inequality of income, and lack of a living wage (Novak, 2000, ¶ 3). Also, the term has been related to the question of what makes up the common good for everyone (Brannigan & Boss, 2001). All of the theories of social justice differ to some extent. However, all social justice theories are based on the notion that justice is related to fairness of treatment and that similar cases should be treated in a similar manner (Munson, 2004). People who take a communitarian approach will put the common good of the community over individual freedoms. Thinking beyond borders to a global economic system and just community, providing equal health care for all people, and preventing global social injustices are issues that those individuals who seek equality must consider.

Theories

In his social contract book *A Theory of Justice*, Rawls (1971) proposed that fairness and equality be evaluated under a "veil of ignorance." This concept means that if people had a veil to shield them from their own or others' economic, social, and class standing, each person would be more likely to make justice-based decisions from a position free from all biases. Consequently, each person would view the distribution of resources in an impartial way. Under the veil, people would view social conditions neutrally because they would not know what their own position might be at the time the veil is lifted. This not-knowing or ignorance of persons about their own position means that they cannot gain any type of advantage for themselves by their choices. Based on this "ignorance" principle, Rawls stated that this view is just (cited in Brannigan & Boss, 2001). Rawls (1971) advocated two principles of equality and justice: (1) that everyone should be given equal liberty no matter what adversities exist for people and (2) that differences among people should be recognized by making sure that the least-advantaged people be given what they deserve or their share for improvements.

Nozick (1974; cited in Brannigan & Boss, 2001) presented the idea of an entitlement system in his book *Anarchy, State, and Utopia* that proposed if individuals can pay for insurance, only then should they be entitled to health care and the benefits of insurance. Nozick emphasized that in order for a system to be just and fair, it must reward only those who contribute to the system (Brannigan & Boss, 2001). People who cannot afford health care insurance strongly disagree with Nozick's entitlement theory.

Later, Daniels explored Rawls's concept of justice further by basing his book *Just Health Care* (1985; cited in Brannigan & Boss, 2001) on the liberty principle. He espoused the idea that every person should be able to exercise freedom and have equal opportunity. Daniels emphasized equal health care and reasonable access to health care services and recommended national health care reform. Daniels and others proposed critical standards for a fair and equitable health care system and provided points of reference, or benchmarks, for this application of fairness in the implementation and development of national health reform.

Distributing and allocating health care resources continue to be major problems in the United States. No matter what theory is applied, there must be a standard by which health care and other resources are distributed. Some ethicists have contended that the following standards need to be applied or considered when distributions are made (Brannigan & Boss, 2001).

- distribute according to market; that is, to those who can afford to pay
- distribute according to social merit
- distribute according to medical need
- distribute according to age
- distribute according to queuing, or first-come, first-served
- distribute according to random selection

Ethical Reflections

- You are the nurse manager in charge of the budget and are told to allocate $10 million to patients for free health care services at a family care clinic where you work. The very generous donor stipulated that a fair and equitable approach to distribution be used and asked for a budget report before the actual distribution was complete. On what basis would you allocate the money, and what distribution plan would you use for health care services?
- Of the three theories of social justice presented—Rawls, Nozick, and Daniels—which one, if any, fits your beliefs and value system? Please explain.

ETHICAL DILEMMAS

A situation in which an individual feels compelled to make a choice between two or more actions that he or she can reasonably and morally justify, or when evidence or arguments are inconclusive, is called an *ethical dilemma* (Beauchamp & Childress, 2001; McConnell, 2002). One action must be chosen because performing both actions would be impossible. Dilemmas may arise from conflicts between nurses and other health care professionals, health care organizational administrators, or patients and family members. The decision to alleviate suffering with palliative pain medications is a real-life dilemma that nurses experience every day (see Ethical Kaleidoscope Box 1-1).

Slippery Slope Argument

Most often the slippery slope argument is a metaphor that is used as a "don't go out without a coat or you'll catch your death" warning with no justification or formal, logical evidence to back it up (Ryan, 1998, p. 341). A slippery slope argument is a hypothetical situation that may be morally acceptable at present, but could presumably slide and become a morally unacceptable situation. For example, Ryan highlighted a metaphor of a runaway train with unintended and frightening destinations when he was referring to the social unacceptability of rational suicide. In other words, the metaphor is intended to point out that when people are given an inch, they will eventually take a mile.

Because slippery slope arguments may move toward illogical extremes, those people or groups who are afraid of a dangerous slide to the bottom of the slope on certain issues must attempt to find evidence that justifies their arguments rather than try to form public opinions and policies based only on alarmist comparisons. One such example is the legalization of voluntary euthanasia. Proponents of the slippery slope argument say that allowing voluntary euthanasia is in itself not morally wrong but that allowing voluntary euthanasia may lead to the eventual allowance of nonvoluntary euthanasia (see Chapter 10). It is the last part of this statement that becomes the slippery slope concern—that members of society should not be allowed to even take the first step of voluntary euthanasia because that first step will lead down a slippery slope to other types of euthanasia, and people will not be able to be stopped. Opponents of the slip-

Box 1-1

ETHICAL Kaleidoscope   "To Give or Not To Give"

Melinda's Ethical Dilemma: Relieving Ms. Spark's Pain
Ms. Spark, a 73-year-old woman, had been diagnosed with terminal stage pancreatic cancer and requested that she be given continuous medications for relief of pain. She explicitly said that she did not want to suffer. Melinda, the RN who was caring for her one day found that Ms. Spark had an order to receive intravenous morphine sulfate both more frequently and in a higher dose then did other patients in Melinda's care in the past. Ms. Spark was moaning, groaning, and had signs of pain and suffering. The family members requested the medicine for her. Melinda could justify giving the pain medication because she did not want Ms. Spark to suffer and, after all, Ms. Spark had requested continuous relief of pain. However, Melinda was terrified that Ms. Spark would quit breathing as a result of her pain relief interventions.

1. What is the central ethical question?
2. What ethical values are involved in this dilemma for Melinda?
3. As you consider all possible outcomes of each action—to give or not to give—what would you do if you were in Melinda's shoes and had to make this decision?
4. What strategies or advice can you offer for other nurses that may be in similar situations?

pery slope argument believe that this type of argument leaves the impression that there is mistrust in peoples' ability to make definitive distinctions between moral and immoral issues.

ETHICAL ANALYSIS IN NURSING

In health care and in nursing practice, ethical dilemmas and moral matters are so ever-present that nurses do not even realize that they are making minute-by-minute moral decisions (Kelly, 2000; MacIntyre, 1996). Nurses have the critical thinking ability and skills to respond to many of the everyday decisions that must be made. To produce a reasoned ethical analysis, it is critical for nurses to listen objectively and carefully to other people and patients and not make hasty conclusions. Personal values, professional values and competencies, ethical principles, and ethical theories are variables that must be considered when a moral decision is made. The questions "What is the right thing to do?" and "What ought I do in this circumstance?" are ever-present in nursing.

The Nurse as Part of the Health Care Team

Times when patients and families are experiencing extreme pain and suffering often coincide with times when decisions need to be made about end-of-life care. Family members may want medical treatment for their loved one while the physician and other providers may be explaining to the family that to continue treatment would be nonbeneficial or futile for the patient. When patients are weakened by disease and illness, and family members are reacting to their loved one's pain and suffering, decisions regarding health care and treatment become challenging for everyone concerned. Members of the health care team may question the decision-making capacity of the patient or family. The patient's decision may conflict with the opinions of the physician or health care team regarding treatment. Nurses who care for particular patients and interact with families sometimes find themselves caught in the middle of these conflicts.

Although nurses frequently make ethical decisions independently, they also act as an integral part of the larger team of decision makers. Most problematic bioethical decisions are not made unilaterally—not by physicians, nurses, or any other person. By participating in extensive dialogue with others on ethics committees and at clinical team conferences, nurses are often part of a larger, team approach to ethical analysis. This team is called an ethics consultation team and usually consists of physicians, the patient's nurse(s), an on-staff chaplain, other nurses, a social worker, a representative of hospital administration, possibly a legal representative, a representative for the patient in question or surrogate decision maker, and others. Nurses often do not agree with physicians' decisions regarding treatment and subsequently may experience intense moral uncertainty and anxiety. When passionate ethical disputes arise between nurses and physicians, nurses are the ones who often seek an ethics consultation. It is within the right and duty of nurses to seek help and advice from the team when they experience moral uncertainty.

Four Topics Ethical Analysis Approach

Jonsen, Siegler, and Winslade's (2002) "Four Topics Method" for ethical analysis is a practical approach for nurses and other health care professionals. The nurse or team begins with relevant facts about a particular case and moves toward a resolution through a structured analysis. In health care settings, resolving ethical problems and dilemmas is usually a case-based or bottom-up, inductive, *casuistry* (pronounced "kazhooistree") approach. The Four Topics Method is called, in jargon, the four-box approach (see Table 1-1) (Jonsen et al., 2002). The Four Topics Method was published first in 1982 in the book *Clinical Ethics: A Practical Approach to Ethical Decisions in Clinical Medicine*. Now the book is in its fifth edition.

This case-based approach allows nurses and other health care professionals to construct the facts of a case in the structured format of the four boxes, which facilitates critical thinking processes about the problems. Every ethical case is analyzed according to four topics: medical indications, patient preferences, quality of life, and contextual features (Jonsen et al., 2002). Nurses and other health care professionals on the team gather information in an attempt to answer the questions in each of the four boxes. The Four Topics Method promotes dialogue between the patient and members of the health care

TABLE 1-1   Four Topics Method for Analysis of Clinical Ethics Cases

Medical Indications	*Patient Preferences*
The Principles of Beneficence and Nonmaleficence	**The Principle of Respect for Autonomy**
1. What is the patient's medical problem? history? diagnosis? prognosis? 2. Is the problem acute? chronic? critical? emergent? reversible? 3. What are the goals of treatment? 4. What are the probabilities of success? 5. What are the plans in case of therapeutic failure? 6. In sum, how can this patient be benefited by medical and nursing care, and how can harm be avoided?	1. Is the patient mentally capable and legally competent? Is there evidence of incapacity? 2. If competent, what is the patient stating about preferences for treatment? 3. Has the patient been informed of benefits and risks, understood this information, and given consent? 4. If incapacitated, who is the appropriate surrogate? Is the surrogate using appropriate standards for decision making? 5. Has the patient expressed prior preferences, e.g. Advance Directives? 6. Is the patient unwilling or unable to cooperate with medical treatment? If so, why? 7. In sum, is the patient's right to choose being respected to the extent possible in ethics and law.

Quality of Life	*Contextual Features*
The Principles of Beneficence and Nonmaleficence and Respect for Autonomy	**The Principles of Loyalty and Fairness**
1. What are the prospects, with or without treatment, for a return to normal life? 2. What physical, mental, and social deficits is the patient likely to experience if treatment succeeds? 3. Are there biases that might prejudice the provider's evaluation of the patient's quality of life? 4. Is the patient's present or future condition such that his or her continued life might be judged undesirable? 5. Is there any plan and rationale to forgo treatment? 6. Are there plans for comfort and palliative care?	1. Are there family issues that might influence treatment decisions? 2. Are there provider (physicians and nurses) issues that might influence treatment decisions? 3. Are there financial and economic factors? 4. Are there religious and cultural factors? 5. Are there limits on confidentiality? 6. Are there problems of allocation of resources? 7. How does the law affect treatment decisions? 8. Is clinical research or teaching involved? 9. Is there any conflict of interest on the part of the providers or the institution?

From Jonsen, A. R, Siegler, M., & Winslade, W. J. *Clinical ethics: A practical approach to ethical decisions in clinical medicine* (5th ed.) New York: McGraw-Hill.

ethics team (Jonsen et al., 2002). By following the outline of the questions, nurses are able to inspect and evaluate the full scope of the patient's situation, as well as the central ethical conflict. Once the nurse or an ethics team has the case facts, the analysis takes place. Each case is unique and should be considered as such, but the subject matter of the dilemma usually involves threads common to other cases, such as withdrawing or withholding treatment and right to life issues (Jonsen et al., 2002).

Although each case analysis begins with facts, the four fundamental principles—autonomy, beneficence, nonmaleficence, and justice—along with the Four Topics Method, are considered together as the process and resolution take place (Jonsen et al., 2002). In Table 1-1, each box includes principles appropriate for each of the four topics. Fairness and loyalty are included in the contextual features box (see Table 1-1). If one wants to see Jonsen's analysis applied to a case study, go to the example at the following Web site: *http://eduserv.hscer.washington.edu/bioethics/tools/cecase.html*.

Frustration, anger, and other intense emotional conflicts between health care professionals and the patient and family may occur. Regrettable verbal exchanges and hurt feelings can result. Openness and sensitivity toward patients and family members are essential during these times. As information is exchanged and conversations take place between nurses, family members, and patients, nurses need to make an attitude of respect a top priority. If respect and sensitivity are maintained, lines of communication are more likely to remain open.

DEVELOPING SAVVY IN INTERNET ETHICS

The Internet has become an unprecedented phenomenon. Almost one billion people have connected to this global electronic community. Of the 6.2 billion people in the world early in 2004, there were 940 million Internet users of all languages (Convea, 2004). Of these 940 million users, 280 million speak English. As nurses and nursing students take advantage of the infinite possibilities of the Internet, they need to know the ethical conduct to use when accessing information on the Internet.

Another critical aspect for nurses and nursing students is the virtual world of patient teaching, nursing information, and health education. Nurses must be able to evaluate the credibility of specific Web sources and the health information they want to use for patient teaching. They also need to teach their patients how to evaluate the credibility of Web sites and health information.

Practical Strategies for Internet Ethics

Many people who use the Internet have already experienced, to some degree, the consequences of unethical computer behavior, such as being the target of someone else's devious acts. Because of the potential for unethical and criminal behaviors, it is imperative that nurses and nursing students understand and practice ethics on the Internet. Respect for one another on the Web and a serious commitment to Web ethics must occur as existing users continue to connect and new users continue to sign on in record numbers each year.

In discussing the importance of Internet ethics, Johnson (2003) identified three particular reasons for understanding and practicing ethical behavior when using the Internet: (1) the virtual world is a relatively new phenomenon, which may not be well understood by adults who attended school before the integration of computers and computer networks; (2) the capabilities of the virtual world require that new ethical considerations be applied because many people see their actions in the virtual world as intangible, and even if the actions are unethical, they do not perceive these actions to be nearly as unethical as they could be in the real world; and (3) often the capabilities of the virtual world and the advanced technology have served as a gateway for misuse; thus many people view their use as low-risk, game-like challenges, rather than misuse (Johnson, 2003, p. 3).

Although many people view computer and virtual world behaviors as intangible or not really existing, the behavior and actions really do exist and cause many problems and concerns. All people who search and use the Internet leave their footprints and traceable evidence. Behaviors that may be viewed as unethical or criminal include

- stealing copyrighted material and credit for intellectual property
- intercepting private e-mail
- displaying pornographical material
- deliberately providing public misinformation
- misusing research material
- improper commercial/personal use of Internet
- stealing credit information (Security Issues on the Internet, n.d., ¶ 4).

Rinaldi (1998) developed a highly regarded set of Internet guidelines, *The Net: User Guidelines and Netiquette*, that include helpful ethical strategies for users. These strategies are everyday manners that form the foundation of respect on the Internet. Seven of the 21 strategic behaviors that Rinaldi (1998) emphasizes for electronic communications, such as e-mails, are highlighted as follows:

- Only capitalize the words you would normally capitalize because capitalizing whole words or sentences gives the appearance of shouting.
- Keep e-mails as short and concise as possible.
- Limit line length to 65–70 characters if possible.
- Always use signatures at the end of the message.
- Avoid sending chain letters.
- Maintain professionalism when e-mailing others.
- Since the emotional aspect of e-mail content is difficult to detect, use emoticons to express feelings, such as ☺ to express humor and ☹ to express sadness, and try to be very careful about how and when you express sarcasm.

Johnson (2003) developed the Three P's of Technology Ethics, which include privacy—respecting one's privacy; property—protecting and respecting one's property;

and a(P)propriate use—using technology appropriately and constructively and not breaking the rules of the government, school, religion, or family. Another code of conduct for usage is the Ten Commandments by the Computer Ethics Institute (2001).

1. *Thou shalt not* use a computer to harm other people.
2. *Thou shalt not* interfere with other people's computer work.
3. *Thou shalt not* snoop around in other people's computer files.
4. *Thou shalt not* use a computer to steal.
5. *Thou shalt not* use a computer to bear false witness.
6. *Thou shalt not* copy or use proprietary software for which you have not paid.
7. *Thou shalt not* use other people's computer resources without authorization or proper compensation.
8. *Thou shalt not* appropriate other people's intellectual output.
9. *Thou shalt* think about the social consequences of the program you are writing or the system you are designing.
10. *Thou shalt* always use a computer in ways that insure consideration and respect for your fellow humans.

Dozens of ethical codes of conduct exist for users of the Internet. However, no matter how many codes exist or what population they serve, the codes are of no use if they are not practiced. Nurses and nursing students need to remember the foremost principal of "respect one another" when accessing the Internet. Box 1-2 discusses the issue of a nursing student stealing another person's paper via the Internet.

Nursing and Health Information on the Internet

There is an overabundance of information on the Internet regarding best health practices and treatment options, but when nurses use the information as a resource for patient teaching, they need to have a certain degree of confidence that the information is credible. Nurses also need to teach their patients how to evaluate Web sites and their content as to soundness and validity.

The power of electronic information has changed the way people are obtaining health information, products, and services. The popularity of electronic health information is astounding. As of 2003, 93 million Americans had searched for at least 1 of 16 major health topics on the Internet, making surfing for health information one of the most popular pursuits for Internet users (Fox & Fallows; Pew Internet & American Life Project, 2003). This statistic was taken from a sample of over 2000 adults. Fox and Fallows also reported the following findings:

- People searching for electronic health information do so to become more informed, to prepare for physician appointments or surgery, to share information with others, and to seek support.

Box 1-2

ETHICAL Kaleidoscope   "Should I Steal This Term Paper?"

Nancy's Term Paper Assignment
Nancy, a nursing student, found a site on the Internet that is a virtual warehouse of old nursing school term papers. She needed a paper on the concept of compassion in nursing. She found a paper on compassion and asked herself "Should I steal this term paper?" Without further thought, however, she downloaded it. She changed the title of the paper slightly, the date, and added her name, then she submitted the paper as her own work.

1. Who do you think is the rightful owner of the paper?
2. Do you think the action is unethical or illegal or both?
3. What are some values and ethical implications that Nancy needed to consider before taking the paper?
4. What is a creative strategy that Nancy's teacher could have used for this assignment to help prevent Nancy and possibly others from finding and using a term paper on the Internet?
5. What are some examples of other similar Web incidents that could be considered illegal or unethical?

- Women are the primary users of Web health information.
- Searching for this information is not an everyday experience.
- Web users find support in Web groups and e-mail.
- People who seek health information and services on the Web find that their relationships with their health care providers change.
- People who search for health information have a difficult time finding the information that is already available.

There have been many third-party regulatory efforts to bring quality and credibility to Internet health care information, including: Quackwatch: Your Guide to Health Fraud, Quackery, and Intelligent Decisions; Health on the Net Foundation Code of Conduct; United States (US) Federal Trade Commission Operation Cure All; and Health Internet Ethics (Schloman, 2002). There are numerous other initiatives in progress.

One worldwide organization, the Internet Healthcare Coalition, was formed by its charter members in 1997 as a response to the World Health Organization's (WHO) recommendations. Before 1997, a WHO working group was formed to control cross-border sales of prescription drugs via the Internet. As this issue began to be addressed by the group, however, the members soon realized that a more extensive look at the virtual world of health needed to be incorporated into their aims. Distinct regulatory approaches needed to be applied to marketers, insurers, health professionals, and others who use the Internet as a venue for health information, products, and services (Internet Healthcare Coalition, 1997).

Later in 1997, when the members formed the Internet Healthcare Coalition, they had the following mission in mind: to strive to see that health care professionals, policy makers, and marketers deliver quality current and budding health information; to strive for self-regulation so that voluntary guidelines can provide an effective way for suitable distribution of credible health information; and to strive for a community of Web members that promotes and provides high-quality and ethical health sources and information for consumers (Internet Healthcare Coalition, 1997; 1998).

Health information encompasses a vast range of information on staying healthy, preventing disease, managing disease, and making health care decisions regarding products and services. Health products may include everything from medications, vitamins and nutritional supplements to medical devices. Health care plans, health care providers, insurers, and health care facilities can also be accessed on the Internet.

On May 24, 2000, the Internet Healthcare Coalition members published their *eHealth Code of Ethics*, with the following vision statement: "to ensure that people worldwide can confidently and with full understanding of known risk realize the potential of the Internet in managing their own health and the health of those in their care" (¶ 1). Many people cannot evaluate Web sites and information adequately. Therefore, coalition members issued this code of conduct for marketers, health professionals, and creators of Web sites in an attempt to enhance a trustworthy environment for consumers of health information, products, and services. Fundamental values of the *eHealth Code of Ethics* (2000) include the following eight concepts:

- candor: disclose beneficial information on the Web site
- honesty: be truthful
- quality: provide accurate and clear health information and provide information that will help consumers judge the credibility of your information, products, and services
- informed consent: respect consumers' rights and how personal data may be collected, used, or shared
- privacy: respect and protect the privacy of others
- professionalism in online health care: respect ethical obligations to patients and consumers and educate patients and consumers about the potential limitations of electronic health information
- responsible partnering: evaluate organizations and sites for their trustworthiness
- accountability: provide ways for consumers to give feedback and evaluate the site, and inquire through specific evaluative questions the extent to which the creators of the site complied with the eHealth Code of Ethics.

With the tremendous growth in health information Web sites, third-party regulatory initiatives are having problems being accepted by these health sites (Schloman, 2002).

Also, some of the evaluation surveys for rating standards being used by some site creators have never been validated. As time goes by, third-party regulators, as well as raters of other systems will make more attempts to create an environment of safe and sound information in the virtual health world.

Schloman (2002) proposed the following questions for consumers to ask and attempt to answer when evaluating health information and Web sites.

- Who created the site?
- Is the purpose and intention of the site clear, including any bias or particular viewpoint?
- Is the information presented accurate?
- Is the information current?
- Is the site well designed and stable? (¶ 22)

Numerous medical universities have Web sites with dependable and sound health information for health care professionals and the general public. Nurses need to follow these guidelines and teach them to their patients. However, all people share in a responsibility to help assure the integrity and soundness of Internet health information. People can accomplish the task by evaluating sites and providing evaluative and meaningful feedback to the creators and marketers.

Case Study: Benefit or Burden: How Much Is Too Much?

Doris Boswell is a 78-year-old female with Alzheimer's disease, rheumatoid arthritis, and type II diabetes mellitus. For the last seven years she has resided at Comfort Rest Nursing Home, but for years before her admittance to the nursing home she lived with her son and his wife. Caring for her became so difficult that her son, John, and his wife could not safely keep her at home any longer. Her son visits every week or as often as possible.

Two years ago, Ms. Boswell developed end-stage renal disease and progressive peripheral neuropathy because of the advancement of her diabetes mellitus. Over time, her dementia has worsened noticeably, but her quality of life remained surprisingly good, despite the presence of her chronic diseases, and her dependence on nursing assistants for feeding and activities of daily living. Although she does not talk, she sometimes cries out in pain.

In the last few months, Ms. Boswell's behavior has changed. She is becoming more irritable by the day and is displaying behavior outbursts when the nurses or anyone else attempt to move her or do anything with her that is not a part of her ordinary daily care. The dialysis treatments have become too burdensome to manage because of her emotional outbursts and resistance.

After a thorough work-up, there was no physical reason for this drastic change in her behavior, so her physician attributed the change to the progression of Alzheimer's disease. Dr. Phillips, her primary physician and medical director of the nursing home, believes that the dialysis is more of a burden than a benefit for Ms. Boswell. Dr. Phillips believes that since he regards Ms. Boswell's quality of life as poor, dialysis treatments are a waste of valuable resources. Without dialysis, Dr. Phillips believes that Ms. Boswell would only live for a month or so. John and the physician discussed the benefit–burden issue, the treatment options, and the outcomes and prognosis of discontinuing dialysis. John was adamant that he wanted his mother to live as long as she could on dialysis, so he told Dr. Phillips that the nursing home administration did not need to worry about money and resources. John informed Dr. Phillips that he would be responsible for the bill and that he had plenty of money. He told Dr. Phillips that his mother would want to live as long as possible.

Case Study Critical Thinking Questions

1. Based on information that you know from the case study, use Jonsen's Four Topics Method to answer the questions in each of the four boxes. Consider the applicable principles that accompany each box.
2. Put yourself in John's place. What would you need to consider if you had to make this same decision about your mother's future? Please explain.

REFERENCES

Aiken, T. D. (2004). *Legal, ethical, & political issues in nursing* (2nd ed.). Philadelphia, PA: F. A. Davis.

American Nurses Association (ANA) (1996, Fall/Winter). Cost containment jeopardizing patient welfare concerns nurses: Survey results. *ANA: Center for Ethics & Human Rights—Communique, 5* (2). Retrieved February 7, 2004, from *http://nursingworld.org/comnque/cmqfw97.htm*

Angeles, P.A. (1992). *The Harper Collins dictionary of philosophy* (2nd ed.). New York: HarperCollins Publishers.

Aristotle. (2002). *Nicomachean ethics* (C. Rowe, Trans.). Oxford: Oxford University Press.

Beauchamp, T. L., & Childress, J. F. (2001). *Principles of biomedical ethics* (5th ed.). New York: Oxford University Press.

Bentham, J. (1988). *The principles of morals and legislation.* (Great Books in Philosophy Series). Loughton, UK: Prometheus Books. (Original work published 1798.)

Billington, R. (2003). *Living philosophy: An introduction to moral thought* (3rd ed.). London, UK: Routledge—Taylor & Francis Group.

Brannigan, M. C., & Boss, J. A. (2001). *Healthcare ethics in a diverse society.* Mountain View, CA: Mayfield Publishing.

Center for Economic Justice and Social Justice. (n.d.). *Defining economic justice and social justice.* Washington, DC: CESJ. Retrieved December 6, 2003, from *http://cesj.org/thirdway/economicjustice-defined.htm*

Computer Ethics Institute. (2001). *The Ten Commandments of computer Ethics.* Retrieved January 19, 2004, from *http://www.cpsr.org/program/ethics/cei.html*

Devettere, R. J. (2000). *Practical decision making in health care ethics: Cases and concepts* (2nd ed.). Washington, DC: Georgetown University Press.

Engelhardt, H. T. (1996). Rights to health care, social justice, and fairness in health care allocations: Frustrations in the face of finitude. *The foundations of bioethics* (2nd ed.). New York: Oxford University Press.

Falikowski, A. (1998). *Moral philosophy for modern life*. Scarborough, Canada: Prentice Hall, Allyn, & Bacon.

Fox, S., & Fallows, D. (2003, July 16). Pew Internet & American Life Project. *Internet health resources*. Retrieved January 13, 2004, from *http://www.pewinternet.org*

Fry, S., & Veatch, R. M. (2000). *Case studies in nursing ethics* (2nd ed.). Boston, MA: Jones & Bartlett.

Fulghum, R. (1986). *All I really need to know I learned in kindergarten: Uncommon thoughts on common things*. New York: Fawcett Books.

Gert, B. (2002, Summer). The definition of morality. In E. N. Zalta (Ed.). *The Stanford Encyclopedia of Philosophy*. Retrieved September 20, 2003, from *http://plato.stanford.edu/archives/sum2002/entries/morality-definition*

Global Reach. (2004) Global Internet statistics 2004. Retrieved September 12, 2004, from *http://www.global-reach.biz/eng/backgrounder.php3?goto*

Guido, G. W. (2001). *Legal and ethical issues in nursing* (3rd ed.). Upper Saddle River, NJ: Prentice-Hall.

Habel, M. (n.d.). Bioethics: Strengthening nursing's role (CE hour #420A). Retrieved February 7, 2004, from *http://www.nurseweek.com/ce/ce420a.html*

Hill, T. E., & Zweig, A. (2003). Editors' introduction: Some main themes of the *Groundwork*. In T. E. Hill & A. Zweig, Eds., In *Immanuel Kant: Groundwork for the metaphysics of morals*. New York: Oxford University Press.

Internet Healthcare Coalition. (1997). Press releases: Internet Healthcare Coalition responds to World Health Organization working group recommendations on medical Internet use. Retrieved January 13, 2004, from *http://www.ihealthcoalition.org/about/ihcc_pr1.html*

Internet Healthcare Coalition. (1998). Internet Healthcare Coalition mission statement. Retrieved January 13, 2004, from *http://ihealthcoalition.org/about/mission.html*

Internet Healthcare Coalition. (2000, May 24). *eHealth Code of Ethics*: International code of ethics. Retrieved January 13, 2004, from *http://www.ihealthcoalition.org/ethics*

Johnson, D. (2003). *Learning right from wrong in the digital age: An ethics guide for parents, teachers, librarians, and others who care about computer-using young people*. Worthington, OH: Linworth Publishing.

Johnstone, M. J. (1999). *Bioethics: A nursing perspective* (3rd ed.). Syndney, Australia: Harcourt Saunders.

Jonsen, A. (1998). *The birth of bioethics*. New York: Oxford University Press.

Jonsen, A. R., Siegler, M., & Winslade, W. J. (2002). *Clinical ethics: A practical approach to ethical decisions in clinical medicine* (5th ed.). New York: McGraw-Hill.

Kant, I. (2003). *Groundwork of the metaphysics of morals* (T. E. Hill & A. Zweig, Eds., A. Zweig, Trans.). New York: Oxford University Press. (Original work published 1785).

Kelly, C. (2000). *Nurses' moral practice: Investing and discounting self*. Indianapolis, IN: Sigma Theta Tau International Center Nursing Press.

Kuhse, H., & Singer, P. (1998). What is bioethics? A historical introduction. In H. Kuhse & P. Singer (Eds.), *A companion to bioethics* (pp. 3–11). Oxford, UK: Blackwell Publishers.

Landauer, J., & Rowlands, J. (2001). *Morality is a guide to living*. Retrieved September 20, 2003, from *http://importanceofphilosophy.com*

MacIntyre, R. (1996). Nursing loved ones with AIDS: Knowledge development for ethical practice. In S. Gordon, P. Benner, & N. Noddings (Eds.), *Caregiving: Readings in knowledge, practice, ethics, and politics*. Philadephia: University of Pennsylvania Press. Reprinted from R. MacIntyre. (1991). Nursing loved ones with AIDS: Knowledge development for ethical practice. *Journal of Home Health Care Practice, 3* (3), 1–10.

Mappes, T. A., & DeGrazia, D. (2001). *Biomedical ethics* (5th ed.). Boston, MA: McGraw-Hill.

McConnell, T. (2002, Summer). Moral dilemmas. In E. N. Zalta (Ed.), *The Stanford Encyclopedia of Philosophy*, Retrieved September 26, 2003, from *http://plato.stanford.edu/archives/sum2002/entries/moral-dilemmas*

Mill, J. S. (2002). *Utilitarianism*. (G. Sher, Trans.). Indianapolis, IN: Hackett Publishing. (Original work published 1863).

Miller, D. (1999). *Principles of social justice*. Cambridge, MA: Harvard University Press.

Munson, R. (2004). *Intervention and reflection: Basic issues in medical ethics* (7th ed.). Victoria, AU: Thomson Wadsworth.

Novak, M. (2000). Defining social justice. *First Things First, 108*, 11–13. Retrieved December 6, 2003, from *http://www.firstthings.com/ftissues/ft0012/opinon/novak.html*

Oddi, L. F., Cassidy, V. R., & Fisher, C. (1995). Nurses' sensitivity to the ethical aspects of clinical practice. *Nursing Ethics, 2*(3), 197–209.

Pence, G. (2000). *A dictionary of common philosophical terms*. New York: McGraw-Hill.

Rawls, J. (1971). *A theory of justice*. Cambridge, MA: Harvard University Press.

Rinaldi, A. (1998). *The net: User guidelines and netiquette*. Electronic communications. Retrieved January 19, 2004, from *http://www.fau.edu/netiquette/net/elec.html*

Rohmann, C. (1999). *A world of ideas: A dictionary of important theories, concepts, beliefs, and thinkers*. New York: Ballantine Books.

Ryan, C. J. (1998). Pulling up the runaway: The effect of new evidence on euthanasia's slippery slope. *Journal of Medical Ethics, 24*, 341–344.

Schloman, B. (2002). Quality of health information on the web: Where are we now? *Online Journal of Issues in Nursing*. Retrieved January 13 2004, from *http://www.nursingworld.org/ojin*

Security Issues on the Internet (n.d.), *Ethics on the web*. Retrieved January 11, 2004, from *http://www.echonyc.com/~ysue/ethics.html*

US Department of Health and Human Services. (2000, November). *Healthy People 2010: Understanding and Improving Health* (2nd ed.). Washington, DC: US GPO.

Varcoe, C., Doane, G., Pauly, B., Rodney, P., Storch, J. L., Mahoney, K., McPherson, G., et al. (2004). Ethical practice in nursing: Working the in-betweens. *Journal of Advanced Nursing, 45*(3), 316–325.

Veatch, R. M. (2003). Is there a common morality? *Kennedy Institute of Ethics Journal, 13*(3), 189–192.

Webnox Corporation. (2000-2003). Pronunciation of casuistry. Retrieved September 28, 2003, from *http://www.hyperdictionary.com/dictionary?define=casuistry&Submit1=Search+Dictionary*

Weston, A. (2001). *A 21st century ethical toolbox*. New York: Oxford University Press.

CHAPTER 2

Values, Relationships, and Virtues

Karen L. Rich, Janie B. Butts

The tiniest hair casts a shadow.

Goethe (1749–1832)

SUMMARY

1. Values are related to the things that people esteem as good or of excellence and they influence how a person's character develops and how people think and subsequently behave.
2. When making moral judgments, people generally tend to believe in a philosophy of ethical relativism—accepting that values differ among people and societies—or ethical objectivism—believing that a universal moral principle exists.
3. The well-being of patients is the central focus of a nurse's loyalty and work as emphasized in the American Nurses Association Code of Ethics.
4. Nurses often experience a disquieting feeling of anguish, uneasiness, or angst in their work that is consistent with what might be called moral suffering.
5. The Moral Ground Model provides a guide for nurses in moving from a groundless, uneducated state of moral functioning to a flourishing moral ground.

6. Flourishing moral ground embodies personal and professional excellence in nursing.

VALUES AND MORAL REASONING

Because ethics falls within the abstract discipline of philosophy, the understanding of ethics can be likened to the view one has when looking through the lens of a kaleidoscope: many vivid patterns and perspectives. The heart of ethics involves a web of patterned connections made up of what people value as good and meaningful in their lives; how they are, how they think, and how they act based on these values; and how they relate to others. Virtue ethics, with its grounding in character development, is the ethical approach that is probably most closely associated with relationship ethics. Therefore, virtue ethics is covered more specifically in this chapter than it was in Chapter 1.

A *value* is something of worth or excellence or "that which is esteemed, prized, or regarded highly" (Angeles, 1992, p. 329). *Values* refer to one's evaluative judgments about what one believes is good or what makes something desirable (Angeles, 1992; Pence, 2000). The things that people esteem as good, or of excellence, influence how a person's character develops and how people think and subsequently behave.

Both professional values, which are often outlined in professional codes, and personal values are integral to moral reasoning in nursing and fall under the domain of normative ethics (see more on normative ethics in Chapter 1). In general, reasoning involves using abstract thought processes to solve problems and to formulate plans (Angeles, 1992). More specifically, *moral reasoning* pertains to making decisions about how humans ought to be and act. Deliberations about moral reasoning go back to the days of the ancient Greeks when Aristotle (trans. 2002), in *Nicomachean Ethics*, discussed the intellectual virtue of practical wisdom as a necessary part of deliberation about what is good and advantageous in terms of moving toward worthy ends. Moral reasoning and decision making for nurses usually occur in the day-to-day relationships between nurses and their patients and between nurses and their co-workers. In other words, the moral reasoning of nurses is often related to their interpersonal relationships.

Two Ethical Perspectives

Ways of ethical thinking, valuing, and reasoning generally fall into two main views: (1) ethical relativism and (2) ethical objectivism or universalism (Brannigan & Boss, 2001).

Ethical Relativism

Relativism as a general term refers to the belief that values differ among persons or societies (Angeles, 1992). According to Brannigan and Boss (2001), there are two types of ethical relativism: ethical subjectivism and cultural relativism. People who subscribe to a belief in *ethical subjectivism* believe "that individuals create their own morality [and that] there are no objective moral truths—only individual opinions" (Brannigan & Boss,

2001, p. 7). Whether actions are right or wrong or good or bad depends on how a person feels about the action. It does not involve an opinion based on reason or factual analysis. What is believed by one person to be wrong might not be viewed as wrong by a neighbor, depending on variations in opinions and feelings. Ethical subjectivism has been distinguished from cultural relativism. Pence (2000) defined *cultural relativism* as "the ethical theory that moral evaluation is rooted in and cannot be separated from the experience, beliefs and behaviors of a particular culture, and hence, that what is wrong in one culture may not be so in another" (p. 12). Those opposed to ethical relativism argue that when it is practiced according to its extreme or literal meaning, it can be dangerous because it may theoretically support ethical relativists in taking exploitative or hurtful actions without justification (Brannigan & Boss, 2001).

Ethical Objectivism

Ethical objectivism is a position in which people believe that universal or objective moral principles exist (Brannigan & Boss, 2001). This view is held by most philosophers and health care ethicists. The theories or ethical approaches to which ethical objectivists generally subscribe include approaches such as deontology, utilitarianism, virtue ethics, natural law theory, and rights-based ethics. Although some ethicists believe that these different theories or approaches are mutually exclusive, they often, in fact, overlap when used in practice. According to Brannigan and Boss (2001), "moral judgment is a whole into which we must fit principles, character and intentions, cultural values, circumstances, and consequences" (p. 23).

Ethical Reflections

- Think about your personal ethical perspective. How does it fit within the context of ethical relativism and ethical objectivism?

Fact/Value Distinction

The 18th century philosopher David Hume (trans. 2000) proclaimed a belief that there is a distinction between facts and values when morality is considered. This fact/value distinction has also been called the "is/ought gap," and it is a position that some people believe is associated with ethical relativism, although others disagree with this position. Hume suggested that a person cannot acknowledge a fact and then make a value judgment based on that fact. One cannot take a fact of what *is* and then determine what *ought* to be. If Hume's view is accepted as valid, people could not logically make assumptions such as (1) if all dogs have fleas (assuming this is a known fact) and (2) Sara is a dog (a fact), therefore (3) Sara *ought not* to be allowed to sleep on the sofa because having fleas on the sofa is a bad thing (a value statement). According to those who believe in the fact/value distinction, the chance of Sara spreading her fleas to the sofa might be a fact if she sleeps on it, but determining that having fleas on the sofa is a bad thing is based only on one's feelings.

Historic and Cultural Periods

Different ethical values, worldviews, and ways of moral reasoning have evolved through history and have different points of emphasis in varying cultural periods. In some cases "what was old becomes new again," as in the case of virtue ethics.

Ancient Greece

In ancient Greece, moral reasoning was usually associated with intellectual virtues and can best be illustrated through what Aristotle (trans. 2002) called the virtue of practical wisdom (*phronesis*). Aristotle's (384–322 BC) conception of *phronesis* can be likened to the virtue of prudence, which is one of Plato's (429–347 BC) four cardinal virtues (Pieper, 1966). Wisdom is focused on the good achieved by being wise; that is, knowing how to act in a particular situation, deliberating well, and acting virtuously, which includes having a disposition that embodies excellence of character (Broadie, 2002). Therefore, in ancient Greece, prudence involved more than having good intentions or meaning well. It included knowing what is what but also transforming that knowledge into well-reasoned decisions. Deliberation, judgment, and decision are the steps in transforming knowledge into action. Prudence becomes truth in action (Pieper, 1966).

The Middle Ages

In the Middle Ages, the time period between the classical era and the Renaissance, the Christian church served as a link between classical Greek and Roman civilization and the gestating modern world (Tarnas, 1991). With the advent of the Middle Ages in Europe, there began to be a more widespread belief in one God rather than many gods. In terms of ethics, the two Catholic saints, Augustine and Aquinas, were major influences during this period.

St. Augustine (354–430 AD) believed that one has a duty to love God and that moral reasoning should direct one's senses in accordance with that duty. Being subject to this obligation is what leads to moral perfection (Copleston, 1950). Generally, St. Augustine believed only in the existence of good. Therefore, according to Augustine, evil is present only when good is missing or has in some way been perverted. In order to move away from evil, one must have the grace of God (Hinson, 1992). Humans were viewed as finite beings who must have the divine aid of grace in order to bridge the gap required to have a relationship with the infinite being of God (Copleston, 1950).

Although it would be too simplistic to say that the moral teachings of St. Thomas Aquinas (1224–1274) are merely a Christianized version of Aristotle's ethical teachings, Aquinas is closely associated with the ethics of Aristotle. Aquinas is placed in the category of a virtue ethicist and, just as Aristotle, he believed that practicing the virtues leads to human happiness (Denise, White, & Peterfreund, 2002). However, whereas Aristotle's moral philosophy was based on humans moving toward an end goal of *eudaimonia* (happiness) through the virtues and philosophical contemplation, Thomas

Aquinas expanded the concept of the end goal of perfect happiness as being grounded only in the knowledge and love of God (Copleston, 1950).

Modern Philosophy

The period of modern philosophy began with two changes in the outlook of people in European societies, changes that led to views of life that differed from those of the Middle Ages. The influence of the Church in society began to diminish while the influence of science began to increase. The scientific revolution began in 1543 with the Copernican theory of the solar system but did not take hold until the 17th century when Kepler and Galileo moved scientific debates to the forefront of society (Russell, 1972).

With these changes came a new emphasis on human moral reasoning, based on people being autonomous, rational, thinking creatures. The duty-based, autonomy-focused ethic of Immanuel Kant, discussed in Chapter 1, was developed during the 18th century Enlightenment when humans believed that they were coming out of the darkness of the Middle Ages into the light of true knowledge. Some scientists and philosophers started to believe that humans could ultimately be perfected. As the belief in empirical science grew, a new way of thinking was ushered in that essentially compared the universe to a machine, which, along with its inhabitants, could be predicted and controlled. People still see evidence of this way of thinking today when cure is highly valued over care and uncertainty is considered something that can be, or needs to be, eliminated in health care.

Postmodern Era

Postmodernism is often considered to have begun about 1950, after the end of World War II (Morris, 2000). However, some people trace its beginning back to the German philosopher Friedrich Nietzsche in the late 1800s. Pence (2000) defined postmodernism as "a modern movement in philosophy and the humanities that rejects the optimistic view that science and reason will improve humanity; it rejects the notion of sustained progress through reason and the scientific method" (p. 43). The postmodern mind is one that is formed by a pluralistic view or a diversity of intellectual and cultural influences. The people who think according to a postmodern philosophy acknowledge that reality is constantly changing and that scientific investigation cannot provide a grand theory that can guide human behavior, relationships, and life. Human knowledge is thought, instead, to be shaped by multiple factors, with storytelling and narrative analysis viewed as core components of knowledge development (Lyotard, 1979; Tarnas, 1991). Postmodernism, along with virtue ethics, has strongly influenced feminist ethics and an ethic of care.

A Kaleidoscope of Ethical Values and Moral Reasoning Often, it is only in hindsight that people are able to analyze and label an historic or cultural era in which there is a converging of norms and beliefs that are held in high esteem or valued by large groups within a society. Like the overlapping of approaches used by ethical objectivists, the influences of historic or cultural eras also build on each other and are often hard to separate. Though mentioning virtue ethics 20 years ago in nursing would have been very unpopular, there has been a resurgence in the popularity of virtue ethics in philosophical circles since the late 1950s and, more recently, within nursing (Crisp & Slote, 1997; Tschudin, 2003). Some Christians still base many of their ethical positions on the philosophers from the Middle Ages. At the same time, it is evident that individualistic, duty-based ethics developed during the Enlightenment remain popular in Western societies because autonomy is highly valued. Narrative ethics, discussed later in this chapter, is also very popular today. The varied historical influences have formed a kaleidoscope pattern of rich and interesting views, values, and perspectives that are evident in the globally connected world that people live in today (see Box 2-1).

Justice versus Care Debate

In 1981, Lawrence Kohlberg reported his landmark research about moral reasoning, which was based on 84 boys he had followed for over 20 years. Kohlberg defined six stages of moral development, ranging from childhood to adulthood. Interestingly, Kohlberg did not include any women in his research but expected that his six-stage scale could be used to measure moral development in both males and females. However, when the scale was applied to women, they seemed to score only at the third stage of the sequence, a stage in which Kohlberg described morality in terms of interpersonal relationships and helping others. Kohlberg viewed this third stage of development as deficient with regard to mature moral reasoning. Because of Kohlberg's exclusion of females in his research and his view of this third stage, Carol Gilligan raised the concern of gender bias. Gilligan, in turn, published an influential book in 1982, *In a Different Voice*, in which she argued that women's moral reasoning is different, but it is not deficient (Gilligan, 1993; Grimshaw, 1993; Thomas, 1993).

While *feminine ethics* is focused on revealing and rectifying the ways that traditional ethical systems fail to reflect the typical moral assertions of women, *feminist ethics* is more directly aimed at using political expressions to address the perceived male-dominated societal oppression or marginalization of women. The distinction that is usually made between the ethics of Kohlberg and Gilligan is that Kohlberg's is a male-

Box 2-1

ETHICAL Kaleidoscope   Is There a Single Truth?

Think of it: zillions and zillions of organisms running around, each under the hypnotic spell of a single truth, all these truths identical, and all logically incompatible with one another.

R. Wright, *The Moral Animal*

oriented *ethic of justice* and Gilligan's is a more feminine *ethic of care*. Gilligan's ethics is one of socially embedded relationships and the emotional responsiveness that is part of those relationships (Blum, 1994). The moral reasoning espoused by Kohlberg is firmly based in rationality whereas Gilligan's view holds that emotion, cognition, and action are intertwined. The Kohlberg–Gilligan justice–care debate is still at the heart of feminine and feminist ethics.

Professional Ethical Codes

The beginning of professional nursing can be traced to 19th century England to the school that was founded by Florence Nightingale, where profession-shaping ethical precepts and values were communicated (Kuhse & Singer, 2001). Nightingale's achievement was a landmark in nursing even though graduates of the school performed below desired expectations in the early days (Dossey, 2000). For the first 30 to 40 years in Nightingale's school, the prospective nurses were trained by male physicians because there were not enough educated nurses to teach nursing. Because of this strong medical influence, early nursing education was focused on technical training rather than on the art and science of nursing as Nightingale would have preferred.

By the end of the 19th century, modern nursing had been established, and ethics in nursing was seriously being discussed (Dossey, 2000; Kuhse & Singer, 2001). The Nightingale Pledge, first administered in 1893, was written under the chairmanship of Lystra Gretter, the principal of a Detroit nursing school, and the presence of the pledge helped establish nursing as an art and a science (Dossey, 2000). The International Council of Nurses (ICN), which has been a pioneer in developing a code of nursing ethics, was established in 1899. By 1900, the first book on nursing ethics, *Nursing Ethics: For Hospital and Private Use*, had been written by the American nursing leader Isabel Hampton Robb (Kuhse & Singer, 2001).

Historically, a primary value consideration in nursing ethics has been the determination of the focus of nurses' work. Until the 1960s, this focus was on the physician, which is not surprising, based on the fact that over the years most nurses have been women and most doctors have been men (Kuhse & Singer, 2001). The focus on nurses' obedience to physicians remained at the forefront of nursing responsibilities into the 1960s, and this assumption was still reflected in the *ICN Code of Nursing Ethics* as late as 1965. By 1973, however, the focus of the ICN code reflected a shift in nursing responsibility from the physician to the patient, where it remains to this day.

Ethical codes are systematic guidelines for shaping ethical behavior that answer the normative questions of what beliefs and values should be morally accepted. However, it must be noted that no code can provide absolute or complete rules that are free of conflict and ambiguity (Beauchamp & Childress, 2001). Because codes are unable to provide exact directives for moral reasoning and action in all situations, some people have stated that virtue ethics provides a better approach to ethics because the emphasis is on a person's character rather than on rules, principles, and laws (Beauchamp & Childress, 2001). Proponents of virtue ethics consider that if a nurse's character is not virtuous, the nurse cannot be depended on to act in good or moral ways even with a professional code as a guide. Professional codes, however, do serve a useful purpose in providing direction to health care professionals although, ultimately, one must remember that codes do not eliminate moral dilemmas and are of no use without professionals who are motivated to act morally. For the code to have more meaning, Benner contended when speaking of the nurse's role in working for social justice, "each of us and each nursing organization" must "breathe life into the code by taking individual and collective action" (Fowler & Benner, 2001, p. 437).

American Nurses Association Code of Ethics

The American Nurses Association (ANA) first adopted its code in 1950 (Daly, 2002). Although it has always been implied that the code reflects ethical provisions, the word "ethics" was not added to the title until the 1985 code was replaced with its sixth and latest revision in 2001 (Fowler & Benner, 2001). The ANA (2001) code contains general moral provisions and standards for nurses to follow, but specific guidelines for clinical practice, education, research, and administration are found in the accompanying interpretive statements (see Appendix A for the ANA Code of Ethics).

The code is considered to be nonnegotiable with regard to nursing practice. Some of the significant positions and changes in the 2001 code include a return to the use of the word "patient" rather than client; an application of the code to nurses in all roles, not just clinical roles; conceding that research is not the only method that contributes to professional development; reaffirming a stance against the participation of nurses in euthanasia; emphasizing that nurses owe the same duties to themselves as to others; and recommending that members who represent nursing associations are responsible for expressing nursing values, maintaining professional integrity, and participating in public policy development (ANA, 2001; Fowler & Benner, 2001).

Fowler (Fowler & Benner, 2001) and Daly (2002), nursing leaders involved in revising the code completed in 2001, have proposed that the new code is clearly patient focused, whether the patient is considered to be "an individual, family, group, or community" (Daly, 2002, p. 98). The nurse's loyalty must be first and foremost to the patient, even though institutional politics is a frequent influence in today's nursing environment. With the expanding role of nurse administrators and advanced-practice nurses, each nurse must be cognizant of conflicts of interest that could potentially have a negative effect on relationships with patients and patient care. Often, nursing has overlooked the responsibility to the patient held by nurses who are not in clinical roles. It is worth noting that nurse researchers, administrators, and educators are indirectly but still involved in supporting patient care. According to Fowler (Fowler & Benner, 2001), "it is not the possession of nursing credentials, degrees, and position that makes a nurse a nurse, rather it is this very commitment to the patient" (p. 435). Therefore, the code applies to all nurses regardless of their role.

One issue that created a vigorous debate during the 2001 revision of the code involved the ethical implications of collective bargaining in nursing (Daly, 2002). Ultimately, those nurses who formulated the revisions decided that it was important for the code to contain provisions supporting nurses who work to assure that the environment in which they work is conducive to quality patient care and that nurses are able to fulfill their moral requirements. Collective bargaining was determined to be an appropriate avenue for more than just negotiating for better salaries and benefits. Now it is also seen as a way to improve the moral level of the environment in which nurses work.

Values and virtues are emphasized in the ANA (2001) *Code of Ethics for Nurses with Interpretive Statements*. Values in nursing encompass an appreciation of what is important for the nurse personally as well as what is important for patients. In the code, the ANA emphasized the importance of moral respect for all human beings, including the respect of nurses for themselves. Self-respect can be thought of as personal regard. Personal regard involves nurses extending attention and care to their own requisite needs. Nurses who do not regard themselves as worthy of care usually cannot fully care for others.

In the code, the ANA (2001) included statements about wholeness of character, which pertains to knowing the values of the nursing profession and one's own authentic moral values, integrating these two belief systems, and expressing them appropriately. Integrity is an important feature of wholeness of character. In a health care system often burdened with constraints and self-serving groups and organizations, threats to integrity can be a serious pitfall for nurses. According to the code, maintaining integrity involves acting consistently with personal values and the values of the profession. When nurses are asked and pressured to do things that conflict with their values, such as falsify records, deceive patients, or accept verbal abuse from others, emotional and moral suffering may occur (see "Moral Integrity" in Chapter 3). A nurse's beliefs, grounded in good moral reasoning, must guide actions even when other people challenge the nurse's beliefs (see Box 2-2). When compromise is necessary, the compromise must not be such that it compromises personal or professional values.

Recognizing the essential dignity of oneself and of each patient is another value that is basic to nursing, and it is given priority in moral reasoning. Pullman (1999) described two conceptions of dignity. One type, called basic dignity, is intrinsic or inher-

Box 2-2

ETHICAL Kaleidoscope   Courage

It is plain that there is no separate essence called courage, no cup or cell in the brain, no vessel in the heart containing drops or atoms that make or give this virtue; but it is the right or healthy state of every man, when he is free to do that which is constitutional to him to do. It is directness—the instant performing of that which he ought.

Ralph Waldo Emerson

ent and dwells within all humans, with all humans being ascribed this moral worth. The other type, called personal dignity, often mistakenly equated with autonomy, is an evaluative type. Judging others and describing behaviors as dignified or undignified are acts of an evaluative nature. Personal dignity is a socially constructed concept that fluctuates in value from community to community, as well as globally. Most often, however, personal dignity is highly valued. The importance of supporting the personal dignity of patients is covered further in the nurse–patient–family relationships section of this chapter.

ICN Code of Ethics for Nurses

In 1953, the ICN adopted its first code of ethics for nurses. (See Appendix B for the most recent ICN *Code of Ethics*.) The code had been revised and reaffirmed many times (ICN, 2000). The four principle elements contained in the ICN code involve standards related to nurses and people, practice, the profession, and co-workers. These elements form a framework to guide nursing conduct and are elaborated in the code, along with practice applications for practitioners and managers, educators and researchers, and national nurses' associations.

A Common Theme of ANA and ICN Codes

A theme common to the ANA (2001) and ICN (2000) codes is a focus on the importance of compassionate patient care aimed at alleviating suffering. This emphasis is threaded throughout the codes but begins from the focal point of patients being the central focus of nurses' work. Nurses are to support patients in self-determination and are to protect the moral environment in which patients receive care. The interests of various nursing associations and health care institutions must not be placed above those of patients. Although opportunities to exhibit compassion in the health care environment are not unique to nurses, nurses must always uphold the moral agreement that they make with patients and communities when they join the nursing profession. Nursing care includes the important responsibilities of promoting health and preventing illness, but the heart of nursing care has always involved caring for patients who are experiencing varying degrees of physical, psychological, and spiritual suffering.

Ethical Reflections

- The ANA Code of Ethics now includes the word "patient" instead of the word "client" in referring to the recipients of nursing care. Do you agree with this change? Why or why not?
- Take a minute to review the ANA Code of Ethics in Appendix A. Would you add any provisions? Would you remove any provisions? If so, please explain.

RELATIONSHIPS

To a disciple who was constantly complaining about others the Master said, "If it is peace you want, seek to change yourself, not other people. It is easier to protect your feet with slippers than to carpet the whole earth."

De Mello, *One Minute Wisdom*

The ANA's 2001 Code of Ethics places the central focus of nursing and nursing relationships on patients. However, the quality of patient care rendered by nurses often depends on the existence of harmonious relationships between nurses and physicians, other nurses, and other health care workers. Nurses who are interested in providing compassionate care must be concerned about their relationships with colleagues as well as with their direct relationships with patients. If nurses view life as a kaleidoscope of interrelationships, all of a nurse's relationships can potentially affect patients.

Moral Suffering in Nursing

Many times nurses experience a disquieting feeling of anguish, uneasiness, or angst consistent with what might be called *moral suffering*. Suffering in a moral sense is similar to the Buddhist concept of *dukkha*, a Sanskrit word translated as "suffering." *Duhkha* "includes the idea that life is impermanent and is experienced as unsatisfactory and imperfect" (Master Sheng-yen, 1999, p. 37). It evolved from the historical Buddha Shakyamuni's belief that the human conditions of birth, sickness, old age, and death involve suffering and *are* suffering. Nurses deal with these human conditions every day. Not recognizing that impermanence, or the changing and passing away of all things, is inherent in human life, the world, and all objects is a cause of suffering.

Moral suffering can be experienced when nurses attempt to sort out their emotions when they find themselves in imperfect situations that are morally unsatisfactory or when forces beyond their control prevent them from influencing or changing perceived unsatisfactory moral situations. Suffering occurs because nurses believe that situations must be changed or fixed in order to bring well-being to themselves and others or to alleviate the suffering of themselves and others.

Moral suffering may arise, for example, from disagreements with imperfect institutional policies, such as a mandatory overtime policy or mandatory on-call policy that the nurse believes does not provide for the nurse's psychological well-being. Nurses may also disagree with physicians' orders that they believe are not in the best interest of their patients or they may disagree with the way a family treats a patient or makes patient care decisions. Moral suffering can result when a nurse's compassion is aroused while caring for a severely impaired neonate that has life-sustaining care withdrawn. These are but a few examples of the many types of moral suffering that nurses encounter.

Another important, but often unacknowledged, source of moral suffering involves nurses who freely choose to act in ways that they themselves would not believe morally commendable if they honestly analyzed their actions. For example, a difficult situation that may cause moral suffering for a nurse would be covering up a patient care error made by a valued nurse who is also a best friend. On the other hand, nurses may experience moral suffering when they act virtuously, doing what they believe is morally right despite anticipated disturbing consequences. Sometimes, doing the right thing or acting as a virtuous person would act is hard, and it is incumbent on nurses to act in virtuous ways consistently; that is, to exhibit habits of excellent character.

The Dalai Lama (1999) proposed that how people are affected by suffering is often a matter of choice or personal perspective. Some see suffering as something to accept and transform, if possible. Although causes lead to certain effects, nurses are often able to change the circumstances or conditions of events so that positive effects occur. One can try to choose and cultivate one's perspective, attitude, and emotions in ways that lead toward happiness and well-being rather than toward suffering.

The Buddha was reported to have stated, "because the world is sick, I am sick. Because people suffer, I have to suffer" (Thich Nhat Hanh, 1998, p. 3). However, the Buddha, in his Four Noble Truths, stated that the cessation of suffering can be made a reality through the Eightfold Path of eight right ways of thinking, acting, and being, which are sometimes grouped under the three general categories of wisdom, morality, and meditation. In other words, suffering can be transformed. When nurses or others react to situations with fear, bitterness, and anxiety, it is important to remember that wisdom and inner strength are often most increased during times of the greatest difficulty. Thich Nhat Hanh (1998) wisely stated, "without suffering, you cannot grow" (p. 5). Therefore, nurses must learn to take their disquieting experiences of moral anguish and uneasiness, that is, moral suffering, and transform them into experiences that lead to more flourishing moral ground.

Nurse–Physician Relationships

In 1967, Leonard Stein, a physician, wrote an article characterizing a type of relationship between physicians and nurses that he called "the doctor–nurse game" (Stein, Watts, & Howell, 1990). The game is based on a hierarchical relationship, with doctors in the superior position. The hallmark of the game is that open disagreement between the disciplines is to be avoided. Avoidance of conflict is achieved when an experienced nurse, who is able to provide helpful suggestions to a doctor regarding patient care, cautiously offers the suggestions in a way that the physician does not directly perceive consultative advice coming from a nurse. In the past, student nurses were educated about the rules of the game while attending nursing school. Over the years, others have given credence to the historical accuracy of Stein's characterization of doctor–nurse relationships (Fry & Johnstone, 2002; Jameton, 1984; Kelly, 2000).

Stein, along with two other physicians, wrote an article revisiting the doctor–nurse game in 1990, 23 years after the phrase was first coined (Stein et. al., 1990). They proposed that nurses had decided unilaterally to stop playing the game. Some of the reasons for this change and some of the ways the change was accomplished have involved nurses' increased use of dialogue rather than gamesmanship, the profession's goal of equal partnership status with other health care professionals, the alignment of nurses with the civil rights and women's movements, the increased percentage of nurses who are receiving higher education, and the joint demonstration projects on collaboration between nurses and physicians. In conjunction with the dismantling of the doctor–nurse game, many nurses have taken a rebellious stance with physicians. These rebellious nurses believe that they need to continue fighting for freedom to establish nursing as an autonomous profession.

However, rather than generating a rebellion full of conflict, the nursing profession might be better served if nurses take a communitarian approach with physicians. It is within communities that morality in general, and bioethics in particular, receive their meaning (Engelhardt 1996; see Communitarian Ethics in Chapter 8). Communities work toward a common good and are held together by moral traditions. Nurses and physicians, as members of the health care community, must work together for the health and well-being of patients, whether those patients are individuals, groups, or communities. When overt or covert battles are waged between nurses and physicians, moral problems arise, and patients are the losers. Some ethicists have contended that the best approach for healing involves actually bringing patients into the community of health care providers (Hester, 2001). If nurses and physicians do not see themselves as members of a common community, the best interests of patients may not be served.

Nurse–Patient–Family Relationships

Unavoidable Trust

When patients enter the health care system, they are usually entering a foreign and forbidding environment (Chambliss, 1996; Zaner, 1991). Intimate conversations and activities, such as touching and probing, that normally do not occur between strangers, are commonplace between patients and health care professionals. Patients are frequently stripped of their clothes, made to sit alone in cold and barren rooms, and forced to wait anxiously for frightening news regarding the continuation of their very being. When patients are in need of help from nurses, they frequently feel a sense of vulnerability and uncertainty. The tension that patients feel when accessing health care is heightened by the need for what Zaner (1991), in discussing patient–physician relationships, called *unavoidable trust*. Zaner's concept can also be applied in other patient–health care professional relationships. Patients, in most cases, have no option but to trust nurses and other health care professionals when they need care.

This unavoidable trust creates an asymmetrical, or uneven, power structure in professional–patient and professional–family relationships (Zaner, 1991). Nurses' responsiveness to this trust must include promising to be the most excellent nurses that they can be. According to Zaner (1991), health care professionals must promise "not only to take care of, but to care for the patient and family—to be candid, sensitive, attentive, and never to abandon them" (p. 54). It is paradoxical that trust is necessary *before* health care is rendered but can only be evaluated in terms of whether or not the trust was warranted *after* care is rendered. Nurses must never take for granted the fragility of patients' trust.

Personal Dignity

In the first provision of the *Code of Ethics for Nurses with Interpretive Statements*, the ANA (2001) included the standard that a nurse must have "respect for human dignity" (p. 7). However, Shotton and Seedhouse (1998) have proposed that the term "dignity" has been used in vague ways. They characterized dignity as being related to persons who are in a position to use their capabilities. In general terms, a person has dignity "if he or she is in a situation where his or her capabilities can be effectively applied" (p. 249). For example, a nurse can enhance dignity when caring for an elderly person by assessing the elder's priorities and determining what the elder has been capable of in the past and what the person is capable of in the present.

A lack of or loss of capability is frequently an issue when caring for patients such as children, elders, and the physically and mentally disabled. Having absent or diminished capabilities is consistent with what MacIntyre (1999) was referring to in his discussion of human vulnerability. According to MacIntyre, people generally progress from a point of vulnerability in infancy to achieving varying levels of independent practical reasoning as they mature. However, all people, including nurses, would do well to realize that all persons have been or will be vulnerable at some point in their lives. Taking a "there but for the grace of God go I" stance may prompt nurses to develop what MacIntyre called the virtues of acknowledged dependence. These virtues include "just generosity," *misericordia*, and truthfulness and are exercised in communities of giving and receiving. Just generosity is a form of giving generously without keeping score of who gives or receives the most; *misericordia* is a Latin word that signifies giving based on urgent need without prejudice; and truthfulness involves not withholding information from others that is needed for their own good. Nurses who cultivate these three virtues can move toward preserving patient dignity and toward working for the common good of a community.

Patient Advocacy

Nurses acting as patient advocates try to identify unmet patient needs and then follow up to address the needs appropriately (Jameton, 1984). Advocacy, as opposed to advice, involves the nurse's moving from the patient to the health care system rather than moving from the nurse's values to the patient. The concept of advocacy has been a part of the ICN and ANA codes since the 1970s (Winslow, 1988). In the *Code of Ethics for Nurses with Interpretive Statements*, the ANA (2001) continues to support patient advocacy in elaborating on the "primacy of the patient's interest" (p. 9) and requiring nurses to work collaboratively with others to attain the goal of addressing the health care needs of patients and the public. Nurses are called on to assure that all appropriate parties are involved in patient care decisions, that patients are provided with the information needed to make informed decisions, and that collaboration is used to increase the accessibility and availability of health care to all patients who need it. The ICN (2000), in the *Code of Ethics*, affirms that the nurse must "share with society the responsibility for initiating and supporting action to meet the health and social needs of the public, in particular those of vulnerable populations" (p. 2).

Nurse–Nurse Relationships

As in the case of nurse–physician relationships, nurse–nurse relationships can be thought of as relationships within a community. Nurses in a nursing community might be what Engelhardt (1996) called "moral friends." According to Wildes (2000), moral friends exist together in communities and use similar moral language. They "share a moral narrative and commitments [and] common understandings of the foundations of morality, moral reason, and justification" (p. 137). Those communities are strongest when moral friends share "common moral traditions, practices, and [a] vision of the good life" (p. 137). In placing patients first in their priorities, nurses in a community work together for a common good, using professional traditions to guide the communal narrative of nursing.

Unfortunately, nurses often treat other nurses in hurtful ways through what some have called lateral or horizontal violence (Kelly, 2000; McKenna, Smith, Poole, & Coverdale, 2003). Lateral or horizontal violence involves interpersonal conflict, harassment, intimidation, harsh criticism, sabotage, and abuse among nurses, and it often occurs because nurses feel oppressed by other dominant groups such as physicians or institutional administrators. Kelly (2000) reported that some nurses have characterized the violence perpetrated by nurses against other nurses who excel and succeed as the "tall poppy syndrome." Nurses who succeed or seem to rise above the crowd are ostracized, or cut down like tall flowers thereby creating a culture among nurses that discourages success.

Lateral violence in nursing is very counterproductive for the profession. A more productive path to moral ground for nurses might be to cultivate the virtue included in the Moral Ground Model (see Figure 2-1 and Table 2-1) that Buddhists call sympathetic joy. Sympathetic joy means that one cultivates experiences of happiness in regard to the good things experienced by others. The nursing community does not benefit from lateral violence, but nurses who cultivate the virtue of sympathetic joy can strengthen the sense of community among nurses. Nurses must support other nurses' successes rather than treating colleagues as "tall poppies" that must be cut down.

However, there are occasions when unpleasant action must be taken with regard to nursing colleagues. In addition to directly advocating for patients' unmet needs, nurses are advocates when they take appropriate action to protect patients from the unethical, incompetent, or impaired practice of other nurses (ANA, 2001). When nurses are aware of these situations, they must deal compassionately with the offending co-workers while assuring that patients receive safe, quality care. Concerns must be expressed to the offending nurse when personal safety or patient safety is not jeopardized in doing so, and appropriate guidance must be obtained from supervisory personnel and institutional policies. Although action must be taken to safeguard patient care, the manner in which a nurse handles situations involving unethical, incompetent, or impaired colleagues must not be a matter of gossip, condescension, or unproductive derogatory talk.

Narrative Ethics

*There are stories and stories . . . There are the songs, also, that
are taught.*
*Some are whimsical. Some are very intense. Some are
documentary . . .*
*Everything I have known is through teachings, by word of
mouth, either by song or by legends.*

Terrance Honvantewa, *Native American Wisdom*

According to one of the foremost modern-day virtue ethicists, Alasdair MacIntyre (1984), narrative thinking and virtue ethics are closely connected. Narrative ethics is also firmly embedded in human relationships. MacIntyre (1984) has proposed that a human is "essentially a story-telling animal"; a person is "a teller of stories that aspire to truth" (p. 216). In order for people to decide what they should do in particular circumstances, they must first identify how they fit within the greater stories of their culture.

Narratives involve stories that are being currently lived, read, watched, heard, discussed, analyzed, or compared. In health care, a good example of a narrative is to think about a patient's particular *case*. A case is the story about a particular patient, but there is much more to the story than is usually known or discussed among the health care providers. Persons are situated within their personal life narratives intersecting and interweaving with the narratives of those with whom they interact. Narratives are very context, or situation, bound. People are not solitary creatures, and as they interact with other people and their environment, they must make choices about what they think and how they will act. Human stories are constantly being constructed. Charon and Montello (2002) stated "[a] narrative approach to bioethics focuses on the patients themselves: these are the moral agents who enact choices" (p. xi). In narrative ethics, the stories of both patients *and* nurses matter.

Ethical Reflections

- Do you believe that stories in books and movies have affected your moral views? If so, in what ways?
- How can stories be used by nurses in their practice?

VIRTUES

Watch your thoughts; they become words.
Watch your words; they become actions.

Watch your actions; they become habits.
Watch your habits; they become character.
Watch your character; it becomes your destiny.

Frank Outlaw

Historic Influences and Tradition

Rather than centering on what is right or wrong, virtue ethics is based on the excellence of one's character and considerations of what sort of person one wants to become. The origin of virtue ethics is generally associated with the ancient Greeks, most notably Plato and Aristotle (see "Virtue Ethics" in Chapter 1). Eastern philosophy, specifically Buddhism, and nursing, through Florence Nightingale, also have a long tradition with virtue ethics. Although it is again popular today, over the years virtue ethics experienced a significant decline in interest in the arenas of Western philosophy and nursing (MacIntyre, 1984; Tschudin, 2003). However, the importance of virtues in the philosophy of Buddhism has remained constant over time.

Many Western philosophers lost interest in the virtues when they became entrenched in the schools of thought popularized during the Enlightenment while, over time, nurses concluded that it was unfashionable to follow the tradition of Nightingale because Nightingale's view of virtues in nursing included a valuing of obedience (MacIntyre, 1984; Sellman, 1997). However, Sellman defended Nightingale in proposing that Nightingale's valuing of obedience must be viewed within the context of the period of time in which she lived. Also, Nightingale's liberal education in Greek philosophy seems to have influenced her use of the virtue of obedience to reflect her belief in the value of practical wisdom as conceived by Aristotle (LeVasseur, 1998; Sellman, 1997). In connecting obedience to practical wisdom, Nightingale's conception became one that approached something akin to intelligent obedience rather than a blind allegiance of nurses to physicians.

Aristotle and the Virtues

Aristotle's (trans. 2002) approach to virtue ethics is grounded in two categories of excellence: one containing intellectual virtues and the other containing character virtues. According to Aristotle, "the intellectual sort [of virtue] mostly . . . comes into existence and increases as a result of teaching (which is why it requires experience and time), whereas excellence of character results from habituation" (p. 111). Although Aristotle divided virtues into those of the intellect and those of character, the two categories of virtues cannot be distinctly separated. Aristotle made this point by proposing that "it is not possible to possess excellence in the primary sense [that is, having excellence of character] without wisdom, nor to be wise without excellence of character" (p. 189).

Buddhist Ethics and Virtues

According to Keown (2001a), Buddhist ethics and health care ethics have a common focus: the alleviation of human suffering. Keown (2001b) also drew a connection between the teleological- or goal-directed ethics of Aristotle and the ethics of Buddhism. Aristotle proposed that the goal for humans is *eudaimonia* or happiness. For the Buddha, the goal was enlightenment or *nirvana*. This Buddhist–Aristotelian connection is illustrated in the virtue-based Moral Ground Model suggested for nursing (see Figure 2-1). In discussing Buddhist virtue ethics, however, it is essential to provide an overview of the Buddha's Four Noble Truths and the Buddhist conception of the Four Immeasurable Virtues.

The Four Noble Truths

That unsatisfactoriness or suffering (*dukkha*) exists as a part of all forms of embodied existence is the First Noble Truth. This suffering is apparent in birth, sickness, old age, and death (Keown, 2001a). Suffering is emphasized in Buddhism, not to suggest a negative outlook toward life but, instead, as a realistic assessment of the human condition. The Second, Third, and Fourth Noble Truths generally suggest the causes of suffering and idea that suffering can be overcome, and propose a path for transforming suffering. The Fourth Noble Truth, or Eightfold Path, is composed of eight *right* practices (Thich Nhat Hanh, 1998). Five of the eight practices have been adapted for nursing in the Moral Ground Model.

The Four Immeasurable Virtues

In Buddhism, there are four virtues that are immeasurable. They are immeasurable because when these virtues are cultivated, it is believed that they will grow in a way that can encompass the whole world, making one's mind loving like a god (Harvey, 2000; Thich Nhat Hanh, 1998). The Four Immeasurables are compassion (*karuna*), loving-kindness (*metta*), sympathetic joy (*mudita*), and equanimity (*upekkha*). Each of these virtues is included in the Moral Ground Model.

A Virtue-Based Nursing Model

The Moral Ground Model has its foundation in Aristotle's approach to virtue ethics, with a proposed path to moral ground adapted from the Eightfold Path of Buddhism. Both the ethics of Aristotle and Buddhism are arguably what can be called teleological philosophies, meaning that they both focus human morality on moving toward a final purpose or goal (Keown, 2001b).

The model implies that nurses may start at a groundless, uneducated state of moral functioning. The path from a groundless, untutored moral state to flourishing moral ground, although modeled in stages, is not linear but occurs in an integrated pattern. The groundless, untutored moral state is one embedded in day-to-day activities in which the nurse is unaware of or unconcerned about the profound moral nature of his or her daily work or is immersed in unsatisfactoriness. Moral suffering is the norm. However, the nurse can move toward flourishing moral ground by traveling along a path of intellectual and moral virtues. The stages of the path are called favorable because they support and facilitate the embodiment of the virtues rather than obstruct movement along the path toward flourishing moral ground.

Murray (1997) stated that narratives, such as novels and literary stories, change us in remarkable ways. From childhood, most people obtain their moral education from stories such as fairy tales and narratives. If nurses remain open to learning through being sensitive to how life stories evolve, are constructed, and can be changed, a *narrative* view of life can educate nurses about intellectual virtues that provide insight into the nature of reality and how to become practically wise. *Insight (sophia)*, a penetrating discernment about the unchangeable truths of reality, is the intellectual virtue that results from a *favorable view*. These truths are that all things are impermanent or passing away, that moral suffering is inherent between the groundless untutored moral state and flourishing moral ground, and that life is characterized by interbeing (a pervasive holism or interconnection of all things). A critical part of this insight is an awareness of the moral nature of the day-to-day work of nurses and that moral suffering can be transformed. *Favorable thought* involves using one's insight into reality in deliberative reasoning and applying the intellectual virtue of practical wisdom (*phronesis*) in directing one's actions. It includes knowing how a person of virtue chooses to act. Emotions regulate insight, knowledge, and the impulse to action.

Web Ethics

The American Nurses Association
http://www.nursingworld.org/

International Council of Nurses
http://www.icn.ch/

The Internet Encyclopedia of Philosophy: Virtue Ethics
http://www.iep.utm.edu/v/virtue.htm

Stanford Encyclopedia of Philosophy: Virtue Ethics
http://plato.stanford.edu/entries/ethics-virtue/

Morality is achieved through choice (*prohairesis*), facilitated by insight, practical wisdom, and evenness of emotional states. Moral virtues (see Table 2-1) and the excellence of the nurse's disposition, or character, are cultivated through habitual practice. The favorables leading to the moral virtues include *favorable communication*: verbal, nonverbal, and written communication that is favorable in moving nurses toward flourishing moral ground; *favorable action*: "the compassionate protection of all [human] beings" (Mizuno, 1987, p. 132); and *favorable livelihood*, which is consistent with being a member of the community of the nursing profession and working to alleviate the suffering and enhance the well-being of other people.

Ultimately, developing and practicing the intellectual and moral virtues leads to flourishing moral ground. *Flourishing moral ground* is likened to the desired goal or *te-*

los of a nurse. It embodies personal and professional excellence in nursing. This state is characterized by an active happiness and well-being that is consistent with an enlightened awareness of the causes of moral suffering, the means of transforming moral suffering, and an awareness of the sacredness of the day-to-day moral nature of nurses' work.

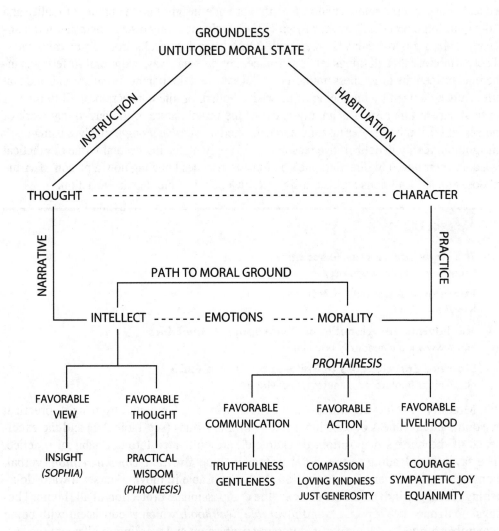

FIGURE 2-1   Moral Ground Model Virtues. © Copyright 2003 by Karen Rich and Janie Butts

TABLE 2-1   Moral Ground Model Virtues

Intellectual Virtues	
Insight:	awareness and knowledge of the moral nature of nurses' day-to-day work and that moral suffering can be transformed.
Practical wisdom:	using deliberative reason to direct actions.
Moral Virtues	
Truthfulness:	refraining from deception through false communication; refraining from self-deception.
Gentleness:	mildness in verbal and nonverbal communication.
Compassion:	the desire to separate others from suffering.
Lovingkindness:	the desire to bring happiness and well-being to oneself and others.
Just Generosity:	giving and receiving based on need.
Courage:	putting fear aside in difficult circumstances to act for a purpose that is more important than one's fear.
Sympathetic Joy:	rejoicing in others' happiness.
Equanimity:	an evenness and calmness of being.

Case Study: Jill Becomes Disheartened

Jill is a 34-year-old attractive, intelligent, and technically competent R.N. who worked for 5 years on a medical–surgical unit of a small hospital. She has generally been well liked by her professional colleagues, and she habitually makes concerted attempts to deliver compassionate care to her patients. Recently, she left her job and began working in the surgical intensive care unit (ICU) of the local county hospital. Jill changed her job because she wanted to gain more varied nursing experience. She was very excited and enthusiastic about her new job, but shortly after Jill began working in the ICU, she began to question her career decision. The more experienced nurses in the ICU are what Jill describes as "abrupt" and "exasperated" when she asks for help in learning ICU patient care and procedures. Jill states that the ICU nurses seem to be "testing my resolve" to "stick it out" and seem to want her to fail at learning how to work in the ICU. She describes many of the surgeons who regularly have patients in the ICU as demanding and impatient with the ICU nursing staff, and Jill is intimidated by them. She mentions being chastised by one of them for asking what he called "a stupid question." There is an air of dissatisfaction among all of the nurses throughout the hospital. Jill says working at this hospital is like no other situation that she has been involved with since becoming a nurse.

Case Study Critical Thinking Questions

1. What do you think might be some of the underlying causes of the ICU nurses' treatment of Jill? Do you believe it is likely that Jill's treatment has anything to do with her personal characteristics?
2. What could Jill do to try to improve her situation?
3. What problems with Jill's delivery of patient care could arise because of the treatment she is experiencing?
4. Do you think that the "air of unhappiness" among all of the nursing staff at the hospital might be directly or indirectly affecting the treatment that Jill is receiving? Might it be affecting patient care hospital-wide? Please explain.
5. If Jill wants to make positive changes at the hospital, what can she do?
6. Review the virtues listed in Table 2-1. Which virtues might the ICU nurses benefit from cultivating? Which virtues would be helpful for Jill to cultivate? Why?

REFERENCES

ANA. (2001). *Code of ethics with interpretive statements.* Washington, DC: ANA.

Angeles, P. A. (1992). *The HarperCollins dictionary of philosophy* (2nd ed.). New York: Harper Perennial.

Aristotle. (2002). *Nicomachean ethics* (C. Rowe, Trans.). New York: Oxford University Press.

Beauchamp, T. L., & Childress, J. F. (2001). *Principles of biomedical ethics* (5th ed.). New York: Oxford University Press.

Blum, L. A. (1994). *Moral perception and particularity.* New York: Cambridge University Press.

Brannigan, M. C., & Boss, J. A. (2001). *Healthcare ethics in a diverse society.* Mountain View, CA: Mayfield Publishing.

Broadie, S. (2002). Commentary. In *Aristotle: Nicomachean ethics: Translation, introduction, and commentary* (C. Rowe, Trans.). New York: Oxford University Press.

Chambliss, D. F. (1996). *Beyond caring: Hospitals, nurses, and the social organization of ethics.* Chicago: University of Chicago Press.

Charon, R., & Montello, M. (2002). Introduction: The practice of narrative ethics. In R. Charon & M. Montello (Eds.), *Stories Matter* (pp. ix–xii). New York: Routledge.

Copleston, F. (1946). *A history of philosophy: Volume I: Greece and Rome.* New York: Image Books.

Crisp, R., & Slote, M. (1997). Introduction. In R. Crisp & M. Slote (Eds.), *Virtue Ethics* (pp. 1–25). New York: Oxford University Press.

Dalai Lama (1999). *Ethics for the new millennium.* New York: Riverhead Books.

Daly, B. J. (2002). Moving forward: A new code of ethics. *Nursing Outlook, 50*, 97–99.

De Mello, A. (1985). *One minute wisdom.* New York: Doubleday.

Denise, T. C., White, N. P., & Peterfreund, S. P. (2002). *Great traditions in ethics* (10th ed.). Belmont, CA: Wadsworth Thomson Learning.

Dossey, B. M. (2000). *Florence Nightingale: Mystic, visionary, healer.* Springhouse, PA: Springhouse Corporation.

Engelhardt, H. T. (1996). *The foundations of bioethics* (2nd ed.). New York: Oxford University Press.

Fowler, M. D., & Benner, P. (2001). Implementing the new code of ethics for nurses: An interview with Marsha Fowler. *American Journal of Critical Care, 10*(6), 434–437.

Fry, S., & Johnstone, M. J. (2002). *Ethics in nursing practice: A guide to ethical decision making* (2nd ed.). Oxford, UK: Blackwell Science.

Geldard, R. (2001). *The spiritual teachings of Ralph Waldo Emerson.* Great Barrington, MA: Lindisfarne Books.

Gilligan, C. (1993). *In a different voice: Psychological theory and women's development.* Cambridge, MA: Harvard University Press.

Grimshaw, J. (1993). The idea of a female ethic. In P. Singer (Ed.), *A Companion to Ethics* (pp. 491–499). Oxford, UK: Blackwell Publishing.

Harvey, P. (2000). *An introduction to Buddhist ethics: Foundations, values, and issues.* Cambridge, UK: Cambridge University Press.

Hester, D. M. (2001). Community as healing: Pragmatic ethics in medical encounters. Lantham, MD: Rowman & Littlefield Publishers.

Hinson, E. G. (1992). Saint Augustine. In I. McGreal (Ed.), *Great Thinkers of the Western World* (pp. 72–75). New York: HarperCollins Publishers.

Honvantewa, T. (1996). [untitled]. In. K. M. Cleary (Ed.), *Native American Wisdom* (p. 40). Barnes & Noble.

Hume, D. (2000). *A treatise of human nature.* (D. F. Norton & M. J. Norton, eds.). New York: Oxford University Press. (Original work published 1739–1740).

International Council of Nurses [ICN]. (2000). *The international council of nurses code of ethics for nurses.* Geneva: ICN.

Jameton, A. (1984). *Nursing practice: The ethical issues.* Englewood Cliffs, NJ: Prentice-Hall.

Kelly, C. (2000). *Nurses' moral practice: Investing and discounting self.* Indianapolis, IN: Sigma Theta Tau International Center Nursing Press.

Keown, D. (2001a). *Buddhism and bioethics.* New York: Palgrave.

Keown D. (2001b). *The nature of Buddhist ethics.* New York: Palgrave.

Kuhse, H., & Singer, P. (2001). What is bioethics? A historical approach. In H. Kuhse & P. Singer (Eds.), *A Companion to Bioethics* (pp. 3–11). Oxford, UK: Blackwell Publishers.

LeVasseur, J. (1998). Plato, Nightingale, and contemporary nursing. *Image: Journal of Nursing Scholarship, 30*(3), 281–285.

Lyotard, J. F. (1979). *The postmodern condition: A report on knowledge* (G. Bennington and B. Massumi, Trans.). Minneapolis, MN: University of Minneapolis Press.

MacIntyre, A. (1984). *After virtue: A study of moral theory* (2nd ed.). Notre Dame, IN: University of Notre Dame Press.

MacIntyre, A. (1999). *Dependent rational animals: Why human beings need the virtues.* Chicago, IL: Open Court.

Master Sheng-yen (1999). *Subtle wisdom: Understanding suffering, cultivating compassion through Ch'an Buddhism.* New York: Doubleday.

McKenna, B. G., Smith, N. A., Poole, S. J., & Coverdale, J. H. (2003). Horizontal violence: Experiences of registered nurses in their first year of practice. *Journal of Advanced Nursing, 42*(1), 90–96.

Mizuno, K. (1987). *Basic Buddhist concepts.* Tokyo: Kosei Publishing.

Morris, D. B. (Nov.–Dec. 2000). How to speak postmodern: Medicine, illness, and cultural change (pp. 7–16). *Hastings Center Report.*

Murray, T. H. (1997). What do we mean by "narrative ethics"? *Medical Humanities Review, 11*(2), 44–57.

Pence, G. (2000). *A dictionary of common philosophical terms.* New York: McGraw-Hill.

Pieper, J. (1966). *The four cardinal virtues.* Notre Dame, ID: University of Notre Dame Press.

Pullman, D. (1999). The ethics of autonomy and dignity in long-term care. *Canadian Journal on Aging, 18*(1), 26–46.

Ridley, M. (1996). *The origins of virtue.* New York: Penguin Books.

Russell, B. (1972). *A history of Western philosophy.* New York: Simon & Schuster.

Sellman, D. (1997). The virtues in the moral education of nurses: Florence Nightingale revisited. *Nursing Ethics, 4*(1), 3–11.

Shotton, L., & Seedhouse, D. (1998). Practical dignity in caring. *Nursing Ethics, 5*(3), 246–255.

Stein, L. I., Watts, D. T., & Howell, T. (1990). The doctor–nurse game revisited. *Nursing Outlook, 38*(6), 264–268.

Tarnas, R. (1991). *The passion of the Western mind: Understanding the ideas that have shaped our world view.* New York: Ballantine Books.

Thich Nhat Hanh (1998). *The heart of the Buddha's teaching: Transforming suffering into peace, joy, and liberation.* New York: Broadway Books.

Thomas, L. (1993). Morality and psychological development. In P. Singer (Ed.), *A Companion to Ethics* (pp. 464–475). Oxford, UK: Blackwell Publishing.

Tschudin, V. (2003). Introductory Paragraph of Scott, P. A. (2003). Virtue, nursing and the moral domain of practice. In V. Tschudin (Ed.), *Approaches to Ethics: Nursing Beyond Boundaries* (pp. 25–32). Edinburgh, UK: Butterworth-Heinemann.

von Goethe, J. W. (1990). Significance. In R. Andrews (Ed.), *The concise Columbia dictionary of quotations* (p. 274). New York: Columbia University Press.

Wildes, K. W. (2000). *Moral acquaintances: Methodology in bioethics.* Notre Dame, IN: University of Notre Dame Press.

Winslow, G. (1988). From loyalty to advocacy: A new metaphor for nursing. In J. C. Callahan (Ed.), *Ethical Issues in Professional Life* (pp. 95–105).

Zaner, R. M. (1991). The phenomenon of trust and the patient–physician relationship. In E. D. Pellegrino, R. M. Veatch, & J. P. Langan (Eds.), *Ethics, Trust, and the Professions: Philosophical and Cultural Aspects* (pp. 45–67). Washington, DC: Georgetown University Press.

CHAPTER 3

Adult Health Nursing Ethics

Janie B. Butts

The most important human endeavor is the striving for morality in our actions. Our inner balance, and even our very existence depends on it. Only morality in our actions can give beauty and dignity to life.

Albert Einstein, *A Letter, "In a Nuclear Age"*

SUMMARY

1. Honesty is about more than just telling the truth. An honest person searches for the truth in a rational, methodical way, and, in the process, has the ability to place emphasis on resolve and action to achieve a just society.
2. Honesty in nursing is about nurses who are honest with themselves and others.
3. Are there ever circumstances when nurses should be ethically excused from telling the truth to their patients? Different levels of disclosure that occur in patient care create uncertainty about truthtelling for nurses. Generally, nurses are obligated by the American Nurses Association's Code of Ethics to be honest in all matters concerning patients and their care.

4. There is a supply-and-demand crisis for organ donation. Utilitarian-based programs to increase the number of organ donors remain challenged, especially in Western countries where such value is placed on autonomy and respect for human dignity.

5. Expert bioethicists are fervently debating the pros and cons of altering the dead donor rule so that patients who have no higher brain function yet still have lower brain function can be considered potential organ donors. The ethical question is: How will changing this rule affect the legal definition and criteria of brain death?

MORAL INTEGRITY

T.G. Plante (2004) stated that, while realizing that no one is mistake free, people who have integrity follow a moral compass, and they do not vary by appeals to act immorally. Most of the time when people speak of a person's integrity, they are referring to the person's quality of character (Cox, La Caze, & Levine, 2001; Plante, 2004). Integrity represents "integration of self . . . maintenance of identity . . . standing for something . . . [and having] moral purpose" (Cox, La Caze, & Levine, 2001, ¶ 3). People with moral integrity pursue a moral purpose in life, understand their moral obligations in the community, and are committed to following through with any constraints that their moral stance may impose on them (Cox, La Caze, & Levine, 2001). To have moral integrity means that a person has integrated several virtues, two of which are closely linked: honesty and telling the truth.

Honesty in Nursing

Honesty is more than just telling the truth. It involves a willingness to diligently dig for truth in a rational, methodical way and having the ability to place emphasis on resolve and action, to achieve a just society (Brannigan & Boss, 2001; Vallee, V., n.d.). In a 2003 Gallup poll, the nursing profession was rated as the most honest and ethical professional group in a survey of many professions (Gallup Organization, 2004). Next were physicians, veterinarians, pharmacists, and dentists. It was some of the business professions, such as HMO administrators, that ranked toward the bottom.

There are many ways that nurses can portray honesty. For example, nurses must stay committed to their promises to patients and follow through with appropriate behaviors, such as telling patients that they will return to their hospital rooms, as promised, to help them with certain tasks. If nurses do not follow through with their commitments, trust may be broken, and patients may see nurses as dishonest.

Honesty is also about being honest with oneself. For example, if a nurse was administering medications and a pill fell on the hospital floor, would the nurse be justified in wiping it off and placing it back in the cup if no one was there to see the action? Nurses might be tempted to wipe off the pill and administer it just to keep from completing a required medication form. If nurses evaluate their problems and make more decisions based on the thought "be honest with myself," it is more likely that they would make rational, trustworthy decisions regarding the care of patients (see more on honesty in Chapter 6).

Telling the Truth in Nursing

Truthfulness was recognized by Aristotle as the mean between imposture (excessiveness) and self-deprecation (deficiency) and is one of the twelve excellences (virtues) that Aristotle identified in his book *Nicomachean Ethics* (trans. 2002). Aristotle emphasized that people need to habitually practice the virtues for the purpose of striving for an integrated moral character and the ultimate goal of happiness and a flourishing human life. Aristotle maintained that people accomplish their ultimate goal of happiness only by exercising rational and intellectual thinking, which he called wisdom or contemplation. Aristotle explained his view of a truthful person as being *the truthful sort* (see Box 3-1).

Truthfulness is "not only what we say but, more importantly, how we say it" (Brannigan & Boss, 2001, p. 126). Truthfulness, translated to telling the truth in the health care arena, is based on the principle of veracity, which means that nurses are ethically obligated to tell the truth and not intentionally deceive or mislead patients (Aiken, 2004). In the *Code of Ethics for Nurses with Interpretive Statements* (ANA, 2001), some parts from Provision 6.1 are stated:

> Virtues such as wisdom, honesty, and courage are habits or attributes of the morally good person . . . For the nurse, virtues and excellences are those habits that affirm and promote the values of human dignity, well-being, respect, health, independence, and other values central to nursing. Both virtues and excellences, as aspects of moral character, can be either nurtured by the environment in which the nurse practices or they can be diminished or thwarted. All nurses have a responsibility to create, maintain, and con-

Box 3-1

ETHICAL Kaleidoscope   The Truthful Sort

We are not here talking about the person who tells the truth in the context of agreements, or anything of that sort . . . but about contexts in which . . . a person is truthful both in the way he talks and in the way he lives, by virtue of being such by disposition. Someone like this would seem to be a decent person. For the lover of truth, since he also tells the truth where it makes no difference, will tell the truth even more where it does make a difference; for there he will be guarding against falsehood as something shameful, when he was already guarding against it in itself. Such a person is to be praised.

Aristotle, ***Nicomachean Ethics***

tribute to environments that support the growth of virtues and excellences and enable nurses to fulfill their ethical obligations (pp. 20–21).

Because of the emphasis in the Western world on patients' right to know about their personal health care, telling the truth has become the basis for relationships between health care professionals and their patients in the last few decades (Beauchamp & Childress, 2001). In the older traditional approach, disclosure or telling the truth was more of a beneficent or paternalistic approach and involved basing actions on the answers to the questions "What is best for the patient to know?" or "If I tell the truth to the patient, will it bring harm?"

Even today, health care professionals, not intentionally meaning to be paternalistic, use various levels of what could be called a beneficent type of deception. This type of deception is used as a mechanism to avoid telling the full truth in an attempt to protect patients from sad and heartbreaking news or to avoid damaging the professionals' own emotions. Nurses or physicians may omit certain information because they do not know the facts, or they may state what they know to be untrue about the situation rather than admit everything they know to be true. Physicians and nurses wonder if patients want them to be so brutally truthful, while patients often wonder if physicians and nurses are telling them the full truth about their diagnosis, treatment, and prognosis.

The ethical question to be asked is: Are there ever circumstances when nurses should be ethically excused from telling the truth to their patients? The levels of disclosure in health care and the cultural viewpoints on telling the truth create too much complexity for a clear line of distinction to be drawn between telling and not telling the truth for nurses. Nurses are obligated by the ANA Code of Ethics to be honest in matters involving patients and themselves and to express a moral point of view when they become aware of unethical practices.

Fry and Johnstone (2002) stated that in some cultures such as the United States, autonomy is so valued that withholding information would be thought of as unjust. Also, under this same autonomy principle, it is assumed that patients have a right not to know their medical history if they so desire. There are cultures, such as those in some Eastern countries, that do not cherish autonomy as other cultures do, and family members will usually decide how much and what information if any, needs to be disclosed to the patient.

Brannigan and Boss (2001) stated that physicians are obligated to tell the truth to their patients unless they have substantial reason to believe that disclosing the truth would cause undue harm, such as causing a patient extreme emotional distress. This circumstance is known as *therapeutic privilege*. Sometimes physicians and nurses become confused about this privilege because they often do not know how much truth to withhold. When physicians exercise this right, they usually base their opinion on data gathered from their interactions with the patient, family, and other health care professionals. Evidence may also come from the patient's medical record, such as documentation of a history of mental and emotional problems.

The complexity of the situation leaves physicians with a difficult decision to make and leaves nurses with moral suffering, especially when patients want to know the full truth, and physicians have decided to disclose only part of the truth—or none of it—to the patient (see Moral Suffering in Nursing in Chapter 2). In these circumstances, nurses must evaluate the situation carefully, as Aristotle stated that people should do, with wisdom and contemplation, before any decision is made. In most circumstances, nurses should not go against the physicians' exercise of therapeutic privilege. Mappes and DeGrazia (2001) emphasized: "When all is said and done, many arguments for individual cases of lying do not hold water. Whether or not knowing the truth is essential to the patient's health, telling the truth is essential to the health of the doctor [and nurse] patient relationship" (p. 92).

An excellent example of telling the truth is from the play *Wit* by Margaret Edson, winner of the 1998 Pulitzer Prize 1999). Susie Monahan, RN, decides to tell the truth to a patient despite a few physicians who chose not to do so (see Box 3-2).

Box 3-2

ETHICAL Kaleidoscope   Susie Monahan, RN, in *Wit*

Susie Monahan was a registered nurse caring for Vivian Bearing, a dying patient with cancer, at a large research hospital. Vivian was receiving large doses of cancer chemotherapy without any success of remission. In fact, the cancer was progressing at an alarming rate. She was near death, but the research physicians wanted to challenge her body with chemotherapy for as long as possible to observe the outcome. Everyone on the medical staff had been cold, technically-minded, and no one had shown any concern for her except for Susie. Vivian had not been informed about the chemotherapy failure or the prognosis that she was dying. One night, Susie found Vivian crying and in a state of panic. Susie first helped to calm her, then shared a popsicle with Vivian at the bedside while she disclosed the full truth to Vivian about her chemotherapy, her prognosis, her choices about Code Blue or DNR, and her imminent death. Susie affectionately explained:

> You can be "full code," which means that if your heart stops, they'll call a Code Blue and the code team will come and resuscitate you and take you to Intensive Care until you stabilize again. Or you can be "Do Not Resuscitate," so if your heart stops we'll . . . well, we'll just let it. You'll be "DNR." You can think about it, but I wanted to present both choices . . . " (p. 67).

Susie felt an urge to be truthful and honest. By giving human respect to Vivian, Susie was showing her capacity to be human.

M. Edson, *Wit*

Ethical Reflections

- You are caring for a woman scheduled for a hysterectomy because of uterine cancer. Her surgeon is known to have a bad surgical record in general but especially in performing hysterectomies. The woman has heard gossip to this effect and asks you about it before her surgery because she is anxious about using that surgeon. You know for a fact that at least one legal suit has been filed against him—a woman with a botched hysterectomy—because you personally know the woman involved in the case. Your choices are that you could be brutally honest and truthful with your preoperative patient; you could give her part of the truth by giving her information that you know to be untrue about certain gossip or not confirming the truth about certain gossip; or you could be totally untruthful by remaining silent or by telling her that you have heard nothing. Discuss these options and any other ideas that you may have in regard to this case. As a nurse who wants to be committed to an ethical nursing practice, what would you do in this very difficult circumstance?
- Other than just verbally telling the truth to patients and others, what are other ways that you can display honesty in an ethical nursing practice? Think of how you would portray honesty in different settings and situations: bedside nursing of patients, documentation, dealing with co-workers, administration, etc.

ORGAN TRANSPLANTATION

Every day in the United States, 70 people receive an organ transplant and another 16 people die while on the organ "wait list" (US Organ Donation and Transplantation, 2004). In 1954, a surgeon named Joseph Murray performed the first successful kidney transplant in Boston (Harvard Medical Schools, 2001; President's Council on Bioethics, 2003). Murray later received a Nobel Prize for Medicine in 1990. The first human heart transplant was performed in 1967 by a surgeon named Christiaan Barnard from Cape Town, South Africa (see Box 3-3).

Organ transplantation is more accepted in the 21st century than it was in the 1950s. The ethical questions regarding removing organs from dead donors then were just as intense and angst-provoking as the ethical questions faced today regarding human cloning. One issue in the 1950s was that, for the first time in history, surgeons were forced to decide criteria for organ recipients in light of a severely sparse supply of organs; in other words, for the first time ever, surgeons were literally choosing who would live and who would die. Another major issue was that many people were dying from organ rejection because of inadequate and harmful antirejection medications (see Box 3-3). It was not until 1978 that the effective immunosuppressive medication, Cyclosporin, was available for use.

Fifty years after the first kidney transplant in 1954, ethical issues regarding organ donation and transplantation are still passionately debated. The issues in the 21st century have shifted to a more diverse set of problems. One major issue is the societal pres-

Box 3-3

ETHICAL Kaleidoscope   Would You Choose the Lion or
Swim From the Crocodiles?

The First Human Heart Transplant

A heart surgeon named Christiaan Barnard and his 19 team members pushed the medical and scientific limits in 1967 to perform the first human heart transplant. Barnard stated: "On Saturday, I was a surgeon in South Africa, very little known . . . [and] . . . On Monday, I was world renowned" (¶ 4).

Barnard transplanted the heart of a 25-year-old female auto-crash victim, named Denise Darvall, into a 55-year-old South African man named Louis Washkansky who at the time was dying of heart disease. For Louis Washkansky, the choice was to live a little longer with the donated heart or die very soon with his diseased heart. Barnard stated:

> For a dying man it is not a difficult decision . . . because he knows he is at the end. If a lion chases you to the bank of a river filled with crocodiles, you will leap into the water convinced you have a chance to swim to the other side. But you would not accept such odds if there were no lion (¶ 18).

There was success with the procedure. The heart began beating during surgery. However, the medication prescribed for preventing rejection of his "new" heart caused Washkansky's immune system to fail. He died 18 days after his surgery.

One News for New Zealanders (2001, Sept. 3). "Pioneer Surgeon Barnard Dies."
http://www.onenews.nzoom.com/onenews_detail/0,1227,55309-1-6,00.html

sure for organ harvesting resulting from the global demand for organs that far outweighs the supply. Another major issue is individuals questioning their own moral beliefs about death and the legal definition of death as it relates to organ donation.

Organ Procurement

As of August 2004, there were more than 86,000 candidates on the wait list for organs in the United States (United Network for Organ Sharing [UNOS], 2004). There is evidence that people are increasingly refusing to donate their organs, which is one of the reasons for the severe imbalance in supply and demand (Kerridge, Saul, Lowe, McPhee, & Williams, 2002; Magee, 2004). Organ donation is a delicate subject for most people. The very thought of donating an organ may lead to individuals having disturbing thoughts about their own death or loss of a body part.

To counterbalance the supply–demand crisis, the US Department of Health and Human Services has implemented new programs to increase organ supply in the last three years. Meanwhile, approximately 6,000 people died in the United States in 2003 while on the wait list for an organ. A societal ethical conflict exists between the national officials' proposals and the values of potential donors. Many program coordinators want to use a utilitarian ethical framework as a basis for setting and accomplishing the goals of increasing organ supply while potential donors, especially in the Western world, value and presently abide by a deontological ethical framework of respect for autonomy and human dignity (see Utilitarianism definition in Chapter 1). With autonomy and decision making as a focus for individuals, utilitarian-based programs find it a challenge to increase the number of organ donors. For a utilitarian approach, some countries use a presumed consent approach, meaning that individuals automatically consent to donating their organs unless they specifically indicate otherwise (Brannigan & Boss, 2001). Another approach is mandated choice, which means that competent individuals would be required to make a choice whether or not they wanted to become an organ donor on license applications, tax returns, and other official state identification records (Taylor, 2004). Once they decide to become a donor, they are bound by the identification cards that they signed; however, a change of mind can be communicated with a patient's written directive that guides the family or guardian of those decisions (Taylor, 2004).

In the United States, donor cards are a legal, but rarely the sole, document used in the organ donation process (Taylor, 2004). Advance directives also are legal documents that are used to express one's desires about organ donation (see Advance Directives in Chapter 10). The UNOS ethics committee has requested that United States citizens use a method called required response, which means that all adults will be required to express their wishes regarding organ donation (as cited in Taylor, 2004). At that time, they will be able to object or willingly agree to donate their organs, plus they have an opportunity to allow a relative to be their designated surrogate.

A financial incentives program for organ procurement in the United States is being studied with great fervor. In the 2004 Joint Commission on Accreditation of Healthcare Organizations (JCAHO) committee report, it was reported that a committee for the Centers for Medicare and Medicaid Services is proposing allowing hospital reimbursement for potential donors prior to their being declared dead. Presently, the Centers for Medicare and Medicaid Services only reimburses hospitals for potential donors after the declaration of death while the donors' bodies are maintained by mechanical ventilation and circulation methods until the organs are harvested.

Illegal Retention or Sale of Human Organs

Some people are convinced that a slippery slope situation will occur with regard to commercial trade in human organs if financial incentives in any form are initiated (see Slippery Slope in Chapter 1). Many people view the commercial trade of human organs as immoral because they see it as a violation of the principle of human rights and dignity (Gillett, 2000). Some ethicists believe that the idea of profiteers legally selling organs could be demoralizing and an act of coercion for many people, especially poor and disadvantaged people. However, several renowned bioethicists (e.g., Faden & Beauchamp,

1986; Veatch, 2003a) have stated that coercion is not involved if a person has been appropriately informed before consenting to selling the organ. The term "coercion" implies that one must use force or a threat of force to move another to engage in an act. Currently, there are two United States' acts that prohibit the sale or purchase of human organs or tissues: the National Organ Transplant Act of 1984 and the Uniform Anatomical Gift Act of 1987, which is an act that each state may exercise (Taylor, 2004; UNOS, 2004).

Stories on the Internet maintain that the illegal trade or sale of human organs (also called the black market of human organs) is thriving, but finding solid evidence has been difficult (Fasting, Christensen, & Glending, 1998). However, some of the stories have been documented. One well-known story that was documented involved profiteers buying kidneys from poor and needy people in India. In exchange, the profiteers managed the financial needs of the donors. As a result, several years ago, India passed a law prohibiting the commercial trade of organs. Another story first emerged in England in 1999, except this hideous story was regarding the retention of organs for research and education (see Box 3-4).

Death and the Dead Donor Rule

An ethical debate that remains unresolved is that regarding when a person's organs can be retrieved in accordance with the legal definition of death. According to the 1981 Uniform Determination of Death Act (UDDA), death is an irreversible cessation of circulatory and respiratory functions and irreversible cessation of all functions of the brain (President's Commission, 1981; as cited in Mappes & DeGrazia, 2001, p. 318; see a full explanation on the definition of death in Chapter 10). The medical community has adopted two guiding moral principles, known as the *dead donor rule*, as the norm for managing potential organ donors. The principles are (1) the donor must first be dead before organs are retrieved and (2) a person's life and care "must never be compromised in favor of potential organ recipients" (Mappes & DeGrazia, 2001, p. 325).

Another ethical issue concerns health care professionals and families. When the potential donor is declared brain dead, the dead patient continues to remain on a mechanical ventilator as if still living, having warm skin, up and down chest movement, and receiving intravenous fluids. This picture leaves health care professionals and families with feelings of ambiguity. Nurses experience moral suffering (see "Moral Suffering in Nursing" in Chapter 2). Normally, once a person is declared dead, medical treatment and ventilation support are suspended. Following a declaration of death for potential organ donors, however, the bodies are maintained physically via ventilation and circulatory support until the organs are harvested.

There is an intensely debated ethical issue surrounding the dead donor rule. Many bioethicists are discussing the pros and cons of altering or overturning the dead donor rule so that organs can be retrieved from patients who have no higher brain function but do have lower-brain function, such as those in a persistent vegetative state (PVS) and babies born with anencephaly (e.g., Koppelman, 2003; Veatch, 2003). Patients with no higher

BOX 3-4

ETHICAL Kaleidoscope   "It Just Broke My Heart"

The Final Report Stated:
"Grotesque" "Unethical and Illegal"

In 1999, British Liverpool authorities discovered that 170 fetal hearts had been removed from babies during post-mortem examinations without parental consent at the Royal Liverpool Children's Hospital Alder Hey (British Broadcasting Company [BBC], 2004). Since 1999, an extended search led to another 2,000 children's hearts, large numbers of brain parts, eyes, 1,500 stillbirth babies and fetuses, and many children's heads and bodies (CNN, 2001). A Dutch pathologist and death expert, Dick van Velzen, was retaining the body parts for research and education. Velzen "lied to parents," "stole records," and "falsified reports" while he was at Alder Hey from 1988 to 1995. Velzen is forever restricted from practicing medicine in the United Kingdom and is facing prosecution.

Paula O'Leary, co-founder of the support group for people affected by organ retention, attended the funeral service of 1,000 stillbirth babies. She stated: "The moment I found out about these unidentified babies, it just broke my heart" (BBC, 2004, ¶ 7). Paula O'Leary's 11-month-old son, Andrew, died in 1981 and had his organs removed without her consent.

From British Broadcasting Company, "Organ Scandal Babies Are Buried,"
2004. Retrieved August 6, 2004, from http://news.bbc.co.uk/1/hi/england/
merseyside/3536970.stm and CNN, "Organ Scandal Report Savages
Doctor," 2001. Retrieved August 6, 2004, from http://www.cnn.
com/2001/WORLD/europe/UK/01/30/alder.hey.02/

---

brain function, such as patients in a PVS, have an intact brain stem and usually breathe without the assistance of mechanical ventilation.

A severe shortage of organs exists for babies. Baby Gabriel who had anencephaly, was the first successful infant heart donor in 1987. The recipient, Baby Paul Holc, survived and thrived (Loma Linda University, 2001). Anencephalic babies are unique in that their brain tissue is usually absent. Baby Gabriel met brain death criteria according to the UDDA definition of brain death, which is the irreversible loss of functioning of the brain. Although Baby Gabriel was legally dead, her organs were maintained by mechanical ventilation until her heart could be harvested. For babies with anencephaly, the challenge is to keep the organs oxygenated until they are harvested. One of the main reasons that anencephalic babies are not considered more often for organ donation is that by the time they meet the brain death criteria, their organs are usually too damaged to be of use.

The issue of organ donation and anencephaly has become intensely debated over time. Several other cases have surfaced in the last few years. "A profound ethical debate developed . . . over the idea of giving breathing assistance to one infant for the benefit of another patient (the organ recipient)" (Loma Linda University, 2001, ¶ 22).

Overturning the dead donor rule and retrieving organs from patients who are still alive by the UDDA definition of death would be a utilitarian ethical framework when viewed from the perspective of longer-term quality of life and the number of people that could be saved. For example, one person's organs may save three or four people. For patients in a PVS, higher brain functioning does not exist. For anencephalic babies, there is usually very little, if any, higher brain function. A question must be considered: if the dead donor rule is altered so that patients without higher brain function but with lower brain function can be organ donors, how will the definition of death be changed to include these patients? Do patients without higher brain function but who are not dead by the current legal definition of death have full moral standing? If persons can breathe on their own, such as those in a PVS, should they be considered dead?

Non–Heart-Beating Organ Donors

Organ donation was originally based on the principle of procuring organs from cadavers. A non–heart-beating donor (NHBD) is one whose heart has ceased at the time that the organ is retrieved (Taylor, 2004). There are two types. Controlled NHBDs are donors who are maintained on mechanical ventilation until their organs are harvested; many times, these donors have advance directives. Uncontrolled NHBDs are donors who have a cardiorespiratory arrest outside the hospital and cannot be resuscitated but have a declaration of death prior to retrieval of their organs. There are two critical NHBD protocols that physicians must follow: there can be no discussion of organ donation or the consent process with family members before the decision has been made by everyone concerned to withdraw life support, and the physician who declares death may not be linked with any organ recovery agency, transplant team, or recovery team (UNOS, 2004). Nurses must adhere to the first protocol.

Social Justice and Organ Transplantation

Social justice is a consideration that cannot be overlooked in the face of scarce health care resources and a scarce supply of organs (Gillett, 2000; see a full explanation of social justice in Theories of Social Justice in Chapter 1). The ethical question is twofold: How are people chosen for the organ "wait list," and how are they chosen to receive the organ? Gillett stated that:

> our ability to act for the benefit of any given individual must be tempered by the requirements of justice. If there is one kidney and more than one possible recipient, some basis has to be found to make the choice between recipients. It is tempting to believe that there must be some ethical way of regulating such choices . . . . The obvious way is to accept the principle of first-come first-served (p. 249).

First-come/first-served may not be an adequate guideline for many people because this method would not address the sickest people first; rather, it is based on a *fairness principle*. Organ coordinators face difficult decisions regarding the allocation of organs, deciding who gets the organ and then justifying the decision. The sickest patients have many more complications and suffer more. However, if they are chosen first, as they often have been in the past, their success rate with the new organ may not be as good as that of a donor chosen based on other criteria. The approach of using the sickest patients first is a *medical entitlement method*, similar to that of medical emergency department triage.

Trying to select organ recipients based on *social worth*, self-destructive behavior, and a potential for rehabilitation is difficult to justify from an ethical perspective. One example of a self-destructive behavior is chronic smoking. Suppose there is a chronic smoker who needs a lung transplant. Would the organ team determine that this smoker is not as worthy to live or to receive an organ as another potential recipient because the person smokes? Is this not a value judgment?

If potential recipients were chosen from a *utilitarian-consequential perspective*, they would receive an organ based on their potential for longer-term survival with a higher quality of life. Gillett (2000) stated about utilitarianism: "Every individual should count for one and nobody for more than one . . . The more one debates the issue, the more it seems the only fair way to determine how to distribute scarce resources" (p. 249).

Ethical Reflections

- How do you think the organ supply could be increased?
- Explore your thoughts on the dead donor rule as it is presently defined and how the rule could be changed to include people who no longer have higher brain function but have lower brain function, such as patients in a PVS. How would changing this rule change societal values and your own values concerning life and death?

MANAGEMENT OF CARE

In this chapter, there are two major sections, one on moral integrity and the other on organ transplantation; these become closely linked when nurses coordinate and give care to potential organ donors, recipients, and their families. According to the Code of Ethics, nurses work within a moral framework of good personal character to promote the principle of beneficence (ANA, 2001). Most of the time, nurses want to have a sense of satisfaction based on their belief that they promote human good, preserve their patients' dignity as much as possible, and maintain a caring environment. Nurses in intensive care units and on transplant teams coordinate organ donations and transplants on a daily basis. The psychosocial impact and outcome of the organ transplantation process for donors, donor families, and recipients are unique.

Pearson, Robertson-Malt, Walsh, and Fitzgerald (2001) conducted a study of the attitudes of intensive care nurses toward brain dead organ donors. Two major themes of caring that emerged from the study were the family and the nurse.

The Family

Of central importance to the nurses in the study was meeting the needs of their patients' families. Some important considerations for nursing care of donor family members were identified as:

- prioritizing the family's needs,
- empathizing with the family's tragedy,
- supporting the family's decisions,
- realizing that caring for the patient shows care for the family,
- encouraging space and privacy for the family to grieve, say their goodbyes, and, hopefully, accept the situation, and
- not intruding on the family's grief (p.135).

The Nurse

A challenge for intensive care nurses is finding meaning in the case of each brain dead patient, including the potential donors (Pearson, Robertson-Malt, Walsh, & Fitzgerald, 2000). In this study, nurses stated that brain dead patients should be treated as if they were alive because this action shows respect for both the patients and their families and were adamant that family members must be shown respect and kindness. A compassionate way to show ultimate kindness is to give excellent care to a family's loved one.

However, nurses often are emotionally drained from feeling a need to clarify the definition of brain death and other medical terms to the families. Nurses also feel emotional strain in regard to their own ambiguities about the definition of brain death. With the ever-increasing organ procurement system, nurses find themselves sometimes suffering morally because of internal moral conflicts regarding the uncertainties of life and death. If nurses take advantage of extra education on organ transplantation nursing care and grieving families, they may be better prepared for managing their own personal emotions and those of families in crisis.

Web Ethics

ORGANIZATIONS RELATED TO ORGAN TRANSPLANTATION

Official US Government Organ Donation and Transplantation
http://www.organdonor.gov

United Network for Organ Sharing
http://www.unos.org

Organ Procurement and Transplantation Network
http://www.optn.org

Case Study: Who Will Receive the Liver?

- Mr. Mann is 50 years old, has been a heavy drinker since high school, and has end-stage liver disease (ESLD) due to alcoholic cirrhosis. He will soon die if he does not receive a liver. He has been unemployed for years, even before his illness, and has received state financial assistance. Mr. Mann has stated that once he receives his new liver he will try to quit drinking on a long-term basis but will make no promises. He is not drinking now because he is in the hospital and knows he must remain abstinent for a period of time before the actual organ transplant and during the recovery process. Mr. Mann is divorced, lives alone, and has two sons who are married and working. Mr. Mann and his two sons are not on good terms.

- Mrs. Bay is 37 years old and has ESLD due to hepatitis B. Mrs. Bay is a wife and a mother of two children, one who is 16 years old and the other 12. The family is well known and active in the community. The family members have a great relationship. The children have stated that they do not want to lose their mother. Mrs. Bay is very sick, but she is not in the hospital. At this time, Mrs. Bay experiences days when she feels very sick and cannot move from the bed. Other days are a little better. Her prognosis is grave, and she was placed on the organ wait list ahead of Mr. Mann.

Based on your knowledge of the two diseases, you know that alcoholic cirrhosis patients with new livers may have a better success rate and longer life than do those suffering from hepatitis B, despite the fact that recovering alcoholics may have a high recidivism (relapsing to their old behavior) rate. Giving hepatitis B patients new livers is controversial, and the success rate is varied. Mr. Mann is at the maximum end of the age range for organ recipients (usually age 50 or more).

Case Study Critical Thinking Questions

What are valid criteria for rank-ordering recipients? Think about the following criteria for allocating organs, some of which were discussed in the chapter. Explore all situations between the two organ candidates. Whom do you choose? Give a full justification for choosing your candidate for the liver.

- The sickest patients: medical entitlement method
- First-come, first-served: fairness principle
- Social worth principle
- Best success rate and long-term outcome: utilitarian–consequential perspective
- Proximity to the area of the hospital where the organ will be transplanted (immediate area, county, region). What about United States versus another country?

REFERENCES

Aiken, T. D. (2004). *Legal, ethical, & political issues in nursing* (2nd ed.). Philadelphia, PA: Davis.

American Nurses Association. (2001). *Code of ethics for nurses with interpretive statements.* Washington, DC: ANA.

Aristotle. (2002). *Nicomachean ethics.* (C. Rowe, Trans.). New York: Oxford University Press.

Beauchamp, T. L., & Childress, J. F. (2001). *Principles of biomedical ethics* (5th ed.). New York: Oxford University Press.

Brannigan, M. C., & Boss, J. A. (2001). *Healthcare ethics in a diverse society.* Mountain View, CA: Mayfield Publishing.

Cox, D., La Caze, M., & Levine, M. (2001). Integrity. In E. N. Zalta (Ed.), *The Stanford Encyclopedia of Philosophy.* Retrieved August 2, 2004, from *http://plato.stanford.edu*

Einstein, A. (1950). A letter: "In a nuclear age," dated November 20, 1950.

Edson. M. (1999). *Wit.* New York: Faber & Faber. (Original publication 1993).

Faden, R., & Beauchamp, T. L., with King, N. (1986). *A history and theory of informed consent.* New York: Oxford University Press.

Fasting, U., Christensen, J., & Glending, S. (1998). Children sold for transplants: Medical and legal aspects (Amnesty International—Danish Working Group for Children). *Nursing Ethics, 5*(6), 518–526.

Fry, S. R., & Johnstone, M. J. (2002). *Ethics in nursing practice: A guide to ethical decision making* (2nd ed.). Oxford, UK: Blackwell Science.

Gallup Organization. (2004). *Public rates nursing as most honest and ethical profession: Image of the clergy recovers to late 1990s level, is still lower than in 2000 and 2001.* Retrieved August 2, 2004, from *http://www.gallup.com*

Gillett, G. (2000). Ethics & images in organ transplantation. In P. T. Trzepacz & A. F. DiMartini (Eds.), *The transplant patient: Biological, psychiatric, and ethical issues in organ transplantation.* Cambridge, UK: Cambridge University Press.

Joint Commission on Accreditation of Healthcare Organizations. (2004). *Health care at the crossroads: Strategies for narrowing the organ donation gap and protection patients.* Retrieved August 6, 2004, from *http://www.unos.org/news/newsDetail.asp?id=336*

Kerridge, I. H., Saul, P., Lowe, M., McPhee, J., &. Williams, D. (2002). Death, dying and donation: Organ transplantation and the diagnosis of death. *Journal of Medical Ethics, 28,* 89–94.

Koppelman, E. R. (2003). The dead donor rule and the concept of death: Severing the ties that bind them. *American Journal of Bioethics, 3*(1), 1–9.

Loma Linda University & Medical Center [LLUMC]. (2001 March). *LLUMC Legacy: Daring to care* (Chapter 4). Loma Linda, California. Retrieved August 4, 2004, from *http://www.llu.edu/info/legacy/Legacy5.html*

Magee, M. (2004). Organ transplantation: A supply and demand crisis. Health politics. Retrieved August 6, 2004, from *http://www.healthpolitics.com/program_transcript.asp?p=prog_48*

Mappes, T. A., & DeGrazia, D. (2001). Biomedical ethics (5th ed.). Boston, MA: McGraw-Hill.

One News for New Zealanders. (2001, Sept. 3). Pioneer surgeon Barnard dies. *http://www.onenews.nzoom.com/onenews_detail/0,1227,55309-1-6,00.htm*

Pearson, A., Robertson-Malt, S., Walsh, K., & Fitzgerald, M. (2001). Intensive care nurses' experiences of caring for brain dead organ donor patients. *Journal of Clinical Nursing, 10,* 132–139.

Plante, T. G. (2004). *Do the right thing: Living ethically in an unethical world.* Toronto, ON: Raincoast Books—New Harbinger Publications.

President's Commission for the Study of Ethical Problems in Medicine and Biomedical and Behavioral Research. (1981). *Defining death* (pp. 33, 73). Washington, DC: Government Printing Office.

President's Council on Bioethics. (2003 January). Organ *Transplantation: Ethical dilemmas and policies.* Retrieved August 6, 2004, from *http://bioethicsprint.bioethics.gov/background/org_transplant.html*

Taylor, G. (2004). Organ/tissue donation & transplantation. Science Museum of Virginia. Retrieved August 6, 2004, from *http://www.smv.org/prog/B2Kprimorgtrans.htm*

United Network for Organ Sharing [UNOS]. (2004). *Organ donation and transplantation.* Retrieved August 6, 2004, from *http://www.unos.org*

US Government Organ Donation & Transplantation. (2004). Retrieved August 6, 2004, from *http://www.organdonor.gov*

Vallee, V. (n.d.). *The roots of sound rational thinking.* Salt Lake City. Retrieved August 4, 2004, from *http://www.plusroot.com/dbook/08Honesty.html*

Veatch, R. (2003a). The dead donor rule: True by definition. *American Journal of Bioethics, 3*(1), 10–11.

Veatch, R. (2003b). Why liberals should accept financial incentives for organ procurement. *Kennedy Institute of Ethics Journal, 13*(1), 19–36.

CHAPTER 4

Reproductive Issues and Nursing Ethics

Janie B. Butts

MARY HAD A LITTLE LAMB

Mary had a little lamb,
Its fleece was slightly gray,
It didn't have a father,
Just some borrowed DNA.
It sort of had a mother,
Though the ovum was on loan,
It's not so much a lambkin,
As a little lamby clone.
And soon it had a fellow clone,
And soon it had some more,
They followed her to school one day,
All cramming through the door.
It made the children laugh and sing,
And thrilled them to the soul,
But there were too many lamby clones,

For Mary to control.
No one else could herd the sheep,
Their imprints didn't vary,
The cloners sought to fix it up
By simply cloning Mary.
So clone they did,
And [newspapers] said it was extraordinary,
But now they don't know what to do
With Mary, Mary, Mary . . .

Unknown

SUMMARY

1. The pro-choice and pro-life debate regarding abortion is about rights—on the pro-choice side, the right of a woman to choose and control her own body; on the pro-life side, the right of a fetus to live. At the center of this rights debate is the question of when the embryo or fetus becomes human life, a person, or ensouled.

2. Reproductive technology leaves some to question whether the family biological structure will weaken as a result of couples using these methods. For others, the technology leaves them with great hope for the future, depending on their beliefs about the conception of human life and when and how it should begin.

3. Genetic counseling and screening are important options for couples who are likely to have a child with a genetic disease. The question to be answered is, with multiple genetic tests available, does society have a moral obligation to provide the couple with the testing that is needed if they choose to make use of it?

4. Women who are infected with HIV need to have a full range of HIV testing and counseling services available to them, although they may also have a moral right not to be tested. Nurses should encourage, not coerce, women to be tested early in pregnancy. If they are infected with HIV, antiretroviral therapy reduces vertical HIV transmission (to the baby) from 25% to less than 2%.

5. Postpartum depression affects 12 to 16% of women who have delivered a child. It is very treatable, but often overlooked. Early detection and treatment may prevent harm to the mother, her baby, or others.

THE MOTHER–INFANT ETHICAL KALEIDOSCOPE

The relationship between a woman and her fetus has been a matter of enormous public moral debate in the last few decades. Cases of cesarean deliveries that were ordered by courts, alcohol and other drug abuse during pregnancy, and pregnant women who have refused blood transfusions in life-threatening conditions have received national attention (van Dis, 2003). Also, abortion and other treatments that tap into the question of whether or not the fetus is viewed as a person are issues of great moral concern.

Since the latter part of the 20th century, there have been astounding advances in reproductive technologies, so much so that the technologies have sparked public ethical scrutiny concerning a woman's private choice (autonomy) versus public regulation and law (Harris & Holm, 2000). Wachbroit and Wasserman (2003) stated that "Genetic technologies seem to promise an ever-increasing control over the creation of children, altering the nature of reproduction in a fundamental way" (p. 139).

Adding greatly to the ethical debate has been the fact that physicians and nurses now consider care and treatment to be for two persons—woman and fetus—instead of just one (Ludwig, 1999). The ethical issue is each person's right to life versus the possibility of bringing harm to one person when treating the other of the two biologically connected persons. In years past, when physicians and nurses cared for a pregnant woman, they considered the mother and fetus as one patient unit with intricate detail. Everything about the care and treatment of the *whole* patient was weighed according to the perceived benefits of the whole compared with perceived combined burdens. Today, physicians and nurses give dual care; that is, they are supposed to consider the best care and medical treatment possible for each person separately and distinctly. With this dual care frame of mind, however, several ethical dilemmas surrounding a person's rights arises. Ludwig (1999) posed these questions:

- What happens when medical therapy is indicated for one patient yet contraindicated for the other?
- When does a fetus or a newborn become a person?
- People have rights. Does a fetus have rights?
- What if maternal decisions seem to be based on unusual beliefs? (¶ 1–5)

The ethical issues are deep and complex with regard to maternal and fetal rights, and the moral debate continues with no agreements forthcoming concerning the mystery of procreation, technology, abortion, and mother–fetal conflict. Nurses sometimes feel as if they are caught in the middle and do not know how to handle the care related to the mother-fetal conflict. Individual nurses need to maintain dialogue of the highest quality among the woman, the family, and other health care professionals because ethical issues that emerge in reproduction are deeply sensitive and, many times, private and confidential. The manner in which nurses interact and intervene with these patients oftentimes will affect their own health and emotional outcomes.

REPRODUCTIVE RIGHTS

A woman's decision to have a baby is one of the most critical decisions she will make in her life. Although a woman may involve significant others, this type of decision is intensely personal and is one that she will hope to make on her own without coercion or mandates from health care professionals or federal or state governments. However, the ethical question to be asked is, "Does a woman have a right to have a child?" Infertility, for instance, is not a life-threatening disorder but can cause undue suffering and shame to the woman or couple. Brannigan and Boss (2001) posed a question: "If there is a right to reproduce, should it include the right to use expensive and scarce medical resources in exercising this right?" (p. 276)

Many times legal rights and moral rights overlap because of the policies that are made into law to enforce certain rights (Brannigan & Boss, 2001). Moral rights include liberty rights and welfare rights. Health care in the United States is a liberty right, which is a right free for people to pursue "without interference from the government or from other people" (p. 33). Liberty rights also include freedom of speech, autonomy, privacy, and others stated in the US Constitution. There are two population exceptions to health care liberty rights— the poor and elderly—and they fall under welfare rights, which are rights or social goods owed to people by the government or by others.

Brannigan and Boss (2001) further pondered the issue of rights and reproductive health care. If there is a right to reproduction, is it a liberty right, a welfare right, or both? Also, does an unborn fetus or child have health care rights? Answers to these questions are unclear, but most experts agree that all health care rights are of critical importance to everyone. Reproductive rights are about human rights, quality health care, choice, liberation from enforced sexual pleasures and abuse, and population growth and distribution (Cook, Dickens, & Fathalla, 2003).

Moral Standing of Humans

Whatever factor signals the end of full moral standing would seem to be relevant as a marker of when full moral standing begins . . . The moral problems with manipulation of sperm and egg cells are often believed to be less troublesome than those arising from manipulating a late-term fetus or postnatal infant. It is important to know why this is so. It must be that, no matter how we attribute moral status to sperm and egg cells, we view them as having a moral standing that is different from the late-term fetus or postnatal infant. If we can identify what it is that is responsible for this perceived shift in moral status, perhaps we can understand better when full moral standing accrues (Veatch, 2003).

When the phrase "moral standing of humans" is mentioned, what comes to mind? In Veatch's (2003) quote he has suggested that whatever it is that causes moral standing to end is what makes it begin. On this topic, he pondered a general question: Could any of the physiological or neurological criteria be the signals of the beginning and ending of moral standing in humans, such as the criteria used for higher brain death, whole-brain death, or the cardiac definition of death? Veatch stated that there is no specific way for people to determine which, if any, criterion is the one that determines when full moral standing begins and ends. He is under the opinion that the question of when full moral standing begins and ends requires a person's religious and philosophical judgment.

ABORTION

Because pro-choice and pro-life debaters justify their claims and arguments on each side, the dilemma seems deadlocked. The origin of this ongoing debate has ethical and legal implications that are distinct. Abortion, especially in the first trimester, is legal in many countries, including the United States. However, intense moral scrutiny, even legal action, has continued to surface since the *Roe v. Wade* decision of January 22, 1973. In *Roe v. Wade*, the US Supreme Court ruled that states could not make any laws that banned abortions in the first or second trimester, except for certain reasons in the second trimester (as cited in Devettere, 2000; *Roe v. Wade,* 2001). The reasons for having an abortion in the second trimester needed to be related to a woman's health or health risks. In the third trimester, states could not make laws banning abortions unless an abortion was absolutely critical to a woman's survival.

In 1971, two years before the *Roe v. Wade* decision, Judith Jarvis Thomson (1998), a philosopher, wrote a classic and well-known article titled *A Defense of Abortion*, which has served as a foundation for the abortion debate. She agreed that every person has a right to life and that this right is extended to fetuses. To make her argument, she stated that she was pretending that a fetus is a person because it becomes a human person some time before birth. However, her conclusive premise was that, even assuming that the fetus has a right to life, the fetus cannot morally infringe on the mother's own right to control her own body or use her body to stay alive.

The definition of *abortion* includes two meanings: to give premature birth before the fetus is capable of sustaining life, as in a miscarriage or spontaneous abortion, or a woman's intentional termination of a pregnancy. This is the core of the pro-choice and pro-life debate. The debaters argue with political fervor and sometimes bitterness about the legality, rightness, or wrongness of a woman's choosing to terminate her pregnancy, but in the pro-choice view, abortion is almost always permissible and can be justified.

Every day 41,237 abortions are performed worldwide, and of those, 3,597 are performed in the United States (Abortion Statistics, 2004). Almost one billion registered abortions were completed worldwide during the last few decades of the 20th century through February 2004 (Johnston, 2004). In the United States alone, from 1943 to February 2004, almost 45 million registered abortions were performed. The self-reported reasons for abortion in the United States include rape, incest, health problems of the mother, youth and immaturity, parental or partner pressure to have an abortion, relationship problems, financial problems, an unwanted baby, fear of disclosure of being pregnant, and worry about anticipated changes a new baby might bring.

The Central Ethical Dilemma

The central ethical dilemma of the abortion debate is *rights*: the right to life of the fetus or the woman's right to control her own body by choosing whether or not to carry a pregnancy to term, have a baby, and parent it (Harris & Holm, 2003). The fetus as person or nonperson remains at the center of most of the pro-choice and pro-life rights debates.

Pro-Choice View

In the pro-choice view, a common argument is that abortion is legally permissible, regardless of the morality involved. A woman has a basic right to make up her own mind about choices of pregnancy or abortion, and her right always prevails over any other right, including any fetal rights (Harris & Holm, 2003). This is based on privacy rights. Personhood is used in the pro-choice view because the rights of a person are at the core of the ACLU, US Constitution and Declaration of Independence, and the worldwide Universal Declaration of Human Rights (ACLU, 2004).

Then there are pro-choice debaters who believe that abortion is morally as well as legally permissible. A fetus that cannot survive outside a woman's body is not considered viable. Therefore, a fetus cannot override the woman's right to choose an abortion when the fetus is not viable outside the womb. With this pro-choice view, there are two general opinions on the beginning of life: the fetus does not have human life until the mother is in the 17th week of gestation, or the fetus has human life when its nervous system has developed.

Pro-choice believers find the two types of morning-after pills acceptable. One type is RU486. This FDA-approved drug is available by prescription as an alternative to a surgical abortion procedure, and can be administered up to 50 days from conception. It must be followed by another drug within 48 hours (U.S. Department of Health & Human Services, 2000). With RU486, the fetus and other tissue are aborted. The other morning-after pill is the FDA-approved emergency contraceptive called Plan B (Planned Parenthood Federation of America, 2004). In May 2004, the FDA rejected the over-the-counter sale of Plan B, and future control will be managed through prescription only (Kaufman, 2004). Plan B has been a popular drug among adolescents because the drug can actually prevent implantation of a fertilized egg if taken within 72 hours of intercourse.

There are two other arguments on the pro-choice side of the debate. One is the pro-choice debater's attempt to argue for the continued protection of legalized safe abortion to prevent women from resorting to unsafe methods. The other argument is based on the thought that human life begins at conception because the genetic code is complete, and human life ends with death. The genetic argument is strictly based on science, and religious and moral beliefs are not taken into consideration at all. A woman making her decision based on the pro-choice genetic argument realizes that her beliefs include the idea that life begins at conception and ends with death. The point in this view is that she makes her own decision and realizes that she has control over her own body whether she's pregnant or not.

Even today, the argument continues as to when a fetus becomes a person—whether it is at conception, when the heartbeat develops, when it is considered viable outside the womb, or when the baby begins the process of thinking. In 1690, John Locke (cited in Harris & Holm, 2003) emphasized that a person should be characterized as one with intelligence, reason, and reflection. With personhood people should have rational thinking and possess the highest possible moral importance (Harris & Holm, 2003). Most pro-choice debaters who hold this view of personhood argue that abortion is permissible only if the fetus or embryo is not considered a rational person with moral reflection and existence. Establishing *when* the fetus becomes a person is the issue.

Pro-Life View

On the side of pro-life debaters, their view on personhood stems from a fundamental pro-life understanding that the fetus is a person. Most pro-life groups argue that life begins at conception and that abortion is immoral and murderous and should be illegal. According to this view, the embryo, from the time of conception and throughout the development of the fetus, has the same right to life that is due each person (Robinson, 2004; Simmons, 2001). Unless a mother's life is threatened, the embryo (or fetus) must be protected because it is worthy of respect yet vulnerable to murder and harm. Some pro-life groups argue that, in special circumstances, the woman may have an abortion, such as in cases of incest or rape or if the infant is severely deformed. However, abortion in the third trimester for anything other than life-threatening reasons should never be allowed.

Robinson (2004) gave an account of the thoughts of some pro-life groups about when personhood begins if not at conception. Among the times given were after the ovum splits into two cells a few hours after conception; 12 days after conception when the fertilized ovum has attached itself to the uterine lining; two weeks from conception when the yellow streak develops, which is the neural tube that protects the backbone and prevents splitting into two embryos (before the yellow streak develops, the embryo may split into identical twins); three weeks from conception as the fetus begins to develop body parts; four weeks from conception when the heartbeat begins (it should be noted that when 3D and 4D ultrasounds, the HDI 3000 and HDI 4000 systems, are performed in high-risk pregnancies, heartbeats are detected very early); six weeks from conception as the first brain waves are sensed; two months and again at three months from conception when the fetus begins to resemble a human being (again the detailed 3D and 4D ultrasounds produce very clear pictures of, fetal development, such as thumb-sucking and smiling [General Electric Medical Systems, 2002]); four months from conception when the fetus has its own characteristics that could be differentiated from other fetuses; 24 weeks from conception when the fetus is said to become viable; 26 weeks from conception when the fetus's higher brain begins to function; and last, at birth, only after delivery and breathing is separate from the woman's body, as evidenced by Genesis 2:7 in the account of how Adam became a person: "God formed the man from the dust of the ground and *breathed into his nostrils the breath of life, and the man became a living being*."

There are two main scripture passages that some pro-life groups use to defend their view against abortion. The verse in Exodus 21:12 is one of the many laws in the Old Testament of the Hebrews. This verse states that anyone who kills another person is to be put to death. According to pro-life believers, this law also applies when it concerns unborn fetuses. The other primary verse is Luke 1:41 in the New Testament. The phrase "the baby in my womb leaped for joy" is the part of this verse used for the argument. Because the baby leaped, pro-life groups strongly believe that fetuses are persons. Neither scripture directly addresses abortion.

There are other passages in the Bible that are used by pro-life believers, but the Catholic Church's position about abortion is a little more complicated (Harris & Holm, 2003). According to the Catholic Church, the whole issue of the morality of abortion stems from the greater question of when the fetus receives a soul. Because there are many interpretations of the Bible, there is great uncertainty. Therefore, the Catholic Church has taken a general stance on the issue, as Harris and Holm (2003) stated: " . . . because killing is such a grave moral wrong, one should act cautiously and presume that there may be ensoulment from conception . . . Abortion and the destruction of embryos should therefore be treated as the killing of an ensouled being" (p. 122).

New Laws Affecting Women's Rights

The National Right to Life Committee and other pro-life groups have campaigned for years for equal rights and protection of the unborn fetus, based on the viewpoint that the fetus is a human life, one that, if not a person yet, has the potential to be a person. Recently, President Bush signed two new acts into law. On November 5, 2003 he signed the "Partial Birth Abortion Ban Act of 2003," and on April 1, 2004 he signed the "Unborn Victims of Violence Act of 2004," also known as "Laci and Conner's Law."

The *Partial Birth Abortion Ban Act of 2003* was placed into law to prohibit physicians from performing partial-birth abortions and thereby killing fetuses (National Right to Life Committee [NRLC], 2003). *Partial-birth abortion* is defined as a physician's deliberate and intentional act of delivering a living fetus vaginally yet only partially for the sole purpose of terminating a pregnancy. Partially means that for head presentation, the entire head needs to be outside the mother's vagina before the fetus can be terminated. For breech presentation, any part of the fetus's trunk past the navel needs to be outside the mother's vagina.

The terms *"intact dilation and extraction"* (intact D & E) and *"partial-birth abortion"* (a nonmedical term) are sometimes used synonymously. Pro-choice debaters have made claims that the term partial-birth abortion does not exist as an official medical term and that, even if it did, the term is too unclear and much too graphic; thus the pro-choice group prefers to use the term intact dilation and extraction. Preferring the opposite, the pro-life group has stated that intact dilation and extraction sounds too clinical.

Three federal courts, New York, San Francisco, and Nebraska, have struck down the federal partial-birth abortion ban for various reasons and have ruled it unconstitutional. The ACLU brought a lawsuit against the ban and presented closing arguments on June 22, 2004, in the case of *National Abortion Federation v. Ashcroft*. The lawsuit is based on two major statements: that "women and their doctors need to be able to make medical decisions free from interference of politicians" and that the ban prevents physicians from performing several abortion procedures in the second trimester of pregnancy (ACLU, 2004, ¶ 1). The court decision is undetermined as of this date.

The *Unborn Victims of Violence Act of 2004* allows any child *in utero* who has been killed or injured to be recognized as a legal victim of a federal crime of violence, such as interstate stalking, kidnapping or bombing (NRLC, 2004). The child *in utero* may be in the mother's womb at any stage of development and is a legal member of the *homo sapiens* species at any stage. The murders of Laci Peterson and her unborn son, Connor, caused Laci's family to speak in strong support for this bill; thus the bill has been informally named Laci and Connor's Law. The language in this law recognizes the unborn fetus as a legal person in the United States. The language "fetus as a legal person," not the act itself, is the disturbing part of the law to pro-choice debaters.

Speaking Out

The legal and moral debates about abortion and women's reproductive rights continue. Elizabeth Cavendish, the interim president of the National Abortion Rights Action League's Pro-Choice America group, stated that the challenge is in getting young people to wake up and see how reproductive rights gained from the *Roe v. Wade* decision are "crumbling piece by piece" (as cited in Paynter, 2004).

Many times, women who are pro-choice and strongly believe in women's reproductive rights receive abortions but do not necessarily want the procedure. They may find themselves in situations of unintended pregnancy where they must have an abortion for reasons already described in this section. Refer to Ethical Kaleidoscope Box 4-1 on

Box 4-1

ETHICAL Kaleidoscope   Pro-Choice Views of Abortion

One woman named Clare was 40 years old with a degree from Cornell University, was a cardiologist, and was very committed to pro-choice beliefs. Clare said...
I had an abortion when I was a single mother and my daughter was 2 years old. I would do it again. But you know how in the Greek myths when you kill a relative you are pursued by furies [sic]? For months, it was as if baby furies were pursuing me.

Quote from Clare: Wolf, N. (1995). Rethinking pro-choice rhetoric: Our bodies, our souls. The New Republic. Retrieved from http://saturn.med.nyu.edu/~yeh/ cf/resource/wolf.html

Radical Pro-Life Activists Should Rethink Their Actions
In Rockford, Illinois, pro-life picketers with 6-foot posters revealed artwork of mutilated and bloody fetuses while they yelled loud appalling and nasty phrases to others. Children of the picketers were present and children not with the group were standing around listening. Emerson, with the Rockford Register (2004), made a profound statement when she said: "[These pro-life anti-abortionists] claim to care about unborn children, yet they verbally and visually assault living children. Some of the fanatics bring youngsters to protest, exposing them to nasty encounters and potential violence. People who are so willing to screw up their own kids don't give a darn about anybody else's children . . . Using the element of surprise, they harass and intimidate. Elsewhere, they have killed people. Their passions are stoked by religious fervor and that they are right and everybody else is wrong.

Quote from Emerson, J. (2004). Radical activists should rethink own choices (¶ 7–10). Rockford Register Star. Retrieved from http://cf.rstar.com

Clare's story rergarding her abortion and, in a different section of the box, a person's view of protestors (as cited in Wolf, 1995).

Just because a woman believes in her right to choose, that does not mean her intentional decision to have an abortion, the loss of her fetus, and the grieving process will not be emotionally traumatizing to her (Burke with Reardon, 2002). Hornstra (1998) spoke of a poem that circulated on the Internet about an aborted fetus that was speaking to its mother from the dead. Toward the end of the poem, the fetus forgave its mother for the abortion. Hornstra stated: "I think all women who have abortions hope this is how our couldn't-be babies feel" (¶ 6). Sometimes women perceive that they cannot express their grief because they fear that no one wants to hear about it. They may believe that they cannot discuss the abortion or loss of their fetus with anyone because it needs to be kept a deep dark secret. Also, women may believe that they do not have permission to grieve for the loss of their fetus, and therefore they experience extreme sorrow. This type of grief is called *disenfranchised* grief (see Ethical Kaleidoscope Box 4-2). When one is not allowed to grieve or must hide it, the grief process is prolonged and far worse. "Such 'impacted' [disenfranchised] grief can even become integrated into one's personality and touch every aspect of one's life" (Burke with Reardon, 2002, p. 51).

Ethical Reflections

- If almost all abortions during the first trimester are considered legally permissible, how should one view a woman's taking a prescribed dose of RU486 to abort a fetus? Would you view RU486 as morally or legally permissible? Both? Neither? Explain your answer.
- After reading all the arguments on rights and human life in this section, what do you believe about abortion? Address your views to the following points:
  - your moral and legal views on abortion,
  - when you think a human life begins,
  - when you think a human life becomes a person.

Please describe these points clearly so that you will clarify your own beliefs and values regarding these issues. Remember that there is no one right answer. These views are your opinions based on your values and what you have read in the literature.

- If you are giving nursing care to a woman who just received a partial-birth abortion (ID & E), first describe your own beliefs concerning partial-birth abortion and then identify psychosocial strategies that you would use in caring for this patient.

ETHICAL ISSUES OF REPRODUCTIVE TECHNOLOGY

On July 25, 1978, Louise Joy Brown, the world's first successful 'test-tube' baby was born in Great Britain. Though the technology that made her conception possible was heralded as a triumph in medicine and science, it also caused many to consider the possibilities of future ill-use . . . The most important question was whether this baby was going to be healthy. Had being outside the womb, even for just a couple of days, harmed the egg? . . . Today [26 years later], the process of 'in vitro' fertilization is considered commonplace and utilized by infertile couples around the world (Basenberg, 2004).

The Brown couple tried to conceive for 9 years before they tried *in vitro* fertilization. Lesley Brown's fallopian tubes were blocked. Reproductive failure can be emotionally and financially devastating to couples. Because of infertility, more than one million babies have been born worldwide with *assisted reproductive technology* (ART) since 1978 (Gosden, Trasler, Lucifero, & Faddy, 2003). Currently, in many Western countries, ART accounts for 1–3% of annual births. The term "ART" refers to the han-

Box 4-2

ETHICAL Kaleidoscope   Disenfranchised Grief: Forbidding the Grief of Abortion

From the words of Tina...
If you regret an abortion, nobody wants to hear about it. After all, there's nothing anyone can do to fix the problem. So you have to tell yourself what happened was good—and everyone around you tells you the same thing. After that, I would never bring up the subject again (p. 55).

From the words of Kathy...
Dear Mom,
I'm sorry I never told you the truth about my abortion for so long. I told you I was having minor surgery—female problems. Remember?...And what really kills me the most is that you and Daddy came to see me that night in the hospital...I was so scared—scared you'd find out what really happened that day. Man, I was hurting inside. And there you two were standing at the foot of my bed extending your love and concern. Mom, didn't you notice I couldn't even look you in the eyes? And over the years the times I turned from you whenever the abortion issue was raised? I can still see your face the moment I finally told you. Eight years later...You never looked up at me...[and] you sat quietly and gently spoke to me. Just as long as I kept my shameful secret, you were willing to keep it too...Oh how I wish you had been able to talk about it...to cry with me, to help me get through that horrible time. You knew it all...but we never talked. I was so desperately alone (pp. 55–56).

Quotes from Burke, T., with Reardon, D. (2002). Forbidden grief: The unspoken pain of abortion (pp. 51, 55, 56). Springfield, IL: Acorn.

dling and management of sperm *and* eggs and every kind of fertility treatment or drug used *only* for the purpose of retrieving eggs to be used in the treatment (CDC, 2001a). Treatments not included under ART include those in which only sperm are managed such as artificial insemination, surgical procedures on women or men, or drugs that involve infertility when eggs are not going to be retrieved.

The three types of ART include *in vitro* fertilization (IVF): extracting the woman's eggs, fertilizing them with sperm, then transferring the embryo through the cervix into the uterus; gamete intrafallopian transfer (GIFT): transferring unfertilized eggs and sperm into the woman's fallopian tubes via a very small abdominal incision; and zygote intrafallopian transfer (ZIFT): fertilizing eggs in the laboratory with sperm then transferring the zygote into the fallopian tubes (CDC, 2001a). Embryos resulting from IVF can be frozen until the time comes that one, or more of them, are needed (Munson, 2004). The embryo is then unfrozen and implanted without significant risks to the fetus.

The concerns over the future of human life and family structure, human cloning, the low success rate of ART, and the cost of reproductive technology give society enough reason to ask a most basic ethical question: whether or not reproductive technology should be used at all (Munson, 2004). The cost of reproductive technology is one that is a global issue of concern because of scarce medical and health care resources. As stated previously in the section on reproductive rights, reproductive health in the United States is currently a liberty right, one that a couple may pursue without interference from any governmental agency provided there are no laws against what is being pursued. However, how do private insurance companies and other reimbursement agencies weigh the priorities of health care resource allocation and distribution between those who are dying and critically ill against those who believe they have an autonomous right to a child? Most reimbursement agencies do not pay for many of these expensive reproductive medical procedures. But what does the future hold for autonomy and rights to reproductive services? How will distributive justice be managed?

Then there are specific ethical issues about reproductive technologies other than the broad ones already mentioned. These issues are divided into five groups: (1) the risks resulting from technology; (2) surrogacy (for donor eggs, embryo donation, or carrying fetuses); (3) the handling of surplus reproductive products, such as eggs that will not be used; (4) the implications of sperm sorting or gender selection; and (5) genetic modification and enhancement (Frankel, 2003; Wachbroit & Wasserman, 2003).

The first group of ethical issues involves risks created as a result of technology. Examples include ART and freezing embryos. Recent studies have found that a congenital abnormality named Beckwith–Wiedemann syndrome occurs at a 4.2-fold increase in ART babies compared with babies who are born naturally (as cited in Gosden et al., 2003). However, other studies do not make a significant link, and Gosden et al. recommended that widespread investigations be conducted. The ethical principles here include beneficence and nonmaleficence, or promoting human good for the couple who strongly desire a baby and doing no harm to the fetus in the process. The ethical question for consideration is, Could there be an acceptable level of risk for fetuses born via ART?

The second group of ethical issues involves third-party involvement through donor eggs and embryos and carrying fetuses through surrogacy. Surrogacy is a particularly good example, such as when a man can fertilize the woman's egg but the woman cannot carry the fetus to term for some reason. In this case, the couple may ask a surrogate woman to carry the fetus to term. This is called gestational surrogacy. Other types of surrogacy include traditional surrogacy in which the surrogate uses her own eggs and is artificially inseminated with semen from the prospective father and carries the fetus to birth; egg donation, where a woman donates her eggs for *in vitro* fertilization with specific semen; and embryo donation, when a couple with a history of past successful pregnancy and delivery donates embryos to prospective couples seeking parenthood for *in vitro* fertilization and implantation.

The ethical issues regarding surrogacy are many. Who "owns" the infant once it is delivered by the surrogate? Who is the mother—the woman who produced the egg or the one who carried the fetus to term and delivered it? Is the meaning of family integrity or biological relationships at stake, or does it matter? Other concerns are legal issues: finding a way to legally pay the surrogate woman for her time and effort because the selling of children is illegal; avoiding treating babies as commodities; and avoiding exploitation of financially needy women (Munson, 2004; Wachbroit & Wasserman, 2003). Munson (2004) stated that surrogacy will very likely increase as population increases. The principles involved are autonomy and nonmaleficence. These principles involve the issues of a couple's feelings about their right to choose, the surrogate's right to choose to be a surrogate, and doing no harm to the outcome of the child, the family biological structure, and individual freedoms.

The third group of ethical issues deals with surplus reproductive products resulting from technology. For example, because the success rate is low for *in vitro* fertilization, a woman may have stored many frozen eggs in an attempt for a successful pregnancy. Once the woman is pregnant, what happens to the remaining eggs? Some eggs may be fertilized, but only a very few are implanted. What happens to the embryos? For people who believe that life begins at conception, is destroying the remainder of the embryos considered murder? Beliefs about the right to life, the point at which life and full moral standing begin, and the question of whether destroying embryos is murder are at the center of this debate, and the principles are autonomy and nonmaleficence.

The fourth group of ethical issues is called sperm sorting or gender selection, which is advanced technology enabling persons to create the kind of child they want to have, or avoid having, for family balancing or to prevent X chromosome-linked or other genetic diseases (Bauer, 2004; Harris & Holm, 2003). The medical procedure is called preimplantation genetic diagnosis (PGD). Family balancing, or evening out gender representation in children, is a concept that is used to help justify and promote the use of gender selection prior to implantation.

Occurring in 1 of every 1000 live births overall, more than 500 X chromosome-linked diseases have now been identified, including hemophilia, Duchenne muscular dystrophy, and X-linked mental retardation. Other genetic diseases that can be identified through

PGD include Fanconi's anemia, thalassemia, sickle cell disease, neurofibromatosis, and many others (University of Minnesota Cancer Center, 2003). Sperm sorting highly increases a couple's chance of having an unaffected child. In Ethical Kaleidoscope Box 4-3, Adam and Molly Nash and their parents' decision to use PGD are highlighted.

The last ethical issue, the fifth group, is inheritable genetic modification (IGM), which is a procedure that is used to modify genes along the germ lines that are transmitted to offspring (Frankel, 2003). Stem cell research could help prevent genetic diseases from ever occurring in families through the generations by modifying the germ lines of the embryos. Also, genetic traits in the embryo can be enhanced with IGM. What if researchers could help a couple create the perfect baby? In 1932, Aldous Huxley suggested in his book

Box 4-3

ETHICAL Kaleidoscope   A Reflection on Molly and Adam Nash

Adam Nash was born in Colorado on August 29, 2000. He had been an embryo that was sorted, screened, and selected from at least 12 embryos from the Nash couple, Lisa and Jack, for the purpose of tissue matching for the Nashes' critically ill daughter, Molly.

Molly Nash was born to the Nash parents on July 4, 1994, with Fanconi's anemia, a fatal autosomal recessive bone marrow failure (aplastic anemia), which is only treatable with a bone marrow transplant from a sibling's umbilical cord blood. The success rate of a bone marrow transplant from an unrelated donor was only 42%, but from a sibling, the success rate increased to 85%.

The Nash couple, with support of physicians, made the decision to have preimplantation genetic testing on their embryos in the hopes of saving their only child. In the process, 12 of Lisa's eggs were fertilized by Jack's sperm via *in vitro* fertilization; 2 of the embryos had Fanconi's anemia and were discarded. Of the remaining 10 embryos, only one matched Molly's tissue. This one became Adam Nash.

From Grady, D. (2000, Oct. 4). Baby conceived to provide cell transplant for his dying sister. New York Times, p. 24. "The Case of Molly Nash," Denver Post, December 14, 2002.

The ethical questions for consideration:

- Were the Nashes justified in creating Adam for the purpose of using Adam to help Molly get well? In other words, should humans be used as a means to an end?
- What could have potentially happened to the nine remaining embryos?
- How was it justified to discard the two embryos that had Fanconi's anemia and keep the one that became Adam? Consider your beliefs regarding when life begins and the moral equality of each life.

Brave New World that genetics and reproductive technology would be society's worst nightmare because of the government involvement in these activities (as cited in Frankel, 2003).

What is the future of genetic modification? No one knows exactly, but Huxley's 1932 perception for the future of genetic technology is strikingly different from Frankel's forecast. Frankel (2003) stated:

> But as we begin the twenty-first century, the greater danger, I believe, is a highly individualized marketplace fueled by an entrepreneurial spirit and the free choice of large numbers of parents that could lead us down a path, albeit incrementally, toward a society that abandons the lottery of evolution in favor of intentional genetic modification. The discoveries of genetics will not be imposed on us. Rather, they will be sold to us by the market as something we cannot live without. (p. 32)

When these genetic issues are mentioned, emotions flare between people divided in their opinions. One side's view is of how great society's future will be with the new developments. The other side's view is how science should not be interfering with nature or God's work. Not only do these genetic issues spark extreme emotions, they also are the most complex of all the ethical issues that people in society face today. The prospect of designing, altering, enhancing, or ending the life of fetuses or embryos is challenging.

In her 1818 book titled *Frankenstein*, Mary Shelley told the frightening story of science gone awry when Victor Frankenstein tried to create a master race but botched the experiment. Although Shelley's story of the superhuman creature was different from genetic technology today, there is a remarkable nonscientific similarity that may leave one with a feeling of being on shaky or fearful moral ground.

The standard principles of autonomy, beneficence, nonmaleficence, and justice should be addressed in the ethics involved with PGD and other genetic manipulation such as IGM. However, the issues seem much more complex than just principle- or even theory-driven justifications. Genetic manipulation is essentially an unexplored territory that leaves nurses and other health care professionals with deep moral suffering (see Chapter 2 for more on Moral Suffering). Frankel's (2003) statement with regard to IGM, which could be applied to all genetic manipulation, is "whether we will shape it or be shaped by it" (p. 36).

Ethical Reflections

- Do you believe that destroying a fetus or embryo is murder?
- Ben and Lynn want to select the gender of their next baby. They currently have a girl, and this time they want a boy to balance the family. Do you think the destruction of their remaining embryos would be for an inconsequential reason—family balancing? Explain your thoughts.
- Do you think that family balancing and the prevention of genetic diseases are reasons that should be considered equal in moral weight in a sperm sorting procedure with resultant destruction of extra embryos?

- Explore your own feelings regarding sperm sorting that involves PGD and genetic modification that involves IGM. Write down your feelings about these two procedures.
- What are ethical strategies that you as a nurse might use if you were caring for two couples using gender selection (sperm sorting), one seeking family balancing and one preventing X-linked mental retardation. Be specific when listing these strategies.

OTHER REPRODUCTIVE SERVICES

The 4D and 3D ultrasound systems that are used today have outstanding qualities that contribute to a physician's diagnostic competency (Koninkligke Philips Electronic, 2003). With high definition imaging, the 4D ultrasound provides almost magazine-quality pictures of fetuses at every stage of development. This high-technology ultrasound has contributed to the debaters' argument about human life. But more important than the debate itself, as Stricherz (2002) stated, women who see their babies so clearly in 4D ultrasounds and see them smiling or thumbsucking are personalizing the fetal face and taking action. They are seeking better prenatal care, thus preventing harm and saving lives. Some women are even changing their minds about having abortions because of seeing the fetal face so vividly. One woman said, "I didn't realize that's something inside of you . . . That's when I decided I was not going to have an abortion. I could see the hands and the feet, and I could hear the heartbeat. It sounded like horses galloping—*da-dum-da-dum-da-dum* (Stricherz, 2002, ¶ 6)."

The woman laughed as she was describing the heartbeat. However, the most important concept to be learned from this quote is whether or not the pregnant woman will care for herself better during her pregnancy as a result of seeing her fetus. Prenatal care is critical to the future health of the child. There are numerous prenatal health issues, but only the critical ethical issues of genetic counseling and testing and HIV testing are included in this section. Postpartum depression is also presented in this section as a postnatal consideration. Alcohol and other drug use as issues are presented in Chapter 5.

Genetic Screening and Testing

To date, 5000 genetic diseases have been discovered and that number increases every day (Munson, 2004). Genes that are causally linked to biochemical, cellular, and physiological defects are responsible for these *genetic diseases*. DNA testing can identify some of these diseases in the fetus, and many new technologies are available. For example, today, Down syndrome can be detected at 16 to 18 weeks of gestation in a blood sample from the pregnant woman or by the older method of amniocentesis. Diseases such as sickle cell, phenylketonuria (PKU), and Tay-Sachs, as well as many others, can be screened with high accuracy. One example is sickle cell disease, which is autosomal recessive. If one parent has the disease and the other is not affected, all four children will be carriers. However, if both parents are carriers, there is a chance that one in four children will have the disease, which makes for a 25% chance overall.

Genetic screening involves professionals counseling individuals or couples about their risk for genetically linked diseases (Munson, 2004). Genetic screening can be useful for couples with a background of genetic disease such as sickle cell anemia because of its inheritance pattern. As Munson pointed out, however, once couples have this information, they often have no idea what to do with it. Should couples decide not to have children at all based on this small 25% chance? Should couples risk their chances and get pregnant anyway with the 25% risk and, if so, should the woman be allowed to have a prenatal genetic test with only a 25% risk involved? And furthermore, if she found out that her fetus had a recessive disease, would she need to consider an abortion? If she would not consider having an abortion, what would be her next step? And last, should there perhaps have been no reason for the prenatal genetic test in the first place?

Couples need to consider these questions before wandering down the path of expensive prenatal testing. There is the possibility that a woman can have embryo selection sometimes called (sperm sorting) via *in vitro* fertilization before implantation of the embryo (see the previous section on reproductive technology). As previously discussed, however, embryo selection means that the remaining embryos will be discarded, diseased or not, unless the couple donates them to other couples or for research purposes. Even when used for research, the embryos are destroyed when used.

There are a variety of prenatal tests that allow for a close inspection of tissue and bone, including ultrasound, radiography, and fiber optics. Prenatal genetic diagnosis, as previously and briefly mentioned, is accomplished through an examination of the fetal DNA. Prenatal genetic diagnosis is commonly performed through amniocentesis at 15 weeks of pregnancy or later or by chorionic villus sampling (CVS) which is performed between 10 and 12 weeks of pregnancy (American Academy of Family Physicians, 2004). CVS carries an average 0.05% risk for fetal foot or toe deformities; with amniocentesis, the risk is that 1 in 200 women will have a miscarriage (Munson, 2004). The most common test used for prenatal genetic diagnosis is a blood test for alpha fetoprotein. It is performed 15 to 20 weeks after conception and predicts spina bifida or anencephaly with high accuracy.

Knowing when to test and when not to test may be the ethical difficulty for health care professionals. Many women want to know prior to delivery that everything is all right, and oftentimes they believe that genetic testing will provide a certain degree of control and comfort for them. Should prenatal testing be done for what would seem like trivial reasons to other people? Will the woman's insurance company pay for these tests? What if she has no insurance and still wants them? Does she have an autonomous right to them just because the technology is available?

Many experts hold two basic views: (1) that prenatal testing should be done if the woman strongly believes in her right to have the procedure and wants it performed, and (2) that the costs of the prenatal testing are very small compared with the costs of raising a child with a genetic disease or debilitating disorder (Munson, 2004). These decisions reach to the very core of family values and biological structure. Stem cell research offers considerable hope for correction of genetic diseases, but until the time comes that it is being fully used, couples must make their decisions based on the technology available to them. Williams, Alderson, & Farsides (2002) conducted a study of when prenatal screening and testing should be conducted. They concluded from the study that testing is appropriate when a couple can depend on accurate information, make an informed choice and decision, and live with the outcome once the decision about prenatal testing is made.

Ethical Reflections

- Do you think that a couple has a right to have a child with a prenatally diagnosed disabling genetic disease? Explain your thoughts.
- Do you think that physicians and nurses should inform couples that are thinking about having a baby about all the genetic tests that are available to them? Why or why not? Explain your thoughts.
- Do you think a mother has a right to know the results of her prenatal genetic tests, whether positive or negative? Explore both sides based on the literature.
- What approaches would you take as a nurse caring for a pregnant mother carrying a fetus with Down syndrome? Consider all the options.

HIV Testing

In 2003, there were 5 million new HIV infections and 3 million deaths worldwide from AIDS (World Health Organization [WHO], 2004). Women account for half and children account for 2.5 million of the 40 million HIV infections in the world. In 2003 alone, 700,000 children worldwide became infected with HIV, most of them through vertical transmission in utero, after delivery, and through breast milk. Because 40% of all pregnancies are unplanned (but not necessarily unexpected), many times women who are infected with HIV do not receive any HIV counseling and testing until some time after they discover that they are pregnant (O'Neill, 2000).

A major ethical dilemma is whether HIV testing should be mandatory for women upon the diagnosis of pregnancy and for newborns once they are delivered. The other major ethical dilemma is whether or not the mother should breastfeed her infant when failure to do so may result in severe physical risk to the infant, especially in developing countries. The principles involved are autonomy, based on privacy, confidentiality, and basic rights; beneficence, based on doing good or acting in the best interest of the mother and fetus; and nonmaleficence, based on doing no harm to either the mother or fetus.

The ACLU (2004) and the US Public Health Service (Centers for Disease Control and Prevention [CDC], 2001b) have opposed mandatory HIV testing of pregnant women and newborns based on the Constitutional right to privacy of each individual. HIV testing must be voluntary. Both agencies agreed that women should have the right to refuse testing and should not be tested without their knowledge but emphasized that testing and counseling be made available universally. According to WHO (2004) however, HIV testing and counseling may occur very late in pregnancy or even during labor.

Regarding the issue of breast milk, there are countless infants who would face health risks if their mothers did not feed them via the breast. They either do not have enough money or do not have access to baby formula or milk. Although research findings are inconclusive concerning antiretroviral therapy for breastfeeding women, WHO (2004) recommended that women should continue their treatment during breastfeeding. Even still, the United Nations group has remained firm on its recommendations that women with HIV should avoid initiating breastfeeding if at all possible (as cited in WHO, 2004).

Practical considerations for nurses caring for women during the perinatal period include promoting the availability of HIV testing and counseling services and encouraging pregnant women to be tested while avoiding coercion in any way. If women wish to be pregnant but are also HIV-infected, nurses need to be sensitive to their wishes and know that they have an enormous decision to make—whether or not to become pregnant in light of their HIV diagnosis. With the antiretroviral drugs and early treatment, HIV transmission from mother-to-infant in the United States is reduced to below 2%; transmission is 25% if treatment is not used (National Institute of Allergy and Infectious Diseases [NIAID], 2004). A woman needs to consider all statistics available, the social contexts, and the medical futures of herself and her child (Kirshenbaum et. al., 2004). What is most important for nurses to remember is that women need to have adequate information and not personal opinions from nurses. Whatever a woman decides, nurses can be supporters of reproductive rights by not interfering with a woman's freedom to make independent decisions about her reproductive choices.

Ethical Reflections

- Discuss confidentiality and issues that are relevant to HIV testing, counseling, and a positive diagnosis of HIV in pregnant women.
- An HIV-infected woman is inclined to breastfeed her newborn, and you are providing nursing care to her. Do you give advice, teach, give options, or listen to her reasons for wanting to breastfeed? Discuss therapeutic communication and identify nursing strategies that you consider important for the woman, her baby, and this nurse–patient relationship.

Postpartum Depression

Misri and Kostaras (2002) stated: "The tragedy of Andrea Yates, the Texas mother convicted of methodically drowning her five children in the bathtub [in July 2001], provides stark evidence for the need to recognize and treat women with severe postpartum depression" (¶ 1). Cheng, a medical director at a women's health center (as cited in Snyder, 2002), stated that long before the Yates case she knew that depression was a misunderstood condition and that mothers with this disorder needed urgent attention. Women can experience various forms of depression after delivery, after having an abortion or miscarriage, after a stillbirth delivery, or even during pregnancy (National Women's Health Information Center [NWHIC], 2004). There are three types of depression associated with pregnancy and delivery: postpartum depression (PPD), postpartum psychosis (PPP), and baby blues.

Yates did not have traditional postpartum depression. She developed postpartum psychosis, a rare but more severe form of depression. PPP requires emergency treatment. Fortunately only 1 in 1000 women who have delivered a child experience PPP (NWHIC, 2004). With this condition, women experience hallucinations, severe insomnia, agitation, suicidal and homicidal thoughts, and extremely bizarre behavior. Jurors in 2002 sentenced Yates to life in prison in the 2001 deaths of three of her children. She was not tried in the deaths of the other two. In January 2005, however, the Yates' capital murder convictions were overturned by an appeals court, which called for a new trial when it ruled: "a prosecution witness' erroneous testimony about a nonexistent TV episode could have been crucial" to the outcome of the jurors judgment and court ruling (Graczyk, 2005, ¶ 1).

After delivery, 12–13% of women have symptoms of PPD, such as strong feelings of sadness, anxiety, stress, lack of motivation, overeating or having no appetite, lack of interest in hygiene and self-grooming, and intense worries over the baby or lack of interest in the baby (NWHIC, 2004). PPD is less severe than PPP, but it too requires treatment and counseling. The *baby blues* affect approximately 50% of women anytime from 1 to 2 weeks after the birth of a child. Mood swings, anxiousness, loneliness, sadness, and feelings of inpatience are a few of the signs and symptoms (Cunningham, 2002). The baby blues usually subside without treatment.

The exact cause of depression after delivery of a child is unknown, but there are contributing factors such as changes in estrogen and progesterone levels, and the thyroid gland; sleep pattern changes; a feeling of being overwhelmed and stressed; feelings of exhaustion; and feelings of loss: loss of control, identity, and sex appeal. Treatment consists of antidepressant medication and psychotherapy. Support groups are excellent and allow women to share stories and feelings with other women who are experiencing similar circumstances and feelings.

Because of the urgency of these depression disorders, postpartum women have a right to be screened and receive early treatment. For physicians and nurses, the key ethical issue is the early recognition of the disorder and prompt treatment to prevent harm to the mother, her child or other children, and others. Providing the type of care and treatment that a mother needs may be considered an issue that borders on paternalistic care because the mother who is experiencing the disorder—or her family—may not always recognize that she needs help. Nonrecognition on the part of a patients or families is exactly the reason that physicians and nurses must be keenly aware of the first signs and symptoms of a woman's depression.

Nurses must never display a negative attitude toward the disorder itself or toward the mother diagnosed with postpartum depression. Recognition of the disorder, treatment, but, more importantly, acceptance of the person is critical so that the mother can return to a functional level, both physically and mentally. A mother may feel guilty about her own depression and believe she is a bad mother. Nurses need to reassure the mother that she has no reason to feel guilty about her depression. An important approach that nurses who work with these mothers can take is to follow up with them in the postpartum period 1 to 2 weeks after the delivery of the baby. Nurses need to have a list of questions to use in the conversation with the mother, and any comments of significance from the mother need to be taken seriously. An appointment with a primary provider needs to be made immediately if signs or symptoms of depression are detected.

Ethical Reflections

- If you were caring for a woman who had just given birth and was about to be discharged, as part of the moral nature of nursing practice, what would you include in your teaching content about postpartum depression, if anything? Be very specific with your strategies.
- As a nurse who cares for postpartum women in a reproductive health center, you have a moral responsibility to be keenly alert to, and to be able to differentiate among, the different kinds of depression that occur in women after giving birth to a child. Please explain how you would distinguish among the three types: the baby blues, postpartum depression, and postpartum psychosis.

MANAGEMENT OF CARE

Ethical and legal issues in reproductive health are incredibly complex and challenging, but at the same time they encourage us with the promise of correcting genetic diseases. Sometimes the possibilities inherent in new genetic technologies, including human cloning, cause people to become apprehensive or fearful. First, nurses caring for child-bearing women must be educated and remain current with reproductive ethics. In the Ethical Reflections presented throughout this chapter, opportunities have been given for nurses to apply the chapter content to reflective questions. In the following Web Ethics box, there are Web sites that will benefit nurses and Web sites for child-bearing women.

Nursing management for child-bearing women is focused on the ethical relationship between the nurse and the woman. Bergum (2004) stated that the nurse should always ask, "What is the 'right thing to do' for oneself and others" (p. 485). The nurse–patient relationship, as Bergum experiences it, is a moral entity. *Relational ethics* is an action ethic that is created within the moral space of a relationship (Jopling, 2000; as cited in Bergum, 2004). A moral space is where the relationship is created, where nurses display responsibility, and where they respond to others. Nurses must be morally responsible to the child-bearing women for whom they care, whether they are caring for them clinically, educating them, or overseeing their care. In so doing, nurses need to remember the dual care framework for pregnant women: woman and fetus.

Web Ethics

ORGANIZATIONS TO HELP CHILD-BEARING WOMEN AND THEIR FAMILIES
National Women's Health Information Center
http://www.4woman.gov

Womens Institute for Fertility, Endocrinology & Menopause
http://www.womensinstitute.org

Center for Reproductive Rights
http://www.reproductiverights.org

ORGANIZATIONS FOR NURSES
CDC's Reproductive Health Information Source
http://www.cdc.gov/reproductivehealth/wh_women.htm

Bergum (2004) has identified four themes to define relational ethics: environment, embodiment, mutual respect, and engagement. No matter what ethical issue is of concern, nurses need to focus on the quality of the moral relationship between nurse and patient. In relational ethics, the first theme, *environment*, is a living system. It is important to understand how the whole environment is affected by actions that each person takes. The living environment is in every nurse, and every action that is taken by nurses affects the outcome of the health care system as a whole. Take, for example, the goal of a health care agency to discharge a woman who had a partial-birth abortion in one day. The patient and agency depend on the responsible and competent actions of nurses and others to meet the goal of a 1-day discharge.

Embodiment is the second theme and is defined as one's having a scientific knowledge, a compassion for human life, and experiencing feeling and emotion for another person. For example, if after a prenatal genetic test a 16-weeks pregnant woman has just been told that her fetus has Down syndrome, the nurse would understand the science behind the test and know what aftercare is called for. Also, the nurse would have a mindful reality of the woman's pain and suffering and would have compassion for her.

Mutual respect is the third theme in relational ethics. Mutual respect is a way for people to exist together and have equal worth and dignity. Mutual respect is difficult to attain many times, but it is the central theme of relational ethics. In the example of the woman and her fetus with Down syndrome, mutual respect could be initiated by the nurse's regard for the woman's feelings, values, beliefs, and attitudes. The word "mutual" means to have a reciprocal and interactive focus, so the woman would need to reciprocate that respect toward the nurse.

The fourth theme, relational *engagement*, is when the nurse and patient can find a few minutes to interact about something that is important to them. The nurse needs to understand the patient's circumstances and vulnerability. An example of engagement for the woman and her fetus with Down syndrome can be accomplished by the nurse's engaging in a conversation with the woman about her feelings concerning the diagnosis and options for her and her fetus.

Dialogue is in the center of the moral space, at the focus of relational ethics, and is the venue for the four themes to emerge. Depersonalization and coldness often surround the health care systems that women use. Nurses must give personalization to child-bearing women by practicing relational ethics. On relational ethics and the moral life, Bergum (2004) stated

> With relational space as the location of enacting morality, we need to consider ethics in every situation, every encounter, and with every patient. If all relationships are the focus of understanding and examining moral life, then it is important to attend to the quality of relationships in all nursing practices, whether with patients and their families, with other nurses, with other health care professionals, or with administrators and politicians (p. 485).

Case Study: Partial-Birth Abortion (ID & E)

Ms. Brown, a 19-weeks pregnant woman age 34, received a prenatal genetic diagnosis of Huntington's disease for her fetus via amniocentesis. The day after the diagnosis, the physician explained two options to Ms. Brown: carrying the fetus to term or having a late-term abortion to terminate the pregnancy. The physician explained how the procedure would be performed. Mr. and Ms. Brown were devastated and needed a few days to process the information. When they returned to the clinic, the Browns informed the physician and nurse that they had decided to have the partial-birth abortion. They made a decision not to have any more children, even after the physician had explained the possibility of embryo selection (sperm sorting) for future children.

Case Study Critical Thinking Questions

1. The day that the physician explained the options to Ms. Brown, you try to establish a genuine ethical relationship with her so that the two of you can have a deeper understanding of the situation. As a nurse, what specific approaches will you use for this relationship?
2. Based on the reading, what ethical issues are at stake? Explain.
3. You are in the room with the physician on the day that the Browns return with their decision to have the abortion. As a nurse, what approaches will you take with the Browns on this day? Consider your own values and beliefs about abortion, especially partial-birth abortion, in light of the fetus's having Huntington's disease.

4. If they decide to have this baby the Browns must think about who would care for their impaired child in the case of their deaths. A person with Huntington's disease is not usually afflicted with symptoms until the middle 30s. Financial demands would also be a problem. Explore all ramifications of a decision to keep the fetus and raise the child, knowing that the outcome would be severe impairment in the child's middle 30s.

5. How can the Browns justify having an abortion when Huntington's disease does not usually affect a person until the middle 30s, well after the child has reached maturity?

6. Explain how each principle—autonomy, beneficence, nonmaleficence, and justice—can guide or be applied in this case. How can you justify each principle?

References

Abortion statistics by US state, race, age and worldwide statistics. (2004). Retrieved July 17, 2004, from http://abortiontv.com/AbortionStatistics.htm

American Academy of Family Physicians. (2004). Prenatal diagnosis: amniocentesis and CVS. Retrieved July 28, 2004, from http://familydoctor.org/144.xml

American Civil Liberties Union [ACLU]. (2004). Reproductive rights. Retrieved July 17, 2004, from http://www.aclu.org/ReproductiveRights/ReproductiveRightsMain.cfm

Bauer, K. L. (2004). Genetics and IVF Institute. [The original high technology infertility and genetic services center, Fairfax, Virginia]. Retrieved July 23, 2004, from http://www.givf.com/ivf/cfm

Bergum, B. (2004). Relational ethics in nursing. In J. L. Storch, P. Rodney, & R. Starzomski (Eds.), *Toward a moral horizon: Nursing ethics for leadership and practice.* Toronto, CA: Pearson—Prentice Hall.

Brannigan, M. C., & Boss, J. A. (2001). *Healthcare ethics in a diverse society.* Mountain View, CA: Mayfield.

Burke, T., with Reardon, D. C. (2002). *Forbidden grief: The unspoken pain of abortion.* Springfield, IL: Acorn.

Centers for Disease Control and Prevention [CDC]. (2001a). *Assisted reproductive technology success rates: 2001 national summary and fertility clinic report.* Retrieved July 22, 2004, from http://www.cdc.gov/reproductivehealth/ART01/section1.htm

CDC. (2001b). Revised recommendations for HIV screening of pregnancy women. [Electronic version]. *Morbidity & Mortality Weekly Report, 50* (RR-19), 59–86. Retrieved July 20, 2004, from http://guideline.gov/summary/summary.aspx?ss=15&doc_id=3053&nbr=2279

Cook, R. J., Dickens, B. M., & Fathalla, M. F. (2003). *Reproductive health and human rights: Integrating medicine, ethics, & law.* Oxford, UK: Clarendon.

Cunningham, F. G., et al. (2001). Neurological and psychiatric disorders. *In Williams Obstetrics,* 21st ed. pp. 1405–1427. New York: McGraw-Hill.

Devettere, R. J. (2000). *Practical decision making in health care ethics: Cases and concepts* (2nd ed.). Washington, DC: Georgetown University.

Frankel, M. S. (2003). Inheritable genetic modification and a brave new world: Did Huxley have it wrong? *Hastings Center Report, 33*(2), 31–36.

General Electric Medical Systems. (2002). *Ultrasound: Then and now.* Retrieved July 18, 2004, from http://www.gehealthcare.com/rad/us/4d/thennow.html

Gosden, R., Trasler, J., Lucifero, D., & Faddy, M. (2003). Rare congenital disorders, imprinted genes, and assisted reproductive technology. *Lancet, 361,* 1975–1977.

Graczyk, M. (2005). Texas mom's murder convictions overturned. *The Associated Press.* Retrieved January 6, 2005, from http://www.comcast.net/News/DOMESTIC//XML/1110_AP_Online_Regional___ National__US_/1d2525cb-b2ce-49f7-9314-7d95d0c36ba7.html

Harris, J., & Holm, S. (2000). Introduction. In J. Harris & S. Holm, *The future of human reproduction: Ethics, choice, & regulation.* Oxford, UK: Clarendon.

Harris, J., & Holm, S. (2003). Abortion. In H. LaFollette, *The Oxford handbook of practical ethics.* Oxford, UK: Oxford University.

Hornstra, D. (1998). A realistic approach to maternal-fetal conflict. *Hastings Center Report, 28*(5), 7–12.

Johnston, W. R. (2004). *Abortion statistics and other data.* Retrieved July 17, 2004, from http://www.johnstonsarchive.net/policy/abortion

Jopling, D. A. (2000). *Self-knowledge and the self.* New York: Routledge.

Kaufman, M. (2004). FDA says Plan B rejection came despite strong recommendations for approval. TheJournalNews.com. *The Washington Post.* Retrieved July 17, 2004, from http://www.thejournalnews.com/print_newsroom/050804/d0108barrmain.html

Kirshenbaum, A., Hirky, A. E., Correale, J., Goldsteim, R. B. Johnson, M. O., Rotheran-Borus, M. J., & Ehrhardt, A. A. (2004). "Throwing the dice": Pregnancy decision-making among HIV-positive women in four U.S. cities. *Perspectives on Sexual and Reproductive Health, 36*(3), 206–213.

Koninkligke Philips Electronics. (2002). *Ultrasound. HDI 4000 system. HDI 3000 system.* Retrieved July 28, 2004, from http://www.ati.com

Ludwig, M. J. (1999). Ethics in medicine: Maternal–fetal conflict. University of Washington School of Medicine. Retrieved July 11, 2004, from http://eduserv.hscer.washington.edu/bioethics/topics/matern.html

Misri, S., & Kostaras, X. (2002). Postpartum depression: Is there an Andrea Yates in your practice? *Current Psychiatry Online, 1*(5). Retrieved July 28, 2004, from http://www.currentpsychiatry.com/2002_05/05_02_postpartum.asp

Munson, R. (2004). *Intervention & reflection: Basic issues in medical ethics* (7th ed.). Belmont, CA: Wadsworth–Thomson Learning.

National Institute of Allergy and Infectious Diseases [NIAID]. (2004). *Fact sheet: HIV infection in women.* Retrieved July 20, 2004, from http://www.niaid.nih.gov/factsheets/womenhiv.htm

National Right to Life Committee [NRLC]. (2003). Final Language Partial Birth Abortion Act as Approved by Both Houses of Congress. Retrieved July 19, 2004, from http://www.nrlc.org/abortion/pba/partial_birth_abortion_Ban_act_final_language.htm

National Women's Health Information Center. (2004). *Postpartum depression.* Retrieved July 29, 2004, from http://www.4woman.gov/faq/postpartum.htm

O'Neill, D. (2000). HIV and pregnancy. *Living +: British Columbia Persons with AIDS Society.* Retrieved July 20, 2004, from http://www.bcpwa.org/issue6/HIVPreg.htm

Paynter, S. (2004 July 2). Pro-choice? Well, now's the time to take action. *Seattle Post-Intelligencer.* Retrieved July 19, 2004, from http://seattlepi.nwsource.com/

Planned Parenthood Federation of America. (2004). Emergency contraception. Retrieved November 7, 2004, from http://www.plannedparenthood.org/ec/

Robinson, B. A. (2004). Abortion. *Ontario Consultants on Religious Tolerance.* Retrieved July 18, 2004, from http://www.religioustolerance.org/abortion.htm

Roe v. Wade: The 1973 Supreme Court decision on state abortion laws. (2001). In R. M. Baird & S. E. Rosenbaum (Eds.), *The ethics of abortion.* Amherst, NY: Prometheus Books. (Reprinted from *United States Reports, 410,* 113–178)

Rosenberg, J. (2004). First test-tube baby—Louise Brown. *Your Guide to 20th Century History.* Retrieved July 22, 2004, from http://history1900s.about.com/od/medicaladvancesissues/a/testtubebaby_p.htm

Shelley, M. (1988). *Frankenstein.* New York: Tor—Tom Doherty Associates Book. (Original work published 1818)

Simmons, P. D. (2001). Personhood, the bible, and abortion). In R. M. Baird & S. E. Rosenbaum (Eds). *The ethics of abortion.* Amherst, NY: Prometheus Books. (Reprinted from P. D. Simmons, *Birth & Death,* Westminster Press, 1983)

Snyder, T. (2002). Cheng writes article on postparum depression. Maryland Department of Health and Mental Hygiene. Retrieved July 26, 2004, from http://www.dhmh.state.md.us/publ-rel/dateline/2002/may02/0502tara.htm

Stricherz, M. (2002). *Bonding with baby: Why ultrasound is turning women against abortion.* Washington, DC. Retrieved July 28, 2004, from http://www.catholiceducation.org/links/search.cgi?query-ultrasound

Thomson, J. J. (1998). A defense of abortion. In R. B. Baker, K. J. Wininger, & F. A. Elliston, *Philosophy and Sex* (3rd ed.). Amherst, NY: Prometheus. (Reprinted from Thomson, J. J., 1971, A defense of abortion, *Philosophy and Public Affairs, 1*(1), 47–66.)

University of Minnesota Cancer Center. (2003). *Transplant biology: Umbilical cord blood research.* Retrieved July 26, 2004, from http://www.cancer.umn.edu/page/research/trsplant/cord13.html

U.S. Department of Health & Human Services. (2000). HHS news: FDA approves mifepristone for the termination of early pregnancy [print media: 301-827-6250]. Retrieved November 7, 2004, from http://www.fda.gov/bbs/topics/news/NEW00737.html

van Dis, J. (2003). The maternal-fetal relationship. *Journal of the American Medical Association, 289*(13), 1696.

Veatch, R. (2003). *The basics of bioethics* (2nd ed.). Upper Saddle River, NJ: Prentice Hall.

Wachbroit, R., & Wasserman, D. (2003). Reproductive technology. In H. LaFollette, *The Oxford handbook of practical ethics.* Oxford, UK: Oxford University.

Williams, C., Alderson, P., & Farsides, B. (2002). "Drawing the line" in prenatal screening and testing: Health practitioners' discussion. *Health, Risk and Society, 4*(1), 61–75.

Wolf, N. (1995). Rethinking pro-choice rhetoric. Our bodies, our souls. *The New Republic.* Retrieved July 15, 2004, from http://saturn.med.nyu.edu/~yeh/cf/resource/wolf.html

World Health Organization [WHO]. (2004). Antiretroviral drugs for treating pregnant women and preventing HIV infection in infants: Guidelines on care, treatment and support for women living with HIV/AIDS and their children in resource-constrained settings. Retrieved July 20, 2004, from http://www.who.int/hiv/pub/mtct/guidelines/en/print.html

Nursing Ethics in the Care of Infants and Children

Karen L. Rich

"Goodbye," said the fox. "And now here is my secret, a very simple secret: It is only with the heart that one can see rightly; what is essential is invisible to the eye."

Antoine de Saint-Exupery, *The Little Prince*

SUMMARY

1. The words "mother" and "mothering person" can be gender neutral.
2. The best-interest standard is generally the ethical approach used in making difficult decisions in the treatment of children.
3. Childhood screening and immunization requirements vary among states, sometimes causing crucial health care disparities.
4. Nurses are in the category of "mandatory reporters" of child abuse. There is legal protection in most states for nurses who are reporting suspected child abuse in good faith.
5. The curtailment of parental rights may discourage pregnant women from seeking treatment for substance abuse problems.

6. The ethics of allowing children themselves or their parents to refuse health care treatments is based on a number of factors. These factors include the severity of the potential harm to the child that may result from the refusal.
7. The Child Abuse Amendments of 1984 are frequently referred to as the Baby Doe rules. Although these rules lack power in actual enforcement, they are influential in decisions regarding the withholding and withdrawing of supportive care involving infants.

MOTHERING

In the book *Ethics for the New Millennium*, the Dalai Lama (1999) emphasized the importance of the ethic of compassion. Empathy, or one's "ability to enter into and, to some extent, share others' suffering" (p. 123), represents compassion (*nying je*) at a basic level. The Dalai Lama stated that Buddhists, and probably other people, believe that compassion can be developed that goes beyond empathy to the extent that it arises without effort and "is unconditional, undifferentiated, and universal in scope" (p. 123). Compassion is a sense of intimacy toward all other feeling and perceiving beings. Persons with this well-developed level of compassion include in the scope of their compassion even those beings that may harm them. According to the Dalai Lama, this profound form of intimacy and compassion can be likened "to the love a mother has for her only child" (p. 123).

All animals are born into an initial condition of vulnerability and dependence. Human infants and children "arrive in the world in a condition of needy helplessness more or less unparalleled in any other animal species" (Nussbaum, 2001, p. 181). Historically, Western ethics has generally ignored human vulnerability and its resultant consequence of creating a need for humans to depend on one another (MacIntyre, 1999). However, some feminist philosophers, such as Virginia Held (1993) and Sara Ruddick (1995), have used the underlying premise of human dependence as the foundation for their views of ethics. In fact, feminist philosophers have proposed that the caring that occurs between a mother and her vulnerable and dependent child can be used as a model for all moral relationships. This model is similar to the model of compassion discussed by the Dalai Lama (1999).

In considering how a feminist approach to ethics might be relevant to the care of infants and children, nurses can think in terms of what Tong (1997) called a care-focused feminist ethical approach. A *care-focused feminist approach* to ethics supports the acceptance of feminine values that have often been marginalized in male-dominated societies. Those values include "compassion, empathy, sympathy, nurturance, and kindness" (Tong, 1997, p. 38). These values and virtues also are ones that are traditionally associated with *good mothering*.

There have been heated debates about the differences between the types of moral reasoning engaged in by males and females (see "Justice Versus Care Debate" in Chapter 2). However, Stimpson (1993) noted that "crucially, both women and men can be feminists" (p. viii). In accepting and using the female model of social relationships that exists between mothers and children, Stimpson stated "a moral agent, female or male, will be [what Held (1993) called] a 'mothering person' " (p. viii).

Held (1993) proposed the concept of *mothering person* as a gender-neutral term used to describe the type of mothering that would occur in a society without male domination. Held stated there are good reasons to believe that mothering should be a practice performed by both women and men. Ruddick (1995) defined a *mother* as one who is capable of doing maternal work as

> a person who takes on responsibility for children's lives and for whom providing child care is a significant part of her or his working life. [She continued] I am suggesting that, whatever difference might exist between female and male mothers, there is no reason to believe that one sex rather than the other is more capable of doing maternal work (pp. 40–41).

In considering ethics involving the care of infants and children, it is hoped that nurses will be interested in supporting mothers and mothering persons, both females and males, who share in the unconditional compassion toward their children as described by the Dalai Lama (1999).

Ethical Reflections

- Do you believe that mothering is an inherently female trait? Why or why not?
- What can nurses do to include patients' fathers in the "mothering" of children?
- Discuss the Dalai Lama's (1999) statement about compassion being similar "to the love a mother has for her only child" (p. 123). Why do you agree or disagree with this statement?

FOUNDATIONS OF TRUST

A boy bathing in a river was in danger of being drowned. He called out to a passing traveler for help, but instead of holding out a helping hand, the man stood by unconcernedly and scolded the boy for his imprudence. "Oh sir!" cried the youth, "pray help me now and scold me afterwards."

Aesop, *Aesop's Fables*

"Children are vulnerable, often frightened small people" (Ruddick, 1995, p. 119). An infant's development of basic trust versus basic mistrust is the first of Erik Erikson's (1950/1985) eight stages of psychosocial development. According to Ruddick (1995), it is the responsibility of mothers to establish the feeling of trust between themselves and their children, because children's trust is ideally founded upon the nurturance and protectiveness of their mothers. Unless there are unusual circumstances, such as some of the examples that will be addressed in this chapter, parents are entrusted with the autonomy to make decisions for their minor children. This autonomy is an endorsement of the trust that free societies place in parents.

Because mothers are trustworthy, mothers and mothering people must be wary when they are judging health care policies and the people involved with meeting their children's needs. This maternal wariness rightly includes a cautious trust of nurses and other health care professionals who interact with and treat their children. However, it is natural for parents to believe that health care professionals have a more complete grasp of the medical facts and probabilities related to their child's situation than they themselves have in many instances. Consequently, parents depend on and trust health care professionals to support or guide them in making difficult health care decisions for their children. Sometimes this trust is similar to the unavoidable trust that was discussed in Nurse-Patient-Family Relationships in Chapter 2.

Ethicists have established standards, which are generally accepted as being morally appropriate, for guiding health care decisions made on behalf of infants and children. The two most commonly accepted ethical standards that underlie surrogate decision making for children are based on *substituted judgment* and a *standard of best interest* (Ross, 1998; see "Deciding for Others" in Chapter 10). The aim of *substituted judgment* is to abide by the preferences that persons had when they *were* competent at a time when they are no longer competent. Thus, some ethicists argue that only a standard of best interest is appropriate when decisions are made for children because the decisions are being made for persons who have never been legally competent; consequently, there is no history of known preferences based on their competent thinking (Jonsen, Siegler, & Winslade, 2002).

The best interest standard is a quality-of-life assessment, and when using it

> a surrogate decision maker must determine the highest net benefit among the available options, assigning different weights to interest the patient has in each option and discounting or subtracting inherent risks or costs. The best interest standard protects another's well-being by assessing risks and benefits of various treatments and alternatives to treatment, by considering the pain and suffering, and by evaluating restoration or loss of functioning (Beauchamp & Childress, 2001, p. 102).

In using the best interest standard, parents must sacrifice their personal goals for their child in favor of the child's needs and interests. Parents are put in a difficult situation when they must be uncompromising in trying to attend to one child's best interest when it may seem to conflict with the best interest of another child or children within the same family (Ross, 1998). Although parents generally have autonomy privileges in decision making for most minor children, it must always be remembered that children have their own *basic dignity* as human beings (see ANA Code of Ethics in Chapter 2). Kahlil Gibran (1923/2000) described an interesting perspective on the soul, or spirit, of children and parental rights (see Box 5-1).

Box 5-1

ETHICAL Kaleidoscope   Gibran "On Children"

Your children are not your children. They are the sons and daughters of Life's longing for itself. They come through you but not from you, and though they are with you yet they belong not to you. You may give them your love but not your thoughts, for they have their own thoughts. You may house their bodies but not their souls, for their souls dwell in the house of tomorrow, which you cannot visit, not even in your dreams. You may strive to be like them, but seek not to make them like you. For life goes not backward nor tarries with yesterday. You are the bows from which your children as living arrows are sent forth. The archer sees the mark upon the path of the infinite, and He bends you with His might that His arrows may go swift and far. Let your bending in the archer's hand be for gladness; for even as He loves the arrow that flies so He loves also the bow that is stable. (pp. 17–18)

Gibran, K. (2000). The prophet. New York:
Alfred A. Knopf. (Original work published 1923)

Ethical Reflections

- What can nurses do to establish trust between themselves and a patient's mothering person(s)?
- What can nurses do or say when they observe parents treating their children as property? What behaviors are seen in this situation?

INFANT SCREENING

State policies for screening infants for genetic diseases have traditionally been based on the availability of presymptomatic treatments that can prevent death and disability at an acceptable cost (Beauchamp & Childress, 2001). With the advances that have occurred in the treatment of HIV, some people have argued that mandatory newborn screening for HIV is now justified. (The issue of HIV screening for pregnant women and newborns was addressed in Chapter 4.)

Another important newborn screening issue is less controversial but equally important. Statistics from the March of Dimes have indicated that two thirds of newborns in the United States are not being screened for congenital conditions that are lethal or neurologically disabling (Mundell, 2004). Only 21 states now require mandatory screening that includes all nine of the tests recommended by the March of Dimes (2004) to prevent these health care problems in children (see Ethical Kaleidoscope Box 5-2).

Box 5-2

ETHICAL Kaleidoscope   Recommended Newborn Screening

- Phenylketonuria (PKU)
- Congenital hypothyroidism
- Congenital adrenal hyperplasia (CAH)
- Biotinidase deficiency
- Maple syrup urine disease
- Galactosemia
- Homocystinuria
- Sickle Cell anemia
- Medium chain acyl-CoA dehydrogenase deficiency (MCAD)
  (March of Dimes, 2004)

March of Dimes, 2004, What You Need to Know, ¶ 6.

Although congenital conditions are rare, many of them can be detected in newborns by a simple heel-stick blood test. If detected too late, the consequences of many of these conditions can be fatal, but if they are detected early, treatment is very successful. Unfortunately, the consequence of not performing comprehensive screening of newborns has sometimes produced tragic results (see Ethical Kaleidoscope Box 5-3). Ironically, all nine of the screening tests together do not usually cost more than $50 to $100 to perform. Nurses must become active politically in working to have more comprehensive tests mandated by each state and in educating the public about this senseless health care disparity in newborn screening among different states.

Box 5-3

ETHICAL Kaleidoscope   A Simple $25 Test

Before Mississippi began mandating the full scope of newborn screening tests recommended by the March of Dimes, a tragic situation happened.

Ben Haygood seemed healthy. "I treated him like a normal kid," said his mother, Robin, 37. "Because that's what I thought he was." Then…checking on Ben at 1:30 [one] morning, she noticed that the toddler was, "I don't know how else to say it—very floppy," she says, "and his breathing was shallow. Something wasn't right." After a desperate 911 call, Ben was helicoptered to a medical center in nearby Tupelo. By then he had stopped breathing, and despite doctors' best efforts, "they never got him back," says Robin. "He died within 12 hours of showing symptoms." …A month later it became almost unbearable when the Haygoods learned that their little boy's death—from a rare but treatable hereditary disease, MCADD . . . could have been prevented with a simple $25 blood test at birth.

Schindehette, S., Atlas, D., Podesta, J.S., Stambler, L., & Duffy, T.,
August 2, 2004, People Magazine, pp. 107–108.

Ethical Reflections

• After his death, Ben Haygood's parents (see Ethical Kaleidoscope Box 5-3) were successful in getting the Mississippi legislature to pass two laws that increased the number of mandatory newborn screening tests performed in their state. Specifically, what actions can nurses take to get state officials to mandate comprehensive newborn screening tests?

IMMUNIZATIONS

During the 20th century, immunization programs were so successful in preventing vaccine-preventable diseases that many Americans are not acquainted with the reality of these illnesses (March of Dimes, 2002). Because immunizations can prevent disease, disability, and death on such a wide scale—and with relatively low financial and physical burdens—the US Department of Health and Human Services (DHHS) designated immunization as a leading health indicator in its publication, *Healthy People 2010* (DHHS, 2000).

Vaccines today are certainly safe and effective, but they are not 100% safe, nor are they 100% effective (Malone & Hinman, 2004). Allen (2002) reported that a November 2000 study showed that 25% of all parents have suspicions regarding some or all vaccines. Reasons for these suspicions vary (see Ethical Kaleidoscope Box 5-4). However, although there may be debate among the public about the benefits versus the risks of immunizations, the broad consensus among public health workers is that, in most instances, a lifetime of suffering can be prevented with only a few minutes of irritation (McKenzie, Pinger, & Kotecki, 2002).

State governments require immunizations to protect the health of their citizens, both individually and as a population (National Network for Immunization Information, 2004). There are immunization laws in all 50 states, although the mandates vary. "As of May 2004, all 50 states allow vaccination exemptions for medical reasons; 48 states allow exemptions for religious reasons; and 20 states allow exemptions for philosophical reasons" (¶ 5). Exemptions for medical reasons are established by physicians, usually based on a child's allergy to vaccine components or because of an immune deficiency. If parents have a sincere religious belief that is contrary to the acceptance of immunizations, religious exemptions are allowed by 48 states (except Mississippi and West Virginia). Twenty states allow exemptions for parents' nonreligious, philosophical objections to vaccines. When exemptions are obtained, children can attend school without immunizations in most states, although parents or

Box 5-4

ETHICAL Kaleidoscope   Parental Opposition to Immunizations

Among the parental reasons for opposing childhood immunizations include beliefs that immunizations:

- are an unwarranted governmental intrusion into family privacy
- eliminate historical childhood illnesses, making them an attack on childhood itself
- dampen the fires of inflammation, and consequently, dampen children's spirits
- may cause autism, asthma, multiple sclerosis

Allen, A., (2002), Bucking the herd, Atlantic Monthly.

guardians may be judged liable in a civil case if, because of their child's lack of immunization, a vaccine-preventable communicable disease is transmitted to another person.

"The National Childhood Vaccine Injury Act of 1986 mandates that all health care providers and institutions record each administration of any vaccine to a child and report any illness, disability, or death resulting from the administration of any vaccine to Health and Human Services" (Guido, 2001, p. 112). The ANA (1997) has published a position statement regarding childhood immunization. A partial list established by the ANA with regard to the role of public health nurses in the immunization of children includes

- developing strategies to remove patient, provider, and system barriers to care
- educating individuals and communities about the importance of immunizations
- designing outreach activities specifically aimed at hard-to-reach populations, such as those who are geographically, culturally, and socioeconomically at risk
- fostering data collection that supports research-based practice (¶ 5).

Ethical Reflections

- Discuss how state disparities and variances in newborn screening and childhood immunization relate to each of the four bioethical principles: autonomy, beneficence, nonmaleficence, and justice.

CHILD ABUSE

Child abuse, which includes physical, sexual, and emotional abuse, as well as neglect, is a form of family violence (Ramsey, 2000). *Family violence* is an "action by a family member with the intent to cause harm to or control another family member" (Allender & Spradley, 2005, p. 908). The most common form of child abuse falls under the category of neglect (Ramsey, 2000). Although all states have mandatory child abuse reporting laws, it is believed that abuse is significantly underreported.

The ethical responsibility of nurses in the care of children includes the responsibility to be alert to the signs of abuse. Nurses, along with all other health care professionals, are considered mandatory reporters of possible abuse (Ramsey, 2000). Situations that signal possible abuse include

- conflict between the explanation of how an incident occurred and the physical findings, such as poorly explained bruises or fractures;
- age-inappropriate behaviors or behaviors that signify poor social adjustment, such as "aggressive behavior, social withdrawal, depression, lying, stealing, thumb sucking" (Ramsey, 2000, p. 59), risk-taking, etc.;
- alcohol and other drug abuse;
- problems in school; and
- suicidal ideation.

The usual responsibility of handling a patient's treatment confidentially is waived in the instance of suspected child abuse, even when the person reporting the abuse is the patient (Ramsey, 2000). Abuse does not need to be confirmed as factual in order to be reportable. The identification of suspected abuse should be promptly reported to the agency designated by each state. There is legal protection in most states for professionals, including nurses, who are reporting suspected abuse in good faith. However, health care professionals may be exposed to legal sanctions if they fail to report suspected abuse to the appropriate agencies.

Corporal Punishment

An analysis of 62 years of research regarding *corporal punishment* (using reasonable force to discipline a child) conducted by Gershoff (2002) revealed that this type of punishment correlates with, but is not directly linked to, negative behaviors such as aggression and delinquency in children. The research findings that were the strongest with regard to the recipients of corporal punishment were for recipients to have the potential to become victims of abuse and, what was perhaps considered to be a positive consequence, recipients may immediately respond to parental expectations. Another analysis of 70 studies published between 1961 and 2000 about the effects of corporal punishment showed that people who received corporal punishment were, essentially, not at an increased risk for emotional or behavioral difficulties, including distorted thinking (Paolucci & Violato, 2004).

The disparity in the negative and/or positive outcomes of corporal punishment—abuse and compliance with parental wishes—is what seems to keep the controversy about the issue alive, according to Gershoff (2002). Gershoff found that 94% of American parents spank their children before the children are 4 years old. This practice is attributed to the historic biblical belief that using physical punishment to ensure obedience to parents ensures obedience to God. Therefore, it is not surprising that corporal punishment occurs most often in the United States in the Bible belt.

Nurses are often in a position to observe parents using physical force, although it may not be blatantly violent, to discipline their children. This may occur, for example, when a mother jerks the arm of a fidgety child while she (the mother) is trying to talk with the nurse. School nurses or other pediatric nurses may be told by children themselves about the type of punishment that they receive. The question arises about how nurses can know what type of punishment or force is excessive: when does corporal punishment become abuse?

In general, nurses must develop and use practical wisdom in reasoning and deciphering what is what in a situation. The whole context of the parent–child relationship must be considered. Does the nurse know the mothering person and the child well? If not, the nurse can try to ask carefully crafted questions to assess the patterns of behavior that the mothering person consistently or inconsistently uses to discipline the child. Assessing stress factors that may be occurring in the family is essential. The nurse can be a valuable advocate for the parent and child in trying to connect stressed mothering persons with resources to help address their problems.

If a child reports parental punishment to the nurse and the nurse is initially unsure how to react to the information, more information should be sought. As Dewey (1910/1997) proposed in the example of a doctor's need to suspend initial judgments when diagnosing a patient, moral imagination can be useful to the nurse (see "Moral Imagination" in Chapter 9). In situations of corporal punishment, unless there are obvious signs of child abuse, a nurse must suspend judgment long enough to assess the situation while not waiting *too* long and overlooking true or reasonable suspicions of abuse.

Maternal Substance Abuse

The effects of maternal substance abuse are detrimental to a fetus or newborn. However, according to research, some pregnant women who abuse drugs do not seem to understand the potential harm that they are inflicting on their unborn children (Perry, Jones, Tuten, & Svikas, 2003). As one would expect, the women who are unaware of the danger that they are posing to their unborn children are those women who are abusing drugs but who do not seek help. This same group of women also was found to be more likely to believe that having a small baby is a positive occurrence. The results of this research underscore the need for wide-scale community education programs about maternal drug abuse. Nurses can be a valuable resource in this effort.

Maternal drug screening is not performed routinely, and testing a woman or an infant without informed consent is considered a violation of a patient's right to privacy (Keenan, 2000). Additionally, if maternal or newborn testing is performed without the mother's consent and the test is found to be positive, any decision to restrict or remove parental rights would be based on illegally obtained evidence. The handling and treatment of maternal drug abuse varies from state to state. Possible scenarios include

- prosecution of a pregnant woman who abuses drugs.
- charging a pregnant woman with drug possession if she is arrested for drug abuse prior to fetal viability

- charging a pregnant woman with distribution of drugs to a minor if she is arrested for drug abuse after the fetus is considered viable
- reduction of parental rights
- priority access to drug treatment centers in some states for known maternal substance abusers

Nurses have an ethical responsibility to recognize maternal substance abuse. Although nurses might personally find a pregnant woman's substance abuse morally objectionable, compassion is warranted. A family rather than an individual person is wounded by the woman's abusive behavior. Although action must be taken to protect a fetus or child that is at risk from maternal substance abuse, nurses must consider that a woman's decision or desire to seek treatment might result in curtailed parental rights. Consequently, a woman's decision to obtain help often involves limited trust toward health care providers.

Ethical Reflections

- If you were an OB/GYN nurse, what action would you take if you suspected that a pregnant patient at the clinic where you work was abusing drugs? What would you do if you suspected that the woman might avoid the clinic in the future if you address the abuse? What, if anything, would you do differently if you believed that the patient might be receptive to receiving help?

REFUSAL OF TREATMENT

Parents sometimes refuse treatment for their children, but children themselves may, in some cases, be deemed to have decisional capacity to refuse treatment based on religious beliefs or other reasons. In general, religious and cultural beliefs are given a lot of respect in health care matters and are protected through liberties granted by the US Constitution (Jonsen et al., 2002). Serious consideration must be given to the wishes of maturing children regarding their health care treatment, and consultation may need to be sought from pediatric mental health practitioners or an ethics committee. Maturing children are usually thought of more in terms of those who are adolescents rather than children aged 12 years and younger (see "Consent Dilemma" in Chapter 6 for a discussion of decisional capacity and adolescents). However, it is reasonable to keep open the possibility that some younger children can be thought of as mature. The following factors must be taken into consideration and carefully weighed when evaluating the extent of autonomy to be granted to minor children in health care decisions, keeping in mind, however, that efforts should be made not to undermine the relationship between a child and the mothering person(s) (Jonsen, et al., 2002).

- The support of the child's request by the child's mothering person(s)
- The severity of the child's condition, such as a child with a terminal and irreversible

condition who refuses additional painful treatment versus a situation such as meningitis in which the child's condition is acute and reversible
- The consequence of direct harm to the child that potentially could result from the child's decision and the child's realistic understanding of the possible consequences
- Fear, distress, or parental pressure as a motivation for the child's decision

Parental autonomy with regard to a child's health care treatment is usually given wide latitude (Jonsen et al., 2002; Ross, 1998). However, some parental refusals are abusive or neglectful. State laws protect children from parental health care decisions based on religious or other beliefs that can result in serious risk or harm to the child (Jonsen et al., 2002). Nevertheless, many states do not prosecute parents for abuse or neglect if they try to refuse treatment based on religious beliefs. In general, the following principles are followed in overriding parental autonomy in the treatment of children.

- The parent or parents are not given the right of parental autonomy if they are deemed to be incapacitated or incompetent.
- As is done when considering respect for the autonomy of a child, the severity of the child's condition and the direct harm to the child that could result from nontreatment should be evaluated. The child *should* be treated even against the wishes of the parents to prevent or cure serious disease or disability.
- Blood transfusions should be given to a child of a Jehovah's Witness when transfusions are needed to protect the child from the serious complications of disease or injury. Court authority need not be sought in an emergency situation; legal precedent protects the safety of the child (see Ethical Kaleidoscope Box 5-5).

Box 5-5

ETHICAL Kaleidoscope   Protection of Vulnerable Children

In the words of a Supreme Court decision about the authority of a Jehovah's Witness parent, "Parents may be free to become martyrs themselves, but it does not follow that they are free…to make martyrs of their children" (*Prince v. Massachusetts, 1944*).

Jonsen, et. al., 2002, Clinical ethics, p. 92

MENTAL ILLNESS AND CHILDREN

When nurses are considering ethical issues surrounding the subject of mental illness and children, one of the primary considerations should be their own sensitivity in recognizing signs of problems with a child's mental health. (See Chapter 7 for additional discussion of ethics in psychiatric/mental health nursing.) Mental illness, with associated impairment, occurs in one in five children and adolescents (Kalb, 2003). Any nurse who works with children is obliged to be educated, at the very least, regarding the basic signs and symptoms of mental illness in childhood, such as the symptoms of depression, which can be manifested differently in children than in adults. Children and adolescents often have more difficulty expressing feelings that are indicative of depression and may exhibit more irritability than depressed adults (Keltner, Schwecke, & Bostrom, 2003). In some instances, a nurse may be the primary link between preventing a child's suicide and helping the child imagine a meaningful future. Another ethical issue involves nurses being active in helping children with mental disorders deal with stigma and the consequent development of what Goffman (1963) referred to as the stigmatized person's "moral career" (see "Stigma" in Chapter 7). One childhood mental disorder that is particularly surrounded by stigma, confusion, and misinformation is attention deficit hyperactivity disorder (ADHD).

ADHD

Some health care professionals and people in the general public have voiced concerns about a progressive trend toward the overtreatment of ADHD in children. Although "ADHD is the most common behavioral condition diagnosed in children" (Dodson, 2001, p. 304; Keltner, Schwecke, & Bostrom, 2003) and is the most well-known childhood mental illness (Kalb, 2003), it is still unrecognized and untreated in most cases (Dodson, 2001). Three to five percent of school-aged children are affected by the disorder (Kalb, 2003). Even when ADHD is recognized, a debate often ensues about whether the disorder should be treated with medication or behavioral therapy (Powell, Welch, Ezell, Klein, & Smith, 2003).

Dodson (2001) listed the following possible causes for the perception by many that ADHD may be overdiagnosed and overtreated:

- increased awareness of the condition by the public
- acceptance of a broader set of diagnostic criteria
- greater appreciation of the course of the illness and its ultimate impact on adult life, which justifies lengthier and uninterrupted treatments
- diminished concern about growth retardation, predisposition to drug use, and long-term effects of stimulant-class medications [and]
- increased treatment of adults (p. 304).

Nurses and other health care professionals need to keep in mind that, as with almost any mental disorder, ADHD can be over- or underdiagnosed and treated. Nurses working with children, such as those working in schools, need to seek a thorough understanding regarding the appropriate assessment of ADHD and treatment options. Some children who have ADHD are required to take medication while they are attending school, although new medications are beginning to make this situation less common.

For any child, having to take medications at school can be a source of stigma, separating the child from the so-called "normals" within the social structure of the school (Goffman, 1963; see Ethical Kaleidoscope Box 5-6). The ethical responsibility of nurses and other health care professionals with regard to ADHD and all childhood mental illnesses involves their interest in the careful evaluation, treatment, and follow-up of each child as well as being alert and active in trying to minimize stigma.

Box 5-6

ETHICAL Kaleidoscope   About Normal

Right now, I don't know what Normal is anymore. That's because Normal has been changing so much, so often, lately. For a long while of lately. I'd like Normal to be okayness. Good health…emotional health, medical health, spiritual health. I'd like Normal to be like that. I'd like Normal to stay, like that. For now though, I know that Normal won't be normal for a little while…but somehow, sometime, even if things are not Normal, they'll be okay. That's because I believe in the great scheme of things and life.

Stepanek, M. J. T. (2002). Hope through heartsongs. New York: Hyperion.

Ethical Reflections

- What specific actions can school nurses take to reduce the stigma of children who are not among the "normals" of the school?
- What interventions can a nurse provide if a mother cries and expresses feelings of guilt with regard to her child's diagnosis of ADHD? How and why would the nature of these interventions be ethically related?

QUALITY OF LIFE

In considering the basis of quality-of-life determinations for newborns and children, it is important to refer back to the ethical foundation that supports ethical decisions, which was mentioned in the beginning of this chapter. There are at least two differences between how quality-of-life decisions are judged for infants and children as opposed to how they are judged for adults (Jonsen et al., 2002; see "Quality of Life" in Chapter 8). Adults are either able to verbalize preferences that reflect their personal evaluations about the quality of their lives or other people have a general idea of those preferences when an adult becomes incapacitated. "In pediatrics, the life whose quality is being assessed is almost entirely in the future, and no expression of preferences is available" (p. 114).

Health care professionals must be aware of any tendencies they may have to judge the quality of life of pediatric patients as lower than the children, to the best of their ability, or their mothering person(s) would judge it. Nurses are not in a position to make major, ethics-laden treatment decisions in the care of infants and children. Even advanced-practice nurses, such as nurse practitioners who work in neonatal intensive care units (NICUs), work in collaboration with other health care professionals. However, all nurses who work with children are potentially very influential in the health care decisions made by parents and others. Moral imagination, practical wisdom, and the good character of the nurse are essential in the compassionate care of children.

WITHHOLDING AND WITHDRAWING TREATMENT

A comprehensive discussion of end of life issues is covered in Chapter 10. This discussion can be used as a basis for considering decisions about withholding and withdrawing treatment for children under 12 years of age. Infants, however, seem to fall into a special class of persons in terms of withholding and withdrawing treatment.

Anyone seriously interested in the study of health care ethics realizes that the analysis of ethics usually cannot be separated from related laws, governmental regulations, and public policies. In evaluating the ethical care of infants in terms of withholding and withdrawing treatment, it may be helpful to understand the circumstances involved with several landmark cases. These cases help to summarize and clarify the usual actions that are expected to be taken with regard to the treatment of infants, although conclusions about the ethical direction provided by these cases are by no means without dispute.

1984 Child Abuse Prevention and Treatment Act Amendments

The 1984 Child Abuse Prevention and Treatment Act Amendments are also referred to as the *Baby Doe Rules* based on the case of Infant Doe who was born in Indiana in 1982. " 'Baby Doe' cases arise when parents of impaired neonates or physicians charged with the care of these neonates question whether continued treatment is worthwhile and consider forgoing treatment in order to hasten death" (Pence, 2004, p. 216). Before presenting a snapshot of Infant Doe's case—and another landmark case, the case of Baby Jane Doe—background and related information will be discussed to provide a better understanding of the social and medical situation surrounding Infant Doe. The following is based on public information about these cases and a history provided by Pence (2004).

NICUs

When NICUs were developed in the 1960s, the goal was to increase the likelihood that premature babies would survive. Many medical and technological advances followed, and researchers are still making great strides in neonatology today. NICUs are often complicated and scary places for parents who are grappling with the trauma of having a severely impaired neonate. Parents frequently must make life and death decisions about their infants within a context that would be highly stressful even in the best of circumstances. NICUs are often scary and emotionally charged places for nurses, too, who feel their heartstrings being pulled from some place deep within themselves as they watch the miracles of life play out before them while also sharing in the experience of some mother's deepest suffering.

1971 Johns Hopkins Cases

In the 1970s, two infants with Down syndrome were "allowed to die" at Johns Hopkins Hospital, based on what some people believe were the selfish motives of the parents (Pence, 2004). A third infant with Down syndrome was referred to Johns Hopkins shortly thereafter because of the hospital's reputation for allowing the other two infants to die. However, at this point the hospital staff presented a more balanced view of the infant's prognosis, which resulted in a different outcome: the third baby was treated and lived.

Infant Doe

Many events happened during the short life of Infant Doe that greatly influenced the precedent that has set the direction for the treatment of impaired newborns. Infant Doe was born on April 9, 1982, and died 6 days later in Indiana (Pence, 2004). The controversy surrounding the care of Infant Doe was based on disagreements about whether treatment should be withheld because the infant had Down syndrome and a tracheoesophageal fistula. The obstetrician who delivered Infant Doe discouraged the parents from seeking surgical correction of the fistula and indicated that the baby might become a "mere blob." Based on the obstetrician's recommendations and their own beliefs, the parents refused care for their infant. Hospital staff and administrators disagreed with this decision and appealed the decision to a county judge. No guardian *ad litem* was appointed for the baby, and an unrecorded, middle-of-the-night hearing was conducted by the judge at the hospital. The meeting resulted in the judge's support of the parents' decision. The hospital staff appealed the decision unsuccessfully all the way to the Indiana Supreme Court. They were in the process of taking the case to the US Supreme Court when Infant Doe died.

The specific details of what followed these events are interesting but are beyond the scope of this chapter. However, the ultimate outcome was that the media attention given to the Infant Doe case precipitated action by the Reagan administration, specifically the US Justice Department and the DHHS (Pence, 2004). Baby Doe Rules were published by the federal government and became effective on February 12, 1984. The Rules were based on Section 504 of the Rehabilitation Act of 1973, which forbids discrimination based entirely on a person's handicaps. The Baby Doe Rules provide for a curtailment of federal funds to institutions that violate the regulations.

According to Pence (2004), "this interpretation by the Justice Department created a new conceptual synthesis: *imperiled newborns were said to be handicapped citizens who could suffer discrimination against their civil rights*" (p. 221; see Ethical Kaleidoscope Box 5-7 for additional information on the case of Infant Doe.) It is noteworthy that the federal Second Circuit Court of Appeals issued a ruling within 10 days of the Baby Doe Rules that made the new Rules essentially unenforceable. This ruling was based on the case of Baby Jane Doe.

Box 5-7

ETHICAL Kaleidoscope   The Case of Infant Doe

The US Civil Rights Commission reviewed the Infant Doe case in 1989, along with other Baby Doe cases, and "the commission concluded that [the obstetrician's] evaluation was 'strikingly out of touch with the contemporary evidence on the capabilities of people with Down syndrome.' "

US Commission on Civil Rights, as cited by Pence, G. 2004.
Classic cases in medical ethics (p. 220). Boston: McGraw-Hill.

Baby Jane Doe: Kerri-Lynn

Baby Jane Doe, Kerri-Lynn A., was born in 1983 at St. Charles Hospital in Long Island, New York. She was transferred to the NICU at the University Hospital of the State University of New York (SUNY) at Stony Brook, NY, because of her complicated condition at birth. Kerri-Lynn was born with spina bifida, hydrocephalus, an impaired kidney, and microcephaly (Pence, 2004). Her parents were lower middle class people who had been married for only four months when Kerri-Lynn was conceived. After Kerri-Lynn was born, there was disagreement among the medical staff and others about whether or not she should be treated or provided with comfort measures (food, hydration, and antibiotics) and allowed to die. The parents decided in favor of withholding aggressive treatment.

The controversy resulted in legal proceedings that eventually included the involvement of the Justice Department and the DHHS. Leaders within these agencies wanted to send representatives to review Kerri-Lynn's medical records to ascertain whether the Baby Doe Rules were being violated. However, the parents and the hospital objected to allowing the government representatives to review the records. Ultimately, a federal appeals court, and then the US Supreme Court, ruled in favor of the parents and the hospital in the case of *Bowen v. American Hospital Association et al.* in 1986 (Pence, 2004).

This ruling essentially removed the teeth from the Baby Doe Rules. The Rules cannot be enforced if the government has no authority to review the individual medical records of infants to determine if the Rules are being violated. The Supreme Court explained that because the parents do not receive federal funds for the provision of medical care, their decisions are not bound by Section 504 of the Rehabilitation Act (Pence, 2004). Baby Jane Doe's parents later decided to allow the surgery to be performed (see Ethical Kaleidoscope Box 5-8). The attorney who had represented her parents reported in 1998 that Kerri-Lynn was 15 years old and living with her parents.

Box 5-8

ETHICAL Kaleidoscope   The Case of Kerri-Lynn

In 1994, B. D. Colen was Lecturer in Social Medicine at Harvard University. He provided an update on Kerri-Lynn.

Now a 10 year old...Baby Jane Doe is not only a self-aware little girl, who experiences and returns the love of her parents; she also attends a school for developmentally disabled children—once again proving that medicine is an art, not a science, and clinical decision making is best left in the clinic, to those who will have to live with the decision being made.

Pence, G. 2004. Classic cases in medical ethics (p. 226). Boston: McGraw-Hill.

Although "in reality [the Baby Doe regulation] does not apply directly to physicians, nurses, or parents, it does get the attention of many" (Carter & Leuthner, 2003, p. 484). The 1984 Child Abuse Prevention and Treatment Act (Baby Doe Rules) generally provides three reasons to withhold treatment from newborns. Confusion remains, however, about whether or not the Rules are an attempt to mandate nutrition, hydration, and medications for all neonates.This confusion, in addition to the compassion that most people feel toward a dying or severely impaired child, is one reason that health care professionals experience moral uncertainty and moral suffering in relation to decisions about withholding and withdrawing treatment from neonates. It is stated in the 1984 Act:

The term "withholding of *medically indicated* treatment" does not include the failure to provide treatment (other than *appropriate* nutrition, hydration, or medication) to an infant when, in the treating physician's . . . reasonable medical judgment:

1. the infant is chronically and irreversibly comatose,
2. the provision of such treatment would
   a) merely prolong dying,
   b) not be effective in ameliorating or correcting all of the infant's life-threatening conditions, or
   c) otherwise be futile in terms of the survival of the infant, or
3. the provision of such treatment would be virtually futile in terms of the survival of the infant and the treatment itself under such circumstances would be inhu-

mane (US Child Protection and Treatment Act of 1984 [italics added] as cited by Carter & Leuthner, 2003, p. 484).

According to Carter and Leuthner (2003), the language in these rules that addresses situations in which aggressive treatment of infants is not required can be interpreted to mean two differing things with regard to nutrition: "(1) every infant should *always* be provided with medical means of nutrition and (2) every infant should receive nutrition appropriate for his/her medical situation" (p. 484).

Carter and Leuthner have proposed that the Baby Doe Rules should not be interpreted to restrict or prevent the withdrawal of nutrition. However, interpretations of the Rules with regard to withholding and withdrawing nutrition, hydration, and medication vary among health care providers and institutions; and, as mentioned previously, health care providers experience moral uncertainty regarding these Rules. When situations arise that precipitate discussions about withholding and withdrawing nutrition and hydration from newborns, the involvement of an ethics committee is recommended. It is also sometimes helpful for health care professionals serving on an ethics committee to obtain consultation from pediatric ethicists.

1993: In the Matter of Baby K

Although the Baby Doe Rules provided a basis for the right of parents to refuse treatment for their severely disabled newborns, the ruling left the unanswered question of whether parents also have the right to insist on treatment for their newborns when medical staff believe the treatment would be futile or useless (see "Medical Futility" in Chapter 10). The landmark case that provided a precedent for this type of situation involved Baby K, born with anencephaly in 1992. Baby K's mother insisted that a hospital provide maximum treatment for her child, including ventilator support. Hospital physicians disagreed with the mother's wishes and proposed that warmth, nutrition, and hydration were all that should be required in Baby K's care. The case was taken to the legal system for resolution. In reviewing this case, judges noted that medical assessments indicated that Baby K was not being subjected to care that would cause her pain or suffering. Judges serving on the US Court of Appeals for the Fourth Circuit ruled in favor of the mother and ordered the hospital to provide the level of care that she requested (In the Matter of Baby "K," 1993).

Ethical Reflections

- Nurses sometimes feel frustrated when they believe they are providing care that is not beneficial to a patient. What types of problems might result for the nurse personally when these feelings arise? What types of problems might occur among a group of nurses working together who are feeling this type of frustration? What type of positive actions and behaviors would you suggest to deal with this frustration?

MANAGEMENT OF CARE

Those who stand for nothing, fall for anything.

Alexander Hamilton

The good character of nurses, other health care professionals, and parents is not the only character that is relevant to the well-being of children. A child's own character development is important too. School nurses are in a special position to help with this and any nurse who works with children would do well to keep in mind the importance of building a child's character and educating others about it as well. Ryan and Bohlin (1999) have proposed that children need to be engaged in "heart, mind, and head" to know "who [they] are" and "what [they] stand for" (pp. xvi–xvii).

The search for the meaning of life overshadows almost all human endeavors in people young and old (see "Life: Meaning and Significance" in Chapter 8). In the fast-paced world of the 21st century, parents are busy trying to provide their families with necessities and physical comforts, and children are often busy playing video games and watching television. There is scarcely time to ponder the greater mysteries of life. Ryan and Bohlin (1999) proposed that "detached from a conception of the purpose of life, virtues become merely nice ideals, empty of meaning" (p. 39). They proposed that adults should not fear stimulating children to ponder the age-old question about why they were born. All children, but particularly children who are ill, think about the meaning of life even when they do not know how to articulate their feelings. Nurses can provide these children with a kind hand and a warm heart during frightening times.

Almost any time is a good time to take the opportunity to educate children in the development of moral and intellectual virtues. As the old saying goes, "it is never too early." Stenson (1999) proposed that there are three ways to help children internalize virtuous habits and strengths of character when they are on their journey from infancy to adulthood. Those three means of internalization, and the order in which they occur, are

1. By example: children learn from what they witness in the lives of parents and other adults they respect (and thus unconsciously imitate).
2. *Through directed practice:* children learn from what they are repeatedly led to do or are made to do by parents and other respected adults.
3. From words: children learn from what they hear from parents and other respected adults as explanations for what they witness and are led to do (p. 207).

Nurses are patient advocates, but they are also role models. Nurses may never know when the example that they show to children and their mothering person(s) may influence the future of a child or may influence the future of nursing.

Web Ethics

National Network for Immunization Information
www.immunizationinfo.org/

March of Dimes
www.modimes.org/

Prevent Child Abuse America
www.preventchildabuse.org/

NICU Issues
http://eduserv.hscer.washington.edu/bioethics/topics/nicu.htm

Case Study: To Feed or Not to Feed?

Baby S is a neonate admitted to the NICU at the county hospital where you work as the nurse manager. Mrs. S had an amniotic fluid embolus during her delivery, and Baby S experienced anoxia. Consequently, Baby S had an Apgar score of 0 at birth. The baby was "successfully" resuscitated but remained unconscious. All of the baby's organs experienced hypoxic insult. Baby S was placed on a ventilator and parenteral nutrition was later initiated. Mrs. S is physically very weak and experiencing extreme grief, along with her husband, over the condition of their infant. They have two other young children, aged 2 and 5 years old. Baby S has been weaned from the ventilator but has remained unresponsive. Mr. and Mrs. S have requested that the hospital staff discontinue their infant's nutrition and hydration. The NICU medical, nursing, and social work staff have not previously experienced a situation quite like the one that is occurring with the S family.

Case Study Critical Thinking Questions

1. You are meeting with the neonatologists, the NICU charge nurse, the infant's primary nurse, the hospital chaplain, and the social worker in the NICU. What do you contribute to the group's discussion with regard to how you think the staff should proceed in providing the best care for Baby S and her family?
2. How do the Baby Doe Rules affect this case?
3. One of the staff RNs makes the comment "I think the mother and father are being selfish about their request to withdraw nutrition from Baby S. I think it is because they don't want to be bothered with taking care of her at home." How do you address these comments?
4. Caring for Baby S and interacting with her family has caused a great deal of emotional and moral suffering for your nursing staff (see "Moral Suffering in Nursing" in Chapter 2). What do you do as the nurse manager to address this situation?
5. As would be expected, Mr. and Mrs. S are also experiencing a great deal of emotional and moral suffering and grief. How would you handle your personal interactions with Mr. and Mrs. S, and what would you do to help educate your staff in working with families in a situation such as this one? What do you know about the grief that parents experience when their infant is extremely impaired or dies? How would you try to help Mr. and Mrs. S?

REFERENCES

Allen, A. (2002, September 1). Bucking the herd. *The Atlantic Monthly.* Retrieved from: http://www. keepmedia.com/pubs/TheAtlantic/2002/09/01/377476

Allender, J. A., & Spradley, B. W. (2005). *Community health nursing: Promoting and protecting the public's health* (6th ed.). Philadelphia: Lippincott Williams & Wilkins.

American Nurses Association (ANA). (1997). *Position statement: Childhood immunizations.* Retrieved from http://nursingworld.org/readroom/position/social/scimmu.htm

Beauchamp, T. L., & Childress, J. F. (2001). *Principles of biomedical ethics* (5th ed.). New York: Oxford.

Carter, B. S., & Leuthner, S. R. (2003). The ethics of withholding/withdrawing nutrition in the newborn. *Seminars in Perinatology, 27*(6), 480–487.

Dalai Lama (1999). *Ethics for the new millennium.* New York: Riverhead Books.

Dewey, J. (1997). *How we think.* Mineola, NY: Dover. (Original work published 1919)

Dodson, W. W. (2001). Attention-deficit hyperactivity disorder. In J. L. Jacobson & A. M. Jacobson (Eds.), *Psychiatric secrets* (2nd ed., pp. 302–309). Philadelphia: Hanley & Belfus.

Erikson, E. H. (1985). *Childhood and society* (35th ed.). New York: W. W. Norton & Company. (Original work published 1950)

Gershoff, E. A. (2002). Corporal punishment by parents and associated child behaviors and experiences: A meta-analytic and theoretical review. *Psychological Bulletin, 128*, 539–579.

Gibran, K. (2000). *The prophet.* New York: Alfred A. Knopf. (Original work published 1923).

Goffman, E. (1963). *Stigma: Notes on the management of spoiled identity.* New York: Simon & Schuster.

Guido, G. W. (2001). *Legal and ethical issues in nursing* (3rd ed.). Upper Saddle River, NJ: Prentice-Hall.

Held, V. (1993). *Feminist morality: Transforming culture, society, and politics.* Chicago: University of Chicago.

In the matter of Baby "K". 832 F. Supp. 1022 (E.D. Va. 1993).

Jonsen, A. R., Siegler, M., & Winslade, W. J. (2002). *Clinical ethics: A practical approach to ethical decisions in clinical medicine* (5th ed.). New York: McGraw-Hill.

Kalb, C. (2003, September 22). Troubled souls. *Newsweek,* 68–70.

Keenan, C. (2000). Maternal versus fetal rights: Part 1. In S. W. Killion & K. Dempski (Eds.), *Quick look nursing: Legal and ethical issues* (pp. 144–145). Thorofare, NJ: Slack.

Keltner, N. L., Schwecke, L. H., & Bostrom, C. E. (2003). *Psychiatric nursing* (4th ed.). St. Louis: Mosby.

MacIntyre, A. (1999). *Dependent rational animals: Why human beings need the virtues.* Chicago: Open Court.

Malone, K. M., & Hinman, A. R. (2004, January 23). *Vaccination mandates: The public health imperative and individual rights.* Retrieved from http://www.cdc.gov/nip/policies/vacc_mandates_chptr13.pdf

March of Dimes (2002, June 18). *Although vaccine benefits are proven, more effort needed to reassure parents.* Retrieved from http://www.marchofdimes.com/printableArticles/791_1595.asp

March of Dimes. (2004). *What you need to know.* Retrieved from http://www.marchofdimes.com/printableArticles/298_834.asp

McKenzie, J. F., Pinger, R. R., Kotecki, J. E. (2002). *An introduction to community health* (4th ed.). Boston: Jones & Bartlett Publishers.

Mundell, E. J. (2004, June 30). Many newborns not getting critical tests. *Health Day.* Retrieved from http://www.keepmedia.com/pubs/HealthDay/2004/06/30/498502

National Network for Immunization Information. (June 09, 2004). *Immunization issues: Exemptions from immunization laws.* Retrieved from: http://www.immunizationinfo.org/immunization_issues_detail.cfv

Nussbaum, M. C. (2001). *Upheavals of thought: The intelligence of emotions.* New York: Cambridge University.

Paolucci, E. O., & Violato, C. (2004). A meta-analysis of the published research on the affective, cognitive, and behavioral effects of corporal punishment. *Journal of Psychology, 138*(3), 197–221.

Pence, G. E. (2004). *Classic cases in medical ethics: Accounts of cases that have shaped medical ethics, with philosophical, legal, and historical backgrounds* (4th ed.). Boston: McGraw-Hill.

Perry, B. L., Jones, H., Tuten, M., & Svikas, D. S. (2003). Assessing maternal perceptions of harmful effects of drug use during pregnancy. *Journal of Addictive Diseases, 22*, 1–9.

Powell, S. E., Welch, E., Ezell, D., Klein, C., & Smith, L. (2003). Should children receive medication for symptoms of attention deficit hyperactivity disorder? *Peabody Journal of Education, 72*(3), 107–115.

Ramsey, S. B. (2000). Abusive situations. In S. W. Killion & K. Dempski (Eds.), *Quick Look Nursing: Legal and Ethical Issues* (pp. 58–59). Thorofare, NJ: Slack.

Ross, L. F. (1998). *Children, families, and health care decision-making.* Oxford, UK: Oxford University.

Ruddick, S. (1995). *Toward a politics of peace.* Boston: Beacon Press.

Ryan, K., & Bohlin, K. E. (1999). *Building character in schools: Practical ways to bring moral instruction to life.* San Francisco: Jossey-Bass.

Stenson, J. B. (1999). Appendix C: An overview of the virtues. In K. Ryan & K. E. Bohlin, B*uilding character in schools: Practical ways to bring moral instruction to life* (pp. 207–211). San Francisco: Jossey-Bass.

Stimpson, C. R. (1993). Series editor's foreword. In V. Held, *Feminist morality: Transforming culture, society, and politics* (pp. vii–ix). Chicago: University of Chicago.

Tong, R. (1997). *Feminist approaches to bioethics: Theoretical reflections and practical applications.* Boulder, CO: Westview.

US Department of Health and Human Services [DHHS]. (2000). *Healthy people 2010: Understanding and improving health* (2nd ed.). Washington, DC: Government Printing Office.

CHAPTER 6

Adolescent Nursing Ethics

Janie B. Butts

*In adolescence we are in many ways like empty but organic
receptacles, fully formed though still growing, waiting to be filled.
And like receptacles we are capable at that stage of life of
receiving with all our being, becoming one with what is within us.*

Colin M. Turnbull, *The Human Cycle*

SUMMARY

1. When implementing any type of prevention education program for adolescents, nurses are faced with the dilemma of choosing which program is appropriate for a particular group. There are a variety of standardized prevention programs for adolescents. Misleading, age-inappropriate, or incorrect information can cause more harm than good and may be a factor in increased unhealthy practices.
2. An increasingly difficult challenge exists for nurses to provide sexual education to adolescents that is ethical, acceptable, and that will be information that they will actually *hear*. Nurses need to know where along the sexual abstinence–safe sex education continuum that information becomes unethical, nonbeneficial, or even harmful.

119

3. Nurses must gain the trust of adolescents by proving themselves to adolescents constantly, being consistent, giving correct information, keeping commitments, and showing concern and caring. These are the tried and true ways of gaining trust.

4. If adolescents ever *really* have autonomous decision-making capacity for consenting to or refusing treatments, it is closely linked to their moral self-development characteristics and how self-directed they are.

5. Information that is gathered in a nurse–adolescent relationship must be kept private and confidential by the nurse. The only exception is when harm or danger threatens the adolescent or others. This exception is called a limit of confidentiality.

6. Nurses need to base their practice with adolescents on a moral framework of virtues that includes trustworthiness, genuineness, compassion, and honesty.

THE AGE OF ADOLESCENCE

"It was the best of times, it was the worst of times, it was the age of wisdom, it was the age of foolishness. . . " is the first statement in Dickens' book, *A Tale of Two Cities* (1993/1859). If this quote could be taken out of the context in which Dickens used it, that is, the turmoil leading up to the French Revolution, it could be used as a quote concerning adolescence. It is through adolescents' best and worst times that they learn to make life decisions and move toward independence. Through these interesting times, adolescents somehow develop their identity and develop their sense of sexuality. Many experts have defined adolescence as an age that occurs during the second decade of life and a period of transition that differs in length for each person (DiClemente, Hansen, & Ponton, 1996; Leffert & Petersen, 1999). Adolescence is a remarkable succession of physical, cognitive, emotional, and psychosocial developmental changes.

Three separate phases, spanning 11 years, have been identified in the adolescent developmental process (Gullotta, Adams, & Markstrom, 2000; Leffert & Peterson, 1999). *Early adolescence* (ages 10–14) is a transitional period from childhood to middle adolescence and is usually marked by the onset of puberty. Adolescents begin puberty with experimentation and discovery. *Middle adolescence* (ages 15–17) is dominated by peer pressure, peer orientation, and stereotypical behaviors, such as following clothing trends and listening to music that is considered acceptable by peers. *Late adolescence* (ages 18–20) usually marks the transition from adolescence to adulthood. Adolescents generally begin to place more importance on their future and their life plans as they move into late adolescence.

Adolescents have a need to find out who they are and a desire to push limits and test unknown waters. Many of the decisions that adolescents make are based on the values that they have adapted from the pressure of peer approval and the exposure to the quickly changing world around them. Mistakes and failures, but also successes, will occur along the way. Adolescents need to be encouraged to make autonomous decisions and express their values and preferences on a continuous basis so that they will evolve to maturity with a defined sense of self.

Risk-Taking Behaviors

As of 2003, there were 1.2 billion adolescents living in the world, that number being the largest number of adolescents ever in the history of the world (United Nations Population Fund [UNFPA], 2004). Forty million of these young people live in the United States (Centers for Disease Control and Prevention [CDC], 2003). Although risk-taking and the feeling of "it's not going to happen to me," or a feeling of invincibility, are the hallmarks of adolescence, new risks and demands are presented every day to these young people like at no other time in history. They are affected by the realities of massive social, economic, political, and cultural changes worldwide.

Health risk behaviors include those behaviors that, according to Lindberg, Boggess, and Williams, "may threaten the well-being of teens and may prevent them from becoming fully functioning members of society" (2000, pp. 1–2). Adolescents who engage in one risky behavior have a tendency to engage in at least one or more other risky behaviors, especially paired behaviors, such as smoking cigarettes and drinking alcohol or smoking marijuana and engaging in risky sexual activities.

In a literature review on adolescents and risk-taking behaviors, McKay (2003) and Cook, Dickens, and Fathalla (2003) found that the origin of most risk-taking behaviors is social rather than medical and that these behaviors can result in injury from accidents, violence, and sexual abuse. The Web Ethics box lists helpful Web sites for nurses, adolescents, and parents seeking information on risky behaviors and ethical issues in the health care of adolescents.

Web Ethics

ORGANIZATIONS TO HELP ADOLESCENTS AND PARENTS
Parenting of Adolescents
http://parentingteens.about.com/

Parenting—Adolescents
http://parentingadolescents.com/archivpa.html

Teen Health (for teens)
http://www.chebucto.ns.ca/health/teenhealth/

Go Ask Alice! (for teens)
Columbia University Health Services
http://www.goaskalice.columbia.edu

ORGANIZATIONS FOR NURSES
Youth Risk Behavior Surveillance System Survey, CDC, 2003
http://www.cdc.gov/yrbss

UNFPA: United Nations Population Fund—
State of the World Population 2003
http://www.unfpa.org

Alan Guttmacher Institute
http://www.agi-usa.org/index.html

Population Reference Bureau
http://www.prb.org

Risk-taking behaviors can often lead to death in adolescents. Six critical health behaviors have been identified and connected to leading causes of death and disability among adolescents in the United States: injury due to violence (including suicide), use of alcohol and other drugs, risky sexual activity, tobacco use, poor dietary habits, and inadequate or inappropriate physical activity (CDC, 2004b). Table 6-1 lists accounts of the risky behaviors that were reported on the 2003 Youth Risk Behavior Surveillance Survey (YRBSS) and, for ages 10–24, the risky behaviors that contributed to the leading causes of death (CDC, 2004b; 2004c; 2004d). It should be noted that the data from the 2003 YRBSS survey were taken only from US high school students who were enrolled in and attending a high school.

TABLE 6-1   Youth Risk Behavior Surveillance Survey (YRBSS) Highlights for 2003

RISK BEHAVIORS FOR US HIGH SCHOOL STUDENTS
(numbers are percentages except where indicated)

Unintentional Injuries and Violence		*Alcohol and Other Drug Use*	
18	Rarely or never wore safety seat belts	75	Had drunk 1 or more drinks on 1 or more days in their lifetime
30	Rode with a drinking driver during the past 30 days	45	Drank alcohol during the past 30 days
17	Carried a weapon during the past 30 days	28	Drank alcohol before the age of 13
33	Were engaged in a fight in the past year	28	Engaged in episodic heavy drinking in the past 30 days
8	Attempted suicide during the past year	40	Had used marijuana 1 or more times in their lifetime
29	Felt so sad that they stopped performing particular activities that were considered "as-usual activities" in the past year	12	Had used inhalants 1 or more times in their lifetime
9	Had been physically forced to have sexual intercourse when they did not want to have sex	11	Had used ecstasy 1 or more times in their lifetime
9+	Had been threatened or injured with a weapon on school property in the last year	10	Had used marijuana before the age of 13
5+	Did not go to school at least 1 or more days during the 30 days prior to the survey because they felt unsafe at school or *en route* to and from school	9	Had used cocaine 1 or more times in their lifetime
		8	Had used methamphetamine 1 or more times in their lifetime
		6	Had used illegal steroids 1 or more times in their lifetime
		3+	Had used heroin 1 or more times in their lifetime

Sexual Behaviors	*Tobacco Use*
37 Did not use a condom during the last sexual intercourse	58 Ever tried cigarette smoking
83 Did not use birth control pills or methods during last sexual intercourse in past 3 months	28 Report regular tobacco usage, including smokeless
47 Ever had sexual intercourse	18 Had smoked a whole cigarette at least once before the age of 13
14 Ever had four or more sex partners	22 Smoked cigarettes regularly during the past month
34 Had sexual intercourse during the past 3 months	10 Smoked cigarettes more than 20 of the 30 days during the last month
900,000 adolescents under the age of 19 become pregnant annually (approximately)	7 Used smokeless tobacco during the last 30 days
15 million new STIs are acquired yearly— 1/4 of these cases are adolescents (3,750,000 adolescents)	15 Smoked cigars during the past 30 days
	4000 American adolescents, ages 12–17, try their first cigarette every day
	6.4 Million adolescents are expected to die prematurely from smoking-related diseases if patterns continue

Dietary Behaviors and Overweight	*Physical Activity*
15 At risk for becoming overweight	75 Did not participate in sufficient physical activity
14 Overweight: 9 million youth are overweight	72 Did not attend physical education class daily
72 Exceed recommendations for saturated fat intake	
83 Drank less than 3 glasses of milk per day in the past 7 days	
78 Do not eat the recommended servings of fruits and vegetables	

LEADING CAUSES OF DEATH IN AGES 10–24 DUE TO INJURIES AND RISKY BEHAVIORS

32 Motor vehicle accident (includes alcohol or other drug use, no seat belts, and/or no helmets, etc.)

28 Other injury

15 Homicide

12 Suicide

1 HIV infection

STI, sexually transmitted infection. From CDC. (2004). *Healthy youth! Health topics: Six critical health behaviors.* Retrieved May 21, 2004, from http://www.cdc.gov/healthyyouth/healthtopics; CDC. (2004). *YRBSS results.* Retrieved May 21, 2004, from http://www.cdc.gov/yrbss/; and CDC. (2004).

Central Ethical Issues At A Glance

The age of adolescence brings with it overpowering family decision-making issues and health concerns, and as a result, complex health care ethical issues arise. As people in society observe the relationships between adults (or parents) and adolescents and see how these two groups seem to be moving swiftly in disharmony through this first decade of the 21st century, they have many perplexing questions. The ethical health care issues of adolescents are focused on rights—the rights that all people expect, especially people in the Western world. Some of those rights include the right of freedom to consent to or refuse treatment, the right to confidentiality and privacy of one's medical record, and the right not to be violated or taken advantage of because of membership in a vulnerable age group. Conducting research with adolescents is a concern because of that vulnerability. In this chapter, research issues are not discussed. Nursing research books include information on the special concerns of vulnerable research subjects. Certain central ethical themes regarding adolescents have become increasingly apparent.

- Prevention education: how, where, and to what extent adolescents receive information and education about prevention
  - *beneficence*
  - *nonmaleficence*
- Trust, privacy, and confidentiality—limits of confidentiality; handling life-threatening illnesses and disorders
  - *respect for autonomy*
  - *beneficence*
  - *nonmaleficence*
- Consent—consenting to treatments without parental or guardian consent; refusal of treatment without parental or guardian consent
  - *respect for autonomy*
  - *beneficence*
  - *nonmaleficence*
- Research with adolescents: a vulnerable population
  - *respect for autonomy*
  - *beneficence*
  - *nonmaleficence*
  - *justice*

Adolescent Relationships and Ethical Issues

Relationships are at the core of an adolescent's life. Because of the value that adolescents place on relationships, nurses would do well to remember that positive and negative relationship skills, that are learned within a family, continue with children into the adolescent stage. It is because of relationships that adolescents experience a kaleidoscope of feelings such as happiness, sadness, excitement, anger, fear, frustration, stress, and even loneliness (Urban Programs Resource Network, n.d.).

Adolescents want and need to be heard and understood; parents want to give their opinions and be heard. Adolescents also want relationships of their own with each other without interference from authority figures. On the other hand, health care and other professionals want to teach adolescents to prevent harm or illness or to manage disease, and media personnel want to grab adolescents' attention by whatever means necessary. Communication is the key issue in adolescent relationships. For instance, in Ethical Kaleidoscope Box 6-1, there are four quotes from people around the world–two from adolescents, one from a young adult, and one from an older parent about their views on the role of communication.

One of the most common "lines" that nurses hear from adolescents is "my parents don't listen to me!" Ironically, parents often say, "my kid won't listen to me!" When it comes to other relationships involving adolescents, similar statements are sometimes made: "my school teacher doesn't listen to my complaints," "that nurse didn't understand my problem," and so on.

Box 6-1

ETHICAL Kaleidoscope   What Are People Saying About Communication?

From the words of Jessica, 17-year-old mother...
I got into sex at 13 because I felt pushed out of the house when my mother had a baby. I found companionship with guys and decided it would be fun to try sex. If I'd had real sex education with feelings, discussions, explanations of contraception and how to get it, I wouldn't have gotten pregnant at 16.

Quote from Jessica, a teenage mom. Lerman, E. (2000). Safer sex: The new morality. Buena Park, CA: Morning Glory.

From the words of an older parent...
My daughter used to be so wonderful. Now I can barely stand her and she won't tell me anything. I feel totally shut out. How can I find out what's going on?

Quote from unknown parent. Wiseman, R. (2001). Queenbees and Wannabees: Helping your daughter survive cliques, gossip, boyfriends, and other realities of adolescence. New York: Three Rivers.

Give Us a Chance to Shine! From the words of Ghana, boy, age 21, Philippines...
...we do not only want to be heard on the media when we have gone to smoke, do drugs, engaged in war of crimes, but most importantly, we want to be heard when we are making great strikes in our world. Let our little efforts towards making the

world a better place for all be heard. We are tired of being showcased as sources of entertainment and fruitless arguments. We have more and can do more than what you perceive of us to the betterment of the world. Give us the chance.

From the words of a boy, age 16, Singapore...
I'm sick of hearing that everything is too sensitive to discuss. If everything is too sensitive, how is the world going to heal? To all those teens and youths who have been told to 'shut up' and 'keep quiet' about 'sensitive issues,' to heck with the social norms. Keep your opinions strong and continue to let your voice be heard.

Last two quotes from UNICEF. (2004, April). Voices of youth: The bimonthly newsletter, 9. Retrieved May 20, 2004, from http://www.unicef.org/voy/news.

Attentive listening, meaning that the nurse is paying attention to what is being said and then giving a signal to the speaker that listening is occurring, is an effective technique for nurses when working with adolescents. Attentive listening helps nurses earn the respect of young people, which is a critical factor in nurse–adolescent relationships. Ways that nurses practice attentive listening include focusing (making eye contact and not allowing the eyes to wander), not interrupting (hearing the speaker in full before commenting and acknowledging the speaker by nods, smiles, or other expressions), and reflecting (summarizing the speaker's thoughts to clarify the meaning).

Ethical Dilemmas Involving Prevention Education

Listening is important but being the "giver" of communication—how, where, and to what extent—is a critical ethical concern for adolescent relationships of all kinds, especially in professional nurse–adolescent relationships. Beneficence and nonmaleficence are the principles that underlie the ethical management of prevention programs involving this age group. The goal of nurses with educational programs is to teach young people the skills they need to make healthy choices and practice healthy behaviors. This aim is consistent with a beneficent approach because nurses promote human good through education. Most education programs for adolescents are prevention–focused. Prevention programs are focused not only on doing "good" but also on doing no harm, or a nonmaleficent approach. An example of an integrated beneficent and nonmaleficent approach is a harm reduction program. In using a harm reduction program, nurses teach adolescents to live safely with certain high-risk behaviors, such as by advocating participation in a needle exchange program for those addicted to intravenous or other needle-requiring drugs.

Nurses who are involved in prevention education must evaluate the program early in the planning phase. Questions to consider are:

• How much information is too much information?
• When and at what age will the information be presented? What types of information are appropriate?
• Where and how should the information be presented to be effective?

Nurses who give information to adolescents may potentially harm them if they choose a wrong or inappropriate prevention education program. This situation poses a critical ethical dilemma for nurses when they must choose among the many standardized and accepted programs that are available for adolescents. For example, nurses may have to choose between teaching sexual abstinence as opposed to teaching the use of safe sexual practices. Choosing an age-inappropriate program for a particular group or choosing information that could easily be misinterpreted could result in an adolescent's being misled, or an adolescent may perceive information differently from the way the educator intended for the message to be received.

Even though alcohol and other drugs are harmful when abused or misused, a small glass of red wine is reported to actually protect the heart against disease (Gulotta et al., 2000). Messages such as this one can be quite confusing to adolescents. In the United States, marijuana is an illegal drug for most people, but for others it is used for medicinal purposes. Thirty-five states have passed legislation that allows for society's recognition of the medicinal value of marijuana, and nine states have totally legalized it for medical use as of 2004 (Gulotta et al., 2000; NORML Foundation, 2004). Adolescents sometimes receive conflicting and incorrect information because of others seeking political or monetary gain. For example, advertisers often show groups of attractive young people socializing and drinking beer. Some companies intend to subtly convey the message that drinking beer makes one more attractive and popular.

There are hundreds of adolescent prevention programs being used in the United States, but the CDC (2004a) reported last year that high school students continue to engage in too many risky behaviors that lead to sexually transmitted infections (STIs), HIV, injury, addiction, depression, chronic disease, and suicide. The trends reveal that adolescents are making slight progress in some areas, such as cigarette smoking and the use of alcohol and other drugs. Although overall drug use is declining very slowly, over the past two years, pre-teens have been inhaling, sniffing, or huffing substances to get high at drastically increased rates (Partnership for a Drug-Free America, 2004). For example, the use of inhalant substances increased in eighth graders from 22% to 26% and in sixth graders from 18% to 26% over the past two years.

There seem to be big gaps in prevention education programs. The increase in inhalant use in preteens is an alarming fact, but it may only be a symptom of problems with prevention programs that convey controversial or inadequate information. Hallfors surveyed adolescents from 104 school districts across the United States (as cited in Manisses Communications Group, 2002). Hallfors found that lack of teacher training, not enough material resources, inconsistent use of lesson plans, and failure to match lesson plans with the appropriate age were factors that could have large negative ramifications for adolescent drug prevention programs across the country.

Because many school nurses plan and implement programs, nurses must know the objectives and content and anticipate the message that will be heard by adolescents who participate in the program. Adolescents will usually assume that the message they hear is correct when school nurses conduct the prevention education program. If adolescents incorporate misinterpreted information into their viewpoints and behaviors, they may be in danger of contracting STIs or HIV, developing a drug habit, or sustaining alcohol- or other drug-related injuries.

Abstinence-Only or Comprehensive Sex Education Programs

One critical issue today is how sexual abstinence programs measure up to comprehensive sexual education programs. In recent years, there has been a much stronger religious and political focus on the teaching of sexual abstinence in schools, homes, and churches than in past years, especially before the sexual revolution movement of the 1960s. In fact, other than through fundamental religious teachings, sexual education was seldom taught in the United States before the HIV and AIDS epidemic began in the 1980s.

The overall ethical concern about sexual education is complex, but, generally, nurses must evaluate at what point along the sexual abstinence–safe sex education continuum the information conveyed becomes unethical, nonbeneficial, or even harmful. Adolescents need sexual education more than ever today. The risk of acquiring HIV or other STIs is very high for adolescents. According to UNFPA (2003), half of all people newly diagnosed with HIV in the world are between the ages of 15 and 24. Most other STIs occur in this age range as well. Said another way, every 14 seconds worldwide, a young person between the ages of 15 and 24 becomes infected with HIV. As noted in Table 6-1, almost 4 million new STIs are acquired each year in the United States by adolescents (CDC, 2004b; 2004c; 2004d).

Pregnancy and abortion rates among adolescents steadily declined in the 1990s. However, 900,000 adolescents become pregnant every year, as shown in Table 6-1 (CDC, 2004b; 2004c; 2004d). In the Sexual Information and Education Council of the United States (SIECUS) report (2002), reasons given for the declining pregnancy rate in adolescents were that adolescents are pursuing and achieving higher levels of education and that many are exposed to comprehensive sexual education programs in schools. Therefore, adolescents learn negotiation skills and effective contraceptive practices.

However, recent statistics worldwide show that adolescents continue to have unprotected sex, and there are three major ethical concerns about the sexual abstinence–safe sex education continuum and adolescents. The first issue that nurses must face is that there is no clear definition of sexual abstinence today. Traditionally, adolescents have equated "having sex" with just intercourse alone. Young people have sought more creative ways, other than coital sex, to express sexual intimacy, such as mutual masturbation, even oral and anal sex, because these types of sex have not been viewed as "traditional sex" (Remez, 2000). The term "sexual abstinence" in recent years has led to dissimilar and ambiguous opinions. A clear definition must be developed for, and then be communicated to, today's adolescents. Meanwhile, parents, educators, and others who teach sexual abstinence continue to say "just say no to sex," "don't have sex before marriage," or "delay the onset of sex." What do these statements mean exactly? Does abstinence mean not having vaginal penetration? Is oral or anal sex all right just as long as one does not participate in penis–vagina intercourse? Is abstinence referring only to a male and female relationship? What about same-sex relationships? How does abstinence apply in those situations?

Based on the CDC's (1988) recommendation not to exchange any bodily fluids, including saliva in exchanges such as french kissing, and to use latex protection where indicated, adolescents are placing themselves at high risk when they have unprotected sexual relations with body fluid exposures. Could abstinence be defined these days as a person's being able to engage in any type of sexual activity just as long as the couple or group is protected with latex and does not exchange body fluids?

Without a clear definition, educators, parents, and others have only vague communication between themselves and adolescents about the meaning of sexual abstinence. What adolescents perceive as the definition of sexual abstinence and what adults are trying to teach as sexual abstinence most likely include a variety of different opinions. Ethically, this vagueness itself can be harmful, not beneficial, because the information may be misperceived. As a result, adolescents are left to their own interpretations. Misinterpreted information may lead to unprotected sex, which, in turn, may lead to an unwanted pregnancy or an STI or infection with HIV.

A second issue is adolescent sexual intimacy, a reality that cannot be denied. In an in-depth study of intimacy and sexual abstinence, Hartwig (2000) contended that long-term abstinence damages individuals' development of their "capacity to love with greater depth and integrity" (p. 3). Although this depth of intimacy can be built upon by other means, Hartwig stated that intimate relationships through sex help people to move past fears and perplexities that sometimes cannot otherwise be overcome.

Early-stage adolescents, ages 13 to 15, may not be capable of managing the strong physical and emotional feelings that go with sexual relationships. Intimate relationships could be injurious to adolescents' emotional development in the short-term, as well as having long-term effects. This issue is a challenge to educators and parents. Hartwig (2000) posed this question to adults: "How does one discourage premature sexual intimacy among those who intensely desire physical sexual intimacy and who often assume they are emotionally mature enough to form intimate relationships without shaming or vilifying sexual intimacy?" (p. 36).

However, according to Hartwig, sometimes adolescents are restricted from learning to eliminate risks when they are exposed solely to abstinence-only programs. Adolescents need what Hartwig called a poetic approach to sexual education and sexual virtue, which complements and balances a moral approach. Poetic intimacy teachings must begin with young children. For adolescents, a process such as this one includes integrating the poetics of sexuality. Examples include exposing adolescents to narratives that highlight tenderness and sensuality and teaching them to practice the use of graceful sexual language, not bad and dirty language. If adolescents are not taught to manage sexual intimacy in a beneficial way, the ethical implication is that harm may result in their developmental and emotional processes. Developing this type of intimacy helps them come to terms with their sexual changes and feelings. Adolescents who learn graceful poetic intimacy develop ways to deepen their desire for intimacy without necessarily having sexual relationships, or they learn to make healthier choices when they decide to have sex.

A third issue is that there is controversy about whether or not abstinence-only programs seem to be working. "It's not a small matter that more and more teens will not have the comprehensive information that could literally save their lives," stated Elizabeth Toledo, the vice president for communications for the Planned Parenthood Federation of America in New York City (as cited in Bowman, 2004, ¶17). Many adolescents are breaking the no-sex pledges that they make to their church leaders, school teachers, and parents. In one survey by researchers at Northern Kentucky University, it was found that 61% of students making abstinence pledges had broken them (*Teens break no-sex vows*, 2003). Moreover, 55% of students who reported that they had kept their pledge stated that they had engaged in oral sex. The views are conflicting. Joanna Mohn, one of the researchers of the national teen pregnancy rates, contended that abstinence is the number one factor in the drop in pregnancy rates (as cited in New study shows abstinence, 2003), and many school and church leaders continue their efforts to teach abstinence-only programs.

Adults in the United States would like to see a comprehensive sexual education program implemented in schools, which includes healthy choices, abstinence, and strategies to be safe. As pregnancy rates have slowly declined over the last decade for adolescents, STIs have remained alarmingly high and of deep concern to public health officials. In a January 2004 poll of 1759 people in the United States, only 15% of adults thought that school officials should teach abstinence alone and not provide information about contraception (Princeton Survey Research Associates; as cited in Bowman, 2004). According to Boonstra (2004), prevention is critical, but prevention must go beyond education. Adolescents need to be able to access health care services that provide them with family planning and STI treatment on a regular basis because many STIs are treatable and curable. Cervical cancer may follow if adolescents are not treated properly for STIs.

This third issue is one of great concern for nurses who work with adolescents. Inconsistency exists across programs. Ethically, nurses need to think about the possible harm that could be done as a result of the type of sexual educational program they choose. Nurses need to evaluate the program early in the planning process by using the guidelines already mentioned in this chapter. It is important for nurses to think about the ways in which adolescents may perceive, interpret, or put into practice the content that is being presented to them. Once nurses can effectively focus on the adolescents who are receiving the message, they need to clarify the message; try to focus on what they are *really* saying to adolescents; and, most of all, attempt to clarify and anticipate as much as possible the message that adolescents are actually hearing. If a nurse takes times to focus on the audience and the content of the message, adolescents will realize that the nurse cares for them and is respecting them for their values and beliefs. As the nurse provides well-defined content and becomes an attentive listener, a reciprocal trusting and respectful relationship is more likely to develop.

- If you were a school nurse planning a prevention education program for your rural middle school students on alcohol, other drugs, and sex, what would you need to consider before actually beginning your program? What is the most effective prevention program that could be used? What ethical considerations should be incorporated into program planning? What message do you think adolescents need to hear? What type of relationship do you hope to establish with the students?

CONFIDENTIALITY, PRIVACY, AND TRUST

Confidentiality, privacy, and trust cannot be viewed as separate entities in a nurse–adolescent relationship. *Confidentiality* is linked with privacy and trust, and usually means that information given to someone is to be kept secret (Blustein & Moreno, 1999). *Privacy* used in this way means for someone to keep information secluded or secret from others. From an ethical standpoint, confidentiality, privacy, and trust are tightly woven with respect for autonomy, the adolescent's right to privacy, and the rights of service. Any breach of confidentiality, privacy, and trust is viewed as a violation of autonomy.

Trust is important to a healthy and respectful relationship. Once trust is broken and mistrust develops, it is very difficult for the informer (nurse) to regain trust. Adolescents will probably refuse to listen to anything that the nurse tries to convey. Trust is a basic need that must be developed in the first stage of life, according to Erik Erikson (1963). If trust is broken early in an individual's life, mistrust carries over in all of the person's relationships.

If adolescents do not trust the nurse, for example, they may not believe the nurse with regard to an informed consent (Blustein & Moreno, 1999). Adolescents may not listen to explanations. The most important way for nurses to gain the trust of adolescents is by proving themselves constantly: being consistent, giving correct information, keeping commitments, and showing concern and caring. These activities, combined together, help show that nurses are *trustworthy*, meaning that nurses are dependable and authentic because they take responsibility for their own behavior and commit to their obligations (Gullotta et al., 2000).

The Clinton administration passed a law called the Health Insurance Portability and Accountability Act (HIPAA) of 1996, which outlined requirements for the protection and privacy of medical records and the confidential information of minors (as cited in Dailard, 2003). More specifically, under the act, if adolescents had consented to their treatment and care, they could be assured of confidentiality with all related records. The act protected adolescents seeking sensitive health services, e.g., pregnancy, abortion, and oral contraceptives. The Clinton administration wanted to make sure that adolescents were allowed every possible avenue to seek the health care that they need for these sensitive issues.

However, early in the Bush Administration, in April 2001, there was a proposal for critical changes to this act. In August 2002, a new law went into effect that somewhat altered adolescents' rights to privacy and confidentiality with regard to their medical records and their right to consent to health care. Under the new law, each state has a right to decide how much privacy, confidentiality, and control adolescents have over their own medical records and treatment. It should be pointed out, however, that most states keep silent on this issue and leave those decisions to health care professionals.

Trust–Privacy–Confidentiality Dilemma

A legal, ethical, and practice issue surfaces when a trusting relationship may exist and the nurse is entrusted with an adolescent's confidential information. Sometimes the sensitive issue and the nature of the information is potentially harmful to the adolescent if it is not reported to proper authorities or others (*Approach to assessing adolescents*, 2004). Adolescents are very concerned about their privacy and what others think of them, especially their parents and peers. Nurses need to ensure that adolescents are examined privately and away from their parents and peers. Many times it is the physical and emotional health outcomes of risky behaviors that force adolescents to seek medical treatment. Because of the sensitive issues involved and the embarrassment that they cause, adolescents want to keep the information secret, especially from their parents.

There are well-established research findings in the United States that reveal the likelihood that adolescents will seek health services for sensitive issues when confidentiality can be maintained (Dailard, 2003). Adolescents can seek family planning services at the state level, such as counseling and contraception through the Planned Parenthood Federation of America, which is federally funded by Title X of the Public Health Service Act, and be guaranteed confidentiality (Planned Parenthood of America, 2004; US Department of Health and Human Services [DHHS], 2004). Each state has a broad range of laws that stem from the federal laws concerning confidentiality and consent of adolescents.

In the United States, the exception to adolescent autonomy over medical records involves the issue of abortion. Seventeen states require no parental involvement in an adolescent's decision to have an abortion. As of April 2004, 33 states require some parental involvement in an adolescent's choice to have an abortion, with 19 states requiring parental consent and 14 states requiring only parental notification (Alan Guttmacher Institute, 2004). Even with required parental consent, 32 of the 33 states with this requirement (all except Utah) have sought ways to work around complete parental involvement by having a judicial bypass, meaning that adolescents may obtain approval from a court to bypass parental involvement. Six of the states permit family members, such as an aunt or grandparent, to be involved in the abortion decision so that adolescents can avoid informing their parents. However, most states allow for exceptions to the parental involvement law when abortions become a medical emergency or when an extraordinary situation exists, such as when the pregnancy was the result of sexual assault or incest.

Limits of Confidentiality

Nurses need to assure adolescents from the beginning that confidentiality is an important component of the nurse–patient relationship. However, confidentiality must never be guaranteed because there are limits (*Approach to assessing adolescents*, 2004). The nurse can assure the adolescent that unless harm or potential threat to the patient or to known others is involved, confidentiality will not be breached. In cases of potential harm, an adolescent must always be given a chance to disclose sensitive or controversial information to parents, guardians, or others involved, as appropriate. If the adolescent refuses to do so, nurses and other health care professionals are obligated to report the following information to state officials according to state laws:

- suicidal ideation
- homicidal ideation
- physical abuse
- sexual abuse
- behaviors that put one at risk of physical harm (*Approach to assessing adolescents*, 2004, ¶ 2)

Nurses must hold to these standards. Even if the situation is not considered a "limit of confidentiality," the nurse should make every effort to involve the parents or guardians if the adolescent is younger than age 14. The lines of confidentiality and consent are even more vague and unclear before the age of 14.

Consent Dilemma

Adolescents under the age of 18 can give consent for their own care in a broad range of circumstances and services. The minors who can consent are those who are over a certain age, mature, legally emancipated, married, in the armed forces, living apart from their parents, high school graduates, pregnant, or already parents (*Approach to assessing adolescents*, 2004). They may also refuse treatment. An adolescent's right to consent to treatment or to refuse treatment is more frequently honored with certain types of services. These services include:

- emergency care
- family planning services, such as pregnancy care and contraceptive services
- diagnosis and treatment of STIs or any other reportable infection or communicable disease
- HIV or AIDS testing and treatment
- treatment and counseling for alcohol and other drugs
- treatment for sexual assault and collection of the medical evidence for sexual assault
- inpatient mental health services
- outpatient mental health services

Deciding whether or not adolescents really have autonomous decision-making capacity is a consideration that is tightly linked to their personal self-directedness and characteristics, what Blustein and Moreno (1999) called moral self-government. The goal during adolescence is development of the moral self, and most adolescents' moral self is not yet fully formed. Blustein and Moreno stated that adolescents have an "emerging capacity," which means that the moral self is evolving but it is not doing so evenly or consistently. Age and the stage of cognitive, emotional, and social development are factors that influence a person's ability to make mature decisions. According to Blustein and Moreno, an adolescent's capacity for decision making does not occur before the age of 15. Some experts have said that adolescents should not take part in significant autonomous decision making before age 14 (*Approach to assessing adolescents*, 2004).

For many years, adults in America have valued the right to control their medical decisions. Adolescents are no different. In most states, these decisions are left up to health care professionals. If a valid consent between a nurse and adolescent takes place, the initial phase should be more of a dialogue and educational exchange. During the consent process, the nurse's responsibility is to evaluate the adolescent's capacity for understanding and appreciating the process, especially when treatments or interventions are anticipated.

The consent process may be more than a single event in time, such as in cancer treatments. It could be that one or both parents were highly involved with the adolescent's initial treatment and consent. Later in the process, adolescents may develop considerable maturity and then have the capacity to consent or not consent to subsequent treatments. Therefore, the adolescent's level of understanding and appreciation of the content of the consent may have progressively increased. Over time, the adolescent can take on more, if not all, of the responsibility in the decision-making process, and dialogue and education need to be continued throughout. During the treatment and consent phases, documentation of the adolescent's progress in development of the moral self is essential.

Ethical Reflections

- A 16-year-old adolescent named Kelly has come to a clinic where you work as a nurse. She has stated that she is at least 12 weeks pregnant but has not told anyone, not even her parents or boyfriend. She is scared of telling her boyfriend for fear of losing him. She wants an abortion, has cash money, and does not want anyone to know about the pregnancy or the abortion. Explore the ethical issues surrounding this situation. Consider the trust–confidentiality–privacy dilemma and the consent dilemma.
- Identify specific nursing strategies that you must consider using with Kelly. The clinic is in a state that does not require direct parental involvement but does require consent by someone of legal age.

HEALTH ISSUES THAT TRIGGER ETHICAL CONCERNS

There are many adolescent health issues that cause nurses to have genuine ethical concerns. Some topics have already been discussed in this chapter, but there are others that are also just as critical to adolescents' health and survival, such as depression and suicidal ideation, substance use and abuse, sexual abuse, and eating disorders. This author realizes that there are many more critical issues that adolescents experience and face every day.

The same guidelines for privacy, confidentiality, and consent that were discussed in the last section apply to these critical health issues. The ethical principles involved with these issues are beneficence (doing good, such as with prevention education) and nonmaleficence (protecting adolescents from harm). The common ethical concern for nurses managing these four health problems is that they are all potentially harmful and may even lead to death if left undetected. In the majority of situations, these problems need to be reported to the proper authorities or other people within the health care system, such as school officials, mental health counselors, or physicians. Because these conditions are considered harmful and fall into the category of "limits of confidentiality," nurses should never promise privacy and confidentiality to adolescents when such information is disclosed to them. The nurse must make it clear and distinct that confidentiality cannot be promised once critical health information, such as suicidal ideation or bulimia, is disclosed. Protection and safety must come first when a health problem is detected.

Depression and Suicidal Ideation

Depression can be closely linked with suicide. Because the age of adolescence is such a time of great emotions and drama, depressive behavior may be hidden in daily displays of extremes (Blackman, 1995, ¶ 4). There are risk factors for adolescent suicidal ideation and attempts, many of which include family disturbances, familial tendency, sexual orientation conflicts, and socioenvironmental problems. However, 90% of suicides occur in adolescents who have had a psychiatric diagnosis.

Obtaining treatment for depression is key to the prevention of suicide. Nurses may be fearful of making a mistake or missing signs of changes in adolescents. In Ethical Kaleidoscope Box 6-2, one nurse, Gail Nelson, expresses her fears and concerns about this very issue (Teen suicide, 2004). If a nurse finds an adolescent who is exhibiting behaviors that look suspiciously like signs of depression or suicidal tendency, first and foremost, the nurse must quickly identify the problem, ascertain the intention of the adolescent, and clearly explain the process of notification while offering hope and the prospect of a treatment plan (American Foundation for Suicide Prevention [AFSP], 2004).

Box 6-2

ETHICAL Kaleidoscope   One Nurse's Fears About
Overlooking a Teen in Trouble

From the words of a nurse...

My greatest fear associated with school nursing and a suspect suicidal student is missing the signs because of lack of familiarity with that student. Not seeing the changes, because I did not know what he/she was like prior to my meeting. Another fear is that my assessment will be discounted by those who know him. Often times, people not attached can see odd behavior clearer than those familiar. I must keep in mind the warning signs, and do what I know is right for that child.

Quote from Gail Nelson, Bulletin Board Forum: Adolescent Suicide. "Teen Suicide," 2004, Retrieved from HyperNews, http://hyper.vcsun.org/

Alcohol and Other Drugs

Adolescents with a family history of abuse are at high risk for developing substance abuse problems, along with those who are depressed, have low self-esteem, and feel like outcasts or that they do not fit in with their peers. An ethical issue that is raised with the use and abuse of alcohol and other drugs is the dilemma of balancing adolescents' rights to autonomy, privacy, and freedom to determine their own actions against the harmful effects of irresponsible use of alcohol and other drugs. Now that prevention drug programs are widespread, adolescents are talking more than ever about substance use and abuse (Banks, 1999). Striking a balance between a nurse's keeping confidential all information learned and protecting the adolescent is a complex and difficult situation. The trust between the nurse and adolescent should not be broken unless there is evidence of impending physical harm, which is considered a limit of confidentiality.

Sexual Abuse

According to Banks (1999), sexual abuse is "an issue which is surrounded by apprehension and fear" (p. 157). Hundreds of thousands of minors are physically or sexually abused each year, most of the time within the family. Sexual abuse, however, may occur outside the home as well. All states have clear laws, policies, and guidelines for child protection from abuse.

Nurses are responsible for critical event changes that are encountered during actual discussions with adolescents. Sexual abuse or other abuses are considered to fall under "limits of confidentiality." Nurses who work with adolescents must report any cases that they encounter to proper officials or health professionals. For example, a school nurse would report the abuse to the principal, or a nurse in an emergency department would report sexual abuse to the physician, mental health worker, or social worker. Before explaining the severity of the situation to the adolescent, nurses should make every effort to help adolescents express their own feelings and reactions about the situation.

Eating Disorders

Physical appearance is one of the most important aspects of self-image for adolescents, but it is especially so for girls. In fact, one third of all adolescent girls in the United States diet (Paige, 2002). Most girls dream and wish for beautiful lean and trim bodies, and many of them tend not to be satisfied with their own bodies.

Two common eating disorders that lead to serious medical complications, and even death, if not treated correctly are anorexia nervosa and bulimia. The physical and emotional outcomes can be disastrous and deadly if these conditions are left untreated. The tragedy is that most adolescents who experience these two disorders are skilled at hiding them until medical problems become severe. Nurses who work closely with adolescents need to be highly skilled in assessing and monitoring adolescents who are at risk for these eating disorders. Other than weight loss, some signs that may alert the nurse to these disorders include the need to be "perfect" or a high achiever, low self-esteem, open displays of intense guilt, signs of depression, or signs of obsession with food, calories, fat grams, or weight (Blackwell, 2002).

For many adolescents, obesity has become a disturbing problem. Adolescents who are obese tend to be very self-conscious of how they look to others, which may lead to a lifelong cycle of anxiety, depression, and overeating (American Psychiatric Association, 2003). Chronic overeating and obesity lead to severe health problems, such as heart disease, hypertension, type 2 diabetes, and respiratory problems.

The fact that these eating disorders exist in many adolescents is a warning that severe emotional hurting is present. In turn, if left undetected or untreated, the emotional distress may progress to more disturbing behavior, such as complete withdrawal, being friendless, expressions of anger and aggression, and self-harm (American Psychiatric Association, 2003).

Ethical Reflections

- As a school nurse, you notice that you have a 15-year-old boy named Eric who keeps to himself and never talks to anyone. Lately, his behavior has become what you would note as extreme: not eating in the cafeteria, keeping his head down at all times, and never making eye contact with anyone. He has completely withdrawn from any social interaction at school. The other teens are making fun of him and his behavior, and these actions just seem to make him go deeper into withdrawal. You believe that he is very depressed, and from literature that you have read recently, you gather that he may be at risk for committing suicide. As a nurse, explore your moral obligations and the specific actions that you would take in this situation.

FACING DEATH

Losing a Loved One

Losing a loved one is a catastrophic tragedy for an adolescent. Healing strategies include simple things for the nurse to do, such as being present, attentive listening, and allowing adolescents to express themselves as long as they need to do so. It is important for nurses to realize that some adolescents do not want to disclose information about their feelings of losing someone, and they need to be alone. Many adolescents turn to prayer, hope, and a belief in absoluteness, or a higher being. Some adolescents heal through self-talk, memories, and dreams. It is a difficult thing for an adolescent to lose a parent. Robert, a 16-year-old boy, expresses his thoughts about the memory of his mother three years after her death (Markowitz & McPhee, 2002) in Ethical Kaleidoscope 6-3. He was only 13 years old when his mother died.

BOX 6-3

ETHICAL Kaleidoscope   "Sometimes I Dream About Her"

From the words of an adolescent boy about the loss of his mother...
Every day I miss her, but it is just something that I've accepted, that I have to deal with and can't change. One time I followed someone [in the car] until she turned, because she had the same color hair as my mom. Even though I knew it wasn't her, there was the fascination of, "What if it was...?" Sometimes I dream about her, but then I wake up...and it knocks me back down to earth. It isn't a sad thing, because it is nice to see her again...The thing that stops me in my tracks is seeing her handwriting. I still have a list of chores she'd written out—there was so much personality in her voice and in her writing, that even though it was just a chore list it is something that is so beautiful to me (Markowitz & McPhee, 2002).

Quote from Robert, age 16. A. Markowitz & S. Mcphee. Adolescent Grief:
"It Never Really Hit Me...Until It Actually Happened." Journal of American
Medical Association, 288 (21), p. 2741.

Although death is expected at some point in life, most of the time people are not prepared for it, especially adolescents. If allowed to grieve appropriately, however, in most cases adolescents will not be permanently scarred, and they will heal. When death is totally unexpected, such as in violence or an accident, screams and loud bursts of "Oh God, why?" and "No!" from adolescents are often voiced. The death of a fellow student may shock others to a state of numbness and disbelief. When adolescents unexpectedly or expectedly lose someone they love, friend or family member, how do they say good-bye, progress through the hurting and pain, and move on?

Adolescents realize that death is a final and irreversible act. When grieving has not progressed appropriately, however, dysfunctional grieving may occur. It is normal for adolescents to live in the present and often not think in terms of consequences. During the grieving process, they may take more risks than usual and harm themselves (National Education Association [NEA], n.d.). They may even seek thrills that are potentially life-threatening. Ethically, the nurse must try to promote beneficence and nonmaleficence by helping adolescents through the 10 stages of grief when they lose a loved one (see Ethical Kaleidoscope Box 6.4). If a long-term nurse-adolescent relationship exists, the nurse must try to help the adolescent overcome barriers to development tasks.

Adolescents Facing Their Own Deaths

Adolescents may be facing their own deaths if they have a terminal illness. In this case, they also may take life-threatening risks to impress their peers or others (NEA, n.d.). Stillion and Papadatou (2002) poignantly stated: "Terminally ill young people find themselves struggling with major issues of identity in the face of a foreclosed future" (p. 302). They ask questions such as "Who am I now?", "Who was I?", "Who would I like to become?", "Who will I be?" and "How will I be remembered by my friends?" (p. 303).

Box 6-4

ETHICAL Kaleidoscope   10 Stages of Grief of Loved Ones

10 Stages of Grief for Loved Ones
-   Stage 1:   Shock
-   Stage 2:   Expression of emotion
-   Stage 3:   Depression and loneliness
-   Stage 4:   Physical symptoms of distress
-   Stage 5:   Panic
-   Stage 6:   Guilt
-   Stage 7:   Anger and resentment
-   Stage 8:   Resistance
-   Stage 9:   Hope
-   Stage 10: Affirmation of reality (NEA., n.d.)

Quote from National Education Association, n.d. Crisis Communications Guide & Toolkit. Tool 32—Children's Concept of Death. Retrieved from http://www.nea.org/crisis/

While struggling with whether or not to engage in intimate relationships and searching for purpose and meaning to their time-limited lives, adolescents with a terminal illness may live almost aimlessly from day to day. They may fear that they will hurt others if they die. "They [adolescents] must learn to live in two worlds—the medical world with the threat of painful treatment, relapse, and death; and the normal world of home, school, and community, with all the challenges that healthy children face" (Stillion & Papadatou, 2002, p. 303).

The central ethical principles involved in this type of nurse–adolescent relationship are beneficence, nonmaleficence, and autonomy. The same grief stages that apply to the death of a loved one are at work here as well, and nurses who are involved with dying adolescents need to first explain the stages to the adolescent. Then, nurses and family members need to be alert to problems that may arise. Extreme behaviors and risk-taking are signs that can alert nurses and family members to take measures to prevent harm (nonmaleficence). Benefiting or doing good for terminally ill adolescents includes maintaining or improving their quality of life as much as possible. Ways to improve quality of life are to allow expressions of their fears and concerns, to be sensitive to meeting cultural and spiritual needs, to have compassion and show benevolence (kindness), and to remember that they experience most of the same challenges that healthy adolescents experience. Nurses must encourage sick adolescents to engage in autonomous decision making as appropriate as they progress through these developmental challenges.

MANAGEMENT OF CARE

In this chapter, there has already been considerable discussion about the ethical management of adolescents concerning consent, confidentiality, prevention, and illness. However, there are some fundamental moral virtues that nurses need to understand and practice consistently in all areas with adolescents. Nurses who base their practice on a moral framework that includes these virtues are more likely to be successful in developing a respectful relationship between themselves and the adolescents with whom they work.

Trustworthiness

Trustworthy nurses, as already defined, are dependable and authentic because they take responsibility for their own behavior and commit to their obligations (Gullotta et al., 2000). For example, a teen girl trusts that a school nurse is going to follow through with an appointment to discuss a sensitive issue, such as the possibility of the girl's being pregnant and her choices.

Genuineness

The adolescent population is more perceptive to how genuine a person is than any other population (Gullotta et al., 2000). *Genuineness* is how credible or real the nurse is. For example, if the nurse makes believe or play acts that there is genuineness in a relationship with an adolescent because of not desiring a genuine relationship, the adolescent will perceive this charade. The pretense may be more damaging to the adolescent than the nurse's admitting the desire not to have a genuine relationship.

Compassion

Compassion means for the nurse to have an understanding of the adolescent's suffering and a desire to take action to alleviate that suffering. The display of compassion is uncommon but is a human quality that nurses need to possess. In the ANA *Code of Ethics for Nurses* (2001) and the ICN *Code of Ethics for Nurses* (2001), compassion and alleviation of suffering are common themes (see Chapter 2).

An example of a compassionate action by a nurse is when a nurse intervenes on behalf of an adolescent who has a hidden hurt. A *hidden hurt* is one that causes a great degree of mental stress, such as when family members or peers tease, make fun of, or bully a person because of a weight problem, poor grades in school, freckles, a big nose, other facial distortions, or other shortcomings (Urban Programs Resource Network, n.d.). The victimized person feels emotionally abused and belittled but, over time, a lowered sense of self-worth will occur, with a display of extremes in behaviors, such as aggression, violence, passiveness, and being withdrawn. An example of a compassionate school nurse is one who takes immediate measures to stop the aggressive behavior and compassionately acts by attempting to establish a trusting relationship with an adolescent who is being bullied or teased continuously. Notifying the school counselor, the principal, and talking with the adolescent's parents are important considerations.

Honesty

The old cliché of "honesty is the best policy" has proved to be good for nurse–adolescent relationships. *Honesty* means being forthright, truthful, and not deceptive. According to Gullotta et al. (2000), "without honesty there can be no relationship" (p. 281). Nurses should express their feelings and emotions in relationships (see "Honesty in Nursing" in Chapter 3). For example, expressing sadness, dissatisfaction, pleasure, or displeasure about an adolescent's behavior is better than trying to cover up feelings. Hiding one's feelings can cause a barrier in the relationship—and irreparable damage.

If nurses practice the virtues of trustworthiness, genuineness, compassion, and honesty with adolescent care, a healthy and respectful relationship between the nurse and adolescent is more likely to develop. However, the adolescent must be able to perceive that the virtues are evident in the nurse's practice, otherwise a trusting relationship between the two may never evolve.

Spiritual Considerations

"One of the most important things we can do to nurture the spiritual growth of our youth is listen to their stories and share with them ours," stated Ingersoll (2000), yet "we have a spiritual emptiness in our society" (¶ 20, ¶1). Spirituality is an essential part of being human (see definition of spirituality in Chapter 10). If adolescents believe in a higher being, or what some may call an absoluteness, they generally voice comfort in living with this belief. For adolescents, spirituality can provide a type of healthy, nonpunitive socialization and acceptance. Nurses can facilitate an adolescent's spiritual growth by remembering the little actions that help adolescents' spirituality, such as attentive listening, being present, or keeping commitments to them. Spirituality transcends all religious beliefs; therefore, nurses generally need to be familiar with different religions.

There are several things that can be done to help adolescents with spiritual growth. It should be emphasized that if nurses help promote adolescents' spirituality, nurses may consciously or unconsciously begin developing their own spiritual growth. Small actions that may help to deliver huge positive consequences are showing love and showing compassion.

Love is difficult to define, but Ingersoll (2000) stated, "many people know it when they feel it" (¶ 55). Showing love, according to Scott Peck, is "the willingness to extend oneself for the purpose of nurturing one's own or another's growth" (as cited in Ingersoll, 2000, ¶ 55). This type of nurturing must be differentiated from charitable acts or unethical and illegal sexual advances.

Compassion is one of the virtues already mentioned in the "Management of Care" section in this chapter. However, for a nurse to promote spiritual growth by practicing compassion, several related virtues emerge:

- forgiveness: always being open to others' situations and reasons for the circumstances
- patience and tolerance: detaching from one's own agenda and outcomes and waiting on and being open to another's agenda
- equanimity: being engaged in a situation with a patient and working toward a patient's well-being without the unhealthy attachment that may cause harm to the relationship
- sense of responsibility: knowing that people are interconnected and that responsibility grows from the interconnectedness
- sense of harmony: remaining in contact with the reality of a situation and with others
- contentment: an intermittent feeling of comfort that comes to a person as a result of practicing and following a spiritual direction (Ingersoll, 2000).

Many Americans have taken a renewed interest in spirituality and would prefer to be labeled as spiritual rather than religious (Ingersoll, 2000). One reason for this interest is that most people believe that spirituality is at the core of human life experience. If nurses talk with adolescents and truly listen to them, spiritual growth may occur for adolescents as well as nurses.

Case Study: An Adolescent Couple with HIV

Alexa was a 17-year-old senior in high school and had been an "A" student in school her whole life. Her goal was to earn a bachelor's degree in science and to one day become a dentist. She had gone steady with Robert for 3 years, but he was 2 years older than she and was already at the local university. Robert was going to be an accountant. They were planning on marriage at some point but were not sure exactly when. They were having unprotected sex on a regular basis, but she was on oral contraceptives so that she would not become pregnant. She did not worry. However, Alexa began to get sick often, such as having no appetite, losing weight, and having nausea, diarrhea, cramping, and other mysterious symptoms. She finally went to her physician. She was diagnosed with HIV. She was shocked! She had never had sex with anyone but Robert. After confronting him, she found out that Robert had been getting high on drugs and having unprotected group sex with boys and girls since he had been in college. Although he too had been having symptoms, he did not know that he had HIV on the night when Alexa confronted him. He was later diagnosed.

Case Study Critical Thinking Questions

1. You are the nurse who is working the day that Alexa finds out that she has AIDS. She is in the clinic for more than one hour with you while you try to counsel her. You have had the formal HIV counseling training, so you go through the official guidelines with her. But several weeks later, after Alexa is more composed and has thought more about her situation, she drops by the clinic and wants to talk with you on a more personal basis. She needs comforting. What approaches are you going to take with Alexa? Please explore the virtues of the nurse and how you might use these to help Alexa. Be specific with your approaches.

2. You know that spiritual promotion for adolescents is also an important consideration. What are methods that you would use with Alexa to promote her spirituality? Be very specific. In doing so, consider her life goals with or without her boyfriend, what might happen to her relationship with Robert, her medical future, and her future in general. Imagine what you might actually say to her and do for her. You might want to imagine a conversation that would take place between the two of you.

REFERENCES

Alan Guttmacher Institute. (2004, April). *State policies in brief: Parental involvement in minors' abortions.* Retrieved June 24, 2004, from http://www.guttmacher.org

American Foundation for Suicide Prevention. (2004). About suicide: Facts—Child and adolescent suicide. Retrieved June 30, 2004, from http://www.afsp.org/index-1.htm

American Nurses Association [ANA]. (2001). *Code of ethics for nurses with interpretive statements.* Washington, DC: Author.

American Psychiatric Association. (2003). News alert: *Obesity can be harmful to your child's mental health; research shows significant risk, impacts.* Press Release No. 03-40. Retrieved June 30, 2004, from http://www.apa.org

Approach to assessing adolescents on serious or sensitive issues and confidentiality. (2004). Retrieved June 24, 2004, from http://pedclerk.bsd.uchicago.edu

Banks, S. (1999). *Ethical issues in youth work.* Routledge: New York.

Blackwell, K. (2002). *Facts about anorexia nervosa. Adolescence: Change and continuity.* Retrieved June 30, 2004, from http://inside.bard.edu/academic/specialproj/darling/adolesce.htm

Blustein, J., & Moreno, J. D. (1999). Valid consent to treatment and the unsupervised adolescent. In J. Blustein, C. Levine, & N. N. Dubler (Eds.), *The adolescent alone: Decision making in health care in the United States.* New York: Cambridge University.

Boonstra, H. (2004, March). Comprehensive approach needed to combat sexually transmitted infections among youth. *The Guttmacher Report, 7*(1), 3–4, 13. Retrieved June 24, 2004, from http://www. agi-usa.org

Bowman, D. H. (2004). Cover story: Abstinence-only debate heating up. *Education Week, 23*(22), 1–2.

Centers for Disease Control and Prevention [CDC]. (1988). Guidelines for effective school health education to prevent the spread of AIDS. *Morbidity & Mortality Weekly Report, 37*(S-2), 1-14. Retrieved June 20, 2004, from http://www.cdc.gov/mmwr/preview/mmwrhtml/00001751.htm

CDC. (2003). National Center for Health Statistics: Health, U.S., 2003 with chart book on trends in health of Americans. Washington DC: CDC. Retrieved May 25, 2004, from http://www.cdc/gov/nchs/ hus.htm

CDC. (2004a). Press release: *Despite improvement, many high school students still engaging in risky health behaviors.* Retrieved June 17, 2004, from http://www.cdc.gov/yrbss

CDC. (2004b). *Healthy youth! Health topics: Six critical health behaviors.* Retrieved May 21, 2004, from http://www.cdc.gov/healthyyouth/healthtopics

CDC. (2004c). *United States: 2003 YRBSS results.* Washington, DC: CDC. Retrieved May 21, 2004, from http://www.cdc.gov/yrbss

CDC. (2004d). Youth risk behavior surveillance—United States, 2003. *Morbidity & Mortality Weekly Report, 53*, (SS-2), 1–98. Retrieved May 21, 2004, from http://www.cdc.gov/yrbss

Cook, R. J., Dickens, B. M., & Fathalla, M. F. (2003). *Reproductive health and human rights: Integrating medicine, ethics, & law.* New York: Oxford University/Clarendon.

Dailard, C. (2003). New medical records privacy rule: The interface with teen access to confidential care. *The Guttmacher Report on Public Policy, 6*(1), 6–7. Retrieved June 24, 2004, from http://www.agi-usa.org

Dickens, C. (1993). *A tale of two cities.* New York: Everyman's Library. (Original work published in 1859)

DiClemente, R. J., Hansen, W. B., & Ponton, L. E. (1996). *Handbook of adolescent health risk behavior.* New York: Plenum.

Erikson, E. (1963). *Childhood and society* (2nd ed.). New York: Norton.

Gullotta, T. P., Adams, G. R., & Markstrom, C. A. (2000). *The adolescent experience.* (4th ed.). San Diego, CA: Academic.

Hartwig, M. J. (2000). *The poetics of intimacy and the problem of sexual abstinence.* New York: Peter Lang.

Ingersoll, R. E. (2000, May). *Spirituality as a counseling resource for adolescents.* MetroHealth presentation. Retrieved June 24, 2004, from http://www.csuohio.edu/casal/spirsyl.htm

International Council of Nurses (ICN). (2000). *Code of ethics for nurses.* Geneva, Switzerland: Author.

Jessor, R., & Jessor, S. (1977). *Problem behavior and psychosocial development: A longitudinal study of youth.* New York: Academic.

Leffert, N., & Petersen, A. C. (1999). Adolescent development: Implications for the adolescents alone. In J. Blustein, C. Levine, & N. N. Dubler (Eds.), *The adolescent alone: Decision making in health care in the United States.* New York: Cambridge University.

Lerman, E. (2000). *Safer sex: The new morality.* Buena Park, CA: Morning Glory.

Lindberg, L. D., Boggess, S., & Williams, S. (2002). Multiple threats: The co-occurrence of teen health risk behaviors. Office of the Assistant Secretary for Planning & Evaluation [Contract No. HHS-100-95-0021]. Retrieved June 17, 2004, from http://www.urban.org/url.cfm?ID=410248

Manisses Communications Group. (2002). Study finds many school districts not using prevention programs effectively. *Alcoholism and Drug Abuse: News for Policy and Program Decision-Makers, 14*(32), 1, 4–5.

Markowitz, A. J., & McPhee, S. J. (2002). Adolescent grief: "It never really hit me…until it actually happened." *Journal of the American Medical Association, 288*(21), 2741.

McKay, S. (2003). Adolescent risk behaviors and communication research: Current directions. *Journal of Language and Social Psychology, 22*(1), 74–82.

National Education Association [NEA]. (n.d.). *Crisis communications guide & toolkit. Tool 32—Children's concept of death.* Retrieved June 30, 2004, from http://www.nea.org/crisis/b4home16.html#Tool32

New study shows abstinence reduces teen pregnancy rates. (2003). *Catholic Exchange.* Retrieved June 21, 2004, from http://www.catholicexchange.com/vm/index.asp?vm_id=53&art_id=18598

National Organization for the Reform of Marijuana Laws. [NORML]. (2004). State by state laws: Marijuana medical use [and] Guide to marijuana laws. Retrieved June 18, 2004, from http://www.norml.org/index.cfm?Group_ID=3376

Paige, J. (2002). *What is an eating disorder and which are most common? Adolescence: Change & continuity.* Retrieved June 30, 2004, from http://inside.bard.edu/academic/specialproj/darling/adolesce.htm

Partnership for a Drug-Free America. (2004). News releases: More pre-teens abusing inhalants. Retrieved June 17, 2004, from http://www.drugfreeamerica./org/Templates/Article.asp?ws=PDFA&vol=1&grp=NewsCenter&cat=News+Releases&top=2004&tit=More+Pre%2DTeens+Abusing+Inhalants+

Planned Parenthood of America. (2004). *Fact sheet: America's family planning program: Title X.* Retrieved August 2, 2004, from http://plannedparenthood.org/library/FAMILYPLANNINGISSUES/TitleX_fact.html

Remez, L. (2000). Oral sex among adolescents: Is it sex or is it abstinence? *Family Planning Perspectives, 32*(6), 298–304.

Sexual Information & Education Council [SIECUS]. (2002). *Teen pregnancy, birth and abortion.* Retrieved June 30, 2004, from http://www.siecus.org

Stillion, J. M., & Papadatou, D. (2002). Suffer the children: An examination of psychosocial issues in children and adolescents with terminal illness. *American Behavioral Scientist, 46*(2), 299–315.

Teens break no-sex vows, study suggests; some say oral sex not sex. (2003). *Christian Century, 120*(26), 14.

Teen suicide. (2004). Bulletin board forum: Adolescent suicide. Quote: Gail Nelson. Retrieved June 30, 2004, from http://www.csun.edu/~webteach/

Turnbull, C. M. (1983). *The human cycle.* New York: Simon and Schuster.

United Nations Population Fund [UNFPA]. (2004). *State of the world population 2003.* Retrieved May 25, 2004, from http://unfpa.org

Urban Programs Resource Network. (n.d.). *Family works: Strategies for building stronger families.* Retrieved June 15, 2004, from http://www.urbanext.uiuc.edu/familyworks

United Nations Children's Fund (UNICEF). (2004, April). *Voices of Youth: The Bimonthly Newsletter, 9.* Retrieved May 20, 2004, from http://www.unicef.org/voy/news

US Department of Health and Human Services. (2004). Office of Family Planning. Retrieved August 2, 2004, from http://opa.osophs.dhhs.gov/titlex/ofp.html

CHAPTER 7

Ethics in Psychiatric and Mental Health Nursing

Karen L. Rich

The Royal Pigeon

Nasruddin became prime minister to the king.
Once, while he wandered through the palace,
he saw a royal falcon.
Now Nasruddin had never seen this kind of a pigeon before.
So he got out a pair of scissors and trimmed the claws,
the wings, and the beak of the falcon.
"Now you look like a decent bird," he said.
"Your keeper had evidently been neglecting you."
"You're different so there's something wrong with you!"

Anthony de Mello, *The Song of the Bird*

SUMMARY

1. Psychiatry is sometimes thought of as a moral discipline rather than a medical discipline because it is often involved with subjective experiences and relationships rather than objective tests and diseases.

147

2. Nurses must be sensitive to the moral implications of using diagnostic labels when referring to patients, because diagnostic labels can be a source of harm and distress for patients.
3. People in society often stigmatize mentally ill persons, and health care professionals sometimes perpetuate this stigma. Even those people who care for mentally ill persons are often stigmatized.
4. Confidentiality and privileged communication are issues of a patient's right to privacy. Confidentiality is usually thought of in ethical terms, whereas privileged communication pertains more to legal protection.
5. In some situations, there are limits to a patient's right to confidentiality and privileged communication, such as when health care professionals have a duty to warn identifiable others of threats made by patients.
6. The decision to involuntarily hospitalize a person is usually based on the person being a danger to self, a danger to others, or, in some states, being gravely disabled.
7. Court proceedings are needed to extend temporary involuntary commitments.
8. Humanistic nursing care is grounded in the belief that through genuine intersubjective experiences and relationships, nurses can help patients be free to become all that they can be.

CHARACTERISTICS OF PSYCHIATRIC NURSING

Although psychiatric/mental health nursing does not have what some nurses perceive to be the glamour and excitement of other nursing specialties such as emergency room nursing, mental health care is extremely important. Most nurses are inspired when they realize that psychiatric/mental health nursing care is focused on the very nucleus of personal identity. However, this realization brings with it an awesome moral responsibility.

According to Radden (2001a), there are three areas that distinguish psychiatry from other medical specialties: the characteristics of the therapeutic relationship, the characteristics of psychiatric patients, and what Radden called the "therapeutic project." Keltner, Schwecke, and Bostrom (2003) have proposed that psychiatric nursing can be divided into three components: "the psychotherapeutic nurse–patient relationship (words), psychopharmacology (drugs), and milieu management (environment), all of which must be supported by a sound understanding of psychopathology" (p. 14). Ethical implications involved with these different aspects of psychiatric care and special issues in mental health are addressed in this chapter.

In general, professional health care practices are made credible because of formal expert knowledge, but the nature of professional–patient relationships, the first distinguishing area of psychiatry, may be even more important in mental health care than in other health care specialties (Radden, 2001a; Sokolowski, 1991). One reason is that facilitative relationships are often the key to therapeutic effectiveness with psychiatric patients. The nurse–patient relationship in psychiatry has been characterized from the perspective of the nurse's "therapeutic use of self," which has been defined as "the ability to use one's personality consciously and in full awareness in an attempt to establish relatedness and to structure nursing intervention" (Travelbee, 1971, p. 19). Radden (2001a) likened the therapeutic relationship to a "treatment tool analogous to the surgeon's scalpel" (p. 53). When nurses are using their personalities to effect changes in patients, it becomes very important that the nurses' behavior reflects moral character.

The second distinguishing feature of psychiatry involves the characteristics of psychiatric patients. Psychiatric patients may be more vulnerable than other patients to exploitation, dependence, and inequality in relationships (Radden, 2001a). A presumed decrease in judgment in psychiatric patients and the stigma associated with mental illness lead to this special vulnerability. A central factor in psychiatric ethics is vulnerability with regard to "treatment refusal, involuntary hospitalization for care and protection, responsibility in the criminal setting, and the set of issues surrounding the criterion of competence (competence to stand trial, competence to refuse and consent to treatment, competence to undertake legal contracts, for example)" (Radden, 2002b, p. 400).

The third distinguishing feature of psychiatric care proposed by Radden (2001a), the therapeutic project, is an important part of the overall relationship between ethics and mental health. The therapeutic project is a major undertaking that involves "reforming the patient's whole self or character, when these terms are understood in holistic terms as the set of a person's long-term dispositions, capabilities and social and relational attributes" (p. 54). As with the nurses' use of self, nurses have an important moral responsibility in working with psychiatric patients in regards to the therapeutic project. Radden stated that there are only a few other societal projects that compare with the impact of the therapeutic project. One is the raising of children, which also places great responsibility on the person who is in a position of power over vulnerable others.

A VALUE-LADEN SPECIALTY

We do not know our own souls, let alone the souls of others.

Virginia Woolf, *On Being III*

The Greek philosopher Socrates said the unexamined life is not worth living. This thought underlies the aim of much of the care that patients receive from psychiatric/mental health nurses. However, one might add two supplementary statements to the famous statement made by Socrates: (1) many people choose not to examine their lives and rather choose to ignore their mental health or mental illness; these lives are still worth living, and (2) even for those who try to examine the content and context of their lives, understanding is often elusive.

Although personal values pervade all discussions of bioethics, an emphasis on values is even more relevant to psychiatric/mental health nursing because it is largely involved with subjective experiences rather than objective diseases. According to Dickenson and Fulford (2000), psychiatry is sometimes referred to as a moral discipline rather than a medical discipline. Human values are generally shared values with regard to the experiences and behaviors addressed by physical medicine. However, in psychiatry, values relating to experiences and behaviors are usually diverse. These diverse values in mental health involve a focus on motivation, desire, and belief as opposed to an agreement, for example, that cancer and heart disease are bad conditions. Problems arise in psychiatric/mental health care when professionals do not know how to use practical wisdom in navigating through value disparities and disagreements with patients and other health care providers.

Seedhouse (2000) proposed that there is often a fundamental values difference between what nurses are traditionally taught about the goals of nursing care and the priorities of the medical model in psychiatry (see Ethical Kaleidoscope Box 7-1). According to Seedhouse, the psychiatric system often relegates nursing priorities to the rank of secondary importance. In mental health organizations, professionals other than nurses sometimes view it as an irritation when nurses try to reinforce the personal worth of patients by trying to find meaning in the patients' behaviors and experiences. However, this statement is not intended to mean that nurses should make negative generalizations about the psychiatric health care system as a whole. Instead, nurses' knowledge of the views of other health care professionals should encourage them to be aware of the values that influence the systems in which they function.

Box 7-1

ETHICAL Kaleidoscope   Possible Priority Disparities

Nursing Priorities:
[Nurses are] supposed to be respectful of all other people's beliefs, treat people as equals, care personally to the extent that [they enter] patients' subjective worlds, uphold their dignity, ensure their privacy, be ethical at all times, nurture all patients and—of course—work for their health (in this case work for their mental health).

Psychiatric [System] Priorities:
The psychiatrist is trained to diagnose and treat mental illnesses supposedly as real and independent of the psychiatrist as [if treating] cold sores and bronchitis.

Seedhouse, D. 2000. Practical nursing philosophy: The universal ethical code (p. 138). Chichester, UK: John Wiley and Sons.

As psychiatric/mental health professionals, it is important to remember that truly knowing ourselves is hard and that understanding what underlies the emotions, words, and behaviors of other persons is often even more difficult. Ethical practice in psychiatry is generally consistent with a foundationally nonjudgmental attitude. This does not mean, however, that nurses should not have thoughts, values, and considered judgments or opinions. It is unrealistic to believe that nurses' values do not affect their work, that is, that the work of nurses can be completely value neutral. The key to moral care is to have moral values. Nurses are responsible for using practical wisdom in their judgments, for being truthful with themselves about their own values, and for being compassionately truthful in their work with patients. Nurses need to take care that their attitude does not degenerate into one of condescension or pity. Keeping a "there but for the grace of God go I" attitude when working in a psychiatric/mental health setting often contributes to compassionate care.

Ethical Reflections

- How to you think the values of our society have helped shape mental health care?
- In what ways do you believe that a nurse's values might have greater ethical implications in psychiatric nursing than in other areas of nursing?
- How might nurses help reconcile disparities in care priorities among psychiatric health care professionals?

MENTAL HEALTH: A SPECIALTY IN CRISIS?

Some people believe that psychiatry is the one health care specialty in which 19th century philosophies continue to exert a strong influence on the approach to practice today (Beresford, 2002). Even in the 21st century, "bad" is often equated with "mad," and many people closely associate dangerous and murderous activities with mental illness. Until the 1950s and 1960s when the discovery of new drug therapies revolutionized the field of psychiatry, mentally ill patients were frequently warehoused in asylums, often for very long periods of time or even for a lifetime (Hobson & Leonard, 2001). At the same time, Freudian psychoanalysis was gaining widespread popularity in hospitals and clinics. Research in the 1950's and 1960's produced new psychotropic medications that ushered in a metamorphosis in psychiatry. The new medications provided a way to manage psychiatric symptoms that had been difficult or impossible to manage before.

However, these drugs were not a "cure all," and there were still many serious side effects related to their use. Because of those drugs, there was a wide-scale release of patients from mental institutions in the 1960s and 1970s, and many of these people eventually became homeless or were jailed (Hobson & Leonard, 2001; Keltner et al., 2003). When patients were released from hospitals, the doors were almost literally locked and barred behind them. The patients were assured that they would receive adequate treatment for their mental illnesses in the community, but society and the medical community did not keep their promises to these patients. Satisfactory community treatment never materialized, and access to care is still a problem in mental health today. Although health care professionals use the term "mental health" when speaking about the specialty of psychiatry, the system of care continues to be based on mental illness (Beresford, 2002).

After the 1970s, patients were still not well managed on the new pscyhotropic drugs, and psychoanalysis had started to lose favor. When in the 1980s and 1990s health maintenance organizations further modified the care and treatment of psychiatric patients, holistic care almost fell apart (Hobson & Leonard, 2001). The payment that psychiatrists received to conduct therapy sessions with their patients was no longer an incentive to provide these services. Now, psychiatrists have been pushed in the direction of focusing on biomedical treatment while nonphysician therapists provide counseling only and are unable to prescribe medications. This trend in treatment began a severe fragmentation in the environment of psychiatric patient care. Physicians and therapists have traditionally not communicated well amongst themselves, often fighting turf battles that further impede the quality of patient care.

Although in recent years there have continued to be many more improvements in the psychiatric medications that are available, medications still provide, at best, a symptom-only treatment, not a cure. Generally, there continues to be a fragmentary divide between those who treat mental illnesses biomedically and those who provide psychological therapy and counseling (Hobson & Leonard, 2001). This fragmentation, or treatment gap, has ethical implications for the quality of care that patients receive. It is in filling this treatment gap that nurses can move forward from a moral perspective.

Nurses are in a crucial bridge, or in-between, position to advance the holistic care of psychiatric patients by assessing their behavior and responses to medications and by providing education and valuable psychological and spiritual care and support. Advanced-practice psychiatric and/or mental health nurse practitioners can prescribe medications as well as provide therapeutic and supportive counseling. However, one of the primary ways that all mental health nurses can affect the ethical environment of psychiatric/mental health care is to act as patient advocates within the imperfect system.

ETHICAL IMPLICATIONS OF DIAGNOSIS

Although it is not always a case of serious proportions, by using mental illness diagnostic categories "people may be locked up, subjected to compulsory (and health damaging) 'treatment' and have their rights restricted" (Beresford, 2002, p. 582). This issue is closely tied to a consideration of the stigma that psychiatric patients face. Pipher (2003), a psychologist, acknowledged that ethical guidelines in clinical mental health practice do not address some of the important moral issues. Disagreement about the application of psychiatric diagnoses is one of these issues. In a qualitative study conducted by Watts and Priebe (2002), the psychiatric patient participants expressed that they perceived the psychiatric system and the labeling involved with psychiatric diagnoses as "an attack on their identity" (p. 446). Because psychiatric diagnoses often represent the boundaries of what is categorized as normal versus abnormal in society along cultural, gender, and class biases, psychiatric diagnoses can perpetuate oppressive power relationships (Crowe, 2000). Consequently, diagnosing patients in psychiatry is a morally charged issue. Psychiatric/mental health advanced-practice nurses are in a position to assign a psychiatric diagnosis to patients, but the assigning of diagnoses is an ethical issue about which generalist nurses must be aware. Crowe (2000) proposed that even when nurses are not responsible for assigning a diagnosis to a patient, they are collaborators in the diagnostic process when they

- provide data and descriptions of observations to enable a diagnosis,
- integrate the nomenclature of diagnosis into the language of mental health nursing practice,
- administer medications which have been determined by psychiatric diagnosis, and
- engage in service user and family education based on psychiatric diagnosis and treatment (p. 585)

In psychiatry, there are often not definitive tests that can be used to diagnose illness, which has led to arguments over the years about the subjectivity of diagnoses (Kahn, 2001). However, the third edition of the *Diagnostic and Statistical Manual of Mental Disorders (DSM)*, published in 1980, radically changed how psychiatric diagnoses were categorized, which began to satisfy some of the critics. The *DSM-III* was the first in a series of the *DSM* manuals to use research as a basis for categorizing diagnoses. The *DSM-IV* went even further in using biological data for diagnostic categories. Diagnosing with the *DSM-IV* is intended to be based on observed data rather than on what is subjective or merely based on theory, although some disagree with this assumption. Many believe that the *DSM* system is a good one. Although practitioners generally identify the same diagnoses when using the system (that is, the system is reliable), others have contended that the *DSM* diagnoses are not always valid or correct. Seedhouse (2000) suggested that those who take an antipsychiatric view (see Ethical Kaleidoscope Box 7-2) believe that the *DSM-IV* is a "house of cards" based on speculative assumptions. Kahn (2001) proposed that practitioners are best served if they remain open minded when using the *DSM* system for diagnosing patients. In other words, the system is useful but not infallible.

Box 7-2

ETHICAL Kaleidoscope   Anti-Psychiatry

Practitioners who have an anti-psychiatry view want:

to focus more on the beliefs and values of their patients and to include the spiritual, political, and socio-cultural dimensions of experience in their practice. This approach indicates that the concept of illness is far too restrictive to assist us in understanding insanity and reminds us that in order to understand mental illness some deconstruction of what constitutes mental illness is necessary (O'Brien, Woods, & Palmer, 2001).

A. O'Brien, M. Woods, & C. Palmer, 2001, The emancipation of nursing practice: Applying anti-psychiatry to the therapeutic community, p. 4, Australian and New Zealand Journal of Mental Health Nursing, 10, 3–9.

In suggesting that there are ethical implications and problems with subjectivity in identifying the psychiatric diagnoses of patients, Pipher (2003) related a story about a young boy with an apparent obsessive-compulsive disorder. The boy's hands were chafed from frequent handwashing, and he insisted that all of his possessions be rigidly organized. The young man might even have qualified for special services at school based on his having a specific diagnosis, but the question became whether or not the diagnosis would ultimately help or hurt the boy. How would a label affect the child's self-perception and the perception of others who might learn about the diagnosis? In the end, Pipher decided that a diagnosis was not necessary in this boy's case. Distraction was used as a treatment, and the child's family physician was available to prescribe appropriate medications as needed.

The point of Pipher's (2003) story was that clinicians must be very careful in labeling patients because health care professionals are often unable to determine what further problems might be triggered by a psychiatric label. According to Pipher, clinicians would do well to ask the following questions before diagnosing psychiatric patients: "Why are we doing this? Will a diagnosis allow clients to get the help they need? Can the diagnosis hurt the client?" (p. 143).

Diagnoses are often generated or changed based on information gathered and reported by nurses. Staff nurses must remember that loosely applied diagnoses that the nurse might offhandedly repeat to others, whether these others are staff, the patient, families, or health care insurers, can be harmful to the best interests of patients. In other words, a psychiatric diagnosis is not something to be applied without skillful and reflective consideration by those who are specially educated to do so. Even then nurses must be aware that often the determination of psychiatric diagnoses is a subjective and inexact science.

Ethical Reflections

- Do you believe that psychiatric nursing is more of an art or a science or that it is no different than other types of nursing? Explain the reasons for your answer.
- What factors make an objective diagnosis difficult in the field of psychiatry? What are some of the moral implications because of this difficulty? How might this difficulty affect nursing care?

STIGMA

The days of telling your patients to "pull themselves together" should be over. It is not our patients who should be pulling themselves together: we should look at ourselves

Bolton, *Reducing the Stigma of Mental Illness*

That people with psychiatric illnesses and conditions are stigmatized by a broad spectrum of society is common knowledge (Bolton, 2003; Green, Hayes, Dickinson, Whittaker, & Gilheany, 2003; Knight, Wykes, & Hayward, 2003; Rosen, Walter, Casey, & Hocking, 2000; Wahl, 2003) (See Ethical Kaleidoscope Box 7-3 for Greek meaning of *stigma*). In fact, some people believe that this stigma even extends to professionals, such as nurses and physicians, who care for psychiatric patients (Bolton, 2003; Halter, 2002). Rosen et al. (2000) defined psychiatric stigma as "the false and unjustified association of individuals who have a mental illness, their families, friends and service providers with something shameful" (p. 19). This negative perception is perpetuated by the media and frequently results in hostility in communities and discrimination by service providers and employers. The flames of fears are fanned and illnesses are left untreated.

Box 7-3

ETHICAL Kaleidoscope   Stigma

The Greeks…originated the term *stigma* to refer to bodily signs designed to expose something unusual and bad about the moral status of the signifier. The signs were cut or burnt into the body and advertised that the bearer was a…blemished person, ritually polluted, to be avoided, especially in public places.

Goffman, E. 1963 Stigma: Notes on the management of spoiled identity (p. 1).
New York: Simon and Schuster.

When referring to people with mental illnesses, the United States Surgeon General stated: "stigma tragically deprives people of their dignity and interferes with their full participation in society" (US Department of Health and Human Services [DHHS], 1999, p. viii). According to the Substance Abuse and Mental Health Services Administration (SAMHSA) report, *Reasons for Not Receiving Substance Abuse Treatment* (as cited in Survey reveals reasons, 2003), stigma is one of the primary reasons that those with alcohol and drug addiction problems do not seek treatment.

Unfortunately, even health care professionals perpetuate the stigma of mental illness. Bolton (2003), a hospital liaison psychiatrist, voiced his distress with regard to health care professionals' negative perceptions of patients with mental illnesses when he stated that those who refer patients to him often say things such as "we've got another nutter for you" (pp. 104–105; see Ethical Kaleidoscope Box 7-4 on societal beliefs about mental illness).

Box 7-4

ETHICAL Kaleidoscope   Stigmatizing Beliefs

Stigmatizing Beliefs About Mental Illness

- People with mental illnesses are dangerous to others
- Mental illness is feigned or imaginary
- Mental illness reflects a weakness of character

- Disorders are self inflicted
- Outcome is poor
- Disorders are incurable
- It is difficult to communicate with people with mental illness

Bolton, J. (2003). Reducing the stigma of mental illness. Student British Medical Journal, 11, 104–105.

Bolton followed up this concern by saying that he no longer accepts this sort of language and stigmatization without tactfully educating the user of such language about its inappropriateness.

Goffman (1963), a well-known sociologist who did landmark work with regard to stigma, contrasted the *normals* of society versus those with a stigma, or those who may also be called the "discreditables." He proposed that those with a particular stigma, for example, mental illness, have common experiences in terms of how they learn to view their stigma and their very conception of self. Goffman described this phenomenon as a common *moral career*. These common experiences, or moral careers, involve four phases that range from having an inborn stigma to developing a stigma later in life. However, regardless of the progression of the moral careers of stigmatized persons, it is a significant point in time when these persons realize that they possess the stigma and are exposed to new relationships with others who also have the same stigma. Goffman proposed that on first meeting others who the stigmatized person must accept as "his own," there is often ambivalence, but eventually a sense of identity develops.

It is important for nurses who practice in mental health settings to understand the meaning of some relationships among psychiatric patients. If nurses become sensitive to the lived experiences of psychiatric patients and the therapeutic value of these patients' relationships with others who are mentally ill, it may ultimately help to create a more supportive environment for these patients. Psychiatric patients, who are marked with a stigma by society, their own families, and even health care professionals, often can find a sense of camaraderie among others who have experienced similar moral careers.

Frequently, nurses find this camaraderie disconcerting and sometimes attempt to minimize the support that psychiatric patients develop among themselves. However, psychiatric patients find encouragement in these relationships, as illustrated by the comments of a former psychiatric patient, Irit Shimrat (2003).

What saved me was the help I got from other patients, and the fact that I was able to help them. By showing each other compassion, by listening to each other, against all odds, we were able to remember that we were still alive . . . When I'm feeling terrified of the world, I can talk to someone else who's been terrified of the world, but who isn't right now, and they can free me from that terror. The stories we tell ourselves about the world and our place in it have a huge influence on how we feel and what we're capable of. When people who have been labeled mentally ill can talk to each other about these stories, without fear of being judged, the feedback we get, and give, can be enormously liberating (p. 18).

Although sound judgment on the part of nurses is essential in assessing safety factors and the therapeutic value of relationships among psychiatric patients, compassionate nursing care involves being sensitive to the stigma experienced by psychiatric patients and how this stigma affects patients' perceptions of others who have lived through similar experiences.

Borderline Personality Disorder

You lived your life like a candle in the wind, never knowing who to cling to when the rain set in.

Elton John and Bernie Taupin, *Candle in the Wind*

Borderline personality disorder (BPD) is probably the most stereotyped and stigmatized psychiatric disorder in North America (Nehls, 1998). Therefore, BPD warrants special consideration in terms of mental health stigma. Although it has been proposed that the very term creates a prejudice and stigma that necessitates a need for changing the name of the diagnostic label (as was done in the past with the term "hysteria"), Nehls proposed that merely changing the name of the disorder does not prevent the same stigma being attached to a subsequent label.

McCann and Ball (2001) stated that the behaviors exhibited by persons with BPD— poor judgment, overdramatizing situations, relational inconsistency, not keeping appointments and then demanding immediate attention, etc.—tend to "engender feelings of anger, irritation, confusion, helplessness, and hopelessness in providers" (p. 194). They contended that these feelings may prompt health care professionals to exhibit nontherapeutic behaviors such as:

- blaming the patient for lack of improvement
- believing that the patient would be better off dead
- failing to return phone calls
- failure to carefully assess the ongoing risk of prescribing medications
- labeling the patient's motivation as the cause of treatment failure
- overzealous use of potentially addictive medications
- arguing with patients
- arguing with other professional staff regarding the patient (p. 194)

Nurses need to be aware of the personal emotions that are engendered by all psychiatric patients while being particularly cognizant of these emotions when they arise in response to interactions with those diagnosed with BPD. Lynn Williams (1998), a woman who professed to have experienced "world-class" symptoms of BPD, but whose condition had improved, wrote a poignant article intended to help health care professionals understand some of the experiences of the disorder (see Ethical Kaleidoscope

Box 7-5). Remembering that these patients are worthy of our concern and worthy of our best nursing care is important with regard to moral psychiatric practice.

Box 7-5

ETHICAL Kaleidoscope   Borderline Personality Disorder

Someone answering to my name was once a terrified, angry person who was showing up in emergency rooms nearly every night and throwing up into a basin, or was being looked for regularly by the police when threatening suicide…But that wasn't the real me. That's not who I want to be. Nor are the other people who are seen through the pathology of borderline personality disorder showing their real selves. As frustrating as these acutely ill people may be, please don't write them off. Maybe, just maybe, you'll be able to help one of them. I'm living proof that—over time—we can be helped.

Williams, L. 1998. A "classic" case of borderline personality disorder,
Psychiatric Services, 49 (2), 174.

Ethical Reflections

- What words or phrases have you heard being used that are stigmatizing to people with mental illnesses? What are the ethical implications when health care professionals use stigmatizing talk?
- In what ways do you believe that the media has contributed to the stigma of mental illness? In what ways might this media influence also affect the way the public views mental health nurses?
- How can nurses help to change negative perceptions of mental illness?

BOUNDARIES

A discussion of boundaries is particularly relevant to psychiatric-mental health nursing because of the particular vulnerability of mentally ill patients and the importance of trust in supporting therapeutic nurse-patient relationships. *Boundary violations* occur when a nurse exceeds the limits of the nurse-patient relationship. Professional boundaries are specifically covered in provision 2.4 of the *Code of Ethics for Nurses with Interpretive Statements* (ANA, 2001). By keeping in mind that the primary concern of nurses' care is "preventing illness, alleviating suffering, and protecting, promoting, and restoring the health of patients," nurses can find guidance in maintaining professional boundaries (p. 11). Nurses must ask themselves if the actions that they take, the words that they say, and the behaviors that they model are in the best interests of patients. In other words, nurses must be very conscious of how their behavior might affect patients and be interpreted by them. It cannot be assumed that psychiatric patients will react the same way that other patients might react to the behaviors of the nurse.

Concepts that underlie nurse–patient boundaries include power, choice, and trust (Maes, 2003). The asymmetry of power in favor of the nurse can place nurses in a position of influencing the decisions of patients. Patients need complete information in order to make choices, and nurses must help patients receive the information that they need. Patients trust nurses to have the knowledge, prudence, and skill necessary to provide them with ethical and competent care; nurses must be faithful to that trust.

Potential violations of nurse-patient boundaries can involve gifts, intimacy, limits, neglect, abuse, and restraints (Maes, 2003). Gifts are often nontherapeutic in psychiatric/mental health nurse–patient relationships, and gifts given to nurses by patients need to be considered in terms of why the gift was given, its value, and whether the gift might provide therapeutic value for the patient. Gifts should not influence the type of care provided by the nurse or the quality of the nurse–patient relationship. General guidelines for the inappropriate acceptance of gifts from patients include situations in which the gift is very expensive; the patient is seeking approval by giving the gift; the gift is given early in the relationship, which may set the stage for lax boundaries; the nurse does not feel comfortable accepting the gift but does so because of not wanting to hurt the patient's feelings; or the nurse is having difficulty setting boundaries (Corey, Corey, & Callanan, 2003). Nurses should never accept money as tips or gifts.

The cultural implications of gift giving also need to be considered. For example, patients from Asian cultures may view giving an inexpensive gift as a sign of gratitude and respect, while nurses responding from a Western perspective may view the taking of a gift from a patient as a boundary violation. If the nurse refused the gift in this situation, the patient would be insulted (Corey et al., 2003). It is important for nurses to keep ethical boundaries in mind, but sometimes inflexibility is damaging to therapeutic relationships. Each situation must be evaluated individually and in accordance with the policies of the employing health care facility

In addition to an obvious violation of intimacy through inappropriate sexual relationships, a violation of intimacy might occur if a nurse inappropriately shares information with others in ways that violate patient privacy. The nature of nurses' work with both patients and colleagues has a very personal element but is not to be confused with the common definition of friendship. Nurses are not discouraged from having a caring relationship with patients, families, or colleagues. However, caring and jeopardizing professional boundaries are two distinct issues. Although carefully chosen self-disclosure is sometimes therapeutic, revealing personal information to patients can also be detrimental to patient care. Nurses are cautioned to observe limits that prevent either the nurse or the patient from becoming uncomfortable in their relationship (ANA, 2001).

Nurses are responsible for providing reasonable care to all patients according to appropriate ethical codes and their state's nurse practice acts. They must do everything possible to prevent or stop patient abuse in whatever form it occurs. Physically, chemically, and environmentally restraining patients can provide a major pitfall for nurses in terms of boundary violations (ANA, 2001). The use of physical, chemical, and environmental restraints is a particularly important issue. It is essential that nurses know the policies of their employer as well as the standards set by accrediting agencies to safeguard patients.

Ethical Reflections

- How would you evaluate whether or not it would be ethical to accept a gift of something that a patient made in an art therapy group?
- Would you accept a gift if you did not feel comfortable telling a co-worker that you had received the gift from a patient? What is the rationale for your answer?

WHOSE NEEDS ARE BEING SERVED?

An issue closely tied to relationship boundaries is whose needs are being served in professional–patient relationships. Counselors need to be aware when they may be placing their own needs before those of their client, as was proposed by Corey (2001) when discussing counselor–client relationships. This assessment and awareness of needs is equally applicable in nurse–patient relationships. It is easy for nurses to unintentionally become absorbed in their own self-interests during day-to-day patient care. Personal needs of the nurse that may be placed before the patient's needs include:

- the need for control and power,
- the need to be nurturing and helpful,
- the need to change others in the direction of our own values,
- the need to persuade,
- the need for feeling adequate, particularly when it becomes overly important that the client confirm our competence, and
- the need to be respected and appreciated (Corey, 2001, p. 44).

Nurses may have to take special care to keep in mind that patients' needs are to be placed first. As is stated in the second provision of the ANA (2001) *Code of Ethics with Interpretive Statements*: "the nurse's primary commitment is to the patient, whether an individual, family, group or community" (p. 9). Because of the psychological nature of their conditions, psychiatric/mental health patients may be particularly vulnerable to nurses placing them in dependent positions.

Psychotropic drugs sometimes make patients more manageable for nurses, which again raises the question of whose needs are being served: the nurse's or the patient's? Similar to the point made with regard to nurses' complicity in the diagnostic labeling of patients, nurses have a very important role in determining the type and amount of medications that are ordered for and administered to psychiatric patients, particularly in hospital settings. Nurses are the professionals who spend the most time with hospitalized psychiatric patients, and physicians often base treatment decisions on nurses' formal or informal comments, reports, and documentation. Again, nurses must be very aware of whose needs are being served and must use careful reflection in determining how they choose to present patients' behaviors and conditions to others.

Ethical Reflections

- What questions might you ask yourself to evaluate your motives before giving p.r.n. medications to a psychiatric patient?

PRIVACY, CONFIDENTIALITY, AND PRIVILEGED COMMUNICATION

Although privacy, confidentiality, and privileged communication are similar concepts, there are important differences to be considered. Confidentiality and privileged communication are issues of a patient's right to privacy; however, confidentiality is usually more associated with ethics, whereas privileged communication pertains more to legality (Corey et al., 2003).

Privacy

The concept of *privacy* began receiving attention in the 1920s when the US Supreme Court addressed the liberty interest of families with regard to decision making about their children (Beauchamp & Childress, 2001). The court's rulings were designed to protect part of a person's private life from state intrusion, which incidentally was also the foundation for the overturning of restrictive abortion laws in 1973. However, the right to privacy cannot be reduced to being viewed in the narrow context of having a right to act autonomously. In addition to autonomy, the rights that fall within the boundaries of privacy include a person's right to be protected by limited physical and informational access by others.

Allen (as cited in Beauchamp & Childress, 2001) described four types of privacy that address limited personal access:

- informational privacy: communication of information
- physical privacy: with regard to personal spaces
- decisional privacy: with regard to personal choices
- proprietary privacy: property interests, including interests with regard to bodily tissues, one's name, etc.

The value placed on privacy varies among situations and people. Sometimes, for example, persons may feel comfortable that others know that they have a psychiatric condition but are not comfortable with their knowing the exact nature of the condition. Nurses need to err on the side of strictly maintaining a patient's privacy unless there is a justifiable reason for privacy to be violated, such as a duty to warn.

Confidentiality

In health care ethics, confidentiality is one of the oldest moral commitments, dating back to the Hippocratic Oath (Gillon, 2001). *Confidentiality*, or nondisclosure of information, involves limits on the communication of "any information a nurse obtains about a patient in the context of the nurse–patient relationship" (Killion, 2000b, p. 36). It includes limits on the communication of information related to any of the five types of privacy previously listed. The Joint Commission on Accreditation of Health Care Organizations (1998) defined confidentiality as "an individual's right, within the law, to personal and informational privacy, including his or her health care records" (p. 139). Confidentiality is one of the most important ethical precepts in psychiatric/mental health nursing because the therapeutic nurse–patient relationship is grounded in trust.

Privileged Communication

Whereas confidentiality involves a professional duty not to disclose certain information, *privilege* provides relief from having to disclose information in court proceedings (Smith-Bell & Winslade, 2003). Patients have a legal right to believe that their communication with nurses will be kept confidential, but there are limits to confidentiality in psychiatric/mental health practice. Limits to both confidentiality and privilege would permit disclosure of information by the nurse when:

- patients are a threat to themselves (suicide, for example) or to identifiable others
- statutes require disclosure, such as those involving the reporting of child abuse, rape, incest, or other crime
- the patient consents to release of the information
- a court mandates the release
- the information is needed for other caregivers to provide care to the patient (Corey, 2001; Killion, 2000b).

Nurses cannot disclose patient information to unidentified or unauthorized telephone callers or to relatives, significant others, or friends of the patient without the patient's consent (Killion, 2000b).

Duty to Warn

In some cases, nurses may have a *duty to warn*, which involves "a duty to disclose confidential information to protect an identifiable victim" (Killion, 2000b, p. 37). Documentation by nurses of repeated patient threats is necessary, but this may not be enough in some cases. Nurses may also have a duty to warn appropriate authorities about threats made by patients or even to warn the person targeted by the threats. This duty is weighed from the perspective of viewing it as a dilemma between respecting a patient's privacy and respecting society's need to be informed about acts that are dangerous to citizens (Everstine et al., 2003). The duty to warn is based on the case of Tarasoff v. Board of Regents of the University of California (see Ethical Kaleidoscope Box 7-6).

Box 7-6

ETHICAL Kaleidoscope   Tarasoff v. Regents

In August 1969 a voluntary outpatient, Prosenjit Poddar, was being counseled at the student health center at the University of California Berkeley campus. The patient threatened to kill a woman (Tatiana Tarasoff) who was unnamed, but who was identifiable to the therapist. The therapist warned the campus police about the threat but the police spoke with Poddar and deemed him to be 'rational' and did not take action to warn Ms. Tarasoff. The therapist continued to pursue the issue, but Ms. Tarasoff was not warned of the threat and was later killed by Poddar. Her family sued the Board of Regents and the university staff for failing to warn the victim. In 1976, the California Supreme Court ruled in favor of the parents. The Court proclaimed: "The protective privilege ends where the public peril begins."

Corey, G., Corey, M. S., & Callanan, P. (2003). Issues and ethics in the helping professions. Pacific Grove, CA: Wadsworth Group–Brooks/Cole.

DECISIONAL CAPACITY

According to Beauchamp and Childress (2001), some people distinguish competence and capacity based on who is making the determination, that is, capacity is assessed by health care professionals, and competence is determined within the court system. Singer (2003) defined competence "as a group of capacities" (p. 152). However, some say that for all practical purposes, the consequences of the determination of capacity versus competence are basically the same (Grisso & Appelbaum, 1998). In psychiatric care, both capacity and competence are related to questions of whether or not patients have a right to consent to and refuse treatment and are closely associated with the issue of autonomy.

Statutory Authority to Treat

Involuntary commitment poses ethical as well as legal problems for psychiatric health care professionals. Based on a general social policy of deinstitutionalization over the last 25 years, involuntary hospitalization decisions can be made only after less restrictive options have failed or have carefully been determined not to be a viable option (Corey et al., 2003). The decision is usually made based on a person being a danger to self, a danger to others, or, in some states, being gravely disabled. Each state jurisdiction has statutes that allow psychiatrists to hold persons involuntarily for psychiatric treatment, and health care professionals are responsible for following their state's particular laws and regulations (Corey et al., 2003; Jonsen, Siegler, & Winslade, 2002; Keltner et al., 2003). If a patient is determined by a psychiatrist to be incompetent (see "Criteria" in competency section), state statutes can be followed for a temporary involuntary commitment. Court proceedings are then initiated to extend the involuntary treatment or commitment. This legal process is expedited while the person is being (temporarily) held involuntarily.

Killion (2000a) outlined this process as beginning with a presumption of competency. However, when it is determined by a psychiatrist that the person exhibits a lack of decision-making capacity, a petition is filed with the court to determine competency. The person receives a court-appointed guardian or legal counsel and undergoes psychological testing procedures. A hearing is scheduled, and evidence is presented with regard to the person's ability to handle personal affairs and to understand the consequences of personal decisions. Negotiations are conducted with the aim of determining the least restrictive alternative. Outcomes of the hearing can result in a dismissal of the petition, the appointment of limited guardianship, or an appointment of complete guardianship. These outcomes may be appealed, and a restoration hearing can be held later if the person's circumstances change and warrant a removal of guardianship. Jonsen et al. (2002) made an important point in stating that this process is often inappropriately called a *medical hold*. However, this psychiatric commitment process does not automatically include an authorization to treat a patient involuntarily for medical, in addition to psychiatric, conditions. A legally authorized appointee must also be specially assigned to make medical decisions other than those that are determined to be for a life-saving emergency, in which an implied consent is sufficient.

Competence and Informed Consent

Competence and informed consent are intricately connected. Informed consent as required by legal authorities is impossible in situations involving incompetent patients (Singer, 2003). A patient, even when involuntarily committed, has a right to refuse treatment, such as psychotropic medications, until or unless the patient has been deemed incompetent by formal legal proceedings. In the case of *Rivers v. Katz,* the New York State Court of Appeals established that there are only limited circumstances in which a patient's right to refuse unwanted treatment can be overridden. A patient's right to refuse medications may be overridden only on the determination that a patient is a danger to self or others. Patients may not be prevented from refusing medications based on health care professionals' desire to create a therapeutic environment, for the convenience of hospital staff, or to facilitate the process of deinstitutionalization.

There are no uniform standards that can be used to determine competence, although it is accepted that incompetence is founded on cognitive impairment (Berg, Appelbaum, & Grisso; as cited in Singer, 2003). Brody (1988) outlined general criteria of competency that are also applicable with regard to psychiatric patients. These criteria include:

- the ability to receive information from the surroundings
- the capacity to remember the information received
- the ability to make a decision and give a reason for it
- the ability to use the relevant information in making the decision
- the ability to appropriately assess the relevant information (pp. 101–102)

To this list Singer (2003) added the capacity to participate constructively in discussion with the caregiver regarding treatment, including the "ability to engage in mutual questioning and answering" (p. 153). Singer called this supplementary capacity of communicative interchange *dialogic reciprocity* (see Ethical Kaleidoscope Box 7-7).

Box 7-7

ETHICAL Kaleidoscope   Dialogic Reciprocity

Dialogic "reciprocity…involves mutual respect for the autonomy and authority of all the participants in a discussion, a respect that…should be accorded to them as a matter of right…Respecting a person's authority in this sense can be thought of as a type of empowerment: empowerment to have one's contribution to the discussion taken seriously, even if it may be subsequently rejected or overridden…In the exercise of dialogic reciprocity we reflect autonomously and critically on our own judgments as well as those of the others with whom we are in dialogue. Therefore, we are open to change, even though the dialogue may result in strengthening our original position." (Singer, 2003)

Singer, B.J., 2003, Mental Illness: Rights, Competence, and Communication, In G. McGee (Ed.), Pragmatic Bioethics, pp. 158–159.

MANAGEMENT OF CARE

Humanistic Nursing

As was mentioned at the beginning of this chapter, some people say that psychiatry is a moral discipline rather than a medical discipline (Dickenson & Fulford, 2000). Ethics in nursing has been distinguished as a special area of ethics based on its grounding in relationships (Austin, Bergum, & Dossetor, 2003; Nortvedt, 1998; Scott, 2003). Yalom (1995), when discussing humanistic or person-centered therapy as advanced by Carl Rogers, said, "experienced therapists today agree that the crucial aspect of therapy, as Rogers grasped early in his career, is the therapeutic relationship" (p. ix). Psychiatric/mental health nursing is morally enriched by humanistic patient–nurse relationships that lead to human flourishing. Three humanistic approaches that were developed in the 1960s and 1970s but are still relevant to psychiatric nursing care today have been included in the proposed strategies for management of patient care.

Person-Centered Approach

The concepts of humanistic psychology and existentialism form the basis of psychologist Carl Rogers' person-centered approach (Corey, 2001). According to Rogers (1980), the development of "person" is the central goal of any person-centered relationship. For a growth-promoting environment to exist in the relationship, three conditions are necessary. Those conditions are (1) genuineness or realness, (2) acceptance, caring, or prizing, and (3) empathic understanding. The nurse who employs the element of genuineness or realness does not maintain a distant professional façade with the patient. The nurse truly experiences the feelings that are occurring in the relationship. The nurse who is exhibiting Rogers' second condition of a therapeutic relationship maintains an attitude of unconditional positive regard for a patient. The patient is prized in a total way and can *be* whatever feelings are occurring. Acceptance of the patient is not conditional. The last of Rogers' facilitative factors, empathic understanding, would include a deep sensitivity to the patient's feelings, both those feelings on the level of awareness and below. The professional nurse is able to sense the personal meanings of the patient's experience and communicate this understanding to the patient.

Humanistic Nursing Practice Theory

Paterson and Zderad first published their Humanistic Nursing Practice Theory in 1976 when nurses were in the midst of assertiveness training as a result of the women's movement in America (Moccia, 1988). However, Moccia proposed that the power that is supported by Paterson and Zderad's theory involves authentic dialogue with patients, students, and other health care professionals. According to Paterson and Zderad (1988), humanistic nursing emphasizes both the art and science of nursing. "Humanistic nursing embraces more than a benevolent technically competent subject-object one-way relationship guided by a nurse in behalf of another" (p. 3). Nursing, rather, involves a responsible searching for nurse–patient two-way interactions that receive their meaning from and are grounded in the nurse's and patient's existential experiences, or the experiences of living. A brief overview of Paterson and Zderad's perspectives on the domain of nursing—person, nurse (nursing), health, environment—provides some clarification of their theory, which can be used imaginatively by nurses in moral psychiatric/mental health practice.

Persons (including patients and nurses) have freedom to make choices; have a personal unique view of the world; are adequate, having the capacity to hope and envision alternatives to what is immediately apparent; have the capacity for authentic presence and intersubjective relatedness; and have meaningful personal histories, although their histories do not control them.

Nursing is an art-science, meaning that nursing is derived from subjective, objective, and intersubjective experiences. Nursing is a form of unique knowledge that is developed through dialogical human processes. Finally, nursing is *being* and *doing*, which focuses on being present with another and engaging in two-way dialogue.

Health does not always mean the absence of disease. The nurse's aim is to provide comfort to patients with comfort conceptualized as a state of being all that one can be at a particular point in time. Nurses try to promote well-being and *more-being* of others, emphasizing that persons are adequate as they are (well-being) but are free to become more than they are (more-being).

Environment, the final part of the domain, focuses on time and space, the here and now or the connectedness of past, present, and future. It also focuses on the nursing situation, which includes the whole world of people and things, a world that is more than just the patient and the nurse; the "all-at-once" or an awareness of all of the emotions, values and experiences that work together to increase wisdom; a community of persons striving toward a common center; complementary synthesis or living out the tension between the objective scientific world and the subjective and intersubjective domains of nursing (O'Connor, 1993; Paterson & Zderad, 1988).

Human-to-Human Relationship Model

The human-to-human relationship model developed by Joyce Travelbee was developed from her experiences in psychiatric nursing and grounded in the philosophy of existentialism. Travelbee (1971) proposed that (1) nurses must possess a body of knowledge and know how to use it, and (2) nurses must learn to use themselves therapeutically if helping relationships are to be established. The phases that lead to the establishment of human-to-human relationships, as described by Travelbee, can be used for ethical practice in psychiatric/mental health nursing. These phases are:

1. The phase of the original encounter. First impressions of both the patient and nurse are perceived. The nurse must be aware of value judgments and feelings.
2. The phase of emerging identities. A bond is established between the nurse and the patient. There is again an emphasis on awareness by the nurse of how the patient is being perceived. Nurses must develop an awareness and a valuing of the uniqueness of others.
3. The phase of empathy. This is a conscious process of sharing in another person's experiences.
4. The phase of sympathy. In this phase, the nurse progresses further than empathy and wants to alleviate a patient's distress.
5. The phase of rapport. Rapport is the end goal of all nursing endeavors; it is a process, an experience, or a happening; it is the human-to-human relationship (Rangel, Hobble, Lansinger, Magers, & McKee, 1998; Travelbee, 1971).

Reducing Stigma

With regard to stigma, Goffman (1963) proposed that those people who are stigmatized often have a turning point in their lives. Sometimes this turning point is recognized when it occurs, but sometimes it is recognized only in retrospect. Goffman stated that the turning point is an

isolating, incapacitating experience, often a period of hospitalization, which comes later to be seen as the time when the individual was able to think through his problem, learn about himself, sort out his situation, and arrive at a new understanding of what is important and worth seeking in life (p. 40).

Because nurses are unaware of when patients are ready to undergo such a significant or potentially life changing event, nurses must constantly cultivate a humanistic environment or milieu that facilitates the personal growth of patients. Smart (2003) wisely stated that he has realized that it is best to think of sanity as occurring along a continuum rather than as a them versus me perspective. Bolton (2003) suggested other ways that stigma can be reduced (see Ethical Kaleidoscope Box 7-8).

Box 7-8

ETHICAL Kaleidoscope   Reducing Stigma

- Examine our own attitudes
- Update our knowledge of mental illness
- Listen to what our patients say about mental illness and its consequences
- Watch out for stigmatizing language
- To be an advocate for those with mental illness
- Add political activism to our daily work
- Challenge stigma in the media

Bolton, J., April 2003, Reducing the stigma of mental illness, Student British Medical Journal, 11, 104–105.

Advocacy

There is often a fragmentation in mental health care when patient treatment is separated into the biomedical sphere of psychiatrists and the psychological sphere of therapists such as psychologists and social workers. Nurses are in a unique position to act as patient advocates in bridging this fragmentary divide through advocacy. *Advocacy* in nursing has been defined as "the active support of an important cause" (Fry & Johnstone, 2002, p. 37). According to Seedhouse (2000), "more than any other branch of nursing, mental health nursing exposes the rift between nursing's nurturing instincts and medicine's/society's insistence that aberrant behaviors are contained" (p. 153). Nurses must try to bring to the forefront the idea that there need not be a sharp distinction between physical or biomedical health promotion and mental health promotion. This integration can be accomplished by nurse-led dialogue among the whole team of health care providers caring for psychiatric patients. Nurses must be open to listen to the feelings, emotions, and goals of all members of the team, while practicing existential advocacy as described by Sally Gadow. According to Gadow (as cited in Bishop & Scudder, 2001), "the nurse as existential advocate does not merely help patients choose what they want—for example, the drug user who wants to be as 'high' as possible while in the hospital. The existential advocate is there to help patients recognize and realize their best selves, given their situation (pp. 76–77)."

Inherent Human Possibilities

Rogers (1980) believed that there is an underlying movement toward inherent possibilities that all human beings exhibit. He proposed that it is a self-actualizing tendency for complete development and that life is an active process that moves toward maintaining, enhancing, and reproducing, even when conditions are not favorable. Rogers compared this view of human flourishing to a story about sprouting potatoes that he observed in his youth. He noticed that even when potatoes were stored in the basement during winter, they would produce pale (as opposed to healthy green) sprouts that twisted toward what little light they might have. Life was still trying to flourish, although conditions were not favorable. Rogers' words very eloquently compare how these potatoes can be likened to psychiatric patients, or any patients, whose lives nurses touch. Rogers said

> In dealing with clients whose lives have been terribly warped, in working with men and women on the back wards of state hospitals, I often think of those potato sprouts. So unfavorable have been the conditions in which these people have developed that their lives often seem abnormal, twisted, scarcely human. Yet, the directional tendency in them can be trusted. The clue to understanding their behavior is that they are striving, in the only ways that they perceive as available to them, to move toward growth, toward becoming. To healthy persons, the results may seem bizarre and futile, but they are life's desperate attempt to become itself (p. 119).

Because psychiatric nursing care is focused on affecting the nature and manifestations of patients' thoughts, emotions, personalities, and behaviors through relationships as well as through biomedical means, ethics pervades good practice. Patients with mental illnesses are stigmatized by large segments of the population, and it is very unfortunate when they are further stigmatized by health care professionals. Nurses who understand and are sensitive to the experiences of psychiatric patients and the cultural implications of psychiatric labeling will be better prepared to take action to improve the public's perception of mental illness. Although mentally ill patients may relate to others in ways that are sometimes difficult to comprehend, nurses, through providing humanistic care, must steadfastly continue to pursue the goal of well-being and more-being with their psychiatric patients

Web Ethics

National Institute of Mental Health
www.nimh.nih.gov

American Psychiatric Nurses Association
www.apna.org

Stigma.org
www.stigma.org

Case Study: Is There a Duty to Warn?

Greg T. is a 25-year-old man hospitalized with a paranoid delusional disorder. When Greg was admitted, he was very angry and vehemently verbalized that he believed that his ex–mother-in-law had been spreading lies about him around the town and accused her of getting him fired from his last job. When Greg's sister, Rose, visited him at the hospital, he gave consent for you, his nurse, and his psychiatrist to talk with her about his condition. At that time, Rose stated that Greg's ideas about his ex–mother-in-law were delusional thinking and that there was no basis in fact regarding his beliefs. His condition has improved with adjustments of his psychotropic drugs (he is no longer actively exhibiting angry and paranoid behavior), and he is being discharged today. When you are talking with Greg today in preparation for his discharge, he tells you "I'm still not finished with my ex–mother-in-law." You ask him what he means by this statement, and he is evasive but answers with cryptic statements that seem to indicate veiled threats against the woman.

Case Study Critical Thinking Questions

1. As Greg's nurse, how would you evaluate the duty to warn in this situation?
2. What actions would you take?
3. Do you believe that Greg should still be discharged today? Please provide a rationale for your answer and discuss what information would be needed to make this decision.
4. How would you document the events of this situation in Greg's medical record? What would be important considerations in writing a good narrative of the event?

REFERENCES

American Nurses Association [ANA]. (2001). *Code of ethics for nurses with interpretive statements.* Washington, DC: Author.

Austin, W., Bergum, V., & Dossetor, J. (2003). Relational ethics: An action ethic as a foundation for health care. In V. Tschudin (Ed.), *Approaches to ethics: Nursing beyond boundaries* (pp. 45–52). Edinburgh: Butterworth-Heinemann–Elsevier Science.

Beauchamp, T. L., & Childress, J. F. (2001). *Principles of biomedical ethics* (5th ed.). New York: Oxford University.

Beresford, P. (2002). Thinking about 'mental health': Towards a social model. *Journal of Mental Health, 11*(6), 581–584.

Bishop, A., & Scudder, J. (2001). *Nursing ethics: Holistic caring practice* (2nd ed.). Sudbury, MA: Jones and Bartlett Publishers.

Bolton, J. (2003, April). Reducing the stigma of mental illness. *Student British Medical Journal, 11,* 104–105.

Brody, B. A. (1988). *Life and death decision making.* New York: Oxford University.

Corey, G. (2001). *Theory and practice of counseling and psychotherapy.* Belmont, CA: Wadsworth Group–Brooks/Cole.

Corey, G., Corey, M. S., & Callanan, P. (2003). *Issues and ethics in the helping professions.* Pacific Grove, CA: Wadsworth Group–Brooks/Cole.

Crowe, M. (2000). Psychiatric diagnosis: Some implications for mental health nurse care. *Journal of Advanced Nursing, 31*(3), 583–589.

Dickenson, D., & Fulford, K. W. M. (2000). *In two minds: A casebook of psychiatric ethics.* New York: Oxford University.

Everstine, L., Everstine, D. S., Heymann, G. M., True, R. H., Frey, D. H., Johnson, H. G., et al. (2003). Privacy and confidentiality in psychotherapy. In D. N. Bersoff (Ed.), *Ethical conflicts in psychology* (3rd ed., pp. 162–164). Washington, DC: American Psychological Association.

Fry, S., & Johnstone, M. J. (2002). *Ethics in nursing practice: A guide to ethical decision making* (2nd ed.). Oxford, UK: Blackwell Science.

Gillon, R. (2001). Confidentiality. In H. Kuhse & P. Singer (Eds.), *A companion to bioethics* (pp. 425–431). Oxford, UK: Blackwell Publishers.

Goffman, E. (1963). *Stigma: Notes on the management of spoiled identify.* New York: Simon & Schuster.

Green, G., Hayes, C., Dickinson, D., Whittaker, A., & Gilheany, B. (2003). A mental health service users perspective to stigmatization. *Journal of Mental Health, 12*(3), 223–234.

Grisso, T., & Appelbaum, P. S. (1998). *Assessing competence to consent to treatment: A guide for physicians and other health care professionals.* New York: Oxford University.

Halter, M. J. (2002). Stigma in psychiatric nursing. *Perspectives in Psychiatric Care, 38*(1), 23–28.

Hobson, J. A., & Leonard, J. A. (2001). *Out of its mind: Psychiatry in crisis—A call to reform.* Cambridge, MA: Perseus.

Joint Commission on Accreditation of Healthcare Organizations. (1998). *Ethical issues and patient rights: Across the continuum of care.* Oakbrook Terrace, IL: Author.

Jonsen, A. R., Siegler, M., & Winslade, W. J. (2002). *Clinical ethics* (5th ed.). New York: McGraw-Hill.

Kahn, M. W. (2001). Introduction to DSM-IV. In J. L. Jacobson & A. M. Jacobson (Eds.), *Psychiatric secrets* (2nd ed., pp. 18–20). Philadelphia: Hanley & Belfus.

Keltner, N. L., Schwecke, L. H., & Bostrom, C. E. (2003). *Psychiatric nursing* (4th ed.). St. Louis, MO: Mosby.

Killion, S. W. (2000a). Competency and guardianship. I. In S. W. Killion & K. Dempski (Eds.), *Quick look nursing: Legal and ethical issues* (pp. 40–41). Thorofare, NJ: Slack.

Killion, S. W. (2000b). Confidential communication—Part I. In S. W. Killion & K. Dempski (Eds.), *Quick look nursing: Legal and ethical issues* (pp. 36–37). Thorofare, NJ: Slack.

Knight, M. T. D., Wykes, T., & Hayward, P. (2003). 'People don't understand': An investigation of stigma in schizophrenia using interpretative phenomenological analysis (IPA). *Journal of Mental Health, 12*(3), 209–222.

Maes, S. (2003). How do you know when professional boundaries have been crossed? *Oncology Nursing Society News, 18*(8), 3–5.

McCann, R. A., & Ball, E. M. (2001). Borderline personality disorder. In J. L. Jacobson & A. M. Jacobson (Eds.), *Psychiatric secrets* (2nd ed., pp. 190–197). Philadelphia: Hanley & Belfus.

Moccia, P. (1988). Preface. In J. G. Paterson & L. T. Zderad, *Humanistic nursing* (pp. iii–v). New York: National League for Nursing.

Nehls, N. (1998). Borderline personality disorder: Gender stereotypes, stigma, and limited system of care. *Issues in Mental Health Nursing, 19*, 97–112.

Nortvedt, P. (1998). Sensitive judgment: An inquiry into the foundations of nursing ethics. *Nursing Ethics, 5*(5), 385–392.

O'Brien, A., Woods, M., & Palmer, C. (2001). The emancipation of nursing practice: Applying anti-psychiatry to the therapeutic community. *Australian and New Zealand Journal of Mental Health Nursing, 10*, 3–9.

O'Connor, N. (1993). *Paterson and Zderad: Humanistic nursing theory.* Newbury Park, CA: Sage Publications, 34.

Paterson, J. G., & Zderad, L. T. (1988). *Humanistic nursing.* New York: National League for Nursing.

Pipher, M. (2003). *Letters to a young therapist: Stories of hope and healing.* New York: Basic Books.

Radden, J. (2002a). Notes towards a professional ethics for psychiatry. *Australian and New Zealand Journal of Psychiatry, 36*, 52–59.

Radden, J. (2002b). Psychiatric ethics. *Bioethics, 16*(5), 397–411.

Rangel, S., Hobble, W. H., Lansinger, T., Magers, J. A., & McKee, N. J. (1998). Joyce Travelbee: Human-to-human relationship model. In A. M. Tomey & M. R. Alligood (Eds.), *Nursing theorists and their work* (4th ed., pp. 364–374). St. Louis, MO: Mosby.

Rogers, C. R. (1980). *A way of being.* Boston: Houghton Mifflin.

Rosen, A., Walter, G., Casey, D., & Hocking, B. (2000). Combating psychiatric stigma: An overview of contemporary initiatives. *Australasian Psychiatry, 8*(1), 19–26.

Seedhouse, D. (2000). *Practical nursing philosophy: The universal ethical code.* Chichester, UK: John Wiley & Sons.

Scott, A. P. (2003). Virtue, nursing and the moral domain of practice. In V. Tschudin (Ed.), *Approaches to ethics: Nursing beyond boundaries* (pp. 25–32). Edinburgh: Butterworth-Heinemann–Elsevier Science.

Shimrat, I. (2003, July–August). Freedom. *Off Our Backs,* 16–18; 55.

Singer, B. J. (2003). Mental illness: Rights, competence, and communication. In G. McGee (Ed.), *Pragmatic bioethics* (2nd ed., pp. 151–162). Cambridge, MA: Massachusetts Institute of Technology.

Smart, D. (2003, April 7). Take action now to banish mental health prejudices. *Pulse-I-Registrar,* n.p.

Smith-Bell, M., & Winslade, W. J. (2003). Privacy, confidentiality, and privilege in psychotherapeutic relationships. In D. N. Bersoff (Ed.), *Ethical conflicts in psychology* (3rd ed., pp. 157–161). Washington, DC: American Psychological Association.

Sokolowski, R. (1991). The fiduciary relationship and the nature of professions. In E. D. Pellegrino, R. M. Veatch, & J. P. Langan (Eds.), *Ethics, trust, and the professions: Philosophical and cultural aspects* (pp. 23–43). Washington, DC: Georgetown University.

Survey reveals reasons why people do not see SA treatment. (2003, November 24). *Alcoholism and Drug Abuse Weekly, 15*(45), 3.

Tarasoff v. Regents of the University of California, 551 P.2d 334 (Cal. 1976).

Travelbee, J. (1971). *Interpersonal aspects of nursing.* Philadelphia: F. A. Davis.

US Department of Health and Human Services, [DHHS] (1999). *Mental health: A report of the Surgeon General—Executive Summary,* Rockville, MD: US DHHS.

Wahl, O. F. (2003). Depictions of mental illnesses in children's media. *Journal of Mental Health,* *12*(3), 249–258.

Watts, J., & Priebe, S. (2002). A phenomenological account of users' experiences of assertive community treatment. *Bioethics, 16*(5), 439–454.

Williams, L. (1998). A "classic" case of borderline personality disorder. *Psychiatric Services,* *49*(2), 173–174.

Yalom, I. D. (1995). Introduction. In C. R. Rogers, *A way of being* (pp. vii–xiii). Boston: Houghton Mifflin.

CHAPTER 8

Ethics In Geriatric and Chronic Illness Nursing

Karen L. Rich

The Fragile Things

*Five-year-old Megan quickly surveyed the display of Willy's
pottery. Her eyes danced over the pots, the pouches, the hand-
woven rugs and feather red rocks perched carefully on the glass.*

*Willy asked, "Megan, what do you like best of all the things you
see here?" Megan looked up, tugged Willy's sleeve, and said, "I
want to touch the fragile things."*

*Mom called this morning at 6 A.M. and said, "Your grandmother
passed away last night." We knew it was coming. She was ninety-
one but the day before she was joking around—correcting my
grammar over the phone and telling the nurses "It sure is hard to
be a princess around this joint sometimes."*

*When I got off the phone I sat by the bed and said, "God, life is
so very frail. I want to touch the Fragile Things."*

L. B. Jones, *Grow Something Besides Old*

SUMMARY

1. Ageism, or discrimination based on chronological age, underlies many ethical issues related to elders.
2. Society often neglects to notice the meaning of elders' lives as scientists work to abolish the biology of aging.
3. Determinations of decisional capacity with regard to elders are sometimes based on prejudiced assumptions rather than facts.
4. Elders may perceive the quality of their lives to be higher than health care professionals perceive it based on observational judgments.
5. Weak or justified paternalism is sometimes a compassionate approach in caring for elderly persons.
6. Focusing on an ethic of dignity rather than a strict ethic of autonomy may be more realistic in caring for some elders, especially in long-term care situations when elderly persons are not completely able to exercise their autonomy.

AGING IN AMERICA

Currently, people are living healthier and longer because of the technological advances that have occurred during the last century in medicine and public health. People in America over the age of 65 years number about 35 million today, and it has been predicted by the United States Census Bureau that nearly 82 million Americans will be over the age of 65 by the year 2050. Life expectancy has increased from 47 years in 1900 to approximately 77.2 years today (CDC, 2004; Peterson, 2002). Although societal factors have increased the quantity of life years, a question remains about how the quality of those years is threatened by chronic debilitating conditions. Often, chronic conditions, which include cerebrovascular disease and Alzheimer's disease, cause elders to lose their most crucial link with others, their voice. A loss of voice to express their individual feelings, desires, and needs is arguably one of the most profound causes of isolation for elders (Smith, Kotthoff-Burrell, & Post, 2002).

Considerations about the loss of the voice of individual elderly persons and the diminished societal recognition of the meaningfulness of their lives underlie many of the ethical issues discussed in this chapter. A large portion of geriatric ethics is based on the relationships that elders have with others, especially on society's perceptions of aging and elders' resultant acceptance of those perceptions.

That we even need to consider a separate subject of geriatric ethics is telling. Often, the lives of elders are set aside from the lives of other adults in the community. It is this overall view of separateness among generations in general and adult generations in particular that makes it necessary to study geriatric ethics and forms the foundation of morals and ethical analysis in relation to elders.

Ageism, a way of thinking that was originally described by Butler (1975), has encouraged young persons in society to view elders as fundamentally different, and, consequently, young people often cease to identify elders as human beings (Agich, 2003).

Just as racism and sexism describe the stereotyping of and discrimination against people because of their skin color or gender, ageism involves the same type of negative perceptions toward older adults based on age. Ageism perpetuates the idea that elders are cognitively impaired, "set in their ways," and "old-fashioned" with regard to their morals and abilities (Agich, 2003; Butler, 1975).

It is disquieting to consider how youth-oriented our Western society is today. When watching television programs, one can see that the target audience is most often young adults and the financially affluent middle-aged baby boomers. Emphasis is placed on keeping or making our bodies beautiful through so-called health supplements and through makeovers and plastic surgery. Beautiful and famous young people are plastered on the covers of magazines, and young athletes are revered. Older actors, and particularly actresses, lament the lack of good roles for them in the movie industry. It is no surprise that, as people age, they often become despondent about the losses they experience with regard to how they look and what they are able to achieve physically. The seemingly vital, active, and glamorous lives of the young people portrayed in the media serve as a stark contrast to what many elderly persons experience. Agich (2003) proposed that "a society that values productivity and material wealth above other values is understandably youth oriented; a natural consequence is that the old come to be seen, and to see themselves, as obsolete and redundant" (p. 54). So, who are the elders in today's society? Savishinsky (1991) stated:

> The class of *the elderly* includes both the rich and poor, sick and well, sane and insane; it also embraces the relatively healthy so-called *young old* between 60 and 75 and the more vulnerable *old old* who are living beyond their eighth decade. Some are intimately connected with family and community, whereas others are cut off from their kin. Some are active and ardent; others are disengaged and hopeless (p. 2).

Our Western model of aging has been primarily formed by the elements of biology and economics. Hillman (1999) called this model a disparaging trap of ageism "that relegates all older people to a category with definite, inescapable handicaps owing to the breakdown of the organism and the exhaustion of its reserves" (p. xviii). When attention is focused on soul (meaning the human psyche), character, or an awareness of how life processes influence older persons, the general public believes that these three concepts are being used to hide the "real truth" about aging and to relieve inescapable despair. It is unfortunate that those people over 50 years old who enthusiastically pursue spiritual growth are often thought to be trying to deny the real truth of aging.

At the end of the 18th century and in the early 19th century, old people were encouraged to view their lives as a pilgrimage and to prepare for death while still participating in service to family and community. However, starting around the 1850s, Western society began to instill the belief that thoughts about death should be avoided and that people should cultivate health and activity as long as possible into old age. The emphasis changed to a focus on valuing "the virtues of youth rather than age, the new rather than the old, self-reliance and autonomy rather than community" (Callahan, 1995, p. 39). These views formed the foundation of the beginning of ageism in the 20th century. The realities of old age were not consistent with the new world view of the morality of self-control; rather, the decay inherent in aging was associated with dependence and failure. Cohen (1988) proposed that although ageism began to be a general social theme after World War II, today it has become focused more on elderly persons who are disabled.

Although people of all ages are haunted by the shadows of their eventual aging and death, it is during one's later years that these issues can no longer be ignored. When one actually does confront the facts of unavoidable aging and death, the mysteries involved can be startling. The feminist philosopher Simone de Beauvior (1972) proposed that "the old are invisible because we see death with a clearer eye than old age itself" (p. 4). Agich (2003) interpreted this statement to mean that old people are set apart from the rest of society because those in society tend to look beyond the elderly persons themselves, who they perceive as close to death, and see the prospect of their own death. The lives of elders are poignant in ways that only they can express, as revealed by the thoughts in this 1887 quote cited by Mencken (1942):

As life runs on, the road grows strange with faces new,—and near the end the milestones into headstones change:—'neath every one a friend.

J. R. Lowell, *On His 68th Birthday*, 1887

Moody (1992) proposed that the modern advances in biomedical technology that have lengthened life for many elderly persons have made it necessary to confront critical ethical questions that society may want to ignore. These questions involve dilemmas about death and dying, the perception of what is meant by quality of life, and decisions about judging the mental and physical functional capacity of old adults. Moody questioned whether or not the typical models or approaches to bioethics, based on rights and duties, fit well when we consider ethics and aging. He asked the question "What ethical ideals are appropriate for an aging society?" (p. 243). According to Moody, focusing on individual autonomy and justice between generations will not provide us with the desired ethical model for engaging in ethics related to elders. Geriatric ethics must involve negotiation, pragmatism, and virtuous practitioners. Principles and rules also must be included, but principles and rules can thwart desired ends if practical wisdom, moral imagination, and character are not a part of the overall scheme.

The issues of autonomy, vulnerability, dependency, and relationships are important to ethics and elders. However, there is another issue that is important to the moral world of elders and those with whom they relate. That issue is related to elderly persons' own feelings about the significance and meaning of their lives. According to Callahan (1995), underlying the strong desire by society and scientists to abolish the biology of aging is "a profound failure of meaning" (p. 39).

Ethical Reflections

- Can an ethicist or nurse apply typical bioethical approaches to situations involving geriatric patients? Why or why not? What is a good approach to geriatric ethics?
- How can nurses combat ageism in their local, state, and national communities? Do you believe that ageism is based solely on age or on the degree of an elderly person's disability? Socioeconomic level? Culture?

LIFE: MEANING AND SIGNIFICANCE

Once, while Mahatma Gandhi's train was pulling slowly out of the station, a European reporter ran up to his compartment window. "Do you have a message I can take back to my people?" he asked. It was Gandhi's day of silence, a vital respite from his demanding speaking schedule, so he didn't reply. Instead, he scrawled a few words on a scrap of paper and passed it to the reporter: "My life is my message."

E. Easwaran, *Your Life is Your Message*

As people age, they often begin to realize the truth of Gandhi's words—that their life is their message—but does Western society support elders in an awareness of the meaning and significance of their lives? In earlier times, tradition was highly valued by society, and the meaning and significance of elderly persons' lives were viewed differently than they are in our morally diverse society today (Callahan, 1995). Elders had an elevated status in communities because their wisdom was prized for its own sake and because their wisdom placed them in a special position of being called upon to perpetuate and interpret societal moral traditions.

However, because we now live in a pluralistic culture that is diverse in moral views, the role of elderly persons in the community-wide passing on of moral traditions is undermined. Therefore, the societal purpose of elders has diminished. Today, elderly persons are important to businesses if they are financially well off, to families if they are willing and able to provide funds and child care to their children and grandchildren, to politicians as a voting block, and to nonprofit agencies as volunteers when the economy forces younger housewives to work rather than volunteer (Callahan, 1995). Some people may believe that these roles for elders make older persons valuable in society. However, on closer inspection, one can determine that it is not age as such that is held in high regard but the accidental features of old age, such as disposable income and free time.

Before exploring various approaches to viewing the meaning and significance of life in old age, it is important to consider what these two terms might mean. According to Cole (1986), *meaning* involves "an intuitive expression of one's overall appraisal of living. Existentially, meaning refers to lived perceptions of coherence, sense, or significance in experiences" (p. 4). Callahan (1995) described meaning as an inner feeling supported by "some specifiable traditions, beliefs, concepts or ideas, that one's life" has purpose and is well structured in "relating the inner self and the outer world—and that even in the face of aging and death, it is a life which makes sense to oneself; that is, one can give a plausible, relatively satisfying account" (p. 33). Callahan described *significance* as "the social attribution of value to old age, that it has a sturdy and cherished place in the structure of society and politics, and provides a coherence among the generations that is understood to be important if not indispensable" (p. 33).

Nurses might question why it is important to nursing morality and ethics for them to consider the pursuit of life meaning and significance by elderly persons. The answer is that nursing ethics is first and foremost about relationships. Morality and ethics for nurses revolve around nurses' helping patients alleviate suffering and move toward well-being. In terms of relationships with elders, nursing ethics also is centered around helping them find and keep their voice or means of expression of desires and feelings. Finding meaning and significance alleviates suffering and promotes well-being for many elderly persons.

Box 8-1

ETHICAL Kaleidoscope   Why Are We Here if We Have to Die?

In the story "The Fall of Freddie the Leaf," a leaf named Freddie questioned a wise older leaf, Daniel, about life and its meaning. When Daniel told Freddie that all of the leaves on their tree and even the tree itself would eventually die, Freddie asked, "Then what has been the reason for all of this? Why were we here at all if we only have to fall and die?"

Daniel answered, "It's been about the sun and the moon. It's been about happy times together, It's been about the shade and the old people and the children [that sat and played beneath the tree]. It's been about colors in Fall. It's been about seasons. Isn't that enough?"

Buscaglia, L. (1982). The fall of freddie the leaf: A story of life for all ages.
Thorofare, NJ: Slack.

Search for Meaning

Viktor Frankl (1905–1997) was a Viennese neurologist and psychiatrist who wrote the influential book, *Man's Search for Meaning,* originally published in 1946. Over 10 million copies of this book have been sold, and it was rated as one of the 10 most influential books by respondents to a survey conducted by the Library of Congress (Greening, 1998). The book is about how Frankl found meaning in his experiences in Auschwitz and other concentration camps during World War II. In the preface to the 1984 edition of the book, Allport stated that Frankl has proposed that "to live is to suffer, to survive is to find meaning in the suffering. If there is a purpose in life at all, there must be a purpose in suffering and in dying" (p. 9).

Frankl (1984) proposed that meaning is the primary motivation in the lives of humans. He determined that the last of his human freedoms in the concentration camps was to choose his attitude toward his suffering. Being in a concentration camp was an unchangeable situation for Dr. Frankl, as is the fact that all people age if they do not die young and the fact that all people eventually die. It is in continuing to make the choices to find meaning in the circumstances that people encounter as their life stories unfold that will eventually form the fabric of a meaningful life when people are old.

Frankl (1984) stated the transitoriness or fleeting nature of life, similar to what Buddhists call impermanence, must not be denied by persons who are interested in putting the search for meaning at the center of their lives. Rather, even suffering and dying can be actualizing experiences. Although no one can supply another person's life meaning, nurses can accompany elderly persons on their journey through the end of life, helping them find meaning and feel that they are significant members of communities.

Updating the Eriksonian Life Cycle

In exploring the moral treatment of elderly persons, Callahan (1995) proposed that the search for common meaning in aging requires looking toward an updated theory of the life cycle as elaborated by Erikson. Erik Erikson's book, *The Life Cycle Completed,* published in 1982, emphasized that all eight stages of the Eriksonian life cycle cannot be distinctly separated but are interrelated. However, after his death in his early 90s, his wife, Joan, used her own ideas and notes made by her husband to update the book. She added new chapters proposing a ninth stage of development and discussed other issues that deal with life and the old–old. Joan Erikson was in her 90s when she wrote this updated book and used her voice to speak for many old–old people about their experiences.

The ninth stage of the life cycle is an extension of the eighth stage, which is described as a time that elders develop despair and disgust vs. integrity. Wisdom is the resultant strength or virtue of both the eighth and ninth stages. The ninth stage is the stage of the lived experiences of persons in their late 80s and 90s. The following are some of the difficulties that Joan Erikson (1997) proposed occur in the ninth stage that make wisdom and integrity hard to achieve.

- Wisdom requires the senses of sight and hearing to see, hear, and remember. Integrity is compared with tact (as in the word "intact"), which is related to touch. In their 90s, elderly persons often lose or have impaired senses of sight, hearing, and touch.

- When persons reach their late 80s or 90s, despair may occur because they realize that life is too short now to try to make up for missed opportunities.
- Despair may occur because the old–old person is just trying to get through the day because of physical limitations, even without the added burden of regrets. However, when persons feel that their lives are not what they wished them to be, the despair is deepened.
- Persons in their 80s and 90s are also likely to have experienced losses of relationships to a greater degree than at any other age. In addition to the suffering directly related to the losses, suffering is generated when the person realizes that "death's door is open and not so far away" (p. 113).

Like virtue ethicists who have drawn connections between the "good life" and being a vital member of a community (Blum, 1994; MacIntyre, 1984), Joan Erikson (1997) said that her husband, Erik, had often proposed that the life cycle cannot be appropriately understood if it is not viewed within the social context or in terms of the community in which it is actually lived. The Eriksons' belief that individuals and society are interrelated and are constantly involved with the give and take of the dynamic woven fabric of community is a key position of communitarian ethicists today. When society lacks a sound ideal of old age, the whole of life is not apparent to communities. If elders are excluded from being among the valued members of a community, they are often viewed as the embodiment of shame instead of the embodiment of wisdom.

Joan Erikson (1997) stated that she was convinced that if persons in their 80s and 90s have developed hope and trust in earlier life stages, they will be able to move further down the path to *gerotranscendence*, a concept she borrowed from the work of Lars Tornstam (1993). Transcendence means "to rise above or go beyond a limit, [to] exceed, [to] excel" (p. 124). Erikson described the experiences of gerotranscendent individuals as:

- feeling a cosmic union with the universal spirit
- perceiving time as being limited to now or maybe only next week; otherwise the future is misty
- feeling that the dimensions of space have been decreased to the perimeter of what the person's physical capabilities allow
- feeling that death is a sustaining presence for the person and viewing death as being "the way of all living things" (p. 124)
- having an expanded sense of self that includes "a wider range of interrelated others" (p. 124).

Erikson then activated the word transcendence into the word transcen*dance* to associate its meaning with the arts and, specifically, "the dance of life [that] can transport us into all realms of making and doing with every item of body, mind, and spirit involved" (p. 127).

- In what ways does society often perpetuate the viewing of elders as the embodiment of shame?
- Joan Erikson (1997) said "to grow old is a great privilege" (p. 128). How can nurses help elderly persons realize this privilege?

MORAL AGENCY

It is generally believed that elders are a vulnerable population because of the natural progression of frailty that usually occurs with old age. Because of this vulnerability, moral agency is often a key consideration in moral relationships with elders. The ability to make deliberate choices and take deliberate action with regard to right or wrong behavior refers to a person's moral agency. Arguments about moral agency generally result from debates about a person's mental capacity with regard to decision making. Whether or not the person is autonomous is usually at the heart of the debate.

Decisional Capacity

Decisional capacity or *incapacity* is the ability or inability to come to what most adults would consider to be reasonable conclusions or resolutions. Decisional capacity can generally be equated with the concept of competence, although competence has more of a legal connotation. Competence is closely tied to formal situations that legally require informed consent. Questions of decisional capacity and competency are associated most often with the three populations of "(a) mentally disabled persons, (b) cognitively impaired elderly persons, and (c) children" (Stanley, Sieber, & Melton, 2003, p. 398). Decisional capacity with regard to minor children and mentally disabled persons is discussed in Chapters 5 and 7, respectively, but the decisional capacity of elders is also an important ethical issue. A problem occurs when nurses become accustomed to thinking about decisional capacity primarily as a means to obtaining consent for invasive procedures that usually occur during inpatient health care admissions. When this type of thinking occurs, the presence of decisional capacity or incapacity of elderly patients in community settings may not be assessed with sufficient sensitivity.

There is no one set of published criteria to be used in all assessments of decisional capacity and competency. A method reported by Beauchamp and Childress (2001) is unique in that it includes a range of the *inabilities* that someone who is incompetent would exhibit as opposed to being based on the person's actual abilities. The standards begin by describing the traits that persons with the least amount of competency exhibit and moves toward those that require higher ability. The standards are:

- inability to express or communicate a preference or choice

- inability to understand one's situation and its consequences
- inability to understand relevant information
- inability to give a reason
- inability to give a rational reason (although some supporting reasons may be given)
- inability to give risk/benefit-related reasons (although some rational supporting reasons may be given)
- inability to reach a reasonable decision (as judged, for example, by what a "reasonable person" would want in a particular situation) (p. 73).

Nurses must be sensitive to the fact that vulnerable and dependent elderly patients are often assumed to be mentally incapacitated or incompetent based on faulty impressions and ageism. When ungrounded assumptions are made based on a persons' frail appearance, for example, elderly patients are often left out of decisions that are important to their well-being. Elders that are physically frail may be left out of decisions ranging from deciding when they want to take a bath in a long-term care facility to health care professionals aiding family members in legally taking away from the older person the decisional capacity to choose among treatment options and manage their financial affairs. Although in most cases family members envision the best interests of the patient as the basis for their actions, this is not always the situation. Occasionally, when the family wants to deem the elder incompetent, family members are more interested in their own self-serving desires than the well-being of the elder. Nurses must be cautiously and wisely alert when assessing situations that affect determinations of decisional capacity.

Autonomy and Paternalism

Autonomy in bioethics is consistent with persons being rational and capable of making their own health care and life decisions. Autonomy, along with beneficence, nonmaleficence, and justice, is one of the four principles of bioethics, which was discussed in more detail in Chapter 1. Since the period of the Enlightenment in the 18th century, autonomy has increasingly become the center of ethical debates. Respecting the wishes and decisions of patients is essential to the underlying framework of bioethics.

Paternalism occurs when health care professionals make choices for patients "in the best interest of the patient" or "for the patient's own good." Over the years, as medical professionals were becoming more highly educated and advances in medical technology were developing at a rapid rate, professionals began to frequently exhibit paternalistic behavior. Doctors and nurses often believed that patients were unable to understand the full extent of their care needs or, worse, there was an underlying lack of respect for a patient's need for personal autonomy because health care professionals believed that their position put them in a justified place of power.

Although some people may consider paternalistic behavior (as discussed later in this chapter) to be justified in some instances, elders are still at risk of being treated in a negative paternalistic manner by health care professionals. Again, this often results from incorrect assumptions about elders' decisional capacity because of their frail appearance and societal ageism. Even when elders are seemingly confused regarding the minor details of a situation, they may retain decisional capacity. In fact, elderly persons may be disoriented to time and place and still retain the capacity to make reasonable decisions regarding their lives. In these circumstances, health care professionals are often tempted to act paternalistically. Instead, the whole perspective of individual situations must be evaluated in terms of the elder's ability to understand the benefits, risks, and consequences of decisions as well as in terms of the overall consistency of the elder's conversations and expressions of wishes over time.

Although health care professionals sometimes are quick to judge elders as incapacitated when their autonomy should rightfully be honored, generally, the excessive paternalistic behavior exhibited by doctors and nurses in the past has caused a backlash resulting in an elevated interest in respecting a patient's autonomy. Therefore, behavior exhibited toward elderly patients falls somewhere along a wide continuum from a point of rigid paternalism to a point of rigid respect for autonomy.

Today, those ethicists who believe that the pendulum has now swung too far in the direction of an overinflated interest in preserving autonomy are concerned that this stance causes people to minimize human relationships, community, and virtues (Agich, 2003; Callahan, 1995; Hester, 2001; MacIntyre, 1984, 1999; Moody, 1992). Hester (2001), a communitarian ethicist, has argued that healing requires communal involvement, not an overdeveloped interest in autonomy. When autonomy becomes the consuming focus in health care, the involvement of communities is often sidelined. In fact, Agich (2003) proposed that societal overemphasis on autonomy with regard to elders creates ambivalence toward those who are aged and dependent. Elderly patients often need the care of nurses not because they lack autonomy but because they have lost physical function.

Rather than focusing on rules and principles such as autonomy, well-being and suffering must be the focal point of care provided to elders. When autonomy is viewed as being constantly under attack, conflict and confusion can be the outcome, and, consequently, elders are not ennobled at a time of their lives in which they are seeking integrity (Agich, 2003). It must be noted that respect for autonomy remains extremely important in bioethics and nursing ethics, but what is needed is a humanistic approach that puts the patient's humanity and well-being at the center of care, not a blind allegiance to rule-oriented behavior.

When health care providers are attempting to champion self-direction by elders, they must not exclude family caregivers from decision making with regard to the care of elders (Agich, 2003). This point is important to emphasize because nurses might inadvertently believe that they must minimize family involvement in order to support an elderly patient's autonomy. However, autonomous elderly patients are not necessarily bound by their family's decisions or recommendations. Often, elders appreciate the caring concern of their family and even the appropriate decisional support provided by trusted nurses. Caregivers, including nurses who are well-known by elderly patients through repeated contact over time, are intimates to the patient, not strangers. When providing decisional support to patients, nurses must use practical wisdom in evaluating whether capricious assumptions and prejudices are influencing the support and direction that they are providing to patients.

Vulnerability and Dependence

In addition to autonomy, vulnerability and dependence are integral to moral agency. In order to facilitate communities working toward the common good of their members, MacIntyre (1999) emphasized that people must acknowledge their animal nature. When it is recognized that human nature is also animal nature, vulnerability and dependence are accepted as natural human conditions, which are inherent human conditions as people move from childhood to adulthood. Barring complicating circumstances, people progress from vulnerability and dependence in childhood to being capable of independent practical reasoning as adults.

As adults, however, humans often may reexperience vulnerability and dependence because of the effects of physical and cognitive changes during aging. According to MacIntyre (1999), ethicists frequently talk in terms of stronger, independent persons benevolently bestowing their virtues on those who are vulnerable and dependent. However, nurses would do well to keep in mind that all people are subject to vulnerability and dependence, even nurses themselves. There is a vast amount to learn from vulnerable and dependent elders if nurses are open to hearing and entering into their patients' life stories (Butts & Rich, 2004).

Dementia

Nurses, particularly those nurses working in home care and long-term care settings, often provide care to patients with dementia. Kitwood (1997) suggested that our evolving culture has supported society and health care communities in treating demented persons as the "new outcasts of society" (p. 44). According to Jenkins and Price (1996), the loss experienced by persons with dementia can be likened to a loss of personhood.

When people become adjusted to demented persons' dwindling capacities, they often begin reacting to demented people as less than persons (Moody, 1992). People with dementia can still be aware of their feelings, even when the person they once seemed to be appears to be withering away. It is reasonable to assume that an extreme sense of vulnerability can occur as a person enters the early and middle stages of a progressive dementia. This occurs when some cognitive ability may still exist in the demented person's awareness of personhood and connectedness to the environment and to others.

Kitwood's (1997) reference to demented persons being the outcasts of society becomes very relevant when those people with dementia lose their dignity in terms of how other people perceive them. Dignity is tied to the relatedness of daily interaction between those people with dementia and their significant others and health care professionals. Dignity is jeopardized when caregivers are too focused on making ethical decisions regarding the care of demented persons and forget to actually relate to the persons themselves (Moody, 1992).

Family and paid caregivers of those people with dementia often become frustrated and anxious. Nurses can serve as mentors to other caregivers when nurses exhibit the virtues of lovingkindness and equanimity when interacting with patients with dementia and their caregivers (see Table 2-1 in Chapter 2). Gentle communication used by nurses also helps to support the overall sense of dignity surrounding the care of patients with dementia. Environmental calm is created with gentle words, an environment of fear and anxiety can be created when loud and harsh words are used. Inexperienced caregivers learn by observing nurses, who must always be aware of their potential to ultimately help or harm patients by the example they set for others.

VIRTUES NEEDED BY ELDERS

May (1986) asserted that aging is a mystery rather than a problem, and as a society, people must focus on how they react to aging rather than how to fix it. That doctors and nurses are in a position of power compared with the seemingly passive beneficiary position of patients is a frequent topic in bioethics. The behavior of health care professionals directed toward aged individuals is very important because elderly persons frequently perceive that the treatment they receive from health care professionals is symbolic of what they can expect from the larger community.

May (1986) has taken the position that even when they are seemingly powerless, elderly persons remain moral agents who are personally responsible for the quality of their moral lives. An ethic of caregiving that is one-sided on the part of doctors and nurses is not the answer to power imbalances between health care professionals and patients.

The following are virtues that May (1986) proposed elders need to cultivate in order to enhance the quality of their moral lives. Nurses who are aware of the continued moral development that occurs in old age can support elderly patients in cultivating these virtues as the patients continue their journey of moral progress.

- *Courage.* Courage is consistent with St. Thomas Aquinas' definition of "courage as a firmness of soul in the face of adversity" (p. 51). Elderly persons need courage in facing the certainty of death and loss in their lives.
- *Humility.* Humility is a virtue needed by caregivers to counteract the arrogance that may develop because of their position of power in relationships with elders. Nurses need to be receivers as well as givers in patient–professional relationships. Nurses can receive the gifts of insight and practical wisdom when they actively listen to the narratives of their elderly patients who have lived many years and experienced many joys and sufferings. However, elderly people also need humility to cultivate graceful acceptance when their dignity is assaulted by seeing and feeling their bodily decay; when they see the looks they receive from young people, looks that reflect that their frailty is noticeable, and often repugnant to others; and when they progressively lose more people and things of value in their lives.
- *Patience.* Although old age sometimes stimulates the emotions of bitterness and anger, a positive conception of the virtue of patience can help combat these reac-

tive emotions. "Patience is purposive waiting, receiving, willing…it requires taking control of one's spirit precisely when all else goes out of control" (p. 52). Patience is the virtue that can help elders bear with the frustrations of their frail bodies rather than curse their fate, such as when they become short of breath trying to walk short distances.

- *Simplicity.* Simplicity is a virtue referred to by Benedictine monks as a moral mark of old age. Simplicity becomes the virtue of a pilgrim who "has at long last learned how to travel light" (p. 53). Simplicity is exhibited when elderly persons experience great joy in the small pleasures of life, such as a meal with friends, rather than in accumulating material possessions.

- *Integrity.* The virtue of integrity represents "an inclusive unity of character" that summarizes all of the other virtues of character in old age (p. 53). Character is a moral structure and requires an overriding virtue when character is "at one with itself" (p. 53). Integrity, or an intactness of character, is the foundation that helps elders remain kind and optimistic in terms of their transcendent connection with the universe, even when loss and impermanence could easily pull them in a more negative direction.

- *Wisdom (Prudence).* Wisdom, or prudence, makes integrity possible through the lessons learned from the experiences of one's past. Prudence was defined by medieval moralists as consisting of three parts: *memoria, docilitus,* and *solertia. Memoria* "characterizes the person who remains open to his or her past, without retouching, falsifying, or glorifying it" (p. 57). *Docilitus* does not represent the passiveness of one who is merely docile but rather is "a capacity to take in the present—an alertness, an attentiveness in the moment" (p. 58). It implies a contrasting state from the need to talk excessively that sometimes serves to separate elders from others. *Solertia* is "a readiness for the unexpected" (p. 58). It provides a contrast to being inflexible with routines (see Ethical Kaleidoscope Box 8-2). However, it should be noted that some amount of ritual helps elders develop strength of character.

Box 8-2

ETHICAL Kaleidoscope   Flexibility and Life

When a man is living, he is soft and supple; when he is dead he becomes hard and rigid. When a plant is living, it is soft and tender; when it is dead, it becomes withered and dry. Hence, the hard and rigid belong to the company of the dead. The soft and supple belong to the company of the living.

Lao Tzu, Tao Teh Ching

- *Hilarity*. A final virtue outlined by May (1986) was another virtue of old age iden-tified by Benedictine monks. *Hilaritas* is "a kind of celestial gaiety in those who have seen a lot, done a lot, grieved a lot, but now acquire that humored detach-ment of the fly on the ceiling looking down on the human scene" (p. 60). It in-volves not taking oneself too seriously. Although depression is more common in elders than at other age periods because of conditions such as naturally lowered serotonin levels, anxiety over fixed incomes, physical, personal and material losses, and disturbed sleep patterns, the monks believed that hilarity is a realistic virtue of old age.

Ethical Reflections

- How can nurses help elderly persons cultivate the virtues identified by May (1986)?
- How important is the personal responsibility of elders for the moral nature of their lives and relationships? As a nurse, how can you affect an elder's personal responsibility?

Box 8-3

ETHICAL Kaleidoscope   Last Acts of Courtesy

Ida was a 79-year-old Alzheimer's patient seen by Dr. Muller, a psychiatrist in the ER, because she became agitated at her foster home. Dr. Muller reported that Ida looked younger than her years and "still showed some of the light that usually leaves the face of the demented. Her score was 7 out of 30" on the Mini Mental Status Exam. "Ida gave little information during the interview, though she showed every sign of wanting to cooperate." Plans were made for Ida to be discharged back to the foster home on Haldol. When Dr. Muller went to say goodbye to Ida, he found her "straightening the sheet and flattening out the pillow on the gurney where she had been placed prior to the interview. She was trying to put [styrofoam cups and food wrappers] into a trash container" but was having difficulty doing so. Dr. Muller stated "I was struck by what was still left of this sweet lady's demented brain and mind—which did not know the year, season, month, or day—that made her want to attempt these last acts of courtesy before leaving the ER." Muller quoted the neu-rologist, Oliver Sacks, who stated "style, neurologically, is the deepest part of one's being, and may be preserved, almost to the last, in a dementia."

Muller, R. (2003). Psych ER. Hillsdale, NJ: Analytic.

QUALITY OF LIFE

What do people mean when they discuss the issue of quality of life? Often, people, including health care professionals, seem to talk about quality of life as if it is a concept that is self-evident. But is it? According to Jonsen, Siegler, and Winslade (2002), determinations of quality of life are value judgments, and value judgments imply variations among those people who are determining value. Jonsen et al. proposed that if it is determined that a patient's quality of life is seriously diminished, a justification can be made to refrain from life-prolonging medical treatments. However, some people find this position problematic because of their views about the sanctity of life. These people believe that because all human life is sacred, life must be preserved no matter what the quality of that life might be.

Many people do believe that treatment can be withheld or withdrawn based on quality-of-life determinations while preserving a reverence for the sanctity of life. Scales have been developed, and measures of physical and psychological functions have been suggested to objectify those determinations. However, even those people who believe that medical treatment can be withheld based on the quality of a life may differ significantly in how they would respond to scales and measurements that are supposed to quantify the quality of their own or others' lives. Studies have shown that at least one group of health care professionals, physicians, frequently rate the quality of a patient's life lower than the patient rates it (Jonsen et al., 2002).

Methods for determining the quality of a life can be divided into categories of personal evaluations and observer evaluations. According to Jonsen et al. (2002), a *personal evaluation* of the quality of life "is the personal satisfaction expressed or experienced by individuals in their physical, mental, and social situation" (p. 107). *Observer evaluation* "is the evaluation by an onlooker of another's experiences of personal life" (p. 108). It is observer evaluations that generate most ethical problems with regard to quality-of-life determinations.

Problems with quality-of-life determinations that are specifically related to elderly patients can arise because of discrimination against patients by health care professionals based on the patient's chronological age, a perception of a patient's "disagreeableness," a patient's dementia, or differences in life goals and values between the professional and the patient (Faden & German, 1994; Jonsen et al., 2002). Decisions regarding treatment must always be made on honest determinations of medical need and the current or previously communicated preferences of patients. If their wishes were not previously communicated, decisions should be based on projections of what loved ones believe the patient would want done or on what it is believed a reasonable person would desire in the way of treatment options. Problems can easily arise, however, when professionals try to project what a "reasonable person" would want in a particular situation. It is at this point that prejudices and biased discrimination based on ageism can enter into observer evaluations.

When acting with regard to elderly patients, special care must be used to remember and focus on the fact that it can be assumed that values and goals are different among people of different age groups (Faden & German, 1994). The values that might be consistent among young health care professionals could be expected to be very different from those values held by old–old adults. Automatic projections of values by nurses and other health care professionals do not support the moral care of elderly persons. Elders may view their lives as having quality when younger persons, still in the prime of their lives, do not readily see the quality there. In addition to using moral imagination in simply stopping to reflect about the dangers of forming automatic assumptions, nurses can conduct a values history with elderly patients when they enter a new health care system. This can be invaluable in trying to assure the ethical treatment of elders. This history must be reevaluated as appropriate.

Ethical Reflections

- A decision not to attempt to resuscitate an unconscious, frail, elderly person, in an emergency room, for example, should not be made based solely on chronological age. What factors must be considered in such a decision?
- Discuss the scenarios of how ageism might affect end-of-life decisions and elders.

Medicalization

Medicalization is a term used to describe an attitude and motivation for action that emphasizes *cure* over *care* in health care professionals' relationships with patients of all ages. Nurse Beverly Hall (2003), in referring to her own treatment for breast cancer, wrote about three examples of medicalization. Her examples included: "(a) giving useless treatments to keep the patient under medical care; (b) demeaning and undermining efforts at self-determination and self-care; and (c) keeping the patient's life suspended by continual reminders that death is just around the corner, and that all time and energy left must be devoted to ferreting out and killing the disease" (p. 53).

As previously discussed, Viktor Frankl (1984) maintained that "man's search for meaning is the primary motivation in his life" (p. 105). Humans embark on the search for meaning in order to alleviate and understand suffering and to move toward well-being. Frankl proposed that inner tension rather than inner equilibrium may result from this search for meaning. He believed that this inner tension is a prerequisite for mental health. Valuing the need to strive toward equilibrium and homeostasis (a tensionless state) is wrong, according to Frankl. This can be especially true when considering elderly persons whose whole being does not generally remain in a state of equilibrium.

Accepting that equilibrium is not necessarily always the healthiest state supports the belief that suffering should not be attacked as if it is something to eliminate at all costs. Rather, well-being often involves the relief of suffering through the acceptance of suffering. In discussing the often misguided goals of a modernist society, Callahan (1995) proposed that the novelist George Eliot had captured this philosophy with the word *meliorism*. The negative concept of meliorism describes "an ethic of action oriented toward the relief, not the acceptance, of pain and suffering" (p. 30).

Although an emphasis on holistic care has helped to eliminate some of the thoughts from the Enlightenment period that compared the human body with a machine (sometimes referred to as *reductionism*), the health care system and health care professionals today often still seem to perpetuate the meliorism proposed by Eliot. This meliorism causes doctors and nurses to work toward curing disease and relieving suffering at all costs. In working with patients of all ages, but especially in patients' later years, attempts must be made to alleviate suffering while realizing that a complete relief or alleviation of suffering is not always possible.

In these instances, the goal of the nurse would be to help facilitate the patient's acceptance of the pain and suffering that cannot be changed. This can be referred to as *transforming acceptance*. Persons who experience transforming acceptance cultivate and exhibit a pervasive calm demeanor and trust that their lives are unfolding as they should. Amid the chaos of caring for persons who are experiencing pain and suffering, a nurse can facilitate a patient's transforming acceptance by acting like the calm person described by the Buddhist monk, Thich Nhat Hanh (2001).

> In Vietnam there are many people, called boat people, who leave the country in small boats. Often the boats are caught in rough seas or storms, the people may panic, and boats can sink. But if even one person aboard can remain calm, lucid, knowing what to do and what not to do, he or she can help the boat survive. His or her expression—face, voice—communicates clarity and calmness, and people have trust in that person. They will listen to what he or she says. One such person can save the lives of many (p. 162).

Transforming acceptance can be the source of a profound life experience for both the patient and the nurse.

Box 8-4

ETHICAL Kaleidoscope   Technological Advances: Blessing, Curse, or Both?

Tithonus was "a Greek hero that craved immortality [and] was finally granted his wish by the gods. Then, to his horror, he realized he had failed to ask the gods for immortal youth. So Tithonus achieved his long life only to endure the miserable frailty and weakness of age until at last the gods took pity on him and converted him into a grasshopper."

Moody, H. R. (1992). Ethics in an Aging Society (p. 19). Baltimore, MD: Johns Hopkins.

Ethical Reflections

- In what ways might elderly patients be more prone to having their health care medicalized than younger patients? What might be some of the reasons why elderly patients' care may be less medicalized?
- Review Thich Nhat Hanh's (2001) story of the Vietnamese boat people. In what ways could you, as a nurse, promote transforming acceptance with a geriatric patient who is experiencing suffering that cannot be completely relieved?
- How is transforming acceptance about more than a patient's personal acceptance of suffering?

CHRONIC ILLNESS

As advances in medical technology and treatment increase exponentially, the length of life of those people who have chronic illnesses also continues to increase. "Lives are saved, but [they are] lives that will be sick until death finally wins out" (Callahan, 1995, p. 20). Chronic illnesses, such as heart disease, cancer, and stroke, as they relate to increased life expectancy are a particular problem for elders. Erlen (2002) proposed that there are three fundamental concerns related to ethics and chronically ill persons. Those three concerns "are lack of control, suffering, and access to services" (p. 416). The three concerns are closely tied to the concept of medicalization discussed in the previous section.

Patients with chronic illnesses frequently feel as if their illnesses are controlling them rather than feeling that they are in control of their own lives. The reality or perception of power imbalances between health care providers and patients (patients often feel vulnerable and dependent) magnify negative feelings that are generated from thinking that one lacks control. Care must be taken by nurses to advocate for the inclusion of chronically ill patients in their own decisions regarding treatment options. This inclusion sometimes leads to situations in which nurses disagree with patients' decisions. However, unless patients may cause harm to others, health care professionals must compassionately allow rational patients to be in control of their own lives.

Suffering related to one's health status can be defined as "the state of severe distress associated with events that threaten the intactness of the person" (Cassell, 1991, p. 33). Chronic conditions produce demands and conflicts to which the ill person must respond. Patient suffering is often related to unrelieved pain, the stigma of chronic illness (see stigma in Chapter 7), and disparities between the consequences of extending life and the quality of life that results from the ability to extend it.

Patients with chronic illnesses usually need greater access to health care services because of exacerbations of the illnesses and the comorbidities that they experience. This increased need for access is often not met by society and health care communities. Disparities that affect elders in the ability to access care are based on factors such as supposed limits in general societal resources, the limited availability of services because of location of providers, and variances in the ability of patients to pay for care.

ASSESSING THE CAPACITY TO REMAIN AT HOME

A problem often faced by nurses working with elders in the community, or those nurses involved with helping to plan discharges of patients from acute care to home care, is assessing the elders' capacity to safely continue to live alone in their own homes. These determinations become particularly difficult when frail elders adamantly want to remain in or return to their homes, and caregivers disagree with the elders' decisions. Caregivers must consider the real and perceived mental incapacities of elders and question the safety of their living situation. Ways to assess cognitive capacity have been covered earlier in the "Moral Agency" section of this chapter and in Chapter 7. If it is believed that an elder is incapacitated, an issue of elder autonomy versus caregiver beneficence may occur. The ethical issue becomes a question of deciding whether or not to act in a way that Beauchamp and Childress (2001) called weak or soft paternalism, which is a concept that was originally suggested by Feinberg.

Weak paternalism involves an intervention by a caregiver based on the principles of beneficence or nonmaleficence that is enacted "to protect persons against their own substantially nonautonomous action(s)" (Beauchamp & Childress, 2001, p. 181). *Nonautonomous actions* are actions that are not based on rational decision making. Persons who are the receivers of weak paternalistic actions must have some form of compromised ability for the weak paternalism to be justified. It is debatable whether or not weak paternalism actually qualifies as paternalism at all. Paternalistic actions are usually not disputed when persons must be protected from harm resulting from circumstances that are beyond their level of comprehension (including a desire based on faulty information when a person is incapacitated). However, an issue of self-harm continues to be an irresolvable problem when elders with intact decisional capacity want to remain at home when it is not safe to do so because of physical limitations. Although family caregivers and health care providers must carefully weigh when and the degree to which weak paternalism is justified in preventing self-harm, elders feel more in control and happiest when they are allowed to make informed, autonomous choices.

LONG-TERM CARE

As in other situations discussed in this chapter, moral relationships between nurses and patients in long-term care facilities are often focused on issues of respect for autonomy. However as previously proposed, focusing too narrowly on respecting autonomy can cause nurses to miss the real day-to-day complexities that make up moral relationships with elders. In many instances, elders are in long-term care facilities because they are no longer able to exercise self-direction in safely caring for themselves. This fact sometimes makes attempts at trying to "preserve autonomy," in a comprehensive sense, a no-win undertaking. Unrealistic goals serve to frustrate nurses and aides who work in long-term care facilities, and, unfortunately, these frustrations can ultimately be directed against elderly long-term care residents.

Pullman (1998) proposed that an *ethic of dignity*, as opposed to an ethic of autonomy, be used in long-term care. With an ethic of dignity, the focus is on the moral character of caregivers rather than on the autonomy of the recipients of care. Of course, autonomy must be respected when it is realistic to do so, but in working with those long-term care residents who are no longer able to exercise their full autonomy, a communal ethic of dignity can provide a compassionate means of care. Even when elders are able to fully exercise their autonomous choices, an ethic of dignity provides an appropriate grounding framework from which to work.

As discussed in Chapter 2, Pullman (1998) divides dignity into basic dignity, which is the dignity inherent in all humans, and personal dignity, which is an evaluative type of dignity decided on by communities but which does not have to be solely tied to autonomy. Personal dignity can be viewed as a community's valuing of the interrelationship of those who are members of the community. Acknowledging the basic and personal dignity of elders through the adoption of an ethic of dignity, includes being able to trust or have "confidence that caregivers will strive to serve the on-going interests of their patients to the best of their abilities" (Pullman, 1998, p. 37). If there is an acknowledged or unacknowledged belief that elderly residents of long-term care facilities need to be independent because being dependent is bad, and if the goal is to minimize the elders' need for care rather than to provide more care, then the relationships between nurses and the elderly residents of long-term care facilities are in trouble from the outset.

Pullman (1998) suggested that long-term care often includes paternalistic interventions from the beginning of patient–health care provider relationships. He defined a *rule of justified paternalism*. That rule is "the degree of paternalistic intervention justified or required, is inversely proportional to the degree of autonomy present" (p. 37). Nurses must be extremely sensitive and aware in ensuring that they cultivate the intellectual virtue of practical wisdom so that errors in judgments are not made regarding how to navigate the waters of autonomy versus justified or weak paternalism in patient care. When elders have the capacity to make choices about treatments and daily living activities, they must have the freedom to make their own personal decisions. Those options include such things as choosing to refuse medications and physical therapy. However, respecting the autonomy of elders does not mean that compassionate nurses should not take considerable time, if needed, to patiently discuss the potential consequences of controversial choices made by elderly persons. Nurses who work from an ethic of dignity are not emotionally detached from their patients but, instead, are willing to risk feeling a personal sense of failure or loss when their elderly patients make choices that a nurse believes are not in the elder's best interest.

Ethical Reflections

- Cohen (1988) said that elders often focus all of their energy toward avoiding "the ultimate defeat, which is not death but institutionalization and which is regarded as a living death" (p. 25). How can nurses help to change the view that residence in a long-term care facility is a "living death"?
- Do you believe that nurses who work in long-term care facilities are stigmatized in any way? If so, what do you believe is the underlying cause of this stigmatization?

ELDER ABUSE

Nurses are frequently the health care professionals who first recognize family violence toward patients (Ramsey, 2000). *Elder abuse* includes "(1) neglect; (2) abuse, both physical and psychological; (3) financial exploitation; and (4) neglect by self or caregiver" (Ramsey, 2000, p. 58). Moral care of elders requires that nurses are interested in recognizing and acting on the signs of abusive situations. Clues that abuse may be occurring include explanations about injuries that seem inconsistent with what the nurse actually sees; delays in seeking treatment for conditions and injuries; and unusual behaviors such as caregivers giving extensive details about the elder's injuries, refusing to allow the elder to be interviewed or treated by the nurse without the caregiver being present, and an unreasonable concern about the cost of treatment. (See Box 8-5 regarding the use of restraints.)

The conditions of abuse are often different for elders than they are for other adults or children (Bergeron, 2000). Older males are more prone to abuse than younger males, but there are limited resources in terms of safe houses for males. Elderly persons who are abused tend to be less accepting of help from police and the court system than younger victims of abuse. This reluctance is particularly prevalent when the abuser is the child of the elder. When an abuser is a spouse, elderly persons are more resistant to seeking a divorce or separation from the spouse than are younger persons. Because of limited financial resources, especially with regard to having a means of generating more income when it is needed, elderly persons usually feel more constrained by their housing and living situations and are reluctant to disrupt the status quo even when they are being abused.

Nurses must take an active role in recognizing the abuse of elders and knowing state statutes regarding the handling of elder abuse. Nurses also have a key role in teaching other health care professionals and the community about recognizing elder abuse. The following list is a guideline for meeting moral responsibility in reporting abuse. Report to:

- Adult Protective Services
- Long-term care ombudsman (usually when an agency or health care provider is involved)

- State licensing board (when health care provider is involved)
- Law enforcement (if required under statute)

When:

- Written or verbal report within 24 hours of incident (Ramsey, 2000, p. 58).

Box 8-5

ETHICAL Kaleidoscope   Use of Restraints
When caring for elders, both chemical and physical restrictions and restraints should be limited to the least amount possible to maintain the safety of patients and caregivers.

AGE-BASED DISTRIBUTION OF HEALTH CARE

There has been substantial debate among bioethicists and philosophers about the need for a societal plan to fairly distribute health care resources among different generations (Callahan, 1995; Daniels, 1988; Moody, 1992). It is a known fact that a large percentage of health care dollars is often spent during an elderly person's last year of life. By 2020, the number of chronically ill Americans is expected to rise to almost 157 million, with a resultant doubling of direct medical costs to treat these conditions, rising to over 10 trillion dollars. This figure will comprise 80% of the total health care spending in America (Partnership for Solutions, 2001; as cited in Lubkin & Larsen, 2002). Currently, no plan for fairly distributing health care dollars has received widespread acceptance in the United States. It is often vulnerable populations such as the very young (neonates) and the very old who are the focus of discussions regarding distribution of health care resources.

Social justice in distributing health care goods according to age has been described as a type of rationing. Moody (1992) defined rationing as a term that fits into discussions related to crisis situations, such as the rationing of gasoline during oil embargoes and butter during World War II. Rationing is based on scarcity of resources and is usually thought of as a temporary situation. The term "rationing" does not accurately define a method that is appropriate to use in making most decisions regarding the distribution of health care resources. In fact, Moody said that America already has an allocation scheme for making decisions regarding health care for elders in the form of the Medicare program, which was established in 1965. The Medicare program has limits with regard to what care and treatment can be provided under the program, but as Moody proposed, these limits are not usually referred to as rationing. American health care practices that can be compared to acts of rationing include "the distribution of organs for transplantation, the practice of triage in admission to hospital emergency rooms, [and] extensive queuing for health care services provided through the Veterans Administration" (p. 199).

Callahan (1995) has proposed that the idea of the "natural life span" and a "tolerable death" might be included in considerations of distributing health care resources to elders. Callahan defined these terms as "a fitting life span followed by a death that is relatively acceptable in its timeliness within that life span" (p. 64). Moody (1992) agreed that using considerations of a natural life span can be helpful in the rationing–allocation debate, but he added that, in the real world, bringing theory and practice together is very difficult and requires prudent political judgment. The debate over allocating health care resources among different generations is a heated one and seems to have no end in sight.

Web Ethics

US Administration on Aging (AOA)
www.aoa.gov

Family Caregiver Alliance
www.caregiver.org

National Institute on Aging
www.nia.nih.gov

National Council on the Aging
www.ncoa.org

The Alzheimer's Association
www.alz.org

National Center on Elder Abuse
www.elderabusecenter.org

Elderhope Ethics and Law
www.elderhope.com/EthicsandLaw.shtml

MANAGEMENT OF CARE

Travelbee (1971) described the human to human relationship as a "mutually significant experience" between a nurse and the recipient of care (p. 123). According to Travelbee, "each participant in the relationship perceives and responds to the human-ness of the other; that is, the 'patient' is perceived and responded to as a unique human being—not as 'an illness,' 'a room number,' or as a 'task to be performed'" (p. 124). Unfortunately, elders often feel dehumanized when interacting with health care professionals, which further compounds the dehumanization that they encounter in society. Travelbee made a profound statement—that if just one health care professional would treat a recipient of care as a human being, this gesture might give the person the strength to cope with 10 other health care professionals who perceive that same person as merely a patient.

Those nurses who are compassionate dedicate themselves to helping others transform or accept unavoidable suffering. It is a challenge to relate to others compassionately, to really communicate to the heart, according to Chodron (1997). "Compassion is not a relationship between the healer and the wounded. It is a relationship between equals" (Chodron, 2001, p. 50).

For many elders, the world is a lonely place. Nurses who have a sincere desire to take action to alleviate or facilitate acceptance of the suffering of this vulnerable group are widening the circle of compassion in the world. Solomon (2001) stated that research has revealed that elders have a higher response to placebo treatment than is normally expected and reported that this higher response has been attributed to the attention that elderly persons receive in connection with participation in research studies. He proposed that elders must be very lonely for this slight attention to provide them with such a lift.

Compassion and healing can be thought of as paired needs of elders. Capra (1982) described healing as a "complex interplay among the physical, psychological, social, and environmental aspects of the human condition" (p. 124). Capra postulated that healing has been excluded from medical science because it cannot be understood in terms of reductionism. Healing suggests a moving toward wholeness that goes beyond a single human being; it is consistent with a belief in the interconnection of all beings and the universe. Healing does not imply curing; it involves a realization that all things cannot be fixed. This idea of healing encompasses the recognition of the nature of impermanence and accepts unpredictability and the inability to strictly control events.

Nurses must establish human to human relationships with elderly patients, incorporating care that recognizes the interplay of many factors that may be affecting the older person's state of well-being. Many factors that affect elders cannot be changed; they must be peacefully accepted and used in achieving integrity. However, there are active healing interventions that nurses can employ.

Dossey, Keegan, and Guzzetta (2000) reported that patients aged 66 to 100 years receive the least amount of touch from health care personnel. The need for physical touch is present at a time when elders are already experiencing significant loss in their lives: loved ones, belongings, and sensory perception. Touch is one form of healing communication that nurses can use to convey compassion to elders. Many elders perceive the nurse's touch as comforting. In her experimental study, Butts (1998; 2001) found that in long-term care facilities the nurse's comforting touch significantly improved female elderly residents' perceptions of five factors: self-esteem, well-being and social status, health status, life satisfaction and self-actualization, and faith and belief when compared with those female elders who did not get touched.

Caring for elders requires dynamic interventions blending art and science. Suffering and loss are inherent in the daily lives of elders, and impermanence forms a glaring presence that is difficult for the aged to ignore. Although there are many approaches to the ethical care of elderly patients, nurses might adopt an approach to care similar to a way of being suggested by Thich Nhat Hanh (1998) based on the Buddhist *Lotus Sutra*. Thich Nhat Hanh stated that the sutra advises one "to look and listen with the eyes of compassion." He further stated that "compassionate listening brings about healing" (p. 86). Compassionate listening by nurses gives individual elders their voice in an often uncompassionate world.

Case Study: Whose Wishes Should Be Honored?

Mrs. Ryan, a frail 85-year-old woman who lived alone, was admitted to a geriatric psychiatric unit because of irritability, confusion, and increasing incontinence. Mrs. Ryan's family stated that she continually refused assistance from her home health aides and became angry when her family and home care nurses tried to reason with her about these refusals. The patient's family had installed child gates in her home to block her entry into her bathroom, trying to force Mrs. Ryan to use a bedside commode. Mrs. Ryan began having frequent "accidents" of incontinence on the floor near the bathroom door while trying to get through the gates. During her hospital admission, a couple of her medications were adjusted, and she subsequently became calm and cooperative with the care she received while in the hospital. When the RN and social worker talked with Mrs. Ryan about the safety risks of her living in her home alone, the patient stated, "I am 85 years old and think that I should be able to decide how I want to live the remainder of my life. I'm willing to take my chances." Mrs. Ryan was often unsure about the correct day of the week when questioned, yet she knew the name of the hospital and the reason that she was admitted for treatment. She was often confused about the names of the hospital staff but was able to state her own name. Her family continued to insist that Mrs. Ryan be admitted to a long-term care facility and requested that the psychiatrist complete the paperwork so that a judge could have the patient declared incompetent. The psychiatrist did not usually seem sincerely interested in his patients, and he had spent little time with Mrs. Ryan. This psychiatrist was usually willing to comply with families' wishes. The RN and social worker disagreed with the decision to declare Mrs. Ryan incompetent and were in favor of allowing her to return home as she wished.

Case Study Critical Thinking Questions

1. Based on the information provided, does it seem that Mrs. Ryan has decision-making capacity? What criteria can be used as a basis for your decision? What needs to be included in a complete assessment of Mrs. Ryan's decision-making capacity?
2. Does safety at home for Mrs. Ryan seem feasible? If so, how might this be accomplished?
3. What could the RN and social worker do to try to resolve the disagreement among the patient, her family, the doctor, and themselves?
4. Is a form of paternalism being used by any of the people involved in this case? If so, is it a form of weak or justified paternalism? Does the approach seem justified?
5. What type of quality-of-life evaluation is most appropriate in this situation? What is your rationale for this choice?

6. How is the issue of Mrs. Ryan's dignity involved in this case?
7. How might the RN and social worker enter into a discussion of life meaning with Mrs. Ryan? With her family? With the physician?

REFERENCES

Agich, G. J. (2003). *Dependence and autonomy in old age: An ethical framework for long-term care* (2nd and Rev. ed.). Cambridge, UK: Cambridge University.

Allport, G. W. (1984). Preface. In V. E. Frankl, *Man's search for meaning: An introduction to logotherapy* (3rd ed., pp. 7–10). New York: Simon and Schuster.

Beauchamp, T. L. & Childress, J. F. (2001). *Principles of biomedical ethics* (5th ed.). New York: Oxford University.

Bergeron, R. (2000, September). Servicing the needs of elder abuse victims. *Policy and Practice, 40*–45.

Blum, L. A. (1994). *Moral perception and particularity.* Cambridge, UK: Cambridge University.

Butler, R. (1975). *Why survive? Being old in America.* New York: Harper & Row.

Butts, J. B. (2001). Outcomes of comfort touch in institutionalized elderly female residents. *Geriatric Nursing, 22*(4), 180–184.

Butts, J. B. (1998). *Outcomes of comfort touch in institutionalized elderly female residents.* Unpublished doctoral dissertation, University of Alabama at Birmingham.

Butts, J. B. & Rich, K. L. (2004). Acknowledging dependence: A MacIntyrean perspective on relationships involving Alzheimer's disease. *Nursing Ethics, 11*(4), 400–410.

Callahan, D. (1995). *Setting limits: Medical goals in an aging society with "a response to my critics".* Washington, DC: Georgetown University.

Capra, F. (1982). *The turning point: Science, society, and the rising culture.* New York: Bantam.

Cassell, E. J. (1991). *The nature of suffering and the goals of medicine.* New York: Oxford University.

Centers for Disease Control and Prevention (2004). *Fast stats a to z: Life expectancy.* Retrieved December 10, 2004 from http://www.cdc.gov/nchs/fastats/lifexpec.htm.

Chodron, P. (1997). *When things fall apart: Heart advice for difficult times.* Boston: Shambhala.

Chodron, P. (2001). *The places that scare you: A guide to fearlessness in difficult times.* Boston: Shambhala.

Cohen, E. S. (1988). The elderly mystique: Constraints on the autonomy of the elderly with disabilities. *Gerontologist, 28* (Supplement, June), 24–31.

Cole, T. R. (1986). *The tattered web of cultural meanings.* In T. R. Cole & S. Gadow (Eds.), *What does it mean to grow old? Reflections from the humanities* (pp. 3–7). Durham, NC: Duke University.

Daniels, N. (1988). *Am I my parents' keeper?* New York: Oxford University.

de Beauvior, S. (1972). *The coming of age* (P. O'Brien, Trans.). New York: Putnam.

Dossey, B. M., Keegan, L., & Guzzetta, C. E. (2000). *Holistic nursing: A handbook for practice* (3rd ed.). Gaithersburg, MD: Aspen.

Easwaren, E. (1992). *Your life is your message: Finding harmony with yourself, others, and the earth.* New York: Hyperion.

Erikson, E. H. & Erikson, J. M. (1997). *The life cycle completed* (extended version). New York: W. W. Norton.

Erlen, J. A. (2002). Ethics in chronic illness. In I. M. Lubkin & P. D. Larsen (Eds.), *Chronic illness: Impact and interventsion* (5th ed., pp. 407–429). Boston: Jones and Bartlett.

Faden, R. & German, P. S. (1994). Quality of life: Considerations in geriatrics. *Clinics in Geriatric Medicine, 19*(3), 541–551.

Frankl, V. E. (1984). *Man's search for meaning: An introduction to logotherapy* (3rd ed.). New York: Simon and Schuster.

Greening, T. (1998). Viktor Frankl, 1905-1997. *Journal of Humanistic Psychology, 38*(1), 10–11.

Hall, B. A. (2003). An essay on an authentic meaning of medicalization: The patient's perspective. *Advances in Nursing Science, 26*(1), 53–62.

Hester, D. M. (2001). *Community as healing: Pragmatist ethics in medical encounters.* Lanham, MD: Rowman & Littlefield.

Hillman, J. (1999). *The force of character and the lasting life.* New York: Ballantine.

Jenkins, D., & Price, B. (1996). Dementia and personhood: A focus for care? *Journal of Advanced Nursing, 24*(1), 84–90.

Jones, L. B. (1998). *Grow something besides old: Seeds for a joyful life.* New York: Simon and Schuster.

Jonsen, A. R., Siegler, M., & Winslade, W. J. (2002). *Clinical ethics: A practical approach to ethical decisions in clinical medicine* (5th ed.). New York: McGraw Hill.

Kitwood, T. (1997). *Dementia reconsidered: The person comes first.* Buckingham, UK: Open University.

Lao Tzu (1989). *Tao teh ching* (J.C.H. Wu, Trans.). Boston: Shambhala. (Original work published 1961)

Lubkin, I. M. & Larsen, P. D. (2002). What is chronicity? In I. M. Lubkin & P. D. Larsen (Eds.), *Chronic illness: Impact and interventions* (5th ed., pp. 3–24). Boston: Jones and Bartlett Publishers.

MacIntyre, A. (1999). *Dependent rational animals: Why human beings need the virtues.* Chicago: Open Court.

May, W. F. (1986). The virtues and vices of the elderly. In T. R. Cole & S. Gadow (Eds.), *What does it mean to grow old? Reflections from the humanities* (pp. 43–61). Durham, NC: Duke University.

Mencken, H. L. (1942). *A new dictionary of quotations on historical principles from ancient and modern sources.* New York: Alfred A. Knopf.

Moody, H. R. (1992). *Ethics in an aging society.* Baltimore: Johns Hopkins University.

Peterson, R. (Ed.). (2002). *Mayo Clinic on Alzheimer's disease.* Rochester, MN: Mayo Clinic.

Pullman, D. (1998). The ethics of autonomy and dignity in long-term care. *Canadian Journal on Aging, 18*(1), 26–46.

Ramsey, S. B. (2000). Abusive situations. In S. W. Killion & K. Dempski (Eds.), *Quick look nursing: Legal and ethical issues* (pp. 58–59). Thorofare, NJ: Slack.

Savishinsky, J. S. (1991). *The ends of time: Life and work in a nursing home.* New York: Bergin and Garvey.

Smith, N. L., Kotthoff-Burrell, E., & Post, L. F. (2002). Protecting the patient's voice on team. In M. D. Mezey, C. K. Cassel, M. M. Bottrell, K, Hyer, J. L. Howe, & T. T. Fulmer (Eds.), *Ethical patient care: A casebook for geriatric health care teams* (pp. 83–101). Baltimore: Johns Hopkins.

Solomon, A. (2001). *The noonday demon: An atlas of depression.* New York: Scribner.

Stanley, B., Sieber, J. E., & Melton, G. B. (2003). Empirical studies of ethical issues in research: A research agenda. In D. N. Bersoff (Ed.), *Ethical conflicts in psychology* (3rd ed., pp. 398–402). Washington, DC: American Psychological Association.

Thich Nhat Hanh (1998). *The heart of the Buddha's teaching: Transforming suffering into peace, joy and liberation.* New York: Broadway.

Thich Nhat Hanh (2001). In R. Ellsberg, Ed., *Thich Nhat Hanh: Essential writings.* New York: Orbis.

Tornstam, L. (1993). Genotranscendence: A theoretical and empirical exploration. In L. E. Thomas & S. A. Eisenhandler (Eds.), Aging and the religious dimension, Westport, CT: Greenwood Publishing Group.

Travelbee, J. (1971). *Interpersonal aspects of nursing* (2nd ed.). Philadelphia: F. A. Davis.

CHAPTER 9

Community and Public Health Nursing and Leadership Ethics

Karen L. Rich

To be a [person] is, precisely to be responsible. It is to feel shame at the sight of what seems to be unmerited misery . . . It is to feel, when setting one's stone, that one is contributing to the building of the world.

Antoine De Saint-Exupery, *A Guide For Grown-Ups: Essential Wisdom From the Collected Works*

SUMMARY

1. Members of a community have a shared interest in a common good.
2. Communities are moral in nature.
3. The epicenter of communitarian ethics is the community rather than the individual perspective of any one person.
4. Using moral imagination helps nurses suspend quick judgments and use empathetic reflection to see "what *could* be."
5. Servant leaders view themselves as servants first and leaders second.
6. A person who exhibits the virtue of just generosity does not give to others merely in proportion to what the giver perceives they are due but, instead, gives to others based on their need.

7. Humans will not achieve true moral progress until people perceive the suffering of others who are not personally known to them as important in their daily lives.

COMMUNITY BUILDING

In their own way, community/public health (C/PH) nurses are contributors to the building of the world. Although the terms "community health nursing" and "public health nursing" are sometimes differentiated, the terms have not been distinguished in this chapter. The following eight tenets of community/public health nursing outlined by the Quad Council of Public Health Nursing Organizations (1999) have been proposed as the primary basis of C/PH nursing care.

1. Population-based assessment, policy development, and assurance processes are systematic and comprehensive.
2. All processes must include partnering with representatives of the people.
3. Primary prevention is given priority.
4. Intervention strategies are selected to create healthy environmental, social, and economic conditions in which people can thrive.
5. Public health nursing practice includes an obligation to actively reach out to all who might benefit from an intervention or service.
6. The dominant concern and obligation is for the greater good of all of the people or the population as a whole.
7. Stewardship and allocation of available resources supports the maximum population health benefit gain.
8. The health of the people is most effectively promoted and protected through collaboration with members of other professions and organizations (pp. 2–4).

The fundamental purpose of C/PH nursing is consistent with the purpose articulated by the United States Department of Health and Human Services (DHHS) (2000) in the national public health agenda outlined in *Healthy People 2010*. The purpose of this national agenda is "promoting health and preventing illness, disability, and premature death" (p. 1). The goals of C/PH nursing are likewise consistent with those of *Healthy People 2010* and include an intention to "increase quality and years of healthy life" and to "eliminate health disparities" among the public (p. 2).

"Population" is the term used to describe the recipients of the health promotion and illness and disability prevention care that is the primary focus of C/PH nursing. In this chapter, a *population* is defined as a group of people who share at least one common descriptive characteristic but who do not necessarily have a collective commitment to a common good. The name or label used to denote the population is often related to the common characteristic(s) of those people who make up the population, such as male alcoholics or pregnant teenagers. People within populations may or may not interact or share in a collective dialogue.

The ethical approach that has been described in this chapter is based on communitarian ethics. A *community* is a group of persons who have a shared interest in a common good, and the various members of the group have the potential to share in a collective dialogue about their common good.

Box 9-1

ETHICAL Kaleidoscope   Community

Community. A word of many connotations—a word overused until its meanings are so diffuse as to be almost useless. Yet the images it evokes, the deep longings and memories it can stir, represent something that human beings have created and recreated since time immemorial, out of our profound need for connection among ourselves and with Mother Earth.

Helen Forsey, 1993, Circles of Strength: Community Alternatives
to Alienation, p. 1.

Membership in the community forms some part of each member's identity. The sharing in a commitment to promote the community's well-being, which transcends individual interests and goals, makes personal relationships within the community moral in nature. Members of a community may or may not share close geographic boundaries; however, if members of a community share some type of geographic boundaries, the primary moral connection among the members is not based solely on that geography. Nurses, patients, and other people in society are usually members of more than one community. A nurse would be a member of the community of registered nurses who are collectively committed to the common good of alleviating patients' suffering and promoting patients' well-being. The same nurse also could be a member of a faith community, a member of a geographic neighborhood community that is interested in the common good of the neighbors, and a member of a parent–teacher organization, which is also a community.

Even when C/PH nurses are working toward health promotion and illness and disability prevention with populations, in moral or ethical terms, they are encouraged to view those people in the target population as members of a moral community. A moral community can be as large as the global community, the members of which are generally committed to the common good of the inhabitants of earth, to a small community of senior nursing students at a university. The common good of a community of nursing students might be related to achieving the primary goal of the students, which is collectively obtaining professional nursing status while maintaining individual physical and psychological well-being. The student community accomplishes its goal through the members' shared commitment to provide emotional support and to help one another in moving toward the successful completion of state board tests. An even smaller community might be a family that is committed to common goals beyond the individual personal goals of family members.

Community-based nursing is the practice of nursing in settings other than in acute care inpatient settings, such as nursing care delivered in homes, ambulatory clinics, or schools. Community-based nursing might be focused on individuals, families, communities, or populations. When care is directed toward communities, the well-being and needs of the individuals that form the communities should not be overlooked. The relationship between individual and community health has been highlighted in statements in *Healthy People 2010* (2000).

> Over the years, it has become clear that individual health is closely linked to community health—the health of the community and environment in which individuals live, work, and play. Likewise, community health is profoundly affected by the collective beliefs, attitudes, and behaviors of everyone who lives in the community. Indeed, the underlying premise of *Healthy People 2010* is that the health of the individual is almost inseparable from the health of the larger community and that the health of every community in every State and territory determines the overall health status of the Nation. That is why the vision of *Healthy People 2010* is "Healthy People in Healthy Communities" (p. 3).

The differentiation of community-based as opposed to non–community-based nursing does not negate the fact that communities can exist in acute care inpatient facilities. However, patients in acute care inpatient settings, other than being a part of a local community of townspeople interested in a common good or being members of the global community, usually are not bound together by an investment in a common good, even when they have a common medical diagnosis. For example, patients might be considered part of a group of end-stage renal disease patients, but the patients are not invested in working together toward a common good and do not enter into a communal dialogue. Therefore, this group of patients would be a population, not a community. However, if a group of patients know one another from weekly visits to a local dialysis unit and are interested in the well-being of one another as a group, a community may exist. Another example of a community may be patients with cystic fibrosis and their families that know one another from frequent hospital admissions and who form a supportive community.

Communities important to nurses' moral relationships include more than patient communities. They might include a group of nurses who work at a particular community-based agency or hospital or, for example, the multidisciplinary group of health care staff who work in an emergency department or for a hospice agency. The staff forms a cohesive group that is concerned about their common goals in providing health care to patients as well as being concerned about the well-being of one another and participating in communal dialogue. The formation of communities of multidisciplinary health care workers facilitates C/PH nurses in the successful fulfillment of the tenet of the Quad Council of Public Health Nursing Organizations (1999) that "the health of the people is most effectively promoted and protected through collaboration with members of other professions and organizations" (p. 4).

COMMUNITARIAN ETHICS

There is no power for change greater than a community discovering what it cares about.

Margaret Wheatley, *Turning to One Another*

Although communitarian ethics can apply to all types of nursing, when one is focusing on C/PH nursing it is essential to keep in mind the eight tenets that distinguish C/PH nursing from other types of nursing before considering the philosophy of communitarian ethics. It is also important to understand that because of the relationships involved, a community has a "moral nature." A population does not. Communitarian ethics is based on the position that "everything fundamental in ethics derives from communal values, the common good, social goals, traditional practices, and cooperative virtues (Beauchamp & Childress, 2001, p. 362). Communitarian ethics is relevant with regard to moral relationships in any community.

The notion that communitarian ethics is based on the model of friendships and relationships that existed in the ancient Greek city-states described by Aristotle was popularized in modern times by the philosopher and ethicist Alasdair MacIntyre (1984) in his book, *After Virtue*. However, in general societal ethics and bioethics, the valuing of and perspective toward community relationships has come to mean different things to different people (Beauchamp & Childress, 2001).

It is noteworthy that some ethicists have tried to draw a strong distinction between ethical approaches that emphasize the value of individualism and autonomy as opposed to the group cohesion and goal-directed behavior emphasized by communitarian ethics. However, it is reasonable to assume that most people are interested in their own well-being as well as being interested in the values and goals of the communities to which they belong. Communitarian ethics as an ethical approach is distinguished because the epicenter of communitarian ethics is the community rather than any one individual (Wildes, 2000). Populations, in general, and moral communities, in particular, are also the starting points for C/PH nursing.

The value of discussing and articulating an approach to communitarian ethics seems to lie in the benefit that can be gained through illuminating and appreciating the relationships and interconnections between people that are often overlooked in everyday life (see Box 9-2). Although personal moral goals are significant, the importance of forming strong communities and identifying the moral goals of those communities must not be neglected in order for both individuals and communities to flourish.

Box 9-2

ETHICAL Kaleidoscope   The Net of Indra

The Buddhist *Avatamsaka Sutra* contains a story about how all perceiving, thinking beings are connected in a way that is similar to a universal community. The story is about the heavenly net of the god Indra. "In the heaven of Indra, there is said to be a network of pearls, so arranged that if you look at one you see all the others reflected in it. In the same way each object in the world is not merely itself but involves every other object and in fact is everything else. In every particle of dust there is present Buddhas without number."

Sir Charles Eliot, as cited in F. Capra (1999). The Tao of Physics (p. 296).

Another important distinction that can legitimately be drawn between communitarian and other popular ethical approaches, such as deontological or rule-based ethics, is based on the proposal of communitarian ethicists that it is natural for humans to favor the people with whom they live and have frequent interactions. Deontologists base their ethics on a more impartial stance toward the persons who are the receivers of their morally related actions.

Nevertheless, from a communitarian perspective, partiality as a way of relating to others does not have to exclude caring about those people who are personally unknown to moral agents. Although it is often easier for people to care about and have compassion for those people who are closest to them in terms of relationships, it is not unrealistic to believe that people also can develop empathy or compassion toward others who are personally unknown to them. Such behavior and expectations are an integral part of Buddhist philosophy, for example. Accepting the notion that humans usually are more partial to those people to whom they are most closely related, while at the same time believing that it is possible to expand the scope of their empathy and compassion to unknown others, broadens the sphere of morality in communitarian ethics.

Nussbaum (2004) suggested that people often develop an "us" versus "them" mentality, especially when violence occurs among various groups and significant cultural differences separate them. People are able to generate sympathy, or fellow-feeling, when they hear about epidemics and disasters occurring on continents that are far away, but it is usually difficult for people to sustain the sympathy for more than a short period of time. People tend to stop and notice others' needs and then soon turn back to their own personal lives. According to Nussbaum, humanity will "achieve no lasting moral progress unless and until the daily unremarkable lives of people distant from us become real in the fabric of our own daily lives" (p. 958) and until people include others that they do not know personally within the important sphere of their lives (see Box 9-3).

C/PH nurses must broaden their scope of concern to include people affected by health care disparities, diseases, and epidemics all over the world.

"All communities have some organizing vision about the meaning of life and how one ought to conduct a good life" (Wildes, 2000, p. 129). C/PH nurses have an important role in bringing populations and communities together to work toward a common humanitarian good. Transforming communities from a "them" versus "us" mentality to one that seeks a common good is possible through education (Nussbaum, 2004). "Children [and people] at all ages must learn to recognize people in other countries as their fellows, and to sympathize with their plights. Not just their dramatic plights, in a cyclone or war, but their daily plights" (p. 959). This need for empathetic understanding is also important in one's own country, state, city, town, or neighborhood. Many people of all ages are suffering in the United States and throughout the world because they lack adequate health care, proper food, and adequate environmental sanitation and housing.

Box 9-3

ETHICAL Kaleidoscope   The Delusion of Separateness

A human being is a part of the whole called by us universe, a part limited in time and space. He experiences himself, his thoughts and feelings as something separated from the rest, a kind of optical delusion of his consciousness. This delusion is a kind of prison for us, restricting us to our personal desires and to affection for a few persons nearest to us. Our task must be to free ourselves from this prison by widening our circle of compassion to enhance all living creatures and the whole of nature in its beauty.

Albert Einstein

The education of communities often occurs through role modeling (Wildes, 2000). Members of communities learn about what is and is not accepted as moral through personal and group interaction and dialogue within their communities. Narratives are told about the lives of exemplars, such as Florence Nightingale in nursing, to illustrate moral living. By her efforts to improve social justice and health protection through environmental measures and her efforts to elevate the character of nurses, Nightingale exhibited moral concern for her local society, the nursing profession, and people remote from her local associations, such as those affected by the Crimean War. In learning from Nightingale's example, communitarian-minded C/PH nurses are in an excellent position to educate the public and other nurses and health care professionals about why they in many ways should assume the role of being their brother's and sister's keepers.

Ethical Reflections

- Have you noticed "us" versus "them" thinking in members of the nursing community? In the community of health care professionals? If so, what effect has this thinking had on relationships between members of the particular community?
- Should one even consider that a community exists when there is "us" versus "them" thinking among the members? Why or why not?
- What patient populations might be particularly susceptible to having other people approach them as "us" versus "them"? How can nurses change this type of thinking?
- To what communities do you belong? What can be identified as the common good of each of these communities?

Moral Imagination

[Persons], to be greatly good, must imagine intensely and comprehensively; [they] must put [themselves] in the place of another and of many others . . . The great instrument of moral good is the imagination.

Percy Bysshe Shelley, *Defense of Poetry*

Some ethicists have associated a communitarian approach to morality with the artistic inquiry involved with having a moral imagination (Fesmire, 2003; Hester, 2001; Johnson, 1993). The foundation underlying the concept of moral imagination, or an artistic or aesthetic approach to ethics, is based on the philosophy of the American philosopher John Dewey (1859–1952).

Imagination, as Dewey proposed it, is "the capacity to concretely perceive what is before us in light of what could be" (Fesmire, 2003, p. 65). Dewey (1934) stated that imagination "is a *way* of seeing and feeling things as they compose an integral whole" (p. 267). *Moral imagination* is moral decision making through reflection that involves "empathetic projection" and "creatively tapping a situation's possibilities" (Fesmire, 2003, p. 65). It involves moral awareness and decision making that goes beyond the mere application of standardized ethical meanings, decision-making models, and bioethical principles to real life situations.

The use of empathetic projection helps nurses be responsive to patients' feelings, attitudes, and values. To creatively reflect on a situation's possibilities helps prevent nurses from becoming stuck in their daily routines and to instead look for new and different possibilities in problem solving that go beyond mere habitual behaviors. Although

Aristotle taught that habit is the way that people cultivate moral virtues, Dewey (1922/1988) cautioned that mindless habits can be "blinders that confine the eyes of mind to the road ahead" (p. 121). Dewey proposed that habit should be combined with intellectual impulse. He stated:

> Habits by themselves are too organized, too insistent and determinate to need to indulge in inquiry or imagination. And impulses are too chaotic, tumultuous and confused to be able to know even if they wanted to . . . A certain delicate combination of habit and impulse is requisite for observation, memory and judgment (p. 124).

Dewey (1910/1997) provided an example of a physician trying to identify a patient's diagnosis without proper reflection. Although Dewey's example is about an individual patient–physician relationship, the example is also applicable for nurses in illustrating the dangers of rushing to conclusions in the practice of the art and science of nursing with both individuals and populations.

> Imagine a doctor being called in to prescribe for a patient. The patient tells him some things that are wrong; his experienced eye, at a glance, takes in other signs of a certain disease. But if he permits the suggestion of this special disease to take possession prematurely of his mind, to become an accepted conclusion, his scientific thinking is by that much cut short. A large part of his technique, as a skilled practitioner, is to prevent the acceptance of the first suggestions that arise; even, indeed, to postpone the occurrence of any very definite suggestions till the trouble—the nature of the problem—has been thoroughly explored. In the case of a physician this proceeding is known as a diagnosis, but a similar inspection is required in every novel and complicated situation to prevent rushing to a conclusion (p. 74).

Dewey (1910/1997) seemed to be trying to make the point that critical thinking requires suspended judgment until problems and situations are fully explored and reflected upon. Moral imagination includes engaging in frequent considerations of "what if?" with regard to day-to-day life events as well as in novel situations. In a public interview on July 22, 2004, immediately after the US Congress released its 9/11 Commission Report, Senator Thomas Kean made a statement with regard to the Commission's findings about the probable causes of the failure to prevent the terrorist attacks on September 11, 2001 (Mondics, 2004). Senator Kean stated that, above all, there was a "failure of imagination" (p. A4).

An important role of C/PH nurses is to provide community leadership and to help create healthy communities through population-based assessment, program planning, program implementation, and evaluation. When assuming this key leadership role, C/PH nurses must continually make choices and decisions that may affect the well-being of large groups of people. Opinions must not be hastily formed, nor should actions be taken without nurses cultivating and using their moral imaginations.

SERVICE LEARNING

Service learning, or "academic experiences in which students engage both in social action and in reflection on their experiences in performing that action" (Piliavin, 2003, p. 235), is ideally suited for supporting the moral development of C/PH nursing students. Kaye (2004) defined *service learning* as "a teaching method where guided or classroom learning is deepened through service to others in a process that provides structured time for reflection on the service experience and demonstration of the skills and knowledge acquired" (p. 7). Service learning is a means for students and teachers to work with community leaders and agencies in collaboratively identifying and working toward a common good. All participants, including teachers, agency administrators, and staff, learn from the students during their interactions with them while the students benefit from developing an increase in community awareness. In service learning "community develops and builds through interaction, reciprocal relationships, and knowledge of people, places, organizations, governments, and systems" (Kaye, 2004, p. 8). Service learning helps fulfill the tenet of C/PH nursing that "all processes must include partnering with representatives of the people" (Quad Council, 1999, p. 3).

Service is usually focused on direct or indirect services, advocacy, or research (Kaye, 2004). In direct services, person to person interactions occur between students and the recipients of the students' work. Direct services may be aimed at students developing a broader awareness of the needs and issues of varying cultures, populations, or age groups; for example, people with AIDS, a homeless population, or elderly persons attending adult day care. A whole community or the environment is the focus of indirect service learning interventions, such as activities aimed at helping to organize and implement a community-wide health education program about safe sex or organizing an effort to decrease pollution of a local waterway. Advocacy—which is a key role of C/PH nursing—combined with service learning involves creating and supporting change in communities to benefit people in the community. Advocacy includes grass roots societal and political activism, such as working to educate a city council about the unmet needs of people with AIDS in the city. Service learning provides an excellent opportunity for students to become involved in community research. Students can participate in developing and conducting surveys and gathering, analyzing, and reporting data regarding issues of public health concern.

Student reflection on service learning experiences is an integral and defining part of service learning. It is in this area that the students' moral imaginations and the development of intelligent habits are cultivated. Reflection helps service learners to consider the "big picture" in working for the good of communities. Reflective experiences can be guided through activities such as journal writing or teacher-led group discussions and processing of experiences. Service learners may benefit from thinking in terms of the intersecting human narratives that exist among themselves, their community collaborators, and the recipients of their services.

Ethical Reflections

- Conduct a literature review about service learning in nursing. Develop suggestions for service learning experiences that focus on each of the following: direct, indirect, advocacy, and research services.
- Explain why service learning is related to ethics in leadership and C/PH nursing.

SERVANT LEADERSHIP

Number five of the eight tenets of C/PH nursing listed at the beginning of this chapter proclaims that "public health nursing practice includes an obligation to actively reach out to all who might benefit from an intervention or service" (Quad Council, 1999, p. 4). Tenet number six includes the directive that "the dominant concern and obligation is for the greater good of all of the people or the population as a whole" (Quad Council, 1999, p. 4). Both of these tenets are closely aligned with the need for servant leadership in C/PH nursing.

In the late 1960s and early 1970s, Robert Greenleaf (2002) was one of several business people who developed and articulated the concept of servant leadership in management. Greenleaf developed the idea of servant leadership after reading the book *Journey to the East* written by Herman Hesse (1956). Hesse's book relates a story about a servant named Leo who is on a journey to the East with a group of men, members of a mysterious League, who are on a mission to find spiritual renewal. Leo brings the group together as a community with his spirit and songs. When Leo decides to leave the group, the small community becomes dysfunctional and disbands. Later, one of the journeymen discovers that, unknown to the journeymen, Leo was really the head of the League that had sponsored their original journey.

Leo was a noble leader who had chosen the role of a servant, a servant whose leadership was of the utmost importance to the sense of community of the journeying group. Greenleaf (2002) proposed that Hesse's story clearly exemplifies a *servant leader* through the portrayal of Leo. He suggested that "*the great leader is seen as servant first*, and that simple fact is the key to his [or her] greatness" (p. 21). In the story, even while Leo was directly in the role of the leader of his Order, he viewed himself first and foremost as a servant (see Box 9-4).

Box 9-4

ETHICAL Kaleidoscope   The Nature of Service

During a Midwestern storm of rain, hail, lightning, and thunder, my mother stopped at the grocery store and asked me to run in for a loaf of bread. As I prepared to get out of the car, I noticed little Janie running down the street. She wore her usual tattered clothes, and her bald head, the result of some condition unknown to me, was unprotected from the hail. Many of our schoolmates teased her, judging her as inferior because of her poverty and appearance. I jumped out of the car and gave her my raincoat. She put it over her head and continued running. I remember thinking, "I am here to help others." I was ten years old.

Susan S. Trout (1997). Born to Serve (p. 13).

Servant leaders who see themselves first as servants, at some later point in time make the choice to lead while serving. Those people who are more concerned with leading *before* serving usually are motivated by a desire for power or to obtain material possessions, although a concurrent secondary motivation to serve is possible. Greenleaf (2002) explained how to distinguish between a servant-first leader and a leader who views service as a secondary or lower priority.

> The difference manifests itself in the care taken by the servant-first [leader] to make sure that other people's highest priority needs are being served. The best test, and difficult to administer, is this: Do those served grow as persons? Do they, while being served, become healthier, wiser, freer, more autonomous, more likely themselves to become servants? And, what is the effect on the least privileged in society? Will they benefit or at least not be further deprived (p. 27)?

When thinking about servant leadership, it is important to note that the role of the *servant follower* is as important as that of the servant leader. If there are no servant followers, or seekers, great leaders are not recognized because there is no one with the awareness to recognize them. "If one is *servant*, leader or follower, one is always searching, listening, expecting that a better wheel for these times is in the making" (Greenleaf, 2003, p. 24).

Covey (2002) defined servant leadership as being consistent with moral authority and proposed that servant leaders and servant followers are, in reality, both followers. They are both followers because both are following the truth. *Moral authority* was described in terms of conscience and includes four dimensions.

1. Sacrifice is the heart of moral authority or conscience. Sacrifice involves an elevated recognition of one's small, peaceful inner voice while subduing the selfish voice of one's ego.

2. Being inspired to become involved with a cause that is worth one's commitment to it. A worthy cause inspires people to change their "question from asking *what is it we want* to *what is being asked of us*" (p. 7). One's conscience is expanded and becomes a factor of great influence in one's life.

3. The inseparableness of any ends and means. Moral leaders do not use unethical means to reach ends; and as the philosopher Kant advocated (see Kantianism in Chapter 1), servant leaders must always treat others as ends in themselves, never as a means to an end.

4. The importance of relationships is enlivened through the development of conscience. "Conscience transforms passion into compassion" (Covey, 2002, p. 9). Living according to one's conscience emphasizes the reality of the interdependence of people and relationships. In relation to this fourth dimension of moral authority, Covey related a story told by a nursing student, JoAnn C. Jones (see Box 9-5).

Box 9-5

ETHICAL Kaleidoscope   "All are Significant"

During my second year of nursing school, our professor gave us a quiz. I breezed through the questions until I read the last one. "What is the first name of the woman who cleans the school?" Surely this was a joke. I had seen the cleaning woman several times but how would I know her name? I handed in my paper, leaving the last question blank. Before the class ended, one student asked if the last question would count toward our grade. "Absolutely," the professor said. "In your careers, you will meet many people—all are significant. They deserve your attention and care. Even if all you do is smile and say hello." I have never forgotten that lesson. I also learned her name was Dorothy (Covey, 2002).

Covey, S., 2002, Servant Leadership, p. 10.

Ethical Reflections

- Reflect and write a narrative about why you want(ed) to become a nurse.
- Was (is) your primary motivation one of wanting to be a servant or a leader? Has your perception of the servant/leadership role changed over time? How?
- If you were a nursing manager of a home health agency, describe how you could see yourself being a servant leader.

JUSTICE

> *To a [disciple] the Master said, "I fear you are doing more harm*
> *than good."*
> *"Why"*
> *"Because you stress only one of the two imperatives of justice."*
> *"Namely?"*
> *"The poor have a right to bread."*
> *"What's the other one?"*
> *"The poor have a right to beauty."*
>
> Anthony De Mello, *One Minute Nonsense*

Justice can be viewed in terms of what rights or resources should be accorded to persons or populations or what is their due. This type of justice was discussed in Chapter 1. Justice also can be approached in terms of involving a duty in relation to "the other," which Pieper (1966) proposed is what distinguishes justice from love. Love does not distinguish between oneself and the one who is loved, whereas justice, as a duty in relation to "the other," highlights the separateness of people and encompasses an approach to justice as (almost) occurring between strangers. With this conception of justice, one views other individuals or people in a population as other than oneself but recognizes that these others have what is their own particular due. Persons are considered just if they provide others with their due, even though they view the other(s) as separate from themselves.

Just Generosity

As discussed in Chapter 2, there is another perspective of justice that is more communitarian in nature: *just generosity*. It is a view of justice that highlights human connections and not separateness. Pieper (1966) went so far as to proclaim that "the subject of justice is the 'community'" (p. 70). Indebtedness is the hallmark of justice, and although the concept of justice as a stand-alone virtue is important to communitarian ethics, the combination of the virtue of justice with the virtue of generosity expands the scope of communitarian justice.

Thinking and acting in terms of the comprehensive virtue of just generosity sometimes requires the use of one's moral imagination to see the larger picture because people are accustomed to thinking in the limited terms of the individual virtues of justice and generosity. Whereas justice involves giving others what they are due, generosity involves giving from a source that is somehow personal. The ability to fuse the single virtues of justice and generosity into a combined active virtue is important in creating flourishing communities.

The virtue of just generosity is based on one's motivation to actively participate in a community-centered network of giving and receiving. A person, or nurse, who exhibits the virtue of just generosity does not give merely in proportion to what the individual receiver or community is perceived as being due but instead gives to persons or communities based on the receivers' or community's need. The giver believes in, and does more than dispassionately allocating or distributing resources. The person possessing the trait of just generosity gives from resources that in some way touch the giver personally, which may not necessarily involve the giving of something that is material or tangible but often involves what might be called giving from one's heart.

Salamon (2003) in her book, *Rambam's Ladder,* adapted the Jewish physician and philosopher Maimonides' (1135–1204) "ladder of charity" for contemporary use. Salamon's book provides a meditation on generosity and underscores that an awareness of the need for giving has become more important than ever in a post 9/11 world. Salamon's ladder of charity starts, as did Maimonides' ladder, with the bottom rung representing the least generous motivation for giving and progressing to the top of the ladder with the top step of the ladder being what Salamon proposed to be the highest form of giving. The eight steps of the ladder are listed below beginning with the lowest.

1. To give begrudgingly.
2. To give less to the poor than is proper, but to do so cheerfully.
3. To hand money to the poor after being asked.
4. To hand money to the poor before being asked, but risk making the recipient feel shame.
5. To give to someone you don't know, but allow your name to be known.
6. To give to someone you know, but who doesn't know from whom he is receiving help.
7. To give to someone you don't know, and to do so anonymously.
8. At the top of the ladder is the gift of self-reliance. To hand someone a gift or a loan or, to enter into a partnership with him or to find work for him so that he will never have to beg again (Salamon, 2003, Introduction).

C/PH nurses can use the ladder of charity as a gauge of the type of giving that occurs within communities while keeping their eyes focused on aiming for the top step of the ladder. C/PH nurses do not directly give money to people and usually do not even give material resources to them; however, nurses' service to others can be substituted for monetary or material giving in the steps of the ladder. Salamon (2003) herself recognized that monetary giving is not always the primary means of generosity.

Nurses might ask themselves whether they give begrudgingly during their work or work from a motivation of a generous servant, hoping to affect the well-being of those in a population or community who will not even know how the (nurse's) service has positively affected them and their health. Must the individual and community recipients of the services of C/PH nurses directly ask for each of their specific needs to be met, or do nurses use their moral imaginations and anticipate needs, reflecting and acting on the big picture that may not be readily apparent to them unless they suspend their initial judgments? When just generosity is consistent with the top step of the ladder, C/PH nurses enter into community partnerships and teach others to be responsible for helping themselves and their communities so that community members and, ultimately, whole communities become self-reliant when possible.

HEALTH DISPARITIES

After the first goal of aiming to "increase quality and years of healthy life" (p. 8), the second goal of *Healthy People 2010* (US DHHS, 2000) "is to eliminate health disparities among segments of the population, including differences that occur by gender, race or ethnicity, education or income, disability, geographic location, or sexual orientation" (p. 11). Eliminating health disparities is a moral issue for C/PH nurses and servant leaders because communitarian ethics is based on building flourishing communities that support the common good of all community members. A major concern of bioethicists is the recognition that people's health and access to health care is adversely affected in proportion to their lack of power and privilege in a society (Sherwin, 1992). Consequently, poverty and the placement of people within the margins of society are key factors in the determination of public health. When some people in communities are suffering or are in need, all in the communities are affected, even if it is in what seem to be imperceptible ways. One must only think about the hypothetical Net of Indra (see Ethical Kaleidoscope Box 9-2) to imagine how this situation can be a reality.

In considering the national public health agenda, people customarily use the limited frame of reference of justice in the form of distributive justice, or the fair allocation of national resources. Whether one approaches the *Healthy People 2010* (2000) agenda with a conceptual outlook of what is fair or what is another's due or from a broader perspective of just generosity, it is important to recognize the justice-related aim of the agenda. The aim is that "every person in every community across the Nation deserves equal access to comprehensive, culturally competent, community-based health care systems that are committed to serving the needs of the individual and promoting community health" (p. 16).

In aiming for practice consistent with the top step of Salamon's (2003) ladder of charity, C/PH nurses need to play a role in helping communities accept the responsibility and develop the capacity to help themselves in resolving problems that lead to health disparities. One coordinated plan to address public health concerns involves four phases or themes: community participation, community mobilization, commitment to social justice, and the leadership challenge (Berkowitz et al., 2001).

C/PH nurses can support members of communities in participating in the validation of suspected problems through investigation and research and in building partnerships to collaborate on policy development. C/PH nurses facilitate community mobilization by educating members of the community regarding health promotion and health protection measures that would be likely to improve the lives of those in the community. Teaching people in the community about how to begin grassroots political efforts to obtain needed resources is an important advocacy role of C/PH nurses. Being committed to social justice requires C/PH nurses to speak out about health disparities to other nurses and health care professionals, to a wide group of community members, and to politicians. In helping communities increase participation, mobilize action, and expand social justice, the leadership challenge for C/PH nurses is to "act as a resource, consultant, facilitator, educator, advocate, and role model" (Berkowitz et al., 2001, p. 53).

A widely accepted approach to organizing communities in efforts to address their health disparity and social justice problems has been based on the thought that health care professionals must appeal to the self-interest of the community and its members (Minkler & Pies, 2002). However, Minkler and Pies argued that this traditional approach often only further divides groups of people by furthering the notion of individualism and separateness that is already a divisive way of thinking in our society. This approach does not support community interest in a common good.

A basic utilitarian philosophy, which advocates the greatest good for the most people as a representation of the common good in local communities, also is not advocated as a simple answer to organizing community activism (Minkler & Pies, 2002). A simple utilitarian perspective does not facilitate a broad approach to envisioning a just society in terms of health disparities. Those leaders who are limited to this view risk being narrowly focused only on the common good of local communities rather than, more importantly, being concerned with the larger society and thinking in a global sense.

Minkler and Pies (2002) adapted a feminist approach to social change (originally proposed by Charlotte Bunch in 1983) as an agenda for trying to eliminate disparities in the equitable distribution of community resources. Historically, feminist philosophers and activists have approached their agenda in terms of the disparities experienced by women. Therefore, a feminist approach can often be applied with other marginalized populations. Minkler and Pies' approach can be used in building a bridge that connects local community efforts to eliminate disparities with efforts that can be used to address more global social concerns. Nurses and other health care professionals working with community members who are involved in organizing to facilitate change can ask: (1) Does [the community organizing effort] materially improve the lives of community members and if so, which members and how many? (2) Does [participating in the organizing process] give community members a sense of power, strength and imagination as a group and help build structures for further changes? and (3) Does the struggle...educate community members politically, enhancing their ability to criticize and challenge the system in the future (pp. 132–133)?

Ethical Reflections

- What is meant by the term "marginalized populations"? Identify populations that may be marginalized in regard to health disparities and discuss why this may be so.
- Reflect on and discuss ways that appeals to self-interest in addressing health disparities might divide people and communities. How might utilitarian appeals limit a broad focus?

INFECTIOUS DISEASES

Public health advances in the 20th century dramatically decreased morbidity and mortality from infectious diseases in the United States, and because of this progress, national health officials began to lose interest in funding and promoting research directed at infectious disease treatment and control (Centers for Disease Control [CDC], 2003). However, people in the government, health care systems, and the general public have begun to recognize that humanity's fight against infectious diseases is neverending (Markel, 2004). Societies are still tormented by diseases that have affected the public's health since ancient times while new infections loom large in the future. In her book about the global collapse of the public health care system, Garrett (2000) stated "we now live in comfortable ignorance about the health and well-being of people in faraway places. But in truth we are never very far away from the experiences of our forebears" (p. xii).

Although President Clinton presented a budget to Congress in 1999 requesting $1.4 billion to support biological and chemical antiterrorism preparedness, the terrorist attacks on September 11, 2001, and the anthrax-laced letters that followed this event, have highlighted the possible dangers of infectious diseases invading society (Farmer, 2001). Paul Farmer, a physician at the Harvard Medical School who also travels to central Haiti to work at the Clinique Bone Sauveur, proposed that the hysteria that ensued from the anthrax letter scare reinforced a point covered in an earlier edition of his book, *Infections and Inequalities*. He stated that "Investing in robust public health infrastructures, and in global health equity in general, remains our best means of being prepared for—and perhaps even preventing—bioterrorism. Indeed, this was the refrain of several of our best public health leaders during the taxing investigations of these [anthrax] attacks" (p. xi).

Still considered to be in its infancy as a disease, the most destructive human epidemic that the world has ever encountered is HIV/AIDS (Hunter, 2003). By 2010, the number of deaths from HIV/AIDS will have risen above the number of deaths from the two world wars combined, and soon it will spiral above the number of total lives lost in all wars. Although in some countries the number of deaths from AIDS has declined, the reality is that "in most countries HIV is spreading like wildfire" (p. 7). The United Nations Security Council has called HIV/AIDS a global security threat. It appears that HIV/AIDS is beginning to destabilize our entire global society and is creating consequences that are much worse than any terrorist could envision.

Stephen Lewis, US envoy to Africa for HIV/AIDS (2004), stated that by the year 2005, the United States will have spent approximately $200 billion on the wars in Afghanistan and Iraq and on the reconstruction of those societies. However, spending only a fraction of that amount on combating HIV/AIDS could help save 3 million lives per year that will be lost to the disease. In the Public Broadcasting Service (PBS) documentary *AIDS Warriors*, Mr. Lewis called this disparity in spending something that "staggers the mind." He reported that a study done by the World Bank predicted that South Africa's economy will collapse within three generations if something is not done to halt the spread of HIV/AIDS in that country.

In conjunction with these horrifying circumstances involving HIV/AIDS, public health professionals and all humanitarians must consider the rapidly advancing re-emergence of tuberculosis (TB). Interestingly, TB has been detected in the mummies of people who lived 5000 years ago, but it continues to be a problem at this point in time and "currently infects a stunning one third of all human beings" (Levy & Fischetti, 2003, p. 228; WHO, 2004). The World Health Organization (WHO) (2004) estimated that 2 million people died from TB in 2002. Annually, 8 to 12 million new cases occur, and the WHO predicts that almost 1 billion more people will become infected with TB by 2020 if aggressive intervention is not initiated (WHO, as cited in Levy & Fischetti, 2003).

So what do these and other infectious disease pandemics and epidemics have to do with ethics and C/PH nursing? Should nurses be their brothers' and sisters' keepers? A nurse must only review the eight tenets of C/PH nursing that were listed at the beginning of this chapter to answer these questions. The words of the poet John Donne (1962) provide a good representation of how infectious disease pandemics are related to ethics in nursing.

> No man is an island, entire of itself; every man is a piece of the continent, a part of the main. If a clod be washed away by the sea, Europe is the less, as well as if a promontory were, as well as if a manor of thy friend's or of thine own were. Any man's death diminishes me, because I am involved in mankind; and there-fore never send to know for whom the bell tolls; it tolls for thee (p. 1107).

Farmer (2001) advocated that "we can no longer accept whatever we are told about 'limited resources' " (p. xxvi). Health care professionals must challenge the often repeated mantra that resources are too limited to fund programs to treat epidemics. According to Farmer, "the wealth of the world has not dried up; it has simply become unavailable to those who need it most" (p. xxvi). He proposed that people must ask to be shown the data that proves that there are fewer resources for public health than there were when effective therapies were not available to treat many diseases. "Our challenge, therefore, is not merely to draw attention to the widening outcome gap, but also to attack it, to dissect it, and to work with all our capacity to reduce this gap" (p. xxvi). Health care professionals and the public must make it clearly known that they are not willing to idly watch when the wealth of nations is being concentrated within limited populations and programs while, on a mass scale, people in other populations die of treatable diseases.

Ethical Issues and HIV/AIDS

HIV Testing

In the United States, the primary issue of ethical concern with regard to testing for HIV is privacy (Beauchamp & Childress, 2001). The ethics of testing are less problematic when testing is anonymous than is the case when there is a greater risk of a person's name and HIV status being associated. Current evidence about the spread of HIV does not warrant a need for universal voluntary or mandatory testing to protect the health of the public, and populations with a low prevalence of HIV have historically produced a high rate of false positive results when they have been screened. Therefore, because of these factors and other concerns about violating personal privacy, universal testing in the United States is not necessary, nor is it cost effective. In other areas of the world where the disease is widespread, such as in certain areas of Africa, widespread testing may make more sense. (Maternal–infant testing for HIV in the United States has been a source of debate and was discussed in Chapter 4.)

Although there is a general consensus that universal testing in the United States is not reasonable, voluntary-selective testing is appropriate for drug users who share needles and for people who practice unsafe sex (Beauchamp & Childress, 2001). However, even when it is voluntary, HIV testing carries with it certain risks and benefits. Since the emergence of HIV, the policy issue that has generated the biggest ethical concern is how to protect the public while respecting individual rights and privacy (Brannigan & Boss, 2001).

Psychological well-being and the opportunity to prevent future infection are among the benefits to those people whose test results are negative (Beauchamp & Childress, 2001). For those people whose test results are positive, benefits include "closer medical follow-up, earlier use of antiretroviral agents, prophylaxis or other treatment of associated diseases, protection of loved ones, and a clearer sense of the future" (p. 298).

Those people who are seronegative have no significant risks from testing; however, the psychological and social risks are significant for people who are seropositive (Beauchamp & Childress, 2001). People who are HIV positive are at a high psychological risk for anxiety, depression, and suicide and are at a high social risk for "stigmatization, discrimination, and breaches of confidentiality" (p. 299). It is the ethical responsibility of health care professionals and other people in society to try to minimize the risks to these individuals. Participating in pre- and post-test counseling, community education, and social and political activism are ways that C/PH nurses can play an important role in minimizing the risk of infection as well as minimizing the risk of negative effects on people who undergo HIV testing.

Informed consent must be obtained for HIV testing and documented in medical records (Dempski, 2000). According to Fry and Veatch (2000):

> Adequate informed consent for testing includes information, comprehension of the information, and voluntariness on the part of the person to be tested. Information that might be conveyed includes the availability and costs of treatment for HIV infection, the lack of a cure for AIDS, possible stigma and discrimination that might threaten the well-being of the person found to be infected with HIV, and the availability of counseling for the HIV-infected (p. 278).

Exceptions to informed consent in HIV testing include situations in which there has been significant occupational exposure (nurses, emergency medical technicians, firefighters, etc.), prior to organ transplant donation, when a coroner needs to determine cause of death, and when testing is needed for emergency diagnostic purposes when the patient is unable to consent and a surrogate is not available (Dempski, 2000). (See Ethical Kaleidoscope Box 9-6 for the American Nurses Association's (ANA) position on HIV testing.)

Box 9-6

ETHICAL Kaleidoscope   ANA Position on HIV Testing

ANA supports:

- HIV testing be either voluntary anonymous or voluntary confidential.
- All HIV testing be conducted with informed consent and pre- and post-test counseling.
- The protection of confidentiality of all HIV-related information to safeguard the client's right to privacy as required by the Code for Nurses.
- The need for continued education of nurses and the public regarding the transmission of HIV/AIDS.
- The position that mandatory testing and mandatory disclosure of HIV status of patients and or nurses will not prevent the transmission of HIV disease and is therefore not recommended.
- The use of and monitoring of universal precautions to prevent the transmission of HIV disease.

ANA opposes:

- Perpetuation of the myth that mandatory testing and mandatory disclosure of HIV status of patients and/or nurses is a method to prevent the transmission of HIV disease.

ANA HIV Resource Task Force. (1997).

Confidentiality

Confidentiality and the duty to warn were discussed in Chapter 7 and have similar applications in ethical relationships with persons infected with HIV. Persons who know or suspect that they have HIV often avoid testing or treatment because of fears about exposure of lifestyle, including sexual practices or drug use; discrimination and stigmatization; and loss of relationships (Beauchamp & Childress, 2001; Chenneville, 2003). As a general rule, a person's HIV status is confidential information (Dempski, 2000). HIV status may be disclosed when persons or their proxies provide written authorization to do so and when health care providers have a need to know, such as workers at a coroner's office or the health care staff of a correctional facility.

Statutory laws must be consulted for direction regarding the duty to warn known sexual partners of individuals with HIV. Of course, before a person's HIV status is disclosed to a known partner or partners, attempts should be made to encourage HIV-positive persons to self-disclose to others who are at risk of infection due to their seropositive status. "In the final analysis, the health professional is expected to weigh the likelihood of harm to other parties against his or her duty to keep confidentiality and act accordingly" (Fry & Veatch, 2000, p. 280). Chenneville (2003) proposed a decision-making model that takes into consideration the premises contained within the *Tarasoff* legal case (see The Duty to Warn in Chapter 7) as well as health care ethics that focuses on the best interest of the person who is seropositive.

The first step in Chenneville's model is to *determine whether disclosure is warranted.* Assess the foreseeability of harm and the indentifiability of the victim. Questions to consider when determining foreseeability include: Does the client use condoms? Is the client impulsive? Is the client aggressive? Submissive? Does the client use substances that decrease inhibitions? Is the client afraid to disclose HIV status because of fear of rejection, discrimination, and so forth? Chenneville's second step, then, is to *refer to professional ethical guidelines*, and the final step is to *refer to state guidelines* (pp. 199–200).

The Duty to Provide Care

In accepting their professional nursing role, nurses make a contract or covenant with the public to provide certain services (Fry & Veatch, 2000). There are only a few situations in which nurses would ethically be permitted to refuse care to individuals with HIV based on the patient being viewed as a danger to the nurse. Each health care institution should have policies that nurses can refer to for guidance in determining when concerns about the risks of care are justified in allowing nurses to refuse to provide care to these patients. One such example or justification often includes nurses who are pregnant. When patients with HIV are considered to pose a significant risk to nurses because of the patients' impaired judgment or altered mental status, security should be provided for all health care workers who are at risk.

Mandatory Treatment of TB

HIV is transmitted by blood, semen, vaginal secretions, and breast milk, but TB is airborne, which makes the treatment of TB a major public health concern in terms of possible infringement on the well-being of others. Patients infected with TB who lack the capacity or desire to adhere to recommended treatment are an ongoing moral problem (Beauchamp & Childress, 2001). Freedom and autonomy are, of course, to be supported when possible. However, when persons infected with TB do not voluntarily adhere to treatment, it is ethically and legally obligatory to mandate treatment because of health threats to others.

Directly observed treatment (DOT), in which the taking of TB medications is directly observed, is one means of ensuring that affected individuals take their medications. The international community has responded to the problem of the spread of TB with coordinated efforts to control it. In 2000, the "Declaration of Amsterdam to Stop

TB" was signed by governments with the highest TB burden. This declaration, along with WHO efforts, supports the international aim of expanding DOT strategies to reach a global target of detecting at least 70% of infectious TB cases by 2005 (Hanson, 2003). The least restrictive and least intrusive measures for reaching treatment goals should be given priority, but if measures like DOT are not effective, detention and quarantine are ethical and may be required for the public's safety (Beauchamp & Childress, 2001).

MANAGEMENT OF CARE

C/PH nurses and other morally minded people who are sincerely interested in the well-being of communities are most likely also interested in creating and preserving peace in those communities, from the local to the global. People who facilitate significant change must realize that power is a factor in the workings of most societies. Chinn (2004) has proposed a plan in which the use of "peace powers" can provide a " 'value map' to think about alternatives [and to provide] specific guidelines for working with others to create meaningful community" (p. 1). Nurses working as advocates and servant leaders in communities can use peace-power processes when fulfilling the eight tenets of public health nursing discussed at the beginning of this chapter. Imbalances of power create disparities in communities (Sherwin, 1992). Chinn (2004) stated "the processes of *Peace and Power* are specifically designed to overcome all types of imbalances of power" (p. 1).

PEACE is an acronym that Chinn (2004) used to represent a way of being that people, particularly nurses, can cultivate in relating to other people in group contexts. PEACE requires nurses to know their values and to act on those values. PEACE actions involve praxis, empowerment, awareness, cooperation, and evolvement.

- *Praxis* is thoughtful reflection and action that occur in synchrony, in the direction of transforming the world.
- *Empowerment* is growth of personal strength, power, and ability, to enact one's own will and love for self in the context of love and respect for others.
- *Awareness* is an active, growing knowledge of Self and others and the world in which you live.
- *Cooperation* is an active commitment to group solidarity and group integrity.
- *Evolvement* is a commitment to growth where change and transformation are conscious and deliberate (pp. 8–9).

Actions arise from the energy of one's power (Chinn, 2004). Power that is commonly used by people who are thought of as powerful in societies is usually based on a hierarchical ideal. It usually involves persons or groups imposing their will on others, often with a readiness to impose penalties on those people who oppose the will of the powerful. In many cases, *having* power is more important to powerful people than what those people can constructively *do* with their power. Chinn called this type of power "power-over," to mean having "power over" other people (pp. 11–12).

However, those nurses who are interested in PEACE must direct their attention toward considerations of the underlying values that support the positive use of power. Chinn (2004) calls this positive type of power *PEACE power*. A partial list of some of the distinctions that Chinn made between "power-over powers" and "PEACE powers" is provided in Table 9-1. Nurses can use PEACE powers to help build and support flourishing communities.

TABLE 9-1   Two Types of Power

Power-Over Powers	*Peace Powers*
The **Power of Results** emphasizes programs, goals, or policies that achieve desired results. Achievement of the goals justifies the use of any means: "I don't care how you do it, just get the job done."	The **Power of Process** emphasizes a fresh perspective and freedom from rigid schedules. Goals, programs, and timetables are used as tools, but are less important than the process itself.
The **Power of Prescription** imposes change by authority; vested interests prescribe the outcome. The attitude is paternalistic: "Do as I say, because I know what is best for you."	The **Power of Letting Go** encourages change emerging out of awareness of collective integrity; leadership inspires a balance between the interests of each individual and the interests of the group as a whole.
The **Power of Division** emphasizes centralization, resulting in the hoarding of knowledge and skills by the privileged few: "What they don't know won't hurt them."	The **Power of the Whole** values the flow of new ideas, images, and energy from all, nurturing mutual help networks that are both intimate and expansive. Practices that nurture group solidarity are regular habits of the group.
The **Power of Force** invests power for or against others and is accomplished by a willingness to impose penalties and negative sanctions. One individual makes decisions on behalf of another individual or group of individuals: "Do it or else."	The **Power of Collectivity** values the personal power of each individual as integral to the well-being of the group. A group decision in which each individual has participated is viewed as more viable than a decision made by any one individual and stronger than a decision made by a majority.
The **Power of Hierarchy** requires a linear chain of command where layer upon layer of responsibilities are subdivided into separate and discrete areas of responsibility: "I don't make the decisions, I just work here." Or, "The buck stops here."	The **Power of Solidarity** shares the responsibility for decision-making and for acting upon those decisions in a lateral network. This process values thoughtful deliberation and emphasizes the integration of variety within the group, while calling forth fundamental values embraced by the whole.

TABLE 9-1   continued

Power-Over Powers	Peace Powers
The **Power of Use** encourages the exploitation of resources and people as normal and acceptable: "If you don't want to work for what we are willing to pay, then quit. There are plenty of people standing in line wanting this job.	The **Power of Nurturing** views life and experience as a resource to be cherished and respected. The earth and all creatures are viewed as precious, deserving of respect and protection, and integral to the well-being of all.
The **Power of Accumulation** views material goods, resources and dollars as things to be used in one's own self-interest, as well as items to gain privilege over others: "I worked for it, I bought it, I own it—*and* I deserve it."	The **Power of Distribution** values material resources (including food, land, space, money) as items to use for the benefit of all, to share according to need. Material goods are valued as a means, not as an end in and of themselves.
The **Power of Expediency** emphasizes the immediate reward or easiest solution. "Oh, radioactive waste? Let's just ship it somewhere else or dump it in the sea."	The **Power of Consciousness** considers long-range outcomes and ethical behaviors. Ethics and morality are derived from values that protect life, growth, and peace, and that are the basis for confronting destructive actions.
The **Power of Xenophobia** (the fear of strangers) rewards conformity and acquiescing to the values of those who hold the balance of power. "Be a team player. Don't make waves."	The **Power of Diversity** encourages creativity, values alternative views, and encourages flexibility. The expression of dissenting views is expected and encouraged. All points of view are integrated into decisions.
The **Power of Rules** relies on policies and laws to dictate what must be done, and to prescribe punishments for breaking the rules. A very few laws or rules are beneficial, but runaway rule-making creates absurd contradictions. "Do it because the law requires it."	The **Power of Creativity** takes into account fundamental laws and rules that govern the society, but values actions and solutions created from ingenuity and imagination. Actions are created to fit each situation, with the knowledge that often there is a better way.
The **Power of Fear** focuses on imaginary future disaster, and extreme actions are taken to prevent that which is feared and to control the behavior of others. "Let's bomb their cities: this will prevent terrorism."	The **Power of Trust** focuses on building genuine human relationships where honest exchange of thoughts and ideas are followed by consistent action. If trust is broken, then the relationship is renegotiated.

Reprinted from Chinn, P. (2004). *Peace and power: Creative leadership for building community* (6th ed., pp. 12–15). Boston: Jones and Bartlett Publishers.

Web Ethics

The Common Good
www.scu.edu/ethics/practicing/decision/commongood.html

Bill and Melinda Gates Foundation
www.gatesfoundation.org

National Service Learning Clearinghouse
www.servicelearning.org

Greenleaf Center for Servant Leadership
www.greenleaf.org

Christian Ethics and the Common Good
www.georgetown.edu/centers/woodstock/report/r_fea74.htm

Case Study: Community Building

Imagine that you will be the administrator for a new residential AIDS hospice that will be opened as an agency of Catholic Charities in the mid-size conservative southern city where you live. The majority of the money for the hospice is coming from a federal grant, but you will need to raise additional funds in order to provide comprehensive care. The hospice will be located in a house in a residential neighborhood, and the location of the hospice is to remain as confidential as possible. The citizens living in the neighborhood are very opposed to having the hospice in their neighborhood. The board of directors of the local Catholic Charities organization provided oversight of the grant application and the plans for the hospice until now. The plans are to create a partnership with the local AIDS task force in providing community AIDS prevention education. It is now time to turn the hospice project over to you, the RN, hired as administrator.

Case Study Critical Thinking Questions

1. You will need a governing body for the hospice. What types of people would you consider and how would you handle the selection process?
2. What types of services would you provide? What ethical issues might affect your decisions about the distribution of resources for the different services?
3. You may have more applicants for admission to the hospice than you have beds available. What criteria will you use to prioritize admissions to the hospice?
4. How would you recruit the staff and volunteers while trying to maintain confidentiality about the location of the hospice? What ethical issues would you include in your staff and volunteer orientation?
5. What would you do to try to build a sense of community that includes the hospice residents, the hospice staff, and the residents of the neighborhood where the

hospice is located? That includes the city? How would building this sense of community be critical to the success of your program?

6. How might the philosophy of communitarian ethics provide you with guidance in developing the plans for the hospice? How might the use of moral imagination be involved?

7. How would you try to minimize the use and effect of "power-over powers" and increase and emphasize "PEACE powers" in trying to build a community within the hospice, the neighborhood, and the city?

REFERENCES

Beauchamp, T. L., & Childress, J. F. (2001). *Principles of biomedical ethics* (5th ed.). New York: Oxford University.

Berkowitz, B., Dahl, J., Guirl, K., Kostelecky, B., McNeil, C., & Upenieks, V. (2001). *Public health nursing leadership: A guide to managing the core functions.* Washington, DC: American Nurses Publishing.

Brannigan, M. C., & Boss, J. A. (2001). *Healthcare ethics in a diverse society.* Mountain View, CA: Mayfield.

Bunch, C. (2003). The reform tool kit. In J. Frideman (Ed.), *First harvest.* New York: Grove.

Capra, F. (1999). *The Tao of physics: An exploration of the parallels between modern physics and Eastern mysticism.* Boston: Shambhala.

Centers for Disease Control [CDC]. (2003). Achievements in public health, 1900-1999: Control of infectious diseases. In P. R. Lee & C. L. Estes (Eds.), *The nation's health* (7th ed., pp. 31–37). Boston: Jones and Bartlett Publishers.

Chenneville, T. (2003). HIV, confidentiality, and duty to protect: A decision-making model. In D. N. Bersoff (Ed.), *Ethical conflicts in psychology* (3rd ed., pp. 198–202). Washington, DC: American Psychological Association.

Chinn, P. (2004). *Peace and power: Creative leadership for building community* (6th ed.). Boston: Jones and Bartlett Publishers.

Covey, S. (2002). Foreword. In R. K. Greenleaf, *Servant leadership: A journey into the nature of legitimate power and greatness* (25th ed.) (pp.1–13). New York: Paulist Press.

De Mello, A. (1992). *One minute nonsense.* Chicago: Loyola University.

Dempski, K. M. (2000). Clients with AIDS and HIV testing. In S. W. Killion & K. M. Dempski (Eds.), *Quick look nursing: Legal and ethical issues* (pp. 56–57). Thorofare, NJ: Slack.

De Saint-Exupery, A. (2002). *A guide for grown-ups: Essential wisdom from the collected works of Antoine De Saint-Exupery.* San Diego, CA: Harcourt.

Dewey, J. (1997). *How we think.* Mineola, NY: Dover Publications. (Original work published 1919)

Dewey, J. (1988). *Human nature and conduct: The middle works, 1899–1924, volume 14* (J. A. Boydston & P. Baysinger, Eds.). Carbondale, IL: Southern Illinois University Press. (Original work published 1922)

Dewey, J. (1934). *Art as experience.* New York: Perigee Books.

Donne, J. (1962). Meditation 17. In Norton Anthology of English Literature, Vol.1, (5th ed.). New York: W. W. Norton.

Farmer, P. (2001). *Infections and inequalities: The modern plagues* (Updated). Berkeley, CA: University of California.

Fesmire, S. (2003). *John Dewey & moral imagination: Pragmatics in ethics.* Bloomington, IN: Indiana University.

Forsey, H. (1993). *Circles of strength: Community alternatives to alienation.* Philadelphia: New Society.

Fry, S. T., & Veatch, R. M. (2000). *Case studies in nursing ethics* (2nd ed.). Boston: Jones and Bartlett Publishers.

Garrett, L. (2000). *Betrayal of trust: The collapse of global public health.* New York: Hyperion.

Greenleaf, R. (2002). In L. C. Spears (Ed.), *Servant leadership: A journey into the nature of legitimate power and greatness* (25th ed.). New York: Paulist Press.

Hanson, C. (2003). *Expanding DOTS in the context of a changing health system.* Geneva: World Health Organization.

Hesse, H. (1956). *The journey to the East.* New York: Picador.

Hester, D. M. (2001). *Community as healing: Pragmatist ethics in medical encounters.* Lanham, MD: Rowman & Littlefield.

Hunter, S. (2003). *Black death: AIDS in Africa.* New York: Palgrave Macmillan.

Johnson, M. (1993). *Moral imagination: Implications of cognitive science for ethics.* Chicago: University of Chicago.

Kaye, C. B. (2004). *The complete guide to service learning: Proven, practical ways to engage students in civic responsibility, academic curriculum, and social action.* Minneapolis, MN: Free Spirit Publishing.

Levy, E., & Fischetti, M. (2003). *The new killer diseases: How the alarming evolution of mutant germs threatens us all.* New York: Crown.

Lewis, S. (2004). *AIDS Warrors* [Television broadcast]. New York and Washington, DC: Public Broadcasting Service.

MacIntyre, A. (1984). *After virtue: A study of moral theory* (2nd ed.). Notre Dame, IN: University of Notre Dame.

Markel, H. (2004). *When germs travel: Six major epidemics that have invaded America since 1900 and the fears they have unleashed.* New York: Pantheon.

Minkler, M., & Pies, C. (2002). Ethical issues in community organization and community participation. In M. Minkler (Ed.), *Community organizing & community building for health* (pp. 120–138). New Brunswick, NJ: Rutgers University Press.

Mondics, C. (2004, July 23). 9/11 report details failure. *The Sun Herald,* A1, A4.

Nussbaum, M. (2004). Compassion and terror. In L. P. Pojman (Ed.), *The moral life: An introductory reader in ethics and literature* (2nd ed., pp. 937–961). New York: Oxford University.

Pieper, J. (1966). *The four cardinal virtues.* Notre Dame, IN: University of Notre Dame.

Piliavin, J. A. (2003). Doing well by doing good: Benefits for the benefactor. In C. L. M. Keyes & J. Haidt Eds.), *Flourishing: Positive psychology and the life well-lived* (pp. 227–247). Washington, DC: American Psychological Association.

Quad Council of Public Health Nursing Organizations.(1999). *Scope and standards of public health nursing practice:* Washington, DC: American Nurses Publishing.

Salamon, J. (2003). *Rambam's ladder: A meditation on generosity and why it is necessary to give.* New York: Workman.

Sherwin, S. (1992). *No longer patient: Feminist ethics & health care.* Philadelphia: Temple University.

Wheatley, M. (2002). *Turning to one another.* San Francisco: Berrett-Koehler.

Wildes, K. M. (2000). *Moral acquaintances: Methodology in bioethics.* Notre Dame, IN: University of Notre Dame.

United States Department of Health and Human Services. (2000). *Healthy people 2010: Understanding and improving health* (2nd ed.). Washington, DC: Government Printing Office.

World Health Organization (2004). Tuberculosis fact sheet no. 104. Retrieved October 24, 2004 from http://www.who.int/mediacentre/factsheets/fs104/en/print.html

CHAPTER 10

End-of-Life Ethical Issues and Nursing

Janie B. Butts

Death has dominion . . . and how we think and talk about dying—
the emphasis we put on dying with 'dignity'—shows how
important it is that life ends appropriately, that death keeps faith
with the way we want to have lived.

Ronald Dworkin, *Life's Dominion*

SUMMARY

1. When individuals rehearse their own death scenario, they can internalize the process and may find a rich meaning to the end of their lives, thus creating a more peaceful death experience.
2. Because suffering and pain are not experiences that most people find tolerable, people often look for ways to die a good death without suffering, which may include a desire for active or passive euthanasia practices.
3. Euthanasia practices, which are sometimes called mercy killings, although still very controversial in most countries including the United States, have been based on the grounds of mercy, autonomy, and justice. Mercy is the duty not to cause further suffering and the duty to act to end existing suffering, autonomy is respect

for a patient's decision, and justice means justification in providing euthanasia to patients who are deemed "unsalvageable."

4. When loved ones no longer have decision-making capacity, someone in the family or a court-appointed person becomes a surrogate decision maker for that patient. There are three standards on which surrogacy is based: the standard of substituted judgment, the pure autonomy standard, and the standard of best interest.

5. End-of-life nursing care involves several principles, which include acknowledging the person's death, alleviating suffering and pain, being respectful of family members' time to grieve, and giving attentive care to the dying person.

What Is Death?

The Ideal Death

Contemporary ethical discussions about death and dying have been related to philosophers attempting to answer captivating questions such as "What is a good death?" and "How will we all die?" More recently, however, the focus of ethicists has been on the challenging issues of readiness to die, acceptance of death, and knowing the right time to die (Battin, 1994; Connelly, 2003; Hester, 2003). Many questions about death are unanswerable, but individuals can develop some sort of subjective notion about the meaning of death. For people to face death more peacefully, they need to come to their own understanding of death and what they think is beyond death, if anything, and develop a personal knowing of death's connection to life (Connelly, 2003). Nietzsche proposed that everyone needs a philosophy of life in relation to death in his notable quote: "He who has a *why* to live [for] can bear with almost any *how* [italics added]" (as cited in Connelly, 2003, p. 51).

Andrew Lustig (2003), a philosopher, stated that he has been amazed at how ethicists are engaging in passionate conversations about the meaning of death, yet, Lustig observed, "it seems very hard for each of us to personalize the truth of [our own] mortality. As the title character in the nonfiction bestseller *Tuesdays with Morrie* puts it, 'Everyone knows they're going to die, but nobody believes it.'" (p. 7). People "talk death" and romanticize death as if it was something ideal rather than a confrontation with mortality.

People use phrases such as "he passed away" to keep from saying the words "he died" or to avoid facing the reality of death (Spiegel, 1993). The term "death anxiety" describes fear of the prospect of dying. The term was proposed by existential philosophers such as Kierkegaard, Heidegger, and Sartre, who stated that it is in facing death and the possibility of nonbeing that a person comes to know oneself best; in other words, a person first has to put death in the proper perspective to attempt to understand any portion of life (as cited in Spiegel, 1993).

Yalom (1980), an existentialist and psychotherapist, stated that individuals avoid facing their own mortality in two ways, or with two defenses. The first defense against death is through immortality projects, where people literally throw themselves into commendable projects, their work, or raising children. People do these activities well, and by doing so, become insulated from death. The second defense is through dependence on a rescuer, believing that another person can provide one with a sense of safety or protection from death. Almost all people want to feel some sense of insulation from elements of threat. Death is one of those elements, and dying is a fearful process. Many times patients look to nurses, physicians, and other health care professionals to fill a rescuer role.

Spiegel (1993), in his studies about death and dying, consulted several hundred people regarding what they most fear about death. This is how Spiegel summed up the responses of people he interviewed.

> Strangely enough, it is not being dead; rather, it is the process of dying. Fears of losing control of your body, suffering increasing pain, losing the ability to do things you love to do, being able to make decisions about your medical care, being separated from loved ones: Those are the ways that fears of dying become real. Death is something that pushes the edge of our comprehension (p. 137).

Death signifies the end to a person's living embodiment. Wanting to die the good death or the ideal death may be everyone's wish at some point in life, even though while a person is alive, death often remains a dark secret. Nurses and other health care professionals need to envisage dying as a process that everyone must face, including themselves. Unfortunately most people will not experience the ideal death. Nancy Dubler (as cited in Hester, 2003) presented what she called a "cinematic" myth of the "Good American Death" when she wrote: "[The good death] includes the patient: lucid, composed, hungering for blissful release—and the family gathers in grief to mourn the passing of a beloved life. The murmurs of sad good-byes, the cadence of quiet tears shroud the scene in dignity.' Unfortunately for many of us, our deaths will not be the spiritual, peaceful 'passing' that we might envision or desire" (p. 122).

For most people, death is a haunting mystery to be discovered rather than a comforting scene with the presence of family members and others hovering over them (Hester, 2003). Instead, patients find themselves, if at all conscious, connected to ventilators and other machines, intravenous lines and meters, and receiving many medications. Technology and medicalization have exacerbated the problem of depersonalization. Family members or significant others experience difficulty communicating with their loved one because of physical technological and environmental barriers. During this perplexing period of time, nurses may be patients' most reliable and consistent contacts. When decisions about life and end-of-life need to be made, family members are often faced with uncertainty about the kind of treatment their loved one would want in particular circumstances. Even when patients have adequate decision-making capacity, they may want input from family members or significant others in treatment decisions. However, family members find it difficult to discuss the uncertainties of treatments with their loved one for two reasons. First, they may have restrictions on their visitation because of hospital policies. Second, they may feel at a loss to help and, therefore, do not want their loved one to know how they feel.

Whatever type of death a person is to experience—a good death; an anticipated death; a sudden unexpected death; or a painful, lingering death—most of the time, people do not have a choice of how they will die. Individuals, meanwhile, need to shift the focus from thoughts "*that* we die" toward "*how* we die" so that people can place considerable thought on future decisions about end-of-life care and what might be best for them (Hester, 2003, p. 122).

The benefit of persons envisioning an ideal death and reflecting on it from time to time is that the image helps them develop a sense of readiness for a peaceful death (Connelly, 2003). The famous American philosopher, Dewey (as cited in Fesmire, 2003), described a similar moral framework that is based on a person's development of intelligent habits through an imaginative *dramatic rehearsal*. Dewey discussed dramatic rehearsal in terms of creative dialogue between two or more people. However, a personal process about one's own ideal death can be imagined and internalized. By reconstructing the ideal death scenario, individuals can imagine the scenario being carried out and, on continued reflection, may later discover a rich meaning with regard to the experience (Fesmire, 2003; Hester, 2003). Persons who imagine an ideal death may have a greater possibility of finding significance in the end point of their lives and then, to some extent, may be able to help shape their dying process (Hester, 2003).

Euthanasia

The thought of extended agony and suffering prior to death provokes a sense of dread in most people. Keeping their emotional, financial, and social burdens to a minimum and avoiding suffering are not always possible (Munson, 2004). O'Rourke (2002) noted that most people go to extremes to avoid suffering when he stated: "Suffering in all its forms is an evil, and every reasonable effort should be made to relieve it" (p. 221). However, an untold number of people die every day with tremendous suffering and pain. For more than 90 years, people have debated whether or not to legalize euthanasia, a process often referred to as "mercy killing."

Until his prison sentence and conviction on a second-degree murder charge, Dr. Jack Kevorkian assisted with more than 100 suicides or mercy killings. From 1990 to 1998, at the request of suffering patients from various parts of the United States, he helped them end their lives (PBS & Frontline, 1998). He has been nicknamed "Doctor Death" because of his euthanasia practices. On November 22, 1998, 15 million viewers of CBS's program *60 Minutes* watched Doctor Death give a lethal injection to a man who was dying with Lou Gehrig's disease. His name was Thomas Youk, age 52. Once this program aired, strong debates surfaced in the media, health care, and legal systems worldwide. Geoffrey Fieger, Kevorkian's lawyer, stated in October 2003 in *The Oakland Press* that most people did not believe that Kevorkian had even committed a crime. Fieger then predicted that Kevorkian would not serve much more time in prison (as cited in Huber, 2003).

Euthanasia, which has come to mean a "good death" or "easy death," has developed a strong appeal in recent years, partly because of the politicization of the right-to-die issues and the association of these issues with the misery and suffering of dying patients.

There are two major types of euthanasia (Munson, 2003). *Active euthanasia* occurs when persons commit an act to end a life (their own or others). This type may include self-administered lethal injections of medications ordered by a physician in physician-assisted suicide. *Passive euthanasia* is when a person allows another person to die by not taking any action to stop death or prolong life. An example of this type may include withholding some type of treatment that would prevent death.

Euthanasia is also categorized as being voluntary and nonvoluntary (Brannigan & Boss, 2001). Voluntary euthanasia occurs when patients with decision-making capacity authorize physicians to take their lives. Also, this type may include the taking of one's own life such as in physician-assisted suicide. Nonvoluntary euthanasia occurs when persons are not able to or do not express their consent about someone ending their lives. A blending of these types of euthanasia may occur, such as voluntary active, nonvoluntary active, voluntary passive, and nonvoluntary passive.

A vigorous debate continues in the United States about whether or not there is a real moral difference between active euthanasia, such as the intentional taking of someone's life, and passive euthanasia, such as withholding and withdrawing life-sustaining treatments (Brannigan & Boss, 2001; Jonsen, Veatch, & Walters, 1998). The action versus omission distinction has caused nurses and physicians to mull over the burdensome question: Is there a moral difference between actively killing and letting someone die?

In her book, *The Least Worst Death*, Battin (2002) argued that euthanasia is a morally right and humane act on the grounds of mercy, autonomy, and justice. The principle of mercy ("mercy killing") is based on two obligations: the duty not to cause further pain and suffering and the duty to act to end existing pain or suffering. The principle of autonomy is based on the thought that health professionals ought to respect a person's right to choose and determine a suitable course of medical treatment. The principle of justice is based on how unsalvageable providers of care believe a permanently unconscious person is; in other words, there is moral justification in providers performing euthanasia on patients that they regard as unsalvageable.

Based on this salvageability/unsalvageability principle, however, a health care provider could justify performing euthanasia on still competent but dying patients if they were regarded as unsalvageable (Battin, 2002). It is in knowing where to draw the line with the principle of euthanasia that providers may face difficult ethical dilemmas. Because of the legal and moral concerns and the potential for a slippery slope to occur, bioethicists, nurses, and health care providers examine acts of euthanasia with grave caution, especially when the acts may increase the scope and meaning of the principle of unsalvageability (see the "Slippery Slope Argument" in Chapter 1). There are, however, many opponents of the slippery slope euthanasia arguments, and they present very convincing viewpoints. Battin (2002), in particular, stated: "But to require the person who chooses to die to stay alive in order to protect those who might unwillingly be killed sometime in the future is to impose an extreme harm—intolerable suffering—on that person, which he or she must bear for the sake of others…[I ask] which is the worse of two evils, death or pain" (p. 119)?

Historical Influences on the Definition of Death

There was widespread fear of being buried alive in the 18th and 19th centuries, especially in Europe, because of inadequate methods for detecting when a person was dead. Documented accounts of people being buried alive exist (Bondeson, 2001). Sometimes, when a body was exhumed, claw marks were found on the inside of the coffin lid (Mappes & DeGrazia, 2001). Bondeson (2001) reported, however, that many people had come to believe exaggerated accounts of premature burial. Bondeson based his conclusions on his detailed historical study of the subject.

Nevertheless, and possibly for good reasons, great fear persisted during that time period. Out of fear of being buried alive, the great composer Frédéric Chopin left a request in his will to be dissected after his death and before being buried (Bondeson, 2001). Even the dying words of George Washington were "Have me decently buried, but do not let my body be put into a vault in less than two days after I am dead" (Death: The Last Taboo, 2003, ¶ intro.).

Although a law was enacted that prevented premature burials, the owners of funeral homes went to the extreme of having their staff monitor dead bodies during the "wait" time (Death: The Last Taboo, 2003). Until the law had taken effect, a variety of special safety coffins were invented with detailed devices to help the dead, once they were buried, to communicate with others above the ground. The devices included such things as a rope extending to the surface of the ground with a bell on the other end, a speaking tube to the outer coffin, a shovel, and food and water.

For years and years, when a person became unconscious, physicians or others would palpate for a pulse, listen for breath sounds with their ears, look for condensation on an object when it was held close to the body's nose, and check for fixed and dilated pupils (Mappes & DeGrazia, 2001). Finally, the stethoscope was invented in 1819, which led to reduced fear, because physicians could listen with greater certainty for a heartbeat through a magnified listening device placed on the chest of the body.

A breakthrough in technology occurred at the beginning of the 20th century when Willem Einthoven, a Dutch physician, discovered the existence of electrical properties of the heart with his invention of the first electrocardiograph (EKG) in 1903, which provided sensitive information about whether or not the heart was functioning. From the middle of the 19th century to the middle of the 20th century, there seemed to be a consensus about determination of death, meaning that when the heart stopped beating and the person stopped breathing, the person had ceased to exist (Benjamin, 2003). People began to change their perceptions of death as technology became integrated into medicine. The 1950s and 1960s brought more uncertainty involving death as physicians kept patients alive in the absence of a natural heartbeat (Death: The Last Taboo, 2003). Then, it became apparent, when transplants were being performed in the 1960s and 1970s, that a diagnosis of death would not necessarily depend on the absence of a heartbeat and respirations. Rather, in the future, the definition of death would need to include brain death criteria.

In 1968, the members of a Harvard Medical School ad hoc committee first attempted to redefine death in terms not only of heart–lung cessation but also in terms of reliable brain death criteria for respirator-dependent patients with no brain function, which the committee members described as patients in irreversible coma (Benjamin, 2003). Back then, this 1968 definition led to confusion about the term "brain death" and to a widespread misconception about whether the human organism, the person, was actually dead. Somehow the term brain death, which technically means death of the brain, came to mean death of a human organism or person. Because of the way some individuals perceived the meaning of the term "brain death," they translated the 1968 definition to mean that two kinds of death existed for human organisms: the traditional heart-lung death and now a new kind of death called brain death. Benjamin (2003) emphasized that ethicists and physicians had not given sufficient attention to clarifying this term before the article was published in 1968.

Definition of Death

Ethicists, physicians, and others continued intense debates about death. It was not until 1981 that members of a President's Commission wrote in the document *Defining Death* that the body was an organism as a whole.

> Three organs—the heart, lungs, and brain—assume special significance—because their interrelationship is very close and the irreversible cessation of any one very quickly stops the other two and consequently halts the integrated functioning of the organism as a whole. Because they were easily measured, circulation and respiration were traditionally the basic 'vital signs.' But breathing and heartbeat are not life itself. They are simply used as signs—as one window for viewing a deeper and more complex reality: a triangle of interrelated systems with the brain at its apex (President's Commission, 1981, p. 33; as cited in Benjamin, 2003, p. 198).

The Commission members sanctioned a definition of death in 1981 in the same document and recommended its adoption by all states (Mappes & DeGrazia, 2001; Youngner & Arnold, 2001). The 1981 definition led to the Uniform Determination of Death Act (UDDA). The committee members required that death be defined in accordance with accepted medical standards. Under the UDDA, a person who is dead is one who "…has sustained either (1) irreversible cessation of circulatory and respiratory functions or (2) irreversible cessation of all functions of the entire brain, including the brain stem…" (President's Commission, 1981, p 73; as cited in Mappes & DeGrazia, 2001, p. 318).

Debates continue to occur concerning the question of which criteria belong in the definition of death and, more specifically, death of the brain. Since this 1981 definition was adopted, criteria for death of the brain have been adopted by almost every state. Veatch (2003) has extended the debate on the definition of death by posing an intriguing question regarding loss of full moral standing of human beings. This statement triggers the question as to when humans should be treated as full members of the human community. Although almost every person has reconciled the thought that some persons have full moral standing and others do not, there is continued controversy about when full moral standing ceases to exist and what characteristics qualify the cessation of full moral standing.

Losing full moral standing is equivalent to ceasing to exist. Various groups have proposed and debated the following four different conceptions of death since the enactment of the UDDA in 1981.

- *Traditional.* A person is dead when he is no longer breathing and his heart is not beating [cardiopulmonary death].
- *Whole-brain.* Death is regarded as the irreversible cessation of all brain functions…no electrical activity in the brain, and even the brain stem is not functioning [death of the brain].
- *Higher-brain.* Death is considered to involve the permanent loss of consciousness…someone in an irreversible coma would be considered dead, even though the brain stem continued to regulate breathing and heartbeat [persistent vegetative state].
- *Personhood.* Death occurs when an individual ceases to be a person. This may mean loss of features that are essential to personal identity or for being a person (Munson, 2004, pp. 692–693).

With whole-brain death, the patient physically may survive for an indeterminate period of time with a mechanical ventilator. Some patients may seemingly have complete loss of brain function only to have the electrical activity of the brain reappear later, even if minimal, which makes the UDDA whole-brain death criteria difficult to use for pronouncing a person dead (Munson, 2004). Veatch (2003) related the peculiarity of such an event: "A brain-dead patient on a ventilator does, of course, make for an unusual corpse. On the ventilator, he is respiring and his heart is beating. But if his whole brain is dead, the law in most jurisdictions says that the patient is deceased" (p. 38).

At the point when the person has met UDDA criteria and therefore is pronounced dead, mechanical ventilation and medical treatment may be discontinued (as cited in Benjamin, 2003). An electroencephalogram (EEG) is a meter device that is used to measure the electrical activity of the brain (Munson, 2004). If a person is on life-sustaining support when in the process of being pronounced dead, such as in whole-brain death, an EEG is needed in addition to the physician's establishing absence of heartbeat and respirations. The following criteria are required to establish whole-brain death (Mappes & DeGrazia, 2001):

- flat EEG with other tests that document the absence of cerebral blood flow
- fixed and dilated pupils
- inability to breathe without mechanical support
- absent brain stem reflexes

Usually, two EEGs with no brain activity, 24 hours apart, are performed on patients before physicians may disconnect them from life-sustaining support (Death: The Last Taboo, 2003). In addition, physicians and nurses must make certain that loss of brain function is not due to mind-altering medications, hypoglycemia, or hyponatremia.

With higher-brain death, or loss of higher-brain function, the patient lives in a persistent vegetative state indefinitely but without the need for mechanical ventilation. A person with higher-brain death may have some functions permanently lost but other functions not lost, which has been the cause for great dispute. Even very minimal brain functioning, such as limited reflexes in the brain stem, is cause for a patient to be diagnosed with higher-brain death or being in a persistent vegetative state (Veatch, 2003). It should be noted that every single neuron must be dead, along with a flat EEG, to meet the criteria for the definition of whole-brain death.

It is because of these situations that questions exist regarding whether or not a person should be treated as one who has full moral standing in the human community. Society, physicians, and nurses have had difficulty defining death by the UDDA definition, which includes the traditional and whole-brain concepts, but the greatest difficulty has been when they have tried to incorporate the concepts of higher-brain and personhood death (Munson, 2004). No definite criteria for either of these concepts—higher-brain or personhood—have been established for defining death. The controversy continues. Meanwhile, Benjamin (2003) posed this question for people to consider: "Exactly what is it that ceases to exist when we say someone like you or me is dead?" (p. 197). Benjamin (2003) and Veatch (2003) affirmed that there will be no answers to questions like this one until ethicists and others can come to some sort of consensus about what life is, when life begins, when life ends, and, then, who does and does not have full moral standing.

ADVANCE DIRECTIVES

An advance directive is "a written expression of a person's wishes about medical care, especially care during a terminal or critical illness" (Veatch, 2003, p. 119). When individuals lose control over their lives, they may also lose their decision-making capacity, and advance directives become instructions about their future health care for others to follow (Devettere, 2000). Advance directives may be self-written instructions or prepared by someone else as instructed by the patient. Critical issues that need to be addressed in any advance directive include specific treatments to be refused or desired; the time the directive needs to take effect; specific hospitals and physicians to be used; what lawyer, if any, to be consulted; and specific other consultations, such as an ethics team, a chaplain, or a neighbor (Veatch, 2003). There are three types of advance directives: living wills, medical care directives, and the durable power of attorney.

A *living will* is a formal legal document that provides written directions concerning what medical care is to be provided in specific circumstances (Beauchamp & Childress, 2001; Devettere, 2000). The living will gained recognition in the 1960s, but the Karen

Ann Quinlan case in the 1970s brought public attention to the living will and subsequently prompted legalization of the document (Devettere, 2000). Although at the time living wills were a good beginning, today they are inadequate. Problems can arise when living wills consist of vague language, contain only instructions for unwanted treatments, lack a description of legal penalties for those people who choose to ignore the directives of living wills, and when living wills are legally questionable as to their authenticity.

A *medical care directive* is not a formal legal document but provides specific written instructions to the physician concerning the type of care and treatments that individuals want to receive if they become incapacitated (Devettere, 2000). The biggest advantage to medical care directives is that physicians use them as a guide to know what incapacitated patients want in terms of specific health care treatments. Convinced that medical care directives are only extended informed consents, attorneys believe that medical care directives are only a minimal improvement over living wills. Other weaknesses of medical care directives are that people cannot possibly anticipate every medical problem that may occur in their future. People change over time and may change their mind about future wishes even after they have delineated the instructions for their medical care directive.

The *durable power of attorney* is a legal written directive in which a designated person is allowed to make either general or specific health care and medical decisions for a patient (Devettere, 2000). This durable power of attorney has the most strength for facilitating health care decisions. However, even with a power of attorney, families and health care professionals may experience fear about making the wrong decisions regarding an incapacitated patient (Beauchamp & Childress, 2001).

In addition to the weaknesses previously stated in this section on advance directives, other weaknesses that may present problems include the fact that very few people ever complete an advance directive, a proxy may be unavailable for decision making, and health care professionals cannot overturn advance directives in the event that a decision needs to be made in the best interest of a patient. The existence of advance directives can be a source of comfort for patients and families as long as they realize the limitations and scope. Ensuring the validity of the advance directive, realizing the importance of preserving patients from unwanted intrusive interventions, and also respecting the possibility that patients may change their minds about their expressed written wishes are several ways that nurses must demonstrate benevolence toward patients and their families.

DECIDING FOR OTHERS

When patients can no longer make competent decisions, families may experience problems in trying to determine a progressive right course of action. The ideal situation is for patients to be autonomous decision makers but, when autonomy is no longer possible, decision making falls to a surrogate (Beauchamp & Childress, 2001). The surrogate, or proxy, is either chosen by the patient, is court appointed, or has other authority to make decisions.

Decisions about treatment options and motives for decisions may be complex and destructive. Before any decisions are made by a proxy, there needs to be appropriate dialogue among the physicians, the nurses, and the proxy (Emanuel, Danis, Pearlman, & Singer, 1995). Proxies may not be able to distinguish between their own emotions and concerns for patients or they may have monetary motives for making certain decisions. It is the responsibility of nurses and physicians to be observant for these kinds of motives or concerns and then to look for therapeutic ways to deliberate with the proxy. There are three types of surrogate decision making (Beauchamp & Childress, 2001; Veatch, 2003).

The standard of *substituted judgment* is used to guide medical decisions that involve formerly competent patients who no longer have any decision-making capacity. This standard is based on the assumption that incompetent patients have the exact same rights as competent patients to make judgments about their health care (Buchanan & Brock, 1990). Surrogates make medical treatment decisions based on what the surrogates believe the patients would have decided were the patients still competent and able to express their wishes. In making decisions, the surrogates use their understanding of the patients' previous overt or implied expressions of their beliefs and values (Veatch, 2003). Before losing competency, the patient could have either explicitly informed the proxy of treatment wishes by oral or written instruction or implicitly made treatment wishes clear through informal conversations with the proxy.

When more than one sibling is involved in the decisions regarding the care of a dying parent, many times misunderstandings occur, and angry feelings over practical, legal, and financial matters become apparent. The siblings will be affected uniquely by their parents' death, depending on several factors: the type of relationship that exists between each sibling and the parent, if and how each sibling has experienced death in the past, each sibling's present life situation and stressors, their past grudges toward siblings, and current sibling relationships. One sibling usually takes charge or the siblings give one sibling the label of speaker for the group. Even when one is empowered, however, the others usually desire an equal voice in the decision-making process. This may be a frustrating process for everyone if the siblings cannot come to a decision. Dialogue is important so that all involved can come to an understanding and avoid further misunderstandings and pain.

The *pure autonomy standard* is based on a decision that was made by an autonomous patient while competent but later drifts to incompetency. This decision is upheld most of the time based on "the principle of autonomy extended" (Veatch, 2003, p. 106). The *standard of best interest* is based on the goal of the surrogate's doing what is best for the patient or what is in the best interest of the patient (Veatch, 2003). The patient represented by the best-interest proxy is a person who has never been competent, for example, an infant or a mentally retarded adult.

MEDICAL FUTILITY

Health care professionals and most other people have accepted and ethically justified withholding and withdrawing treatments that have been deemed as futile or extraordinary.

The term "futile" represents pointless or meaningless events or objects (O'Rourke, 2002). When a health care provider cannot have reasonable hope that a treatment will be of benefit for a terminally ill person, the medical treatment is considered to be *futile care*. Treatments that may be considered medically futile include cardiopulmonary resuscitation (CPR), medications, mechanical ventilation, artificial feeding and fluids, hemodialysis, chemotherapy, and other life-sustaining technologies. When proxies are the spokespersons for patients, one of the nurse's responsibilities is to make sure that communication remains open between the health care team and the decision maker for the family. Everyone needs to have a chance to express feelings and concerns about treatment options that are viewed as medically futile (Ladd, Pasquerella, & Smith, 2002).

PALLIATIVE CARE

Palliative care consists of comfort care measures that patients may request instead of aggressive medical treatments when their condition is terminal. Nurses are probably the most active of all the health care professionals in meeting palliative needs of dying patients. Palliative care has become an organized movement through official associations and organizations since the 1990s. The World Health Organization ([WHO], 2003) has defined palliative care as "an approach that improves the quality of life of patients and their families facing the problems associated with life-threatening illness, through the prevention and relief of suffering by means of early identification and impeccable assessment and treatment of pain and other problems, physical, psychosocial and spiritual" (¶ 1).

When nurses provide palliative care, they do not hasten or prolong death for these patients; rather, they try to provide patients with relief from pain and suffering and help them maintain dignity in the dying experience. Palliative treatment may include a patient's and family's choice to forego, withhold, or withdraw treatment. Some patients will have a do not resuscitate (DNR) order, which is a written physician's order that is placed in a patient's chart. Each hospital and agency has specific policies and procedures for how a DNR order is to be written and followed. A critical moral violation to informed consent may occur if a physician writes a DNR order on a patient's record without discussing the order and decision with the patient, family members, or proxy (O'Rourke, 2002). A DNR order needs to be justified by one of three reasons: there is no medical benefit that can come from CPR, a person has a very poor quality of life before CPR, and a person's life after CPR is anticipated to be very poor (Mappes & DeGrazia, 2001).

Unofficial—and unauthorized—"slow codes" have been practiced and can be described as "going through the motions" or as giving half-hearted CPR to a patient whose condition has been deemed futile. In the past, slow codes were initiated by nurses when DNR orders were not written on the chart of a terminally ill patient. However according to the American College of Physicians (1994), a slow code is an unethical practice and physicians and nurses should never initiate them.

Right to Die and Right to Refuse Treatment

A patient's gaining autonomy over the dying process has evolved gradually over time, and today well-informed patients with decision-making capacity have an autonomous right to refuse and forego recommended treatments (Jonsen, Siegler, & Winslade, 2002). Most of the time there are no ethical or legal ramifications if a person decides to forego treatments. The courts uphold the right of competent patients to refuse treatment (Jonsen et al., 2001; Mappes & DeGrazia, 2001). Nevertheless, health care professionals need to make certain that the patient's decision is truly autonomous and not coerced. However, health care professionals may find it very difficult to accept a competent patient's decision to forego treatment.

Sometimes, in a patient's mind the burdens of medical treatments outweigh the benefits (O'Rourke, 2002). A patient's perceived burden is a concern for nurses, physicians, and patients because physical pain and emotional suffering from treatments or the prolongation and dread of carrying out treatments may be too much to bear. Other views of burden consist of the economic, social, and spiritual burdens on a patient and family. Whether at the end of life or not, adult autonomous patients with competent decision-making capacity may refuse medical treatments at any time in life and may base their refusal on religious or cultural beliefs.

Withholding and Withdrawing Life-Sustaining Treatment

Notable legal decisions led to many questions regarding the right to die and the right to withhold and withdraw life-sustaining treatments. Specifically, there were two legal cases that generated landmark decisions about withholding and withdrawing treatments (Brannigan & Boss, 2001; Jonsen et al., 1998). The case of Karen Ann Quinlan in 1975 led to the right to discontinue a mechanical ventilator (Jonsen et al., 1998; *In re Quinlan, New Jersey*). In the case of Nancy Cruzan in 1990, the judges of the US Supreme Court established three conditions: the patient has a right to refuse medical treatment; artificial feeding constitutes medical treatment; and if the patient is mentally incompetent, then each state must document clear and convincing evidence that the patient's desires were for discontinuance of medical treatment (Jonsen et al., 1998; *In re Cruzan, Missouri*).

Nurses need to give compassionate and excellent care to patients. No matter what decision is made, family members and patients need to feel a sense of confidence that nurses will maintain moral sensitivity with a course of right action. In the *Code of Ethics with Interpretive Statements*, Provision 1.3, the ANA (2001) has taken the position that nurses ethically support the provision of compassionate and dignified end-of-life care as long as nurses do not have the sole intention of ending a person's life.

Alleviation of Pain and Suffering in the Dying Patient

Attempting to relieve pain and suffering is a primary responsibility for nurses and providers of care, which makes the whole arena of palliative care an ethical concern. Patients fear the consequences of disease, that is, they fear pain, suffering, and the process of dying. Also, they fear unnecessary suffering. Most of the time, it is the nurse who administers the pain medication and evaluates a patient's condition between and during pain injections (see "Management of Care" in this chapter).

Rule of Double Effect

The rule of double effect (RDE) is defined as the use of high doses of pain medication to reduce the chronic and intractable pain of terminally ill patients even if doing so hastens death (Quill, 2001). Although now used in secular settings, this rule is based on the same principle that was practiced in medieval times in the Catholic Church (Marker, 1996). The use of opioid analgesics frequently is used when applying the RDE. There are many bioethicists (e.g. Fohr, 1998; Marker, 1996) who are convinced that opioids and other medications play only a minimal role in hastening death, even unintended death of patients. Instead, Fohr (1998) has emphasized that because of a "myth" that exists regarding the RDE in terms of end-of-life issues, physical pain and suffering are vastly undertreated.

Even so, when the rule is applied, nurses need to be aware that the hastening of death must be a possible foreseen effect but assure that it is not intended. In Provision 1.3 of the *Code of Ethics for Nurses with Interpretive Statements*, the ANA (2001) supports nurses in their attempts to relieve patients' pain, "even when those interventions entail risks of hastening death" (p. 8). According to Quill (2001), critical aspects of the rule are: "the act must be good or at least morally neutral"; "the agent must intend the good effect and not the evil effect (which may be "foreseen" but not intended);" "the evil effect must not be the means to the good effect;" [and] "there must be a "proportionally grave reason" to risk the evil effect" (p. 67).

Nurses may have conflicting moral values concerning the use of high doses of opioids, such as morphine sulfate and other medications. In times when nurses feel uncomfortable, they need to explore their attitudes and opinions with their supervisor and, when appropriate, in clinical team meetings. Individually evaluating each patient and circumstance is essential.

TERMINAL SEDATION

Terminal sedation (TS) is a phrase that did not appear in the literature until the 1990s, but even today, there is no clear consensus regarding its meaning (Marker, 2003). Whether TS should be used as a palliative treatment or not still remains to be answered. McStay (2003) stated: "In 1997, the U.S. Supreme Court [Judges O'Connor, Ginsberg, &, in part, Breyer] tacitly endorsed terminal sedation as an alternative to physician-assisted suicide thus intensifying…the 'right to die' controversy" (McStay, 2003, p. 45). TS remains ethically controversial because of the perception of its being a "last option" alternative and a compromise for physician-assisted suicide, but it seems to be moving toward a social and an ethical acceptance (Quill, 2001; McStay, 2003). TS is defined by Quill (2001) as " . . . when a suffering patient is sedated to unconsciousness, usually through the ongoing administration of barbiturates or benzodiazepines. The patient then dies of dehydration, starvation, or some other intervening complication, as all other life-sustaining interventions are withheld" (p. 181).

When the word "terminal" is used, there is an understanding among the health care team and family members that the outcome, and possibly a desired outcome, is death (Sugarman, 2000). TS has been used in three situations: to provide relief of physical pain, to produce unconsciousness before withdrawing artificial food and fluids, and to relieve suffering (McStay, 2003). The practices of producing unconsciousness and withholding or withdrawing artificial food and fluids lead to an unresolved question of whether or not these two practices occur as a single action (McStay, 2003). Nurses must evaluate the moral, ethical, and legal implications of these practices, especially as a single action, and then understand the underlying principles for the practices.

Although the ANA (2001) did not address TS directly in the *Code of Ethics for Nurses with Interpretive* Statements, there is a statement that nurses are to give compassionate care at the end of life. It should be emphasized, according to the code, that nurses are not to have the sole intent of ending a person's life. Nurses need to evaluate the intentions of physicians' orders to the extent possible and the intentions of their own actions when giving care to patients in questionable TS situations. Understanding the moral and ethical implications will guide nurses in their individualized direction. Even though TS has been tacitly endorsed by the judges of the US Supreme Court, there is a question as to its legal acceptance, and great controversy continues over whether or not TS is considered a euthanasia practice.

PHYSICIAN-ASSISTED SUICIDE

Society has reacted with everything from moral outrage to social acceptance with regard to physician-assisted suicide. Physician-assisted suicide is defined as "the act of providing a lethal dose of medication for the patient to self-administer" (Sugarman, 2000, p. 213). The only state in the United States to legally allow physician-assisted suicide today is Oregon, which passed the Death With Dignity Act in 1994. With certain restrictions, patients who are near death may obtain prescriptions to end their lives in a dignified way (Ladd et al., 2002).

During a 20-year dispute over euthanasia practices, under certain guidelines, the practice of euthanasia was allowed in the Netherlands (Boyd, 2003). In February 2002, a Dutch law was passed that permitted voluntary euthanasia and physician-assisted suicide. In the discussions of euthanasia in the United States, the scope has been limited to only physician-assisted suicide, whereas in the Netherlands, the discussion has a much wider perspective.

Special guidelines relating to the Death With Dignity Act in Oregon were written by the Oregon Nurses Association for nurses who care for patients who choose physician-assisted suicide (cited in Ladd et al., 2002). The guidelines include maintaining support, comfort, and confidentiality; discussing end-of-life options with the patient and family;

and being present for the patient's self-administration of medications and during the death. Nurses may not inject the medications themselves, breach confidentiality, subject others to any type of judgmental comments or statements about the patient, or refuse to provide care to the patient. It is critical to note that the ANA (2001), in the *Code of Ethics for Nurses with Interpretive Statements*, plainly stated that nurses are not to act with the sole intent of ending a person's life.

RATIONAL SUICIDE

> The idea of saving people vs. allowing people to die or commit suicide is at the very essence of one of the most debated and controversial dilemmas today. As long as there is difficulty in determining rationality in suicide, this controversy will remain. Moral progress in nursing necessitates that nurses ponder these ethical uncertainties…with patients who are contemplating rational suicide. Meanwhile, nurses should never be caught off-guard in relation to the ethical and political changes in health care for fear of losing their power and voice (Rich & Butts, 2004, p. 277).

Rational suicide is a self-slaying based on reasoned choice and is categorized as voluntary active euthanasia. Siegel (1986) stated that the person who is contemplating rational suicide has a realistic assessment of life circumstances, is free from severe emotional distress, and has a motivation that would seem understandable to most uninvolved people in the person's community.

To morally accept the act of a person's committing rational suicide seems outrageous to most people, and the very thought of it weighs heavily on their hearts, even today. No matter what people think morally about suicide, an enormous public health crisis exists because worldwide there are an estimated one million suicides a year, or one every 40 seconds (WHO, 2000). In the United States, there are an estimated 30,000 suicides per year (Centers for Disease Control [CDC], 2000).

Should people be criticized for making a choice of rational suicide? More and more people view rational suicide as a rational alternative to life, especially when they are faced with unbearable pain, suffering, or loneliness (O'Rourke, 2002). However, the terms "rational" and "suicide" seem to contradict each other (Engelhart, 1986; Finnerty, 1987). David Peretz (as cited in O'Rourke, 2002), a noted psychiatrist and suicidologist, gave his interpretation of why rational suicides seem to be occurring and more accepted in society when he stated:

> Under the unprecedented stress of recent decades, denial mechanisms are breaking down and we have become increasingly vulnerable to the threats of intensely painful feelings of anxiety, fear, panic, rage, guilt, shame, grief, longing and helplessness. In order to avoid being overwhelmed, we seek new ways to adapt…I believe that the growing concern with a good death, death with dig-

nity and the right-to-die reflect this search…If our deepest known fear is of being destroyed, and we cannot deal with that fear, we take refuge in planning death and rational suicide. We find comfort in the illusion, 'It will not be done to me…I will do it myself' (pp. 206–207).

Peretz thinks that this motivation is unethical, dangerous, and harmful because it leads a person to a false sense of omnipotence.

Two other elements may contribute to rational suicide but are also unrealistic and unethical, according to Peretz (as cited in O'Rourke, 2002). One element is that people who are advocates of rational suicide believe strongly that personal autonomy is the goal of human life, and, therefore, if a person cannot have complete personal autonomy, life is not worth living. The other element is an act of self-destruction, which has a potential to mythologize rational suicide. Peretz stated that by mythologizing an object, it is given false power. Advocates of rational suicide promote self-destruction as a way to realize a false sense of freedom from serious human problems, such as physical suffering, loneliness, or frailty.

For nurses to endorse any suicide seems contradictory to good practice, because traditionally nurses and mental health professionals have intervened to prevent suicide. Many times nurses are guided by their cultural, religious, and personal beliefs in how they respond to patients who are thinking about suicide. Does a nurse have a right to try to stop a person from committing rational suicide; in other words, to act in the best interest of a patient? Or is a nurse supposed to support a person's autonomous decision to commit rational suicide, even when that decision is morally and religiously incompatible with the nurse's perspective? If the nurse knows of the plan for rational suicide, would care toward that patient be obligatory? In other words, would nurses be obligated to render care despite their own conflicts in values. What actions could the nurse take at this point?

According to Rich and Butts (2004) there are no clear answers to this ethical dilemma but interventions become unique to each situation. Interventions may include everything from being asked to provide information regarding the Hemlock Society to being asked about lethal injections. Autonomy and beneficence need to be considered when nurses are deciding on interventions for persons who are planning rational suicide. Nurses are closely involved with more end-of-life ethics as the issue of voluntary active euthanasia is becoming increasingly popular.

UNCERTAIN MORAL GROUND FOR NURSES

Nurses first must sort out their own feelings about euthanasia and dying before appropriate moral guidance and direction can be offered to patients and families. The sights, sounds, and smells of death can be an emotionally draining experience for nurses. At the same time, nurses must meet the needs of patients and families. Every day nurses face disturbing moral conflicts, such as whether or not they should keep giving a continuous morphine sulfate infusion to a dying patient for comfort in light of the risk of depressed respirations or whether or not they should assist in withdrawing or withholding artificial nutrition and fluids or other life-sustaining interventions. When nurses experience personal value and professional moral conflicts, they may find themselves on uncertain moral ground.

Barbara Couden (2002), a registered nurse, wrote a vivid description of her emotional experiences with loss and death in intensive care. She stated that at times she just wanted to run (see Ethical Kaleidoscope Box 10-1). She also portrayed her experiences of physical and emotional exhaustion; periods of fatigue, guilt, and sometimes relief when death finally came; tearfulness and sadness, and her own intense feelings of grief and loss. Couden experienced unexpressed grief and unresolved personal losses, along with the losses of her patients, until she had no emotions left to express toward her patients and no energy left to spend on them.

Box 10-1

ETHICAL Kaleidoscope   "Sometimes I Want to Run"

From the words of Barbara A. Couden...
Sometimes I want to run. It's work not to recoil from the rawness of life in those rooms. It is probably easier to behave as a starchy, mechanical nurse who staves off discomfort with a cheerful cliché. However, people deserve to experience hospitalization, grief, or even dying at its very best. To provide less isn't care at all. So I give my open heart and plunge into their circumstances, even though really I'm no one special to them—just there by default. In return, they honor me with the privilege of sharing their pain, struggle, and the richness of life, death, and love. In some way, we each live on in the other's memory: endeared by shared suffering, strivings to nurture hope, and our individual attempts to love.

So there are nights that I reflect on my heartfelt efforts, smell death on my clothes, and feel dampness where the tears of grieving loved ones have pressed against my face. Sometimes it seems that my role as a nurse is to absorb the feelings of others: pain, sadness, and loss. I'm sitting up in bed tonight, waiting for mine to dissipate.

Quote From Couden, B. A. (2002). "Sometimes I want to run": A nurse reflects on loss in the intensive care unit, pp. 41–42, Journal of Loss and Trauma, 7(1), 35–45.

After she sought ways to deal with her crisis, she discovered three important aspects of her emotional work. First, she has had to face her own grief and loss, which includes continuous expressions of loss through tears and discussions. Second, she had to find ways to deal with her own intense feelings of grief and loss before she "could dare to give them [her feelings] utterance" (p. 42). She cries and expresses her own grief with patients and, as she does, the environment becomes a unique environment for her and her patients as they exchange their emotions. She also finds ways to pamper herself. Her third aspect of emotional work is her mannerisms toward her patients and her feeling good about the way she responds to her patients. Couden confirmed her feelings about the way she responds to her patients when she saw her therapist emotionally moved by her own stories.

Relationships with patients are at the heart of nursing ethics. However, Maeve (1998) stated that these relationships become quite complex because of the accompanied interrelational experiences and emotions. Most nurses share in patients' emotional experiences of pain, suffering, and joy and do not just give superficial care and then forget about it. The care that nurses provide to their dying patients becomes an essential component of their own lives, and the stories that they remember about their patients become interwoven into their own life stories. Maeve (1998) studied nine nurses who worked with suffering and dying patients. As Maeve listened to the nurses' stories, she realized that moral issues about practice and relationships were dominant where suffering and dying patients were concerned.

Three major themes were identified from the study (Maeve, 1998). One was "tempering involvement," which meant that nurses had a dilemma or conflict about becoming involved: how much involvement, setting limits, setting boundaries to distinguish their lives from their patients' lives, and becoming embodied, such as when nurses may actually live in the experience with their patients (p. 1138). The second theme was "doing the right thing/the good thing," which involved education, experience, courage, moral dilemmas, and past regrets for a few of their performances or decisions with patients (p. 1139). "Cleaning up" was the third theme that emerged, and this theme marked the end of the involvement with the patient (p. 1140). This period of time was for a nurse to reflect on experiences and clean up grief.

In one Japanese study of 160 nurses, Konishi, Davis, and Aiba (2002) studied withdrawal of artificial food and fluid from terminally ill patients. The majority of the nurses supported this act only under two conditions: if the patient requested withdrawal of artificial food and fluids and if the act relieved the patient's suffering. Nurses agreed that comfort for the patient was of great concern. One nurse in the study stated: "[Artificial food and fluid] AFF only prolongs the patient's suffering. When withdrawn, the patient showed peace on the face. I have seen such patients so many times" (Konishi et al., 2002). In the same study, another nurse who was experiencing moral conflict with a decision to withdraw artificial food and fluid stated: "Withdrawal is killing and cruel, I feel guilty" (Konishi et al., 2002).

Other end-of-life issues may be reasons for moral conflicts, as well. Georges and Grypdonck (2002) conducted a literature review on the topic of ethical issues in terms of how nurses perceive their care to dying patients. There has been a deficiency of systematic research on this topic specific to nurses' moral conflicts. However, Georges and Grypdonck outlined some of the moral dilemmas that are particularly related to nurses and end-of-life care. Some of the moral problems of nurses found in the literature were:

- Communicating truthfully with patients about death because they were fearful of destroying all hope in the patient and family

- Managing pain symptoms because of fear of hastening death
- Feeling forced to collaborate with other health team members about medical treatments that in the nurses' opinion are futile or too burdensome
- Feeling insecure and not adequately informed about reasons for treatment
- Trying to maintain their own moral integrity throughout relationships with patients, families, and co-workers because of feeling that they are forced to betray their own moral values.

Although a conscientious nurse has an obligation to provide compassionate and palliative care, the nurse also has a right to withdraw from treating and caring for a dying patient as long as another nurse has assumed that care. When care is such that the nurse perceives it as violating personal and professional morality and values, the professional nurse must pursue alternative approaches to care.

MANAGEMENT OF CARE

The Compassionate Nurse With a Dying Patient

Nurses find themselves on uncertain moral ground when attempting to sustain dying patients, but they must be honest with patients and give sufficient information concerning advance directives and medical treatment options. However, the most important aspect is to offer support to dying patients by relating to their fear of death and by alleviating pain and suffering. Family members also need to support their loved one and often learn support strategies from talking with nurses and observing how nurses interact with the patient. When dying patients experience the compassionate acts of nurses and family members, death can be a positive experience for them. Nurses must remember that it is the little things that they can do for patients and their family members that make a big difference in the dying process.

Nurses need to realize that medical treatments aimed at relieving pain and suffering can coexist with palliative care, and nurses' compassionate acts are essential to this cohesive coexistence (Ciccarello, 2003). One particular compassionate act is for nurses to teach individuals and patients in community and hospital settings about treatment decisions at the end of life, such as life-sustaining treatments and palliative care with symptom management. Nurses also can teach patients about advance directives and surrogate decision making.

Physical and Emotional Pain Management

Understanding and actually upholding aggressive pain management precepts may be the most challenging moral dilemma that nurses face when caring for dying patients. Because of lack of understanding regarding the issues and fears of patient addiction or death, pain and suffering have been vastly undertreated in many cases. Miller, Miller, and Jolley (2001) alerted health care professionals to the importance of applying three basic precepts when attempting to control pain: first, nurses and physicians need to follow the WHO's "Pain Ladder" protocol for palliative pain management (see next section); second, it is important to treat pain early because, once pain is out of control, it is more difficult to treat; and third, addiction is not to be feared in patients who have a terminal illness, for rarely do dying patients become addicted to pain medications when drugs are administered properly.

Types of Pain There are two major types of pain that have been described by Miller et al. (2001): nociceptive and neuropathic. Nociceptive pain involving tissue damage occurs with two types of pain: somatic (musculoskelatal pain) and visceral (organ pain—the most common type of pain). Once nurses have performed a thorough pain assessment, the Pain Ladder by WHO (2003) is an excellent approach that can be taken (see Web Ethics box in this chapter for Web site information). At the first sign of a patient's pain, as a first step, nurses should administer oral nonopioid medications, given that a primary provider has ordered pain relievers. The next progressive step involves use of mild opioids such as codeine. Then the last step involves use of strong opioids such as morphine sulfate.

A variety of other pain medications can be used for neuropathic pain that is described either as dysesthesias (burning or electrical sensations) or lancinating pain (shooting, stabbing, or knifelike pain) (Miller et al., 2001). Pain medications and treatment options for these types of pain include antidepressants, anticonvulsants, sedatives, nerve blocks, epidural catheters, and others.

Web Ethics

ORGANIZATIONS TO HELP PATIENTS AND FAMILIES
End of Life Choices
http://www.endoflifechoices.org/microsite

Advance Directives
http://partnershipforcaring.org/Advance/content.html

Spiritual Care Program
http://spcare.org

ORGANIZATIONS FOR NURSES
National Hospice & Palliative Care Organization
http://www.nhpco.org

End of Life Nursing
http://www.aacn.nche.edu/elnec

Spiritual Care in Nursing
http://www.about.com/library.weekly/aa080101a.htm

WHO's Pain Ladder
http://www.who.int/cancer/palliative/painladder

Because pain and symptom control are complex and ethically challenging areas that nurses face in the care of dying patients, nurses need to recognize and evaluate their own moral conflicts and the impact of these conflicts on the care of their patients. A major ethical issue that nurses must evaluate is the issue of their giving high-dose pain medication to dying patients to alleviate suffering when the medication may in fact, but unintentionally, hasten death. Nurses also need to be aware of the moral conflicts that patients and family members experience when it comes to the impact of the relief of pain and suffering during end times. Sharing in each patient's experience of pain and emotional suffering will provide a better experience for nurses and their patients during the death process.

Core Principles for End-of-Life Care

Benner, Kerchner, Corless, and Davies (2003) delineated core principles for end-of-life nursing care, which are based on a central thought of "death as a human passage" (p. 558). The core ethical principles are taken from the work of Benner et al. on the Expert Panel on End-of-Life Care at the American Academy of Nursing. The group's core principles are ethical approaches that nurses can take in caring for dying patients and are summarized in the following points.

- Because death is an essential human passage, nurses must acknowledge and respect the passage. Nurses, significant others, and patients themselves have an impact on how that passage occurs.
- Always consider whether or not patients actually desire an optimal level of pain management and sedation to relieve pain and suffering and respect their wishes. Patients may wish for a balance between alertness and level of comfort so that they can chat and feel the presence of others.
- Palliative care should be comprehensive and flexible for pain and symptom management. Treatments are warranted to enhance quality of life.
- Avoid offering treatment options or any other options that are unrealistic. Dying patients are very limited as to their choices and options and do not need to be offered treatment options that do not have any beneficial effects.
- Be respectful of the time that patients and family members need for coming to terms with the realization of death. Each person and family member is unique.
- Be respectful of time that is needed for family members or significant others to grieve, to come to terms with their loved one's death, and for their own spiritual practices.
- Give attentive end-of-life care to dying patients so that the ones who are grieving can witness the nurse's impact on the facilitation of human passage. The sight of well-cared-for dying loved ones promotes emotional and physical well-being among the grieving family members and significant others.
- Avoid universal prescriptions and expectations for dying patients. Every death and death narrative is unique.

Spiegel (1993) captured the importance of following these core principles in end-of-life care. The following passage describes how people feel about unfinished business and caring for one another during the dying process.

There is such an absoluteness to death. Harsh words cannot be taken back. Promises unfulfilled can never be completed. One cannot even say goodbye. Facing the absoluteness of death can be a tremendous stimulus to life. If it is important, do it now...Say what you mean to say. Settle old grievances. Accomplish what needs doing, sooner rather than later...Death is so overwhelming that it is rather humbling. There seems to be so little one can do about it. Strangely enough, we always resort to the same comfort: our sense of caring about one another. In some sense, we huddle together. Our bond of caring forms a kind of talisman against the power of death. Although, ultimately, each of us has to face death alone, it is a tremendous relief to do some of the work with someone else. A good hug or some shared tears may not save a life, but it will make you feel more alive (pp. 144–145).

Spiritual Considerations

Spirituality is one of the most important aspects of end-of-life nursing care, but often nurses feel helpless when it comes to providing the right type of spiritual care for their patients. Meaningful experiences, especially during end-of-life times, are important for nurses in their care of patients because nurses feel that they touch patients' lives in some way through generous or compassionate acts. One such way may be the facilitation of spirituality. Spirituality has become more essential to nursing care since it has been included in the definition of palliative care, yet many people in the United States and Europe fall outside of a faith or religious network (Walter, 2003). The committee members of the Life's End Institute (2003) stated that most Americans believe that end-of-life spiritual care is an important part of the dying process, but they believe it is inadequately met.

Today, the Joint Commission on Accreditation of Healthcare Organizations ([JCAHO], 2000; as cited in Taylor, 2003) mandates that a spiritual assessment be conducted for each hospitalized patient. Furthermore, in the International Council of Nurses ([ICN], 2000) *Code of Ethics*, Element 1, and the ANA's (2001) *Code of Ethics for Nurses with Interpretative Statements*, Provision 1.3, phrases are included relating to the importance of nurses' promoting an environment that enables patient spirituality.

In her book, *Spiritual Care: Nursing Theory, Research, and Practice*, Taylor (2002) explored spirituality in nursing and portrayed spirituality as a deeply personal and integral part of a person's life. Several definitions of spirituality exist in nursing (e.g., Dossey & Guzzetta, 2000; as cited in Taylor, 2002; Narayanasamy, 1999). Spirituality as defined by Dossey and Guzzetta (2000) is "a unifying force of a person; the essence of being that permeates all of life and is manifested in one's being, knowing, and doing;

the interconnectedness with self, others, nature, and God/Life Force/Absolute/ Transcendent" (p. 7).

In a notable study, Stephenson and Draucker (2003) explored spirituality by conducting interviews with hospice patients. Participants in the study identified what they thought were characteristics that health care workers should display in spiritual care. They identified these characteristics as "good" qualities of humankind, which are "being kind, living the life of a good Christian, living the Golden Rule, and being attentive to those in need" (p. 57). Stephenson and Draucker concluded that intently listening to patients' stories and displaying the good qualities of humankind are ways that nurses and other health care professionals need to approach spiritual care with dying patients.

The studies of Taylor (2003) and Stephenson and Draucker (2003) have a few similarities in their findings about the spiritual needs of dying patients. Taylor (2003) studied the expectations of patients and family members regarding spiritual needs and care from nurses. An in-depth tape-recorded interview was conducted with 28 adult patients with cancer and their family caregivers. Six categories, and, consequently, specific nursing interventions, are listed in the priority of responses and they are "kindness and respect," "talking and listening," "prayer," "connecting," "quality temporal nursing care," and "mobilizing religious or spiritual resources" (Taylor, 2003, p. 588).

The category with the most responses was "kindness and respect," and a few responses regarding this theme included "just be nice," "giving loving care," and "a smile does a lot" (Taylor, 2003, pp. 587–588). For the next category, talking and listening, the responses varied widely because some patients enjoyed the superficial chatter, and others, especially the African Americans, were pleased about nurses' sharing their own deep religious experiences as comforting measures. Another category, prayer and the nurse's offering to pray with patients, varied widely in responses according to individualized beliefs. The category of connecting is identified by certain characteristics, such as nurses' being authentic and genuine, having physical presence, and having symmetry with patients. Symmetry with patients means that patients want to have a sense of working with nurses in a notion of friendship. Giving quality temporal nursing care, another category, was identified as the mechanisms that support the spirit of the person, such as keeping the room clean and not allowing the patient to suffer. The last category is mobilizing religious or spiritual resources. Nurses can facilitate mobilization by consulting chaplains, having Bibles in the room, and having other religious materials available as needed.

There are no completely "right" ways to help a person die because of individualized dying processes (Benner et al., 2003). Nursing care depends on each situation. Stories told by family members and dying patients are particularly significant to the understanding of death and are central to paying proper tribute to human passage. As Benner et al. (2003) pointed out, "death forever changes the world of those who experience the loss of the person dying" (p. 558). The involvement of nurses in decisions about death becomes more complex every day as more technology is incorporated into the dying process. Family members and patients must be involved with all ethical decisions that are made.

Case Study: End of Life with Mary Lou Warning

Mary Lou Warning, a widow of age 73, was admitted to the emergency department (ED) after her oldest son, Tom, found her disoriented and confused. He had taken her refilled prescriptions to her house on his way home from work. The ED physician and her primary provider agreed that they could not rule out a stroke and therefore wanted to admit her for "observation only." Tom thought, "This seems minor enough!" So, Tom went home to rest for the night once the papers were signed. She was admitted to a regular room. During the night, alone in her room, her stroke extended, and, when the registered nurse made one of her visits, she found Ms. Warning breathing but unresponsive to commands and pain. She immediately called the ED physician to check her and asked another nurse to call her primary physician and her son. Ms. Warning had five sons and one daughter, all of whom lived out of town except for Tom. An occlusive stroke was diagnosed after CT and MRI scans. Treatment was probably not going to be helpful because of the degree of damage. The ED and primary physicians were making preparation to send her to the intensive care unit (ICU) and were preparing themselves for how they were going to approach Tom. The primary physician informed Tom that she might not live, but, if she did, he and his siblings had to make some decisions about whether or not they wanted her to be on a mechanical ventilator, if it came to that decision. Also, he told Tom that at the present time she was in an unconscious state, which could mean an indefinite existence, and they needed to think about what types of treatment, if any, they wanted for her. The physician thoroughly explained the treatment options and the siblings' options to withdraw or withhold treatment for their mother. He explained to Tom that her prognosis was poor and that, if she lived, she probably would never regain consciousness. Meanwhile, Tom frantically called all of his siblings to tell them to "come fast" and that decisions needed to be made "now" regarding their mother's end-of-life care. Tom was pacing back and forth with distress and fear because no one in his family had ever discussed these issues among themselves or with his mother. When all of the siblings arrived the next day, they made a decision for the physician to withdraw all medications and intravenous fluids and requested no treatments of any kind. A DNR order was put in place.

Case Study Critical Thinking Questions

1. You are the nurse who is caring for Ms. Warning in the ICU. Before bedtime, you keep a daily journal of all of your experiences. The day you had to discontinue all of her treatments, you went home to reflect and write down the day's event and your feelings in an effort to express pent-up emotions concerning the day. Imagine becoming part of this experience, then dramatically rehearse this whole event as if you were that nurse, experiencing the event, seeing the sights and sounds, and feeling the intense emotions. Please complete this journaling process as an exercise.

2. What is the role that medical futility plays in this situation and in the family's decision?

3. The primary physician mentioned to Tom that Ms. Warning could need a mechanical ventilator at some point. Explain this statement by explaining the difference in the two levels and significance of death of the brain. Discuss nursing ethical implications involved with both types.

4. What ethical role could you as a nurse take to help support Tom and his siblings?

5. How could an advance directive have helped Tom's distressed state of mind when the physician presented him with "options"? Which one of the advance directives would have been the most suitable in Ms. Warning's case? Please explain.

6. What type of nursing care does Ms. Warning need to receive? In answering this question, explore the ethical issues that you as a nurse must face. Please explain your answer.

7. In Ms. Warning's case, the siblings came to a unified decision. However, if the siblings had not come to a consensus about a course of action for their mother, there could have been disagreement and arguing between them. Consider the nature of "equal voice" for each of them and how they might view the equality of their input compared with their siblings. If they could agree on one spokesperson for them, what approach might they take to channel their equal voice to one sibling spokesperson? Do you think the siblings would consider appointing the eldest son, Tom, to be the spokesperson to represent them? Please discuss this issue.

8. On which principle will surrogate decision making be based in Ms. Warning's case? Please define this principle and discuss why this particular principle is best for this particular patient.

REFERENCES

American College of Physicians. (1992/Updated1994). Do-not-resuscitate orders. *Ethics Manual.* Retrieved December 28, 2003, from http://www.imc.gsm.com/demos/dddemo/consult/resusama.htm

American Nurses Association. (2001). *Code of ethics for nurses with interpretive statements.* Washington, DC: Author.

Battin, M. P. (1994). *The least worst death: Essays in bioethics on the end of life.* New York: Oxford University.

Beauchamp, T. L., & Childress, J. F. (2001). *Principles of biomedical ethics* (5th ed.). New York: Oxford University.

Benjamin, M. (2003). Pragmatism and the determination of death. In G. McGee, *Pragmatic bioethics* (2nd ed.). London: Bradford Book—MIT.

Benner, P., Kerchner, S., Corless, I. B., & Davies, B. (2003). Attending death as a human passage: Core nursing principles for end-of-life care. *American Journal of Critical Care, 12*(6), 558–561.

Bondeson, J. (2001). *Buried alive: The terrifying history of our most primal fear.* New York: W. W. Norton.

Boyd, A. (2003). *American Medical Student Association Physician-assisted suicide: For and against.* Retrieved December 5, 2003, from http://www.amsa.org/bio/pas.cfm

Brannigan, M. C., & Boss, J. A. (2001). *Healthcare ethics in a diverse society.* Mountain View, CA: Mayfield.

Buchanan, A. E., & Brock, D. W. (1990). *Deciding for others: The ethics of surrogate decision making.* New York: Cambridge University.

Centers for Disease Control and Prevention [CDC]. National Center for Injury Prevention and Control. *Suicide: Fact Sheet.* Suicide in the United States. Retrieved December 6, 2003, from http://www.cdc.gov/ncipc/factsheets/suifacts.htm

Ciccarello, G. P. (2003). Strategies to improve end-of-life care in the intensive care unit. *Dimensions of Critical Care Nursing, 22*(5), 216–222.

Connelly, R. (2003). Living with death: The meaning of acceptance. *Journal of Humanistic Psychology, 43*(1), 45–63.

Couden, B. A. (2002). "Sometimes I want to run": A nurse reflects on loss in the intensive care unit. *Journal of Loss and Trauma, 7*(1), 35–45.

Death: The last taboo. (2003). Australian Museum. *What is death?* Retrieved December 5, 2003, from http://deathonline.net/what_is/

Devettere, R. J. (2000). *Practical decision making in health care ethics: Cases and concepts* (2nd ed.). Washington, DC: Georgetown University.

Dossey, B. M., & Guzzetta, C. E. (2000). Holistic nursing practice. In B. M. Dossey, L. Keegan, & C. E. Guzzetta (Eds.), *Holistic nursing: A handbook for practice* (3rd ed., pp. 5–26). Rockville, MD: Aspen.

Dworkin, R. (1994). *Life's dominion: An argument about abortion, euthanasia, and individual freedom.* New York: Vintage Books—Random House.

Emanuel, L. A., Danis, M., Pearlman, R. A., & Singer, P. A. (1995). Advance care planning as a process: Structuring the discussions in practice. *American Geriatrics Society, 43*, 440–446.

Engelhardt, H. T. (1986). Suicide in the cancer patient. *Cancer, 36*(2), 105–109.

Fesmire, S. (2003). *John Dewey and moral imagination.* Bloomington, IN: Indiana University.

Finnerty, J. L. (1987). Ethics in rational suicide. *Critical Care Nursing Quarterly, 10*(2), 86–90.

Fohr, S. A. (1998). The double effect of pain medication: Separating myth from reality. *Journal of Palliative Medicine, 1*, 315–328.

Georges, J. J., & Grypdonck. M. (2002). Moral problems experienced by nurses when caring for terminally ill people: A literature review. *Nursing Ethics, 9*(2), 155–178.

Hester. D. M. (2003). Significance at the end of life. In G. McGee (Ed.), *Pragmatic bioethics* (2nd ed.). London: Bradford Book—MIT.

Huber, S. W. (2003, October 3). Fieger to appeal for Kevorkian's release. *The Oakland Press: Online Edition.* Retrieved November 21, 2003, from http://theoaklandpress.com/stories/031704/loc_20040317067.shtml

Jonsen, A. R., Siegler, M., & Winslade, W. J. (2002). *Clinical ethics* (5th ed.). New York: McGraw-Hill.

Jonsen, A. R., Veatch, R. M., & Walters, L. (1998). *Source book in bioethics.* Washington, DC: Georgetown University.

Konishi, E., Davis, A. J., & Aiba, T. (2002). The ethics of withdrawing artificial food and fluid from terminally ill patients: An end-of-life dilemma for Japanese nurses and families. *Nursing Ethics, 9*(1), 7–19.

Ladd, R. E., Pasquerella, L., & Smith, S. (2002). *Ethical issues in home health care.* Springfield, IL: Charles C. Thomas.

Life's End Institute. (2003). Missoula demonstration project: Community engagement. Retrieved November 8, 2004, from http://www.lifes-end.org/community.phtml

Lustig, A. (2003). End-of-life decisions: Does faith make a difference? *Commonweal, 130*(10), 7.

Maeve, M. K. (1998). Weaving a fabric or moral meaning: How nurses live with suffering and death. *Journal of Advanced Nursing, 27,* 1136–1142.

Mappes, T. A., & DeGrazia, D. (2001). *Biomedical ethics* (5th ed.). Boston, MA: McGraw-Hill.

Marker, R. L. (2003). International Task Force on Euthanasia and Assisted Suicide. *Assisted suicide: The continuing debate.* Retrieved December 28, 2003, from http://www.internationaltaskforce.org/cd.htm

McStay, R. (2003). Terminal sedation: Palliative care for intractable pain, post Glucksberg and Quill. *American Journal of Law and Medicine, 29*, 45–76.

Miller, K. E., Miller, M. M., & Jolley, M. R. (2001). Challenges in pain management at the end of life. *American Family Physician, 64*(7), 1227–1234.

Munson, R. (2004). *Intervention & reflection: Basic issues in medical ethics* (7th ed.). Victoria, AU: Wadsworth-Thomson.

Narayanasamy, A. (1999). ASSET: A model for actioning spirituality and spiritual care education and training in nursing. *Nurse Education Today, 19*, 274–285.

O'Rourke, K. (2002). *A primer for health care ethics: Essays for a pleuralistic society* (2nd ed.). Washington, DC: Georgetown University.

Quill, T. E. (2001). *Caring for patients at the end of life: Facing an uncertain future together.* New York: Oxford University.

Public Broadcasting System & WGBH/Frontline. (1998). The Kevorkian verdict: The chronology of Dr. Jack Kovorkian's life and assisted suicide campaign. Retrieved December 21, 2003, from http://www.pbs.org/wgbh/pages/frontline/kevorkian/chronology.html

President's Commission for the Study of Ethical Problems in Medicine and Biomedical and Behavioral Research. (1981 July). *Defining death: Medical, legal, & ethical issues in the determination of death* (chapter quotes, pp. 33, 73; whole document 84 pages plus 6 appendices). Washington, DC: Government Printing Office.

Rich, K. L., & Butts, J. B. (2004). Rational suicide: Uncertain moral ground. *Journal of Advanced Nursing, 46*(3), 270–283.

Siegel, K. (1986). Psychosocial aspects of rational suicide. *American Journal of Psychotherapy, 40*(3), 405–418.

Spiegel, D. (1993). Detoxifying dying. *Living beyond limits: New hope and help for facing life-threatening illness.* New York: Random House—Times Books.

Stephenson, P. L., & Draucker, C. B. (2003). The experience of spirituality in the lives of hospice patients. *Journal of Hospice and Palliative Nursing, 5*(1), 51–58.

Sugarman, J. (2000). *20 common problems: Ethics in primary care.* New York: McGraw-Hill.

Taylor, E. J. (2002). *Spiritual care: Nursing theory, research, and practice.* Upper Saddle River, NJ: Prentice Hall.

Taylor, E. J. (2003). Nurses caring for the spirit: Patients with cancer and family caregiver expectations. *Oncology Nursing Forum, 30*(4), 585–590.

Veatch, R. M. (2003). *The basics of bioethics* (2nd ed.). Upper Saddle River, NJ: Prentice Hall.

Walter, T. (2003). Historical and cultural variants on the good death. *British Medical Journal, 327*, 218–220.

World Health Organization [WHO]. (2003). *WHO definition of palliative care.* Retrieved December 10, 2003, from http://www.who.int/cancer/palliative/definition/en/print.html

WHO. (2003). *WHO's pain ladder.* Retrieved January 1, 2004, from http://www.who.int/cancer/palliative/painladder

WHO. (2000). *Suicide statistics.* Retrieved December 6, 2003, from http://www.befrienders.org/suicide/statistics.htm

Yalom, I. D. (1980). *Existential psychotherapy.* New York. Basic.

Youngner, S. J., & Arnold, R. M. (2001). Philosophical debates about the definition of death: Who cares? *Journal of Medicine and Philosophy, 26*(5), 527–537.

American Nurses Association's
Code of Ethics for Nurses — Provisions

Approved as of June 30, 2001

1. The nurse, in all professional relationships, practices with compassion and respect for the inherent dignity, worth and uniqueness of every individual, unrestricted by considerations of social or economic status, personal attributes, or the nature of health problems.
2. The nurse's primary commitment is to the patient, whether an individual, family, group, or community.
3. The nurse promotes, advocates for, and strives to protect the health, safety, and rights of the patient.
4. The nurse is responsible and accountable for individual nursing practice and determines the appropriate delegation of tasks consistent with the nurse's obligation to provide optimum patient care.
5. The nurse owes the same duties to self as to others, including the responsibility to preserve integrity and safety, to maintain competence, and to continue personal and professional growth.
6. The nurse participates in establishing, maintaining, and improving healthcare environments and conditions of employment conducive to the provision of quality health care and consistent with the values of the profession through individual and collective action.

7. The nurse participates in the advancement of the profession through contributions to practice, education, administration, and knowledge development.
8. The nurse collaborates with other health professionals and the public in promoting community, national, and international efforts to meet health needs.
9. The profession of nursing, as represented by associations and their members, is responsible for articulating nursing values, for maintaining the integrity of the profession and its practice, and for shaping social policy.

Reprinted with permission from the American Nurses Association, *Code of Ethics for Nurses with Interpretive Statements,* Washington, D.C.: American Nurses Publishing, 2001

The ICN Code of Ethics for Nurses

THE ICN CODE OF ETHICS FOR NURSES

An international code of ethics for nurses was first adopted by the International Council of Nurses (ICN) in 1953. It has been revised and reaffirmed at various times since, most recently with this review and revision completed in 2000. The ICN Code of Ethics is also available in French [pdf file] Spanish [pdf file] German.

Preamble

Nurses have four fundamental responsibilities: to promote health, to prevent illness, to restore health and to alleviate suffering. The need for nursing is universal.

Inherent in nursing is respect for human rights, including the right to life, to dignity and to be treated with respect. Nursing care is unrestricted by considerations of age, colour, creed, culture, disability or illness, gender, nationality, politics, race or social status.

Nurses render health services to the individual, the family and the community and co-ordinate their services with those of related groups.

THE CODE

The *ICN Code of Ethics for Nurses* has four principal elements that outline the standards of ethical conduct.

Elements of the Code

1. Nurses and people

The nurse's primary professional responsibility is to people requiring nursing care.

In providing care, the nurse promotes an environment in which the human rights, values, customs and spiritual beliefs of the individual, family and community are respected.

The nurse ensures that the individual receives sufficient information on which to base consent for care and related treatment.

The nurse holds in confidence personal information and uses judgement in sharing this information.

The nurse shares with society the responsibility for initiating and supporting action to meet the health and social needs of the public, in particular those of vulnerable populations.

The nurse also shares responsibility to sustain and protect the natural environment from depletion, pollution, degradation and destruction.

2. Nurses and practice

The nurse carries personal responsibility and accountability for nursing practice, and for maintaining competence by continual learning.

The nurse maintains a standard of personal health such that the ability to provide care is not compromised.

The nurse uses judgement regarding individual competence when accepting and delegating responsibility.

The nurse at all times maintains standards of personal conduct which reflect well on the profession and enhance public confidence.

The nurse, in providing care, ensures that use of technology and scientific advances are compatible with the safety, dignity and rights of people.

3. Nurses and the profession

The nurse assumes the major role in determining and implementing acceptable standards of clinical nursing practice, management, research and education.

The nurse is active in developing a core of research-based professional knowledge.

The nurse, acting through the professional organisation, participates in creating and maintaining equitable social and economic working conditions in nursing.

4. Nurses and co-workers

The nurse sustains a co-operative relationship with co-workers in nursing and other fields.

The nurse takes appropriate action to safeguard individuals when their care is endangered by a co-worker or any other person.

Suggestions for use of the *ICN Code of Ethics for Nurses*

The *ICN Code of Ethics for Nurses* is a guide for action based on social values and needs. It will have meaning only as a living document if applied to the realities of nursing and health care in a changing society.

To achieve its purpose the *Code* must be understood, internalised and used by nurses in all aspects of their work. It must be available to students and nurses throughout their study and work lives.

Applying the Elements of the *ICN Code of Ethics for Nurses*

The four elements of the ICN Code of Ethics for Nurses: nurses and people, nurses and practice, nurses and co-workers, and nurses and the profession, give a framework for the standards of conduct. The following chart will assist nurses to translate the standards into action. Nurses and nursing students can therefore:

- Study the standards under each element of the Code.
- Reflect on what each standard means to you. Think about how you can apply ethics in your nursing domain: practice, education, research or management.
- Discuss the Code with co-workers and others.
- Use a specific example from experience to identify ethical dilemmas and standards of conduct as outlined in the Code. Identify how you would resolve the dilemma.
- Work in groups to clarify ethical decision making and reach a consensus on standards of ethical conduct.
- Collaborate with your national nurses' association, co-workers, and others in the continuous application of ethical standards in nursing practice, education, management and research.

ELEMENT OF THE CODE # 1: Nurses and People

Practitioners and Managers	*Educators and Researchers*	*National Nurses' Associations*
Provide care that respects human rights and is sensitive to the values, customs and beliefs of people.	In curriculum include references to human rights, equity, justice, solidarity as the basis for access to care.	Develop position statements and guidelines that support human rights and ethical standards.
Provide continuing education in ethical issues.	Provide teaching and learning opportunities for ethical issues and decision making.	Lobby for involvement of nurses in ethics review committees.
Provide sufficient information to permit informed consent and the right to choose or refuse treatment.	Provide teaching/learning opportunities related to informed consent.	Provide guidelines, position statements and continuing education related to informed consent.
Use recording and information management systems that ensure confidentiality.	Introduce into curriculum concepts of privacy and confidentiality.	Incorporate issues of confidentiality and privacy into a national code of ethics for nurses.
Develop and monitor environmental safety in the workplace.	Sensitise students to the importance of social action in current concerns.	Advocate for safe and healthy environment.

ELEMENT OF THE CODE # 2: Nurses and Practice

Practitioners and Managers	*Educators and Researchers*	*National Nurses' Associations*
Establish standards of care and a work setting that promotes quality care.	Provide teaching/learning opportunities that foster life long learning and competence for practice.	Provide access to continuing education, through journals, conferences, distance education, etc.
Establish systems for professional appraisal, continuing education and systematic renewal of licensure to practice.	Conduct and disseminate research that shows links between continual learning and competence to practice.	Lobby to ensure continuing education opportunities and quality care standards.
Monitor and promote the personal health of nursing staff in relation to their competence for practice.	Promote the importance of personal health and illustrate its relation to other values.	Promote healthy lifestyles for nursing professionals. Lobby for healthy workplaces and services for nurses.

ELEMENT OF THE CODE # 3: Nurses and the Profession

Practitioners and Managers	Educators and Researchers	National Nurses' Associations
Set standards for nursing practice, research, education and management.	Provide teaching/learning opportunities in setting standards for nursing practice, research, education and management.	Collaborate with others to set standards for nursing education, practice, research and management.
Foster workplace support of the conduct, dissemination and utilisation of research related to nursing and health.	Conduct, disseminate and utilise research to advance the nursing profession.	Develop position statements, guidelines and standards related to nursing research.
Promote participation in national nurses' associations so as to create favourable socio-economic conditions for nurses.	Sensitise learners to the importance of professional nursing associations. Lobby for fair social and economic working conditions in nursing.	Lobby for fair social and economic working conditions in nursing. Develop position statements and guidelines in workplace issues.

ELEMENT OF THE CODE # 4: Nurses and Co-Workers

Practitioners and Managers	Educators and Researchers	National Nurses' Associations
Create awareness of specific and overlapping functions and the potential for inter-disciplinary tensions.	Develop understanding of the roles of other workers.	Stimulate co-operation with other related disciplines.
Develop workplace systems that support common professional ethical values and behaviour.	Communicate nursing ethics to other professions.	Develop awareness of ethical issues of other professions.
Develop mechanisms to safeguard the individual, family or community when their care is endangered by health care personnel.	Instil in learners the need to safeguard the individual, family or community when care is endangered by health care personnel.	Provide guidelines, position statements and discussion fora related to safeguarding people when their care is endangered by health care personnel.

DISSEMINATION OF THE *ICN CODE OF ETHICS FOR NURSES*

To be effective the *ICN Code of Ethics for Nurses* must be familiar to nurses. We encourage you to help with its dissemination to schools of nursing, practising nurses, the nursing press and other mass media. The *Code* should also be disseminated to other health professions, the general public, consumer and policy making groups, human rights organisations and employers of nurses.

GLOSSARY OF TERMS USED IN THE *ICN CODE OF ETHICS FOR NURSES*

Co-operative relationship	A professional relationship based on collegial and reciprocal actions, and behaviour that aim to achieve certain goals.
Co-worker	Other nurses and other health and non-health related workers and professionals.
Nurse shares with society	A nurse, as a health professional and a citizen, initiates and supports appropriate action to meet the health and social needs of the public.
Personal health	Mental, physical, social and spiritual well -being of the nurse.
Personal information	Information obtained during professional contact that is private to an individual or family, and which, when disclosed, may violate the right to privacy, cause inconvenience, embarrassment, or harm to the individual or family.
Related groups	Other nurses, health care workers or other professionals providing service to an individual, family or community and working toward desired goals.

Copyright © 2000 by ICN - International Council of Nurses,
3, place Jean-Marteau, CH-1201 Geneva (Switzerland)

ISBN: 92-95005-16-3

Index